KERRANG!

THE DIREKTORY OF

HEAVY
METAL

THE INDISPENSABLE A–Z GUIDE TO
ROCK WARRIORS &
HEADBANGIN' HEROES!!!

D1439375

222 052

HOW TO USE THIS BOOK

1. Do not drop the book.
2. Open the book.
3. Read the book.

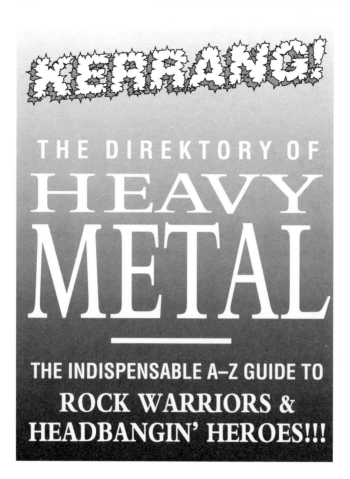

KERRANG!

THE DIREKTORY OF

HEAVY METAL

THE INDISPENSABLE A–Z GUIDE TO
ROCK WARRIORS &
HEADBANGIN' HEROES!!!

Edited by Neil Jeffries

First published in 1993 by
Virgin Books
an imprint of Virgin Publishing Ltd
332 Ladbroke Grove
London W10 5AH

© *Kerrang!* 1993

A catalogue record for this title is available from the British Library

ISBN 0 86369 761 5

DESIGN BY: Caroline Fish

WRITTEN BY:
Jason Arnopp, Paul Harries, Neil Jeffries, Howard Johnson,
Alison Joy, Mörat, Matthias Penzel,
Neil Perry, Dave Reynolds, Chris Watts, Ray Zell

PHOTOS BY:
Steve Callaghan, Robert Ellis, Harrison Funk, Joe Giron,
Martyn Goodacre, Ross Halfin, Paul Harries, Mark Leialoha,
Katia Natola, Ray Palmer, Neal Preston, Steve Rapport, Ed Sirrs,
Gus Stewart, Geoff Swaine, David Wainwright, Chris Walter,
Frank White, David Willis

INVALUABLE ASSISTANCE BY:
Louise Millar, Jon Moore and Skarlet

TYPESETTING: by us lot!

Repro by Colour Systems, 90/92 Pentonville Road, London N1.

Printed and bound in Great Britain by Butler and Tanner, Frome,
Somerset.

EDITOR'S EXCUSES

YOU HAVE to remember, right, that we at the world's leading Heavy Metal weekly – that's **Kerrang!** *– are only human. (Well, most of us are, er... mostly human.) So we may not have included your favourite band in this book. Life's like that sometimes. But the point is, we know who we've left out and why – because there wasn't bloody room, that's why! So apologies to the Galactic Cowboys, to Blazon, to Raging Fuck Death and to the Cheesy Comestibles... not to mention Dwight Yokam. Nevertheless, there are nearly 600 names in this book which is a damn sight better than a poke in the eye with a shitty stick. Some of them, we know, are bogawful. But even the very worst are still amusing in their bogawfulness. And if you think the names are bogawful, you should hear some of the music...*

Special thanks to all those who have gone before so that we might come from behind and steal your glory. You know who you are...

Extra special thanks to James Hetfield Esquire for sending us wot he writ and writting us wot he sent. But let's read the next couple of pages and show some respect: this is, after all, the guy who wrote the riff to 'Enter Sandman' – although obviously not in joined-up writing...

"FUCK, MY HEAD HURTS !!"
THE WORDS HEARD EVERY SATURDAY ~~MORNING~~ AFTERNOON
AT THE ~~HOUSE~~ REMAINS LARZ & I CALLED HOME.
—THE YEAR: 1982—

UP AT THE CRACK OF NOON, DISCOVERING THAT YOU
~~FELL ASLEEP~~ PASSED OUT WITH YOUR SHOES ON,
BUT NOT YOUR PANTS !? THAT YOUR TURNTABLE (WHATS THAT?)
STILL WORKS AFTER YOU'VE BARFED UP HALF THE
LIQUOR STORE ON IT. THAT YOUR ~~FRIENDS~~ PARTNERZ
IN CRIME, AFTER SETTING THE COUCH ON FIRE, HAVE EATEN
ALL YOUR FOOD (KETCHUP SAMWICHEZ: ENOUGH TO LAST YOU THE
WHOLE WEEK). AND THAT THE BEER YOU JUST DRANK TO
UNSTICK YOUR TONGUE FRUM THE ROOF OF YOUR MOUTH, WAS
USED AS AN ASHTRAY & SPITOON LAST NITE.

YES ! THE FRISCO BAY HEADBANGERS KNEW WHERE WE
LIVED (SO DID THE COPS) AND KNEW HOW TO ENJOY MUSIC !
EVERY FRIDAY NITE AT THE METALLIPAD THE FURNITURE
WOULD GO INTO THE GARAGE, (STORED AWAY SAFE FRUM ANY MORE
TORCHINGS)) ALL EXCEPT THE STEREO; OUR HOST FOR THE EVENING.
A COUPLE NEW MOTORHEAD POSTERS WENT UP ON THE WALLS,
NOT ONLY BECAUSE WE DUG THE MUSIC (NOT TO MENTION HOW CUTE THEY WERE)
BUT THEY COVERED UP THE NEW HOLES IN THE WALLS FRUM
LAST WEEKS SESSION, THEN THE LOCAL METALHEADZ WOULD
COME OVER AND HAVE FUN AT EVERYONES EXPENCE !!

FUKIN-METAL !!
ITS A WAY OF LIFE
BEYOND JUST MUSIC ITS AN ATTITUDE,
IT ~~STARTS~~ STIRS UP SOMETHING FOR EVERYONE AT DIFFERENT LEVELS.
I ~~RECALL~~ REMEMBER CLIFF (BURTON !!) ASKING THIS GIRL WHY
SHE WAS WEARING A RATT T-SHIRT. HER REPLY WAS "DUH,
CAUSE THEY'RE SO HARDCORE." WHAT THA FUK ?!!! WE JUST
LOOKED AT EACH OTHER AND FELT LIKE SHOVING HER HEAD
INTO THE TOUR BUS SPEAKERS WHILE DISCHARGE CRUSHED
HER TINY GROUPIE BRAIN ! BUT I GUESS TO HER RATT (GOD, I
~~HOPE THEY'RE~~ HOPE THERE NOT IN THIS METAL DIREKTORY) WOULD SOUND HEAVY
COMPAIRED TO SAY ... NELSON (NO, NO, I WONT LOOK .....OH SHIT, THEY ARE !
KERRANG HAS REALLY LOST IT NOW) THERE YOU GO ! PEOPLE HAVE
DIFFERENT IDEAS OF WHAT METAL IS. AS LONG AS IT ~~EXPLORE~~
STIRS UP AN EMOTION , (LIKE KILLING NELSON)

METAL HAS SURVIVED ITS DOWNFALLS OVER THE YEARS. FRUM CRITICS CALLING IT "SOME SORT OF NOISE FOR THE BRAIN DEAD", COURT ROOM CASES BLAMING IT FOR SATANIC VIOLENCE AND TEEN SUICIDES, OZZY REMOVING HEADS OFF CUTE LITTLE ANIMALS, KISS REMOVING THIER MAKE-UP (OFF THIER CUTE LITTLE HEADS), TO THE ALWAYS EXTREMELY UNBIASED NATIONAL INQUIRER OF HEAVY METAL ..... KERRANG.

BUT WHEN YOU FEEL IT HIT A NEW LOW, NEW BANDS COME ALONG SMASHING THROUGH EVEN MORE BOUNDRIES SET ONLY BY YOUR OWN MIND. TRYING NEW IDEAS YET STICKING TO THE LOGIC OF PLEASING YOURSELF FIRST, FEARLESS, UNSAFE AND NOT AFRAID TO LET YOU KNOW HOW THEY FEEL.

CALL IT WHAT YOU WILL; THRASH, SPEED, HARDCORE, BLACK METAL, GRINDCORE, GRUNGE, SPEEDCORE, ACID METAL, FUNK METAL, FUCK METAL ....., WHO CARES!! AS LONG AS THE ATTITUDE LIVES.

FRUM THE SUTTLE MOTORHEAD, THE COMPLEX RAMONES, THE RADIO FRIENDLY VENOM, THE AUDIBLE NAPALM DEATH, THE LOVE & HAPPINESS OF BLACK SABBATH, THE SOBER GIRLSCHOOL, TO THE LEVITY OF METALLICA (who?), ATTITUDE DOES LIVE AND HOPEFULLY DRIPS FRUM THESE PAGES (NO, THATS NOT WHY THE PAGES ARE STUCK TOGETHER).

DIG IN.

JAYMZ

4/16/93

P.S. ALL JOKES TAKEN PERSONALLY WERE THEN INTENDED TO PISS YOU OFF. (JOKE). ...... SEE, IT WORKS

P.S.S. I HAD NOTHING TO DO WITH THE SELECTION OF METAL BANDS IN THIS BOOK. KANSAS IS JUST TOO HEAVY FOR MY TASTE.

Lee AARON

Canada, vocalist (1981-present)

FIRST RATE singer forever in search of songs

and a band to do justice to her voice. Having once modelled for *Oui* magazine, she has spent much of her career trying to establish musical credibility. After her lively second album, 'Metal Queen' (Attic, 1984), she supported Bon Jovi in Europe in 1985 but stardom has always eluded her.

Recommended album:
CALL OF THE WILD *(Roadrunner, 1985 – KKKK)*

OUI! OUI! It's Lee!

ABATTOIR

USA, five-piece (1983-1988)

LOS ANGELES band who opened for both W.A.S.P. and Metallica, then featured on the 'Metal Massacre IV' compilation. Singer John Cyriss and guitarist Juan Garcia formed Agent Steel, bassist Mel Sanchez eventually joined Evildead. Abattoir made two LPs then quit.

Recommended album:
VICIOUS ATTACK *(Roadrunner, 1985 – KKK)*

ACCEPT

Germany, four-piece (1977-present)

QUINTESSENTIAL BOMBASTIC German Metallers at their best in the early '80s as a five-piece featuring Udo Dirkschneider (vocals), Wolf Hoffman (guitar), Herman Frank (guitar), Peter Baltes (bass) and Stefan Kaufmann (drums), they drew on the style of Judas Priest (who they once supported) with hysterically high-pitched vocals and screaming dual guitars.

'Restless And Wild' was their finest work and is cited as inspirational by numerous Thrash bands. Sadly, the group toned down their style for 'Metal Heart' and the singer quit to front a new, similar outfit called, cunningly, U.D.O.! Replacements included Rob Armitage, David Reece and Jim Stacey, but the band fell apart at the end of the '80s. 1992 saw them reform as a quartet (the aforementioned line-up minus Herman Frank) for 1993's superbly-titled comeback album, 'Objection Overruled'.

Recommended albums:
RESTLESS AND WILD *(HM Worldwide, 1982 – KKKKK)*
BALLS TO THE WALL *(Portrait, 1984 – KKKK)*

ACID REIGN

UK, five-piece (1988-1991)

THRASH ACT with a sense of humour – a rare commodity – that ultimately was their own downfall when trying to broaden their fan-base. Original line-up featuring H (vocals), Kev (guitar), Gaz (guitar), Ian (bass) and Ramsey (drums) presented a bizarre, sometimes undisciplined stage act. Gaz and Ian were replaced by Mac (ex-Holosade bassist) and Adam (ex-Lord Crucifier guitarist). New line-up supported Nuclear Assault (in UK) and Exodus (in Europe) but never achieved their early promise. Adam quit (joining Gaz and Lee Dorrian in Cathedral; Ramsey later did the same), Kev joined Lawnmower Deth, and Acid Reign announced it was all over in January 1991. One posthumous collection followed, plus a farewell Marquee show on October 28 that year.

Recommended album:
OBNOXIOUS *(Music For Nations, 1990 – KKKK)*

AC/DC

Australia/UK, five-piece (1973-present)

UNDOUBTEDLY ONE of the Top Three HM acts in the world today – alongside Guns N' Roses and Metallica – AC/DC rose to that point employing a combination of uncomplicated hard rock and dogged determination. On their way up they've had to endure the tragic death of a frontman... but have lost few fans.

ANGUS YOUNG on stage with the late great Bon Scott

AC/DC were formed in Sydney, Australia by two brothers, Malcolm Young (born January 6, 1953) and Angus (born March 31, 1959). Both had been born in Glasgow, Scotland but the family emigrated to Australia in 1963. Three years later their elder brother George enjoyed worldwide success as a member of the Easybeats, a band which also included Harry Vanda who helped George produce many of the subsequent AC/DC records. Malcolm spent 1971/72 as a member of Newcastle, New South Wales band the Velvet Underground after they relocated to nearby Sydney.

AC/DC debuted on December 31, 1973 at the Chequers Club in Sydney, Australia with a line-up also featuring Dave Evans (vocals), Larry Van Knedt (bass) and Colin Burgess (drums).

Three more drummers and another bassist passed through the line-up, but more importantly, in September 1974, Evans refused to play a gig at short notice and AC/DC gave the job to their driver, one Bon Scott (born July 9, 1946, Kirriemuir, Scotland).

Scott had emigrated to Australia in 1951. After five consecutive years as the under-17 drum champion with the Perth Pipe Band, he spent some time behind bars for assault and battery, a conviction which contributed to him being refused entry to the army on the grounds that he was 'socially maladjusted'. Instead in 1965 he joined the Spectors (as drummer/ sometime singer). Next he fronted the Valentines (as singer) in 1966, and jazz/blues band Fraternity (1970-1974).

Scott then consolidated an AC/DC line-up which lasted three years and featured Phil Rudd (drums, born May 19, 1954, Melbourne) and Mark Evans (bass, born March 2, 1956, Melbourne). AC/DC had already recorded a single, 'Can I Sit Next To You', before Scott arrived but his vocals were to grace the band's first two Australia/New Zealand-only released LPs, 'High Voltage' and 'TNT'.

AC/DC caught on quickly by touring almost non-stop Down Under, with their combination of a rock solid rhythm section, Bon's lascivious but good-humoured stage persona and Angus' outrageous stage act. Following his sister's advice, Angus wore his short-trousered school uniform, then following his basic instinct he never stood still. The live show never failed and Australian sales of 100,000 for each of the albums was enough to secure worldwide media interest and a UK/US deal with Atlantic. The label's first move was to relocate the band to Barnes, West London, in January 1976, and book them club dates. They debuted at the now demolished Red Cow pub in Hammersmith.

In May, Atlantic released 'High Voltage', a compilation of tracks from their two Australian LPs, and the band supported Back Street Crawler for nine dates. In June, whilst Punk exploded and the media falsely declared heavy rock a dead duck, they began their first headlining tour. By the end of 1976 they were back in Australia having released another LP, 'Dirty Deeds Done Dirt Cheap', and played their US debut club dates.

June 1977 saw the arrival of a new bassist: Englishman Cliff Williams (born December 14, 1949, Romford, Essex) and the new line-up recorded the 'Let There Be Rock' LP. Pinpointing AC/DC's success to particular songs is difficult but this album contained one, 'Whole Lotta Rosie', which perhaps did more than any other. The album failed to produce a hit single, however, a task which fell to 'Rock 'N' Roll Damnation' from 'Powerage' in July 1978. Once this song opened up American radio, the sky was AC/DC's only limit. A live album 'If You Want Blood – You've Got It' was released in February 1979, followed five months later by what many still consider to be their finest studio record, 'Highway To Hell'.

It was to be the last to feature Bon Scott, as after a heavy drinking session and a night spent asleep in a friend's car, he was found unconscious then pronounced dead at King's College Hospital – on February 20, 1980. A coroner would later record a verdict of death by misadventure, stating that the singer had 'drunk himself to death'. His final gig had been at the Southampton Gaumont on January 27.

AC/DC were quick to replace him, announcing the appointment of Brian Johnson (born October 5, 1947) in March. Johnson was the former frontman with UK band Geordie, a Glam Rock act in the style of Slade who had made three albums and had four UK Top 40 singles. His first task was to help the band finish sessions for the 'Back In Black' album, which turned into their most successful ever – selling over 10 million copies in the USA alone. Subsequent releases never matched it for consistency of song content or sales, but the band's stature as a live act grew and grew.

The pressure of touring and accompanying alcoholic indulgences took its toll on some: with Phil Rudd retiring in May 1983 (replaced by

IN THEIR OWN WORDS...

"The biggest bonus about being in this band is the fact that I can get into their gigs without paying for a fucking ticket. Honestly! Now and again I've forgotten I'm singing and I just stop and watch the band because I think they're just fucking great!"
– Brian Johnson
Kerrang! 11, March 11-24, 1982

"A gig is a gig is a gig, right? Whether it be 20,000 people or 20, it's still the atmosphere. If it all fell through, then we'd probably turn around and start back on the pubs again. Pretty stupid, aren't we?!?"
– Brian Johnson
Kerrang! 97, June 27-July 10, 1983

"I just heard the other day that we'd sold 30 million albums around the world. So we're asking, where's the money?!?"
– Malcolm Young
Kerrang! 378, February 8, 1985

"The critics might not like us – as Angus said the other day, 'We put out the same album every year with a different cover!' Ha! But the kids still like it and that's all we're worried about."
– Malcolm Young
Kerrang! 111, January 9-22, 1986

"We're still as tough as ever – there's definitely NO BALLADS! Actually, I don't mind hearing a ballad every now and then. Like once a year, maybe..."
– Angus Young
Kerrang! 159, October 24, 1987

"When he was alive, all people would say about Bon was that he was this creature straight from the gutter; no one would take him seriously. Then after he died, all of a sudden he was a great poet. Even he himself would have been laughing at that..."
– Angus Young
Kerrang! 309, September 29, 1990

"There's not a day goes by when I don't pick up a guitar. And I'm getting there. I've got two fingers going now!!!"
– Angus Young
Kerrang! 413, October 10, 1992

AC/DC

Simon Wright – ex-A II Z and Tytan – until he went to Dio in December 1989); Malcolm being unfit to tour in 1988 (he was briefly replaced on the 'Blow Up Your Video' tour by cousin Stevie Young (ex-Starfighters); and Cliff Williams whose place was taken temporarily by Paul Greg on the US leg of the 1991 tour. But AC/DC gradually dried themselves out and the band that Malcolm returned to was much healthier. Stronger, too, with the addition of Gary Moore, Firm *et al* drummer Chris Slade.

Slade (born October 30, 1946) made his debut on 'The Razor's Edge' and secured his place on the extensive world tour which followed, parts of which were recorded for the long overdue 'Live' double album. The story continues...

AC/DC 1993 vintage: still about to rock!

ALBUMS

HIGH VOLTAGE (Albert, Australia only, 1975 – KKK) Raw with more promise than power. 'Little Lover' and 'She's Got Balls' later lifted onto the worldwide release of same title.

TNT (Albert, Australia only, 1975 – KKK) Stronger than debut. Bulk of it resurfaced on...

HIGH VOLTAGE (Atlantic, 1976 – KKKK) "Inimitable blend of relentless rock 'n' roll and humour" – Kerrang! 74, AC/DC retrospective, August 9-22, 1984.

DIRTY DEEDS DONE DIRT CHEAP (Atlantic, 1976 – KKK) "Hilarious lyrics (but) lumbering down the beaten track" – Kerrang! 74.

LET THERE BE ROCK (Atlantic, 1977 – KKKKK) "Brilliant... HM classic... It'll stay fresh forever" – Kerrang! 74.

POWERAGE (Atlantic, 1978 – KKKK) "More of the same... The pace barely slackens!" – Kerrang! 74.

IF YOU WANT BLOOD – YOU'VE GOT IT (Atlantic, 1978 – KKKKK) "Did the impossible and translated the band's electrifying show onto vinyl" – Kerrang! 74.

HIGHWAY TO HELL (Atlantic, 1979 – KKKKK) "Polished and streamlined... a more precise delivery. Bon Scott's last..." – Kerrang! 74.

BACK IN BLACK (Atlantic, 1980 – KKKKK) "First with Brian Johnson... AC/DC rocketing back in style... with a touch of commerciality" – Kerrang! 74.

FOR THOSE ABOUT TO ROCK (WE SALUTE YOU) (Atlantic, 1981 – KK) "Several of the songs didn't work... Rather tedious" – Kerrang! 74.

FLICK OF THE SWITCH (Atlantic, 1983 – KKK) "Not as satisfying as 'Back In Black', but a considerable improvement on 'For Those...' " (Kerrang! 50, September 8-21, 1983)

FLY ON THE WALL (Atlantic, 1985 – KKK) "The glorious anthemic tunes we have come to expect... but no killers" – Kerrang! 97, June 27-July 10, 1985.

WHO MADE WHO (Atlantic, 1986 – KKK) "Compilation soundtrack to Steven King's 'Maximum Overdrive' movie. Includes three new songs: 'Who Made Who', 'D.T.' and 'Chase The Ace' " – Kerrang! 122, June 12-25, 1986.

BLOW UP YOUR VIDEO (Atlantic, 1988 – KKKK) "Songs played with almost spartan clarity. No clutter..." – Kerrang! 171, January 23, 1988

THE RAZOR'S EDGE (Atco, 1990 – KKK) "Shows the whole concept of AC/DC showing its age badly" – Kerrang! 308, September 22, 1990

LIVE (Atco, 1992 – KKKKK) "Just about all of AC/DC's classic tracks... only failing is that the tracks are separated... Crowds fade in and out" – Kerrang! 415, October 24, 1992

Bryan ADAMS

Canada, singer/guitarist (1979-present)
UNCOMPLICATED BUT incredibly gifted
songwriter now, ironically, plagued by the
success of the 1992 mega-hit single
'(Everything I Do) I Do It For You'. Although
always a rocker at heart, his credibilty has been
forever dented by this cringeworthy ballad.
Previous to it, he'd spent five years and three
albums struggling to raise a profile above the
cult level. Then in '85, 'Run To Me' broke him
and his fourth album, 'Reckless', worldwide.
1987's 'Into The Fire' was a lacklustre follow-up,
and the subsequent 'Waking Up The
Neighbours' ('92) suffered at the hands of over-
zealous 'Mutt' Lange production. Nevertheless,
this modest geezer-next-door remains one of
the rock world's most engaging live performers.
Recommended albums:
RECKLESS *(A&M, 1985 – KKKKK)*
LIVE! LIVE! LIVE! *(A&M, 1988 Japanese import*
– KKKKK)

AEROSMITH

USA, five-piece (1970-present)
'GOOD EVENING people, welcome to the
show!', is the openin' yelp and
introduction from ol' plunger lips
Steven Tyler on Aerosmith's
eponymous '73 debut. It's a
welcome, my friends, to a show
that (despite a few ins, outs, ups
'n' downs!) never ends!

The legendary, once infamous, 'Boston
bad boys' actually have their roots in Sunapee,
New Hampshire. Back in the summer of 1970,
some local tykes with a vision stopped pissin' in
the wind with their various outfits an' formed a
band who actually flirted with the idea of bein'
called the Hookers (!) before sensibly settlin' for
the less provocative Aerosmith. Ray Tabano
once played guitar alongside Joe Perry but,
stampin' a claim on Boston as their local turf,
their line-up soon settled as Tyler – who
originally played drums with Perry and Hamilton
in an oufit called the Jam Band – (vocals), Joe

Perry (guitar), Brad Whitford (guitar), Tom
Hamilton (bass) and Joey Kramer (drums). They
would tout their goods everywhere and
anywhere – literally! Aerosmith meant business.

It was a show at New York club Max's Kansas
City that swayed Columbia record label
executive Clive Davis to sign Aerosmith, a move
which resulted in the release of their self-titled
debut in '73. It laid the foundations for a sassy,
no-frills, hard-rockin' formula that – unlike most
mega-bands who suffer dodgy periods
artistically – has rarely deviated from total
brilliance up to the present day. Constant coast-
to-coast touring and a second LP release, 'Get
Your Wings' ('74), kept the 'Smith fuse burnin',
but it was the leap in sophistication of '75's
'Toys In The Attic' which was the explosion. Yet
although 'Toys...' remains the band's biggest
sellin' opus (quintuple platinum), it was the
follow-up 'Rocks' which
most deem to be the
definitive Aero-offering. On
its release in '76, Aerosmith
– along with Kiss – were
America's hottest home-
grown rock attraction.

After a recuperative period in
early '77 (their first rest – EVER!) a slightly
frazzled Aerosmith recorded 'Draw The
Line'. This release hardly matched the
band's previous success, and in
retrospect many a rock historian has
considered 'Draw The Line' to be the start of
somethin' of a decline for our heroes – despite
the fact that it was probably more frenetic than
their whole back catalogue put together! Press-
wise, Aerosmith's first British jaunt that year,
including the Reading Festival, pretty much
found the sofa-lipped Tyler bein' the butt end of
Jagger impersonator jibes, but at least the Brit
concert-goers ignored that and bothered to let
the music do the talkin'...

1978 saw Aerosmith splattered across the big
screen playing the Beatles' 'Come Together' as
the Future Villain Band in all-time turkey movie
'Sgt. Pepper's Lonely Hearts Club Band'. But at

"We still piss all over the opposition"
– Steven Tyler
Kerrang! 27, October 21-November 3, 1982

"If you're the Hookers you should come out looking like whores, y'know. So when we came across Aerosmith it was great – it doesn't mean a thing!" – Steven Tyler Kerrang! 33, January 13-26, 1983.

"I don't like way (Tyler)'s always phoning me up in the morning when I'm asleep! You just tell him I've got the utmost respect for him... providing he's standing at least 20 feet away from me!" – Joe Perry Kerrang! 70, June 14-27, 1984.

"Our previous label CBS ... were obviously a bit fed up with cheques going direct to drug dealers!" – Steven Tyler Kerrang! 106, October 31-November 13, 1985.

"What Heavy Metal image? We're an R'n'B band." – Joe Perry Kerrang! 127, August 21-September 3, 1986.

"We've cleaned up now... well, our minds are just as filthy as ever!" – Joe Perry Kerrang! 152, August 6-19, 1987.

"I mean, the last time we came to England – 10 years ago – all we were worried about was finding the best bottle of wine and the best cocaine. I mean, I did no sight-seeing, I did no shopping, and fuck the music man, let's get high!" – Steven Tyler Kerrang! 159, October 24, 1987.

"I think I had my drink for next Christmas... about seven years ago." – Joe Perry Kerrang! 254, September 2, 1989.

"You get fucked and you learn." – Joe Perry Kerrang! 302, August 11, 1990.

AEROSMITH

least that song was a hit and the saving grace for Aerosmith. Then came the sizzlin' and conspicuously live for a live album (if you know what I mean...) 'Live Bootleg' double package. But all was not well in the Aero-camp. Bein' road rats tested-true-and-tried, the sudden lack of constant tourin' did not suit their individual temperaments. Mind-screwin' chemical stimulants probably weren't a bonus either.

Thus, and heartbreakingly, durin' the recording and after the completion of '79's 'Night In The Ruts', Joe Perry and Brad Whitford bailed out respectively for solo careers. Perry forming his mercurial Joe Perry Project and Whitford teamin' up with ex-Ted Nugent singer Derek St Holmes for the inspirationally monickered... um, Whitford/St Holmes.

Virtual unknown guitarists Jimmy Crespo and Rick Dufay took on the awesome and unenviable task of fillin' Perry and Whitford's size nines, and while '80's 'Greatest Hits' album plugged the gap for a couple of years, the new duo had their trial by fire on '82's 'Rock In A Hard Place'. It might not have had the depth and flair of the classic line-up, but credit where it's due, this platter seriously bruised the rectal area, and Perry himself still curses himself for not being on it!

So to Valentine's Day 1984, when Perry and Whitford (Spinal Tap style!) cruised backstage after a 'Smith Boston show: love must have been in the air cos by April it was announced that the original line-up would re-unite for – what else – the Back In The Saddle tour. *YAAY!* Aerosmith signed to Geffen, but the mucho Zeppy debut for that label, 'Done With Mirrors' ('85) , complete with the sleeve ingeniously printed back-to-front (!), by their own standards was perhaps the nearest Aerosmith ever got to an off-day. The remedy and boost to their re-launch came when producer Rick Rubin and rappers Run DMC asked Steve 'n' Joe to guest on their cool cover of the Aero-classic 'Walk This Way'. It was a Rap/Metal barrier-breakin' crossover, along with a video humorously stressin' the point. MTV, of course, lapped it up. Aerosmith were back in vogue.

The release of the slick and somewhat calculated (for them) 'Permanent Vacation' ('87) saw them continue on a roll, and with singles 'Dude (Looks Like A Lady)' and 'Angel', enjoyin' hit action for the first time in aeons. It seemed Steve and Joe losin' their 'Toxic Twins' tag along with their drug and alcohol habits was paying off big time. Next the 'Biodegradable Brothers' soared to even higher heights when

AEROSMITH: from attics to cellars and back to the top...

'89's acclaimed (by every bugger except da *Big K!*'s reviewer!) 10th studio album 'Pump' leap-frogged 'Permanent Vacation's triple platinum mark, ultimately matchin' the 'Toys...' quintuple status! The scarily candid 'The Making Of Pump' vid and a globe-devouring tour accompanied it. And in April of 1993, with the Boston rock giants well and truly back in the saddle and relishin' every sore, Aerosmith showed they were still able to 'Get A Grip'...

ALBUMS:

AEROSMITH *(CBS, 1973 – KKKKK) Hard-drivin', rootsy, raw to the bone R'n'B...*
GET YOUR WINGS *(CBS, 1974 – KKKK) More sensitive than debut, but when it kicks it kicks!*
TOYS IN THE ATTIC *(CBS, 1975 – KKKKK) A1 class rock personified. Packed with hits.*
ROCKS *(CBS, 1976 – KKKKK) As above... but heavier! An absolute all-time hard rock classic.*
DRAW THE LINE *(CBS, 1977 – KKKKK) Looser, but stunningly effective. Nice 'n' ratty funk riffs.*
LIVE BOOTLEG *(CBS, 1978 – KKKKK) Warts an' all live recordings from '76 and '77 tours plus a few more ancient in concert rarities.*
NIGHT IN THE RUTS *(CBS, 1979 – KKKKK) Under-rated. Many fine songs, strong blues influence injected by Joe Perry.*

ROCK IN A HARD PLACE *(CBS, 1982 – KKKK) Mean 'n' moody guitars by Crespo and Dufay, songs unmistakably by Aerosmith.*
DONE WITH MIRRORS *(Geffen, 1985 – KKKK) "Hats off to Ted Templeman for brill production and for bringing the rawness back." – Kerrang! 107, November 14-27, 1985*
PERMANENT VACATION *(Geffen, 1987 – KKKKK) "Instant aural orgasms... the best thing Aerosmith have done since 'Rocks'." – Kerrang! 153, August 20-September 2, 1987*
PUMP *(Geffen, 1989 – KKKKK) "A saucy, slick parody of 'Permanent Vacation' that lives up to its model only spasmodically." – KKK in Kerrang! 255, September 9, 1989*
GET A GRIP *(Geffen, 1993 – KKKK) "Rates above 'Pump' because it shows a harder approach, and, ballads aside, is much less sweet, but the latter half disappoints.' – Kerrang! 440, April 24, 1993*

COMPILATIONS ETC:
GREATEST HITS *(CBS, 1980)*
CLASSICS LIVE *(CBS, 1986) New material.*
CLASSICS LIVE 2 *(Columbia, 1987) Ditto.*
GEMS *(Columbia, 1988)*
ANTHOLOGY *(Raw Power, 1989)*
PANDORA'S BOX *(Columbia, 1991) Superb triple CD/cassette. Hits, rarities and out-takes.*

AGENT STEEL

USA, five-piece (1984-1988)
"I LIKE to think of myself as the Steven Spielberg of Heavy Metal," was one of the choicer quotes from singer John Cyriss – a man who apparently believed himself to be from another planet, and signed his autographs, '2011'. Also featuring guitarist Juan Garcia, who went on to form Evildead, Agent Steel recorded two albums and an EP, before relocating to Florida and replacing Garcia with musical nomad James Murphy for what was to be their final tour, in Europe. Murphy later referred to the other band members as 'a bunch of wankers'. Rumours that John Cyriss later became a shaven-headed Buddhist monk were never fully substantiated.
Recommended album:
UNSTOPPABLE FORCE
(Music For Nations, 1987 – KKKK)

AGNOSTIC FRONT

USA, five-piece (1982-1992)
FORMED BY Vinnie Stigma (guitar) and Roger Miret (vocals), Agnostic Front typified New York's Hardcore scene. Powerful, aggressive and brutally uncompromising, and that was just the band members! Like a lot of bands of their ilk, they came from the wrong side of town, and that was exactly what came across in their music. Heavily tattooed Miret used to breed and fight pit-bulls (he is now a sworn vegetarian) and spent two years of a four year sentence in jail for drug-running. Many fans thought they had become too Metal with their final 'One Voice' opus, but there is no doubt they will be sadly missed. Played their last gig at the famous CBGB's club in their home town on December 20, '92. Or did they? Rumours persist...
Recommended album:
LIBERTY AND JUSTICE FOR
(Rough Justice, 1987 – KKKK)

ALCATRAZZ

USA, five-piece (1983-1987)
FORMED BY ex-Rainbow singer Graham Bonnet after he split from MSG in 1983. The debut album 'No Parole From Rock 'N' Roll' featured Swedish guitar hero Yngwie J Malmsteen, who left after a year to be replaced by former Frank Zappa fret frazzler Steve Vai. The band signed to Capitol and made 'Disturbing The Peace' (1985) and 'Dangerous Games' (1986) before calling it a day.
Recommended album:
NO PAROLE FROM ROCK 'N' ROLL *(Rocshire, 1983 – KKKK)*

ALICE IN CHAINS

USA, four-piece (1987-present)
ARGUABLY THE most original (and disturbing) of the new breed of Metal bands, with a crunching sound and uncompromising style that would have come to worldwide attention even without the coincidental 'advantage' of originating from Seattle. It took them two years from forming to get a deal, but when Columbia pushed the contract towards manager Susan Silver's pen (April 1989) they did so because they recognised the seeds of something very special in Alice In Chains' music – not because they were attempting to ride on the coat-tails of either Nirvana's success (the release of their first album, 'Bleach', was still two months away) or the Seattle scene. (That city's Sub Pop label was burgeoning rapidly, but the whole explosion was still set on a longish fuse...)

No, Alice In Chains had something darker and more powerful: the double-edged sword of Jerry Cantrell's guitar and Layne Staley's impassioned, sometimes desperate vocals. The pair of them were writing songs on the weirder side of comfortable, with many of their lyrics telling grim tales that could only have been inspired by the use of heroin. Come 1993, the band were claiming that their use of the drug was all in the past and refused to condone the practice, but an impact had already been made.

After embarrassingly glammy origins under the name Diamond Lie, Alice renamed and

restyled. Things began slowly in the USA, gigging only around their home city (originally with a different singer, Nick Pollock, now of My Sister's Machine), before Staley's arrival stabilised the line-up as: himself, Cantrell, Mike Starr (bass) and Sean Kinney (drums). After the deal was inked, Columbia released the 'We Die Young' EP in June 1990 as a prelude for the full-length Alice debut 'Facelift', out two months later. To promote it the band did their first gigs out of town, making it all the way to the East Coast for dates supporting Iggy Pop. The set then included unrecorded songs 'Dirt' and 'Rooster'. Audience reaction was indifferent. Back in Seattle things went better and a US-only in concert video, 'Live Facelift', was filmed at the end of the year.

January 1991 saw the band gaining momentum. They were nominated for an American Music Award (Favourite Heavy Metal Artist), filmed by

IN THEIR OWN WORDS...

"We never sat down and planned out a sound that's this dark or claustrophobic. It's pretty much a release for us. We dig aggressive, moody music; the stuff that moves you and whips you around."
– Jerry Cantrell, *Kerrang! 333, March 23, 1991*

"We never tried to follow in the footsteps of a distorted feedback, grunge band. It was only after we changed our name to Alice In Chains and had been jamming on this material for well over a year that bands like Mother Love Bone and Nirvana came out."
– Layne Staley, *Kerrang! 333, March 23, 1991*

"It's public knowledge that Layne and I had some (drug) problems. That's way over, that's already been taken care of. 'Dirt's music is the final nail in that coffin."
– Jerry Cantrell, *Kerrang! 416, October 31, 1992*

ALICE IN CHAINS

Cameron Crowe as the bar band in his 'Singles' movie, and – more importantly – released the single 'Man In The Box' which began a 26 week climb into the Top 20.

By now the 'buzz' about Alice had reached Europe where the band toured for the first time as the opening act on the Megadeth/Almighty tour. Their European live debut was the first night of that tour at London's Marquee club, part of *Kerrang!*'s 10th anniversary celebrations.

Back in the States in February they were nominated for a Grammy then headed off in May on the 'Clash Of The Titans' tour as the sometimes overlooked opening salvo before the big gun barrage of Slayer, Megadeth and Anthrax. But all later spoke of the band fondly, as have so many other peers and elders...

In August 1991, Alice In Chains began a prestigious – if on paper, unlikely – five month slot on the Van Halen tour before taking time out in November to record an acoustic EP 'Sap'. Deemed a little too weird by Columbia for European audiences, it was never formally released here but sold well on import. The band's next release, the single 'Would?' (originally on the 'Singles' movie soundtrack) came out in the States in August 1992, then five months later in the UK where it followed the American precedent and turned Alice into a chart and radio-play band. Alice's second album, 'Dirt', had already been a hit since its release in September 1992, not least being voted the *Kerrang!* Critics' Album Of The Year.

Bassist Starr quit immediately prior to the band's January 1993 visit to the Europe. For the dates, including a sell-out UK leg, his touring replacement was former Ozzy Osbourne Band man Michael Inez. For Alice In Chains, the future – as they say – is history.

ALBUMS:
FACELIFT (Columbia, 1990 – KKKK) "A trip you won't be able to avoid getting sucked into. Slow and foot-stompingly heavy..."
– Kerrang! 302, August 11, 1990
SAP (Columbia, 1991 – KKK) "Five-song EP... a stop gap... a mildly interesting diversion."
– Kerrang! 381, February 29, 1992
DIRT (Columbia, 1992 – KKKKK) "Very nearly a masterpiece... nightmarish trip through a cycle of self-abuse and tortuous struggles..."
– Kerrang! 412, October 3, 1992

The ALMIGHTY

UK, four-piece (1988-present)

THE ALMIGHTY's rise through the ranks has been relentless and brutal. Originally the brainchild of Belfast-born Ricky Warwick, the band was conceived following his unceremonious departure from New Model Army. Ricky wasted little time in establishing the Almighty as a glorious thundercloud over the British club scene. The original blueprint of post-Zodiac proto-punk has been bullied and pummelled into shape over the course of three studio albums for Polydor and celebrated in October 1990 with the release of a live set ('Blood, Fire & Live') as the band made the gradual transition to larger venues. Recruiting Canadian guitarist Pete Friesen (ex-Alice Cooper band) in March 1992 revitalised the

RICKY WARWICK (the Almighty): a bloodbath warhorse and no mistake...

Almighty's crushing bloodbath of volatile riffs and pro-power lyrics. They triumphed as the opening act on that year's Castle Donington rock festival and have established themselves as an internationally streamlined warhorse.
Recommended albums:
BLOOD, FIRE & LOVE *(Polydor, 1989 – KKKK)*
POWERTRIPPIN' *(Polydor, 1993 – KKKKK)*

ANACRUSIS

USA, four-piece (1986-present)
ULTRA COMPLEX techno Metalheads who make most VoiVod songs sound like Extreme acoustic ballads.
Cautiously recommended album:
MANIC IMPRESSIONS *(Metal Blade, 1991 – KKK)*

ANGEL

USA, five-piece (1974-1981)
INTIALLY FEATURING a line-up of Frank Dimino (vocals), Gregg Giuffria (keyboards), Barry Brandt (drums) and former Bux duo Punky Meadows (guitar) and Mickey Jones (bass), Angel were conceived in Washington DC as a majestic Pomp Rock band, taking their cue from Yes, Deep Purple and ELP.

Discovered by Kiss' Gene Simmons and snapped up by Casablanca Records upon his advice, Angel were to spend the rest of their career in their labelmates' shadow.

The progressive Metal blitzkrieg of 'Angel' and 'Helluva Band' earnt them a cult following, leading to the readers of influential rock magazine *Circus* voting Angel the best new band of 1976. But despite solid touring Angel were mysteriously denied any kind of sales breakthrough at retail for their recorded work, a fact which irritated Casablanca so much that they insisted that Angel turn their attention towards a more commercial line in songwriting by third album, 'On Earth As It Is In Heaven'.

Replacing Jones with Felix Robinson for 'White Hot', Angel spent virtually all of 1978 on the road, yet even blockbusting bubblegum pop rock such as the ensuing 'Sinful' album, released the following year, failed to even get anywhere near Gold status. Then a double-live package, 'Live Without A Net', proved to be Angel's epitaph at the turn of the new decade.

Best remembered more for their magical stage show and heavenly Glam image, various reformations of the group have been made in recent years, none of which have gone beyond the recording of half-assed demos. In solo ventures Gregg Giuffria has far and away been the most successful, with Giuffria and then House Of Lords.
Recommended albums:
ANGEL *(Casablanca, 1975 – KKKKK)*
SINFUL *(Casablanca, 1979 – KKKK)*

ANGEL WITCH

UK, three-piece (1980-1990)
CLASSIC NWOBHM act featuring Kevin Heybourne (guitar and vocals), Kevin Riddles (bass) and Dave DuFort – brother of Girlschool's Denise – (drums). Toyed with occult imagery and featured a strongly Sabbath-influenced sound. Reformed mid- and late-'80s but were at their best early on.
Recommended (debut) album:
ANGEL WITCH *(Bronze, 1981 – KKKK)*

The ANGELS

Australia, five-piece (1975-1992)
LED BY nutter vocalist Doc Neeson, the Angels are a national institution in the barn-sized bars Down Under with their uncompromising riff-led rock 'n' roll. Yet they have remained criminally overlooked outside their native land, sometimes trading as Angel City or the Angels From Angel City (!). Axl Rose has sung their praises and Great White covered 'Face The Day' but the rest of the world still can't see the light.
Recommended albums:
FACE TO FACE *(Albert, Australia, 1978 – KKKKK)*
BEYOND SALVATION *(Chrysalis, 1990 – KKKKK)*

ANNIHILATOR

Canada, five-piece (1985-present)
THE BRAINCHILD of guitarist extraordinaire Jeff

Waters, Annihilator have come to be known for precise and skillfully schizoid Metal, along with sleeve imagery depicting strange little girls called Alice.

Between '85 and '86, the original Ottawa-based line-up recorded two well-received demos, but the ultimately frustrated Waters decided to relocate to Vancouver. There, he met the people who were destined to cut the 'Alice In Hell' album with him; most notably singer Randy Rampage, a known alcoholic and ex-DOA man. The album made a strong impact, but Rampage quit during an '89 tour, to be replaced by Coburn Pharr, formerly with LA also-rans Omen. He left in 1991 to be replaced by the relatively soberly named Aaron Randall.

Recommended albums:
ALICE IN HELL (Roadrunner, 1989 – KKKK)
NEVER NEVERLAND (Roadrunner, 1990 – KKKK)

ANTHRAX

USA, five-piece (1981-present)
FROM HESITANT origins, New York Thrash band Anthrax grew into one of the late '80s Big Four – along with their West Coast contemporaries Metallica, Slayer and Megadeth. Although yet to enjoy major commercial success, Anthrax have at least progressed well from early days when they presented a leather-jackets-and-jeans tough-guy image...

This was instigated by original vocalist Neil Turbin, who fronted a line-up completed by Scott Ian (guitar), Dan Spitz (guitar), Dan Lilker (bass) and Charlie Benante (drums), and which recorded the rather clichéd 'Fistful Of Metal' LP. It ranks low by later standards, and all-round changes soon followed...

Lilker (later of Nuclear Assault) and Turbin were ousted, and the band quickly became uncomfortable with the idea that he was once a part of Anthrax. In a later issue of *Kerrang!* Scott Ian marvelled disbelievingly: "The guy had his picture taken with a knife!".

Into the Anthrax fold by way of replacement came bassist Frank Bello and ex-Bible Black man Joey Belladonna (real surname Bellardini), whose comparatively melodic voice was first heard on 1986's 'Armed And Dangerous' EP, followed later in the year by the full-blown

ANTHRAX (Scott Ian): riff-kruncher and face-puller extraordinaire

IN THEIR OWN WORDS...

ANTHRAX

'Spreading The Disease' opus, which caused major ripples on the Metal pond, with such fine tunes as the unbelievably crunchy 'Madhouse' (a promo video for which was banned on grounds that it was making fun of the mentally wayward), 'Medusa', and the highly stompy opener 'A.I.R.'.

The album made it into the lower reaches of the *Billboard* Top 200, and Anthrax (managed by their US Megaforce label mogul Johnny Z) subsequently landed support slots with W.A.S.P. and Black Sabbath. Scott Ian and Benante helped form the cult band S.O.D. shortly after recording '...Disease', but they found less and less time for the side project as a European tour with Metallica loomed. The pairing was predictably explosive, although the tour as a whole was ended by the death of Metallica's bassist Cliff Burton.

1987 saw Anthrax move to Island Records and release 'Among The Living'. With it came a change of image that seemed overly premeditated to some, stirring many a debate:

bermuda shorts, merry face-pulling, and lyrics/photo-shoots revolving around comics, Stephen King novels and skateboarding. Whatever their opinion on the band's look and interests, few could deny the new album's potency. The first side in particular is jam-packed with great songs, and 'I Am The Law' managed to penetrate the UK's Top 40 singles chart. A further single, 'I'm The Man', made a fair impression with its humorous cross-breeding of Metal and Rap.

After lengthy touring with 'ATL', 1988's 'State Of Euphoria' LP, despite receiving an OTT six-K review in *Kerrang!*, was less exciting, failing even to equal its predecessor in terms of songwriting, production or general spirit. It was nevertheless supported by tours with Iron Maiden, Ozzy Osbourne and Kiss.

Resurrection was eventually achieved with their fifth studio album, 'Persistence Of Time', delayed by a studio fire in late '89, and finally released the following summer. It heralded a decided return to form, with Ian's patented mega-moshy guitar enjoying the mix's spotlight once again, and Anthrax went on to support Iron Maiden in Europe.

In 1991, the band furthered their previous flirtations with Rap, by collaborating with Public Enemy on a new single version of 'Bring The Noise'. It was an excellent pointer to crossover possibilities between the two musical genres, and despite (outside) fears of racial clashes, the bands subsequently toured together without problems. The single was then included on both bands' current albums. Anthrax's was 'Attack Of The Killer B's', dubbed 'the longest EP ever', due to the fact that it was originally meant to be one! It was the band's last album for Island. They signed next to Elektra, and parted ways with Belladonna, confirming rumours that the band's democracy had been unbalanced for some time. Belladonna's replacement turned out to be Armored Saint man John Bush, who set about writing songs with them for their 1993 comeback...

ALBUMS:

FISTFUL OF METAL (Music For Nations, 1984 – KK) "Great debut... Next time around we may have a klassik on our hands." – Kerrang! 62, February 23-March 7, 1984.

SPREADING THE DISEASE (Island, 1985 – KKKK) "There's NOT a better example of the (Thrash) genre around." – Kerrang! 106, October 30-November 13, 1985.
AMONG THE LIVING (Island, 1987 – KKKKK) "MOSH! MOSH! MOSH! AHHH! VVRROOOMM!" – Kerrang! 142, March 19-April 1, 1987.
STATE OF EUPHORIA (Island, 1988 – KKK) "After 'ATL's enormous majesty, this poses the question: how did Anthrax manage to lose the plot?" – Kerrang! 204, September 10, 1988.
PERSISTENCE OF TIME (Island, 1990 – KKKK) "The ultimate payback... To the poseurs who dismiss Anthrax as not moody enough..." – Kerrang! 304, August 25, 1990.
ATTACK OF THE KILLER B'S (Island, 1991 –

KKKK) "A treasure trove of tidy-sized trinkets." Kerrang! 346, June 22, 1991.
THE SOUND OF WHITE NOISE (Elektra, 1993 – KKKKK) "Anthrax have finally made the record that's been welling up in them like the veins in Scott Ian's shaved head." Kerrang! 444, May 22, 1993

ANTI-NOWHERE LEAGUE

UK, four-piece (1980-present)
THOROUGHLY OBNOXIOUS biker/punk band led by vocalist Nick 'Animal' Karmer. Earned themselves a loyal and unruly following with the likes of 'I Hate People'; and the attention of the Obscene Publications Squad who seized and destroyed copies of their debut single (a cover of Ralph McTell's 'Streets Of London') because of its now-infamous B-side, 'So What'. Split for a while after 1987's change of image, with the band swapping dirty black leather for clean white shirts, but since have Metallica covered 'So What' the League have returned to foul-mouthed form.
Recommended (debut) album:
WE ARE THE LEAGUE (WXYZ, 1982 – KKKKK)

ANVIL

Canada, four-piece (1980-present)
DILDO-BRANDISHING vocalist/guitarist Lips was obsessed by sex, Heavy Metal and, er... sex. These three (!) obsessions made for great interviews and occasionally great records but the lusty vocals and breakneck guitars never quite translated into MTV-fuelled superstardom.

Anvil are still playing clubs in Toronto, but the newest line-up can't touch the over-the-top,

LIPS OF Anvil: would you buy a used anything off this man?!?

chainsaw-handed, Very Metal, original.
Recommended (first two) albums:
HARD 'N' HEAVY *(Attic, 1981 – KKKK)*
METAL ON METAL *(Attic, 1982 – KKKKK)*

APRIL WINE

Canada, five-piece (1972-1985)
ONCE UPON a time, April Wine were among the
biggest three Canadian acts, chasing the coat-
tails of Heart and Rush – but their music was
never the equal of either. Unsure whether to
play lame hard rock or tough AOR, their 15
albums usually ended up in the depressingly
grey area in the middle. They were promoting
'Harder Faster' – one of their better efforts –
when they played the first Donington festival in
1980 but never really took off outside Canada
and the States. An early '90s reformation
seems, thankfully, to have failed.
Recommended album (if only for the title):
HARDER FASTER *(Capitol, 1979 – KKK)*

ARMAGEDDON

UK, four-piece (1975)
BRILLIANT UNKNOWNS whose career ended
when their singer, ex-Yardbirds man Keith Relf,
died in a bizarre electrocution accident. Their
sole legacy is a timeless, skull-crushingly heavy
album of eerie hard rock that should be plucked
from any bargain bin immediately.
Highly recommended album:
ARMAGEDDON *(A&M, 1975 – KKKKK)*

ARMORED SAINT

USA, five-piece (1983-1992)
GIFTED BUT unlucky band who, over the course
of five albums, changed from Speed/Thrash to
Power Metal without offending fans or critics.
Guitarist Dave Pritchard died from leukemia in
February 1990, then, towards the end of 1992,
following their best album (see below), singer
John Bush left to replace Joey Belladonna in
Anthrax. The band have since folded...
Recommended album:
SYMBOL OF SALVATION *(Metal Blade, 1991 –
KKKK)*

ASaP

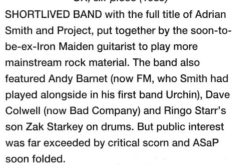

UK, six-piece (1989)
SHORTLIVED BAND with the full title of Adrian
Smith and Project, put together by the soon-to-
be-ex-Iron Maiden guitarist to play more
mainstream rock material. The band also
featured Andy Barnet (now FM, who Smith had
played alongside in his first band Urchin), Dave
Colwell (now Bad Company) and Ringo Starr's
son Zak Starkey on drums. But public interest
was far exceeded by critical scorn and ASaP
soon folded.
One album:
SILVER AND GOLD *(Enigma, 1989 – KK)*

ASIA

UK, four-piece (1982-present)
ORIGINALLY A 'supergroup' featuring ex- members of Yes (guitarist Steve Howe and keyboard
player Geoff Downes), ELP (drummer Carl
Palmer) and King Crimson (bassist/singer John
Wetton). After a huge hit with 'Heat Of The
Moment', the band went downhill from being a
big time AOR band with progressive leanings to
a sad collection of wannabes trading on
an outdated concept as original members
left and took musical credibility with them.
Recommended album:
ASIA *(Geffen, 1982 – KKKK)*

ATOM SEED

UK, four-piece (1989-present)
ALTHOUGH INITIALLY plagued by comparisons
to the Red Hot Chili Peppers or Faith No More,
(they once even, perhaps unwisely, supported
the Chilis on a UK tour), the Atom Seed rapidly
built up a strong following with their intense live
shows and gradually developed their own style.

After these and their indie debut 'Get In Line'
album, the Seeds were hotly tipped to be the
brightest hopes in British rock, a phrase which
is usually the kiss of death for any good band
and sadly proved no different in this case. It
brought them a promising major deal with
London/Slash which ended in 1992 with no

albums ever being released and the band virtually back at square one. They split up early in 1993 having never been given a real chance to fulfil their obvious potential.

Recommended album:
GET IN LINE *(Heavy Metal, 1990 – KKKKK)*

AUTOPSY

USA, three-piece (1988-present)
EXPONENTS OF bassy Gore Metal, with all the interview verbosity of the corpses they growl about, Californians Autopsy began creating their messy wares after drummer (and eventual vocalist) Chris Reifert left 'Scream Bloody Gore'-era Death, and gathered two like-minded musos around him.

Over the course of three albums and two EPs, with song titles like 'Necrocannibalistic

Vomitorium', the band found no favour with any censorship groups whatsoever. Unfortunately, neither have they sent a staggering number of music fans into ecstatic paroxysms...

(Not particularly) recommended album:
ACTS OF THE UNSPEAKABLE *(Peaceville, 1992 – KK)*

AVENGER

UK, four-piece (1982-1986)
'HOT AND Heavy Express', a track on a Neat Records live 12", represented Avenger's recording debut. Links with NWOBHM heroes Blitzkrieg meant press recognition yet both of the band's albums ('Blood Sports' and 'Killer Elite') were hampered by horrendous production problems, despite the obvious musical ability displayed on each.

Recommended album:
KILLER ELITE *(Neat, 1985 KKK)*

AXXIS

Germany, five-piece (1984-present)
ALMOST UNKNOWN pomp-ish Metallers who opened for Black Sabbath in 1989 the UK on their 'Headless Cross' tour. Having made four albums (one live) they've now let the perms grow out and sharpened up their act.

Recommended album:
THE BIG THRILL *(Electrola, 1993 – KKK)*

BABY ANIMALS

Australia, four-piece (1990-present)

FRONTED BY unlikely rock heroine Suze DeMarchi, Baby Animals trotted onto the UK scene in 1990, when import copies of their debut album sneaked in by carrier pigeon. A proper UK release didn't follow until after the band had opened for Bryan Adams, but by then the band's mixture of hard driving rock and super smooth softer songs was well known.

BABY ANIMALS' Suze DeMarchi: she's got balls!

The band toured hard in Britain, and Suze showed she was all woman by regaling a *K!* journalist with tales of her bad moods and PMT. That aside, DeMarchi is indisputably one of the very few positive role models for female musicians. She wouldn't be seen dead in a Gaultier bustier and wields a mean guitar. Femininity and balls?! She's gottit!

Highly recommended album:
BABY ANIMALS *(Imago, 1991 – KKKKK)*

BABY TUCKOO

UK, five-piece (1982-1987)

FAMOUS-FOR-15-minutes mob featuring singer Rob Armitage, a big teaser from Barnsley with plenty of gunpowder in his barrel. Fellow Yorkshireman Andy Barrott added guitar, but aside from a shared *K!* cover with Chrome Molly in February 1987, Baby Tuckoo remained sadly overlooked.

Recommended album:
FORCE MAJEURE *(Music For Nations, 1986 – KKKK)*

The BABYS

UK/USA, four/five-piece (1975-1981)

FORMED IN London but enjoyed all their success in the United States. When signed by Chrysalis, the band was initially a four-piece, with vocalist John Waite joined by Michael Corby (bass), Wally Stocker (guitar) and Tony Brock (drums). Corby had departed by the time third album, 'Head First', was issued in 1979, after which not one but two Americans were drafted in – Ricky Phillips (bass) and Chicago-born Jonathan Cain (keyboards).

The latter formed a good songwriting partnership with Waite, taking The Babys into another dimension on their final two releases, 'Union Jacks' and 'On The Edge', after which Cain was headhunted by Journey and Waite went off to pursue a lucrative solo deal. Later, the pair were to team up once more in the successful, but ultimately ill-fated, Bad English.

Recommended albums:
THE BABYS *(Chrysalis, 1976 – KKKK)*
UNION JACKS *(Chrysalis, 1980 – KKKK)*

BABYSITTERS

UK, four-piece (1983-1987)

ABSURD BUT brilliant trashy rock 'n' rollers who infested the thrivin', but for the most part unrecognised, London Glam scene of the early-to mid-'80s.

Recommended album:
BABYSITTERS *(Heavy Metal, 1985 – KKKK)*

BACHMAN-TURNER OVERDRIVE

Canada, four-piece (1973-1979)
THANKS TO those cuddle-mungous DJs
Smashey and Nicey, these now defunct Canuck
heavy(over)weights are now universally known
for their rock-tastic hit 'You Ain't Seen Nothin'
Yet', Yet, at their peak (the third and fourth
albums, below) BTO were actually a fiercely
uncompromising hard rock/boogie band, led by
Randy Bachman's gruff vocals and crunching
rhythm guitar. Both were sadly missing in '84
when the band reformed briefly without him to
support Van Halen.
Recommended albums:
NOT FRAGILE *(Mercury, 1974 – KKKK)*
FOUR WHEEL DRIVE *(Mercury, 1975 – KKKK)*

BAD BRAINS

USA, four-piece (1980-present)
RAGING RASTAFARIAN outfit who completely
threw early audiences by going from flat-out
Hardcore Punk into melodic Reggae several
times during the same set.

They were originally best known for the
ludicrously fast single 'Pay To Cum', but
frontman HR soon became a predominant
feature in the band because of his unusual
vocal style and outrageous back-flips on stage.
Unfortunately he had a habit of leaving the band
in favour of religion and appalling solo projects,
so they eventually replaced him with ex-Faith
No More singer Chuck Mosley. The line-up was
unproductive and the band split again, until
early 1993 and reports of gigs in New York with
only two original members surviving.
Recommended album:
ROCK FOR LIGHT *(Line, 1983 – KKKKK)*

BAD COMPANY

UK, four/five-piece (1973-present)
FORMED AS a quartet from the ashes of blues
rock legends Free, featuring the latter's peerless
singer Paul Rodgers and drummer Simon Kirke,
plus ex-Mott The Hoople guitarist Mick Ralphs
and veteran bassist 'Boz' Burrell. That line-up
recorded the eponymous '74 debut album and

worldwide
featuring
worldwide
hit 'Can't
Get
Enough'.
Although
some saw
the band
as a soul-
less
variation
of Free,
Bad

*BAD COMPANY's Paul Rodgers: 'peerless'.
Nice flares, too…*

Company were far more successful (especially
in America) and their records helped define
AOR, and in particular the style adopted by
Foreigner – although Bad Co's sound was much
rawer. Bad Company were also much admired
by Led Zeppelin, who offered them support
slots and eventually a place on their Swan Song
label.

After third LP, 'Run With The Pack' (Island,
1976), internal friction grew and the band lost
creative flair and although they enjoyed success
with the fifth record, 'Desolation Angels' (Swan
Song, 1982), the band soon fell apart. Rodgers
left to work with Jimmy Page in The Firm, and
was replaced by Brian Howe (ex-Ted Nugent).
Howe is a great singer but the band lost focus.
Expanding to a five-piece with varying sidemen
didn't help, either. Today, 10 albums old, the
band makes more than respectable music but is
very much trading on past glories.
Recommended albums:
BAD COMPANY *(Island, 1974 – KKKKK)*
STRAIGHT SHOOTER *(Island, 1975 – KKKKK)*

BAD ENGLISH

UK/USA, five-piece (1989-1991)
ORIGINALLY DUBBED ONE of AOR's most
spectacular supergroups, but almost inevitably,
any hoped-for longevity went out the door come
second album, 'Backlash'.

Comprised of vocalist John Waite, bassist
Ricky Phillips (both formerly of The Babys),

guitarist Neal Schon (ex-Santana and Journey), keyboard player Jonathan Cain (ex-Babys *and* Journey!) and drummer Deen Castranova (previously with the Wild Dogs), the band's self-titled debut album proved the perfect blend of radio-friendly rockers and lush ballads. One of the best of the latter, 'When I See You Smile', even hit the US Number One spot.

But the pressure of that success, coupled with ego clashes, led to rows over the form 'Backlash' should take, and then a split in the ranks. Schon and Castranova departed to form Hardline, whilst Phillips played bass on some of the Coverdale/Page tracks. Waite, meanwhile, plotted to restart his solo career with the help of former Whitesnake guitarist Adrian Vandenberg.
Recommended album:
BAD ENGLISH *(Epic, 1989 – KKKK)*

BAD NEWS

UK, four-piece (1982–1987)
SPOOF ROCK band put together by Channel 4's 'Comic Strip' crew Adrian Edmonson, Rik Mayall, Nigel Planer and Peter Richardson, and allegedly based on a cross between W.A.S.P. and Brick Outhouse. Two hilarious TV programmes, 'Bad News' and 'More Bad News', passed into legend, and unlike the Spinal Tap movie were far more than simply a collection of music biz in-jokes.

Remarkably, some of their songs were better than those of 'real' Metal bands and they played sell-out shows at the London Marquee and Hammersmith Odeon, supported Iron Maiden on a UK tour, and were first on the bill at Donington Monsters of Rock in 1986. Scenes of the band being bottled off stage (for 'More Bad News') had to be enhanced because they went down surprisingly well. 'Warriors Of Ghengis Khan' has since been covered by various bands, including Acid Reign.
Recommended to accompany both videos:
BAD NEWS *(EMI, 1987 – KKKK)*

BADLANDS

USA, four-piece (1988-1992)
FORMED BY singer Ray Gillen (after brief stints with Black Sabbath and Blue Murder) and ex-Ozzy Osbourne guitarist Jake E Lee, the band aimed to recreate the feel of hard driving Blues music as written by Led Zeppelin, Humble Pie and early Bad Company. Their debut almost succeeded, but the second, 'Voodoo Highway' (Atlantic, 1991) failed badly and the band split acrimoniously after Lee criticised Gillen in *Kerrang!* and said he had been replaced by a girl. Farewell UK dates, featuring Gillen, proved otherwise (!) but slanging matches between the two continued, occasionally on stage. Tales of a fresh start with a new (male) singer persist...
Recommended album:
BADLANDS *(Atlantic, 1989 – KKKK)*

BALAAM AND THE ANGEL

UK, four-piece (1983-1992)
UNFAIRLY HERALDED as Cult copyists when they first terrorised the pubs in white pyjamas, the three Morris brothers (Mark – bass/vocals, Jim – guitar, Des – drums) and later recruit guitarist Ian McKean steered their poignant Goth Metal around the world with some success. A split with Virgin Records in 1991 upset the applecart but they returned with the 'No More Innocence' mini-LP (Intensity, '91) then re-released those six plus five new ones as 'Prime Time' (Bleeding Hearts, '93).
Recommended album:
LIVE FREE OR DIE *(Virgin, 1987 – KKKKK)*

BANG TANGO

USA, five-piece (1989-present)
PERHAPS THE last of the really original and exciting LA-based rock bands, with the rasping vocals of Joe Lesté and songs wrapped around the funk-fuelled bass of Kyle Kyle.

Their indie debut, 'Live Injection' (1989), prompted GN'R comparisons then their first full blooded studio affair, 'Psycho Café', met a wealth of favourable reviews. Toured the US with Britny Fox and Bad English, then made the darker, Gothier 'Dancin' On Coals' before another live set, 'Ain't No Jive Live', in 1992.
Recommended album:
PSYCHO CAFÉ *(Mechanic/MCA, 1989 – KKKK)*

Jimmy BARNES

Australia, singer (1984-present)

SCOTTISH-BORN gravel-voiced belter who shot to stardom Down Under fronting national institution, Cold Chisel. After that band split, his solo success was assured and, initially, well deserved. He made three albums of polished, but respectably heavy AOR, then Lost It... eventually having his hair cut and taking the Michael Bolton route. Well and truly souled out. Sad.

Recommended album:
FREIGHT TRAIN HEART *(Geffen, 1988 – KKKK)*

BARON ROJO

Spain, four-piece (1981-1989)

PRONOUNCED 'ROKKO', the (Red) Barons delivered quality Heavy Metal while struggling against an often unfavourable political climate. Criticising the same – usually in Spanish lyrics – didn't help at home or abroad.

Recommended album:
METAL MORPHOSIS *(Chapa Disocs, 1983 – KKK)*

BATHORY

Sweden, three-piece (1983-present)

ONCE DESCRIBED in *Mega Metal Kerrang! 6* as "just about the most diabolically nasty that Metal is likely to get", Bathory's eponymous, black-sleeved debut hit the racks in 1984. It was indeed evil stuff, even outdoing the mighty originators of the genre, Venom, in terms of Satanic horror.

Album number two, 'The Return', was recorded while enigmatic mainman Quorthon and his sidemen were drunk, and it showed. Things improved with 1987's 'Under The Sign Of The Black Mark' – unthinkably extreme in places, while introducing an epic, Gothic feel. 'Blood Fire Death' furthered this element quite well, but subsequent albums stretched it to tedious lengths...

Recommended album:
UNDER THE SIGN OF THE BLACK MARK *(Under One Flag, 1987 - KKKK)*

BE BOP DELUXE

UK, four-piece (1972-1978)

POETIC BUT punchy, semi-Prog Rock band led by Wakefield-born Bill Nelson, who as a vocalist/frontman was an astonishing guitarist/lyricist!

Recommended album:
AXE VICTIM *(Harvest, 1974 - KKKK)*

Jeff BECK

UK, guitarist, (1968-present)

ALTHOUGH RARELY choosing to play in a HM style, Beck is undoubtedly one of its finest exponents. Since leaving the Yardbirds in the late '60s he has prefered either R'n'B or jazz, but what he can do to a Fender Stratocaster is nobody's business. He remains a largely unsung hero (except amongst those who have tried to figure out how he does it) and a major influence on the likes of Ritchie Blackmore, Gary Moore and Joe Perry. None of these, and few others, would dispute his ranking among the very best as evinced by the triple-CD career-best box set 'Beckology' (Epic, 1992). Otherwise, sample...

Recommended albums:
BLOW BY BLOW *(Epic, 1975 – KKKK)*
GUITAR SHOP *(Epic, 1989 – KKKK)*

Jason BECKER

USA, guitarist (1987-present)

HYPERFAST WIDDLER discovered by Shrapnel label boss Mike Varney. Debuted on 'Speed Metal Symphony', the first of two Cacophony albums alongside Marty Friedman (now Megadeth), and solo on 1988's instrumental album, 'Perpetual Burn'. But his most accessible, if less technical work, was done for David Lee Roth's 'A Little Ain't Enough'. Sadly, Becker was too ill to join Roth's touring band.

Recommended album (with Cacophony):
SPEED METAL SYMPHONY *(Roadrunner, 1987 – KKK)*

Pat BENATAR

USA, solo artist (1979-present)

BORN PATRICIA Andrzejewski and operatically

trained, Pat Benatar's first three albums were a major attraction on the international soft rock scene. Practically everything the diminuitive chanteuse recorded turned to platinum, and, alongside husband and guitarist Neil Geraldo, she forged a tough path to stadium success. Her later albums matured dramatically, although a Blues album was tepidly received by critics and fans alike. Despite a dated image, some of her work still stands as a tribute to the Hollywood rock industry of the '80s.
Recommended album:
SEVEN THE HARD WAY (Chrysalis, 1985 – KKKK)

The BEYOND
UK, four-piece (1987-present)
DESPITE THEIR standard Thrash Metal origins, Derby's The Beyond have mutated along proggier, more adventurous lines since signing to EMI in 1991. The deal's on hold following a debut album too arty and confused for a major market but their career has yet to run its course.
Recommended album:
CRAWL (EMI, 1991 – KKK)

Jello BIAFRA
USA, singer/lyricist (1978-present)
PERHAPS THE most influential figure ever to deal in Anarcho Rock, Jello Biafra originally hit the headlines as vocalist for the legendary San Fransisco Punk band, the Dead Kennedys. A constant thorn in authority's backside, he ran for mayor in 1979 and pushed the limits of politics in rock further each year, until the eventual demise of the 'Kennedys around the time of a 14 month court case ending in August '87. The band were cleared of the charges against then ("distribution of harmful matter to minors" in the shape of a 'Penis Landscape' poster by award-winning artist HR Gieger, given away with the DK's 'Frankenchrist' album) in what turned out to be an immensely important case for the rock world.

While running the successful Alternative Tentacles record label, Biafra (real name Eric Boucher) has continued to work tirelessly for freedom of speech and anti-censorship, while putting out some stunning records, both spoken word and with bands such as Ministry, DOA, and NoMeansNo.
Recommended albums:
LAST SCREAM OF THE MISSING NEIGHBORS (Alternative Tentacles,1989- KKKKK) with DOA
I BLOW MINDS FOR A LIVING (Alternative Tentacles, 1991-KKKKK) spoken word

BILL AND TED
USA, Rock Dudes, (1989-present)
ABSOLUTLEY NO relation to Wayne and Garth although they may have watched 'Wayne's World' when younger. Bill (Alex Winter) and Ted (Keanu Reeves) are from California, dude, and have starred in two movies, 'Bill And Ted's Excellent Adventure' (1989) and its totally bigger budget follow-up 'Bill And Ted's Bogus Journey' (1991). Excellent!
Recommended watching:
BOTH THE ABOVE but not their garage band, Wyld Stallyns.

BITCH
USA, four-piece (1982-1987)
HEAVILY IMMERSED in S&M imagery and led by singer Betsy Weiss (once dubbed "Rob Halford's little sister"), Bitch initially found it hard to live up to their own hype, being only a very average Metal band. First two albums – 'Damnation Alley' ('82) and 'Be My Slave' ('83) – were followed in 1987 by 'The Bitch Is Back', with a refined sound and a less hysterical image. However, in an attempt to be taken more seriously, Bitch changed their name to Betsy on the eve of LP number four in 1988. Oddly enough they haven't recorded since...
Recommended album:
THE BITCH IS BACK (Metal Blade, 1987 – KKK)

BLACK CROWES

USA, six-piece (1989-present)

FIERCELY SINGLE-MINDED troupe formed by Atlanta, Georgia-born singer Chris Robinson (born December 20, 1966) and his brother Rich (rhythm guitar, born May 24, 1969). The pair write 99 per cent of the band's material and refuse to compromise it in any way to appease current trends or record company pressure. Instead, the Black Crowes smoke pot and write music from their hearts to please their ears, and claim to tolerate the 'music business' only as a means to that end. Stating as much in the media has led many to accuse the Robinsons and their band of arrogance and naivety, but this early in their career, the Black Crowes are a major force.

The Robinsons are the sons of Stan Robinson (who had a minor hit in the USA in 1959) and Nancy (née Bradley), a Nashville country singer. While growing up, the boys were always surrounded by music and their drift into it was as inevitable as it was natural. Their first working band was an outfit called Mr Crowe's Garden, who earned $50 for their first gig in Chattanooga in 1984. The cheque bounced, the Robinsons bounced higher.

A reliable bass player proved hard to find, and they dispensed with the services of half-a-dozen before enlisting Johnny Colt in 1988. They then invited drummer Steve Gorman to join, after meeting him whilst recording a demo in an adjacent studio. Finally, after playing at a party in Nashville, they were impressed enough by another band's guitarist, Jeff Cease, to invite him into the fold to toughen up their sound.

In May 1989 the quintet changed their name to the Black Crowes and were signed to Def American by A&R man George Drakoulias. Although the label's roster has broadened considerably since, initially the band were very much an oddity amongst some (very) Heavy Metal bands, including Slayer. Label boss and producer Rick Rubin had little time for the band, who released their debut in March 1990. It was produced by Drakoulias and featured help from ex-Allman Brothers Band man Chuck Leavell on piano. The album was named 'Shake Your Money Maker' after an old Blues song made popular by Fleetwood Mac, and entered the US charts at a modest Number 174. But constant touring – including lengthy stints opening for Aerosmith, Robert Plant then Heart in the US – coupled with the popularity of singles like 'Jealous Again' and 'Hard To Handle' (a cover of Otis Redding's 1968 hit) saw the album climb into the *Billboard* Top Five and sell five million copies. They also visited Europe, making their UK debut at the Marquee June 7, '90 before seven dates supporting the Dogs D'Amour.

After closing 1990 by headlining a two-month US tour of 1,000-plus capacity venues the band began 1991 on the road once again, this time as a six-piece with piano player Ed Hawrysch, opening for ZZ Top. Offstage the band were named Best New American band in the prestigious annual *Rolling Stone* magazine awards, but on the tour things weren't going so well. The ever-outspoken Chris had taken to making onstage comments about the commercialisation of rock 'n' roll in general and the sponsorship of the ZZ Top tour by brewers Budweiser in particular. He ignored repeated warnings from the headliner's management to desist, and so on

IN THEIR OWN WORDS...

"Rick Rubin hated us when he signed us. No money was involved. We literally had my two guitars which we used on the first record... Def American wouldn't pay to rent any other equipment." – Rich Robinson, Kerrang! 392, May 16, 1992

"Music just exists in your mind. You can't see it, you can't touch it. It just comes to your ears. That's pure art..." – Chris Robinson, Kerrang! 392, May 16, 1992

"When we came to record 'The Southern Harmony...' we had all these songs we'd written on tour – then we get home and our mind-set is different so we wrote another record!" – Rich Robinson, Kerrang! 410, September 19, 1992

"The creative part of this band is just as heavy as painting, sculpting, playwriting... The only thing I can't connect it to is acting, cos I don't see it as an act, trying to fool people..." – Chris Robinson, Kerrang! 409, September 12, 1992

"We love music so much. We listen to all kinds of music, we form opinions on music. It's a philosophy, a way of life." – Rich Robinson, Kerrang! 410, September 19, 1992

BLACK CROWES

March 25, the Crowes were told to leave the tour. Undeterred, Chris continued to speak out in press interviews... The band again visited Europe bringing their marathon road trek to an end at Hammersmith Odeon after 22 months on the road with hardly a break. The schedule took its toll on Cease, who was dismissed and replaced by Marc Ford, formerly of LA's Burning Tree. Cease had failed to mature musically and was still struggling to reproduce the album solos while the rest of the band were jamming.

Yet, almost as soon as they were home they were keen to work again and December found them setting up in a house to record their second album. In all, they spent just eight days recording the basic tracks for 'The Southern Harmony And Musical Companion' with a handful more added for a few overdubs. The eight days were also interrupted by Christmas and because the Robinsons had to rush to a hospital where their mother underwent multiple bypass heart surgery.

Amazingly, the band's creative processes survived unharmed and the ensuing album was met with almost universally ecstatic reviews when released in May 1992. The record proved to all who would listen that the band were far more than the Faces copyists they had been branded (their sound is actually much closer to Humble Pie, for example). True, they were heavily influenced by music of the early '70s, but they built upon such patterns out of respect not plagiarism.

Within months, the band were touring in the USA again, this time taking with them a weird stage set made up of a few Persian rugs, a couple of mirrorballs and an old fishing net festooned with dozens of lightbulbs. Once again, the Black Crowes were turning their back on tradition and doing something their own way. Set-lists would change every night, and most nights they would deliberately not play hits like 'Hard To Handle' or 'She Talks To Angels', preferring to extend others into adventurous jams, or premiere brand new material. But the Crowes like it that way and if you don't care for it, then the band are sorry for you, but don't really care either...

ALBUMS

SHAKE YOUR MONEY MAKER *(Def American, 1990 – KKKKK) "The garage sound ain't exactly lush but it kicks like a mule. The sheer excellence of the songs does the rest."* – Kerrang! 279, March 3, 1990

THE SOUTHERN HARMONY AND MUSICAL COMPANION *(Def American, 1992 – KKKKK) "Records like this ain't released every day. Hell, records like this ain't released every year..."* – Kerrang! 391, May 9, 1992

BLACK FLAG

USA, five-piece (1978-1986)
HARDCORE PUNK band originally lead by Dez Cadena (vocals) and Greg Ginn (guitar). Many of their original fans seemed to prefer this line-up, but vocal duties were taken over by Henry Rollins and the band's sound got considerably heavier. Black Flag played their first UK gigs in 1981, supporting bands like the Exploited and the Damned and playing an all-day Punk festival in Leeds called 'Christmas On Earth'. The band frequently met a very hostile reception and Rollins was knocked out cold by a skinhead at a show at London's legendary 100 Club.

Ironically, Black Flag were sadly missed after they split up and are now cited as a major influence by many Hardcore bands.
Recommended albums:
EVERYTHING WENT BLACK *(SST, 1982-KKKK)*
DAMAGED *(Roadrunner, 1982-KKKKK)*

BLACK 'N BLUE

USA, five-piece (1982-1988)
HAVING SPENT moonlighting stints behind the drums with Kevin Wet, Wild Dogs, and Movie Star, skinbasher Jaime St James decided to swop his sticks for a microphone when restructuring the band with guitarist Tommy Thayer and changing its name to Black 'N Blue.

B'NB's first demo tape, made in '82, created such a buzz that Geffen signed them almost immediately. Relocating to LA and signing to a major label so quickly, as James was to admit a few years down the line, "really f**ked Black 'N Blue up", for rather than capturing their raw aggression on their planned live mini-LP, Geffen sent them to Germany to record their 1984 eponymous debut with Dieter Dierks, then insisted Bruce Fairbairn handled 'Without Love' the following year.

Black 'N Blue didn't really find their feet until they hooked up with Gene Simmons in 1986 for the very Kiss sounding 'Nasty Nasty', and the follow-up, 'In Heat'. Then the band appeared to disintegrate, with Thayer moving on to Harlow

and St James recording demos with Wet Engine and American Man projects.

However, Thayer and St James hooked up once more, playing the parts of Ace Frehley and Peter Criss in LA Kiss tribute band Cold Gin during 1992, with the possiblity of working together in a new act looking very likely.
Recommended album:
NASTY NASTY *(Geffen, 1986 – KKKK)*

BLACK OAK ARKANSAS

USA, six-piece (1966-1979)
TAKING THEIR name from their town and state of origin, Black Oak Arkansas grew into a major US concert draw in the '70s and even had a day's holiday named in their honour in Arkansas. Made at least 14 albums before swaying from their Southern Boogie roots and disintergrating in a gospel-flavoured mess. Their main appeal was larger-than-life frontman Jim Dandy who managed to combine an outrageous ego (witness the song 'Jim Dandy To The Rescue'), with sexual innuendo ('Hot Rod') and, er... a washboard. He was a protoytpe Dave Lee Roth crossed with an archetype Ozzy Osbourne (Black Oak actually supported Black Sabbath in the UK in 1974). The band also featured drummer Tommy Aldridge, who went on to work with Pat Travers, Ozzy Osbourne and David Coverdale in Whitesnake amongst others. Aldridge was not one of only two founder members involved in '84's short-lived reformation.
Recommended album:
HOT 'N' NASTY *(Atlantic, 1974 – KKKK)*

BLACK SABBATH

UK, four-piece (1969-present)
A BAND if not for whom... you wouldn't be reading this book. It's impossible to overstate the influence of this quartet either in defining the Heavy Metal genre, or setting the standards for all that followed. Although wholesale personnel changes since 1979 have marred more recent output and threatened the credibility of subsequent line-ups, they have

only increased the reputation of the original: Ozzy Osbourne (vocals, born 'John', December 3, 1948), Tony Iommi (guitar, born February 19, 1948), Geezer Butler (bass, born 'Terry', July 17, 1949) and Bill Ward (drums, born May 5, 1948).

The four came together in 1967 in Birmingham playing heavy Jazz/Blues variations, under the collective moniker of Polka Tulk, then Earth. After featuring a second guitarist and (briefly) a saxophonist, they cut back to a quartet and changed their name to Black Sabbath. The handle came after the song, inspired by Butler's interest in occult author Dennis Wheatley. The new name and the adoption of Satanic imagery – as an opportunist gimmick – proved a masterstroke. After signing to Philips Records and releasing an unsuccessful cover of US band Crow's hit 'Evil Woman', they transfered to Philips' burgeoning 'progressive' label, Vertigo. In April 1970, they recorded their eponymous debut in less than a day's studio time for just £600 – yet the record, released in 1970, remains one of the best examples of dark, doomy Metal ever made. For the follow-up, 'Paranoid' – initially to be called 'War Pigs' but retitled even after the sleeve artwork was complete because 'Paranoid' had become a Top Five UK hit – the songwriting improved (arguably to an all-time peak) and the relentless sound had been refined

without sacrificing any of the power. The third album 'Master Of Reality' was a similar if marginally inferior work. All three were produced by Rodger Bain, who also worked with Budgie.

But, come the fourth album, titled simply 'Vol 4', the Sabs opted to produce themselves and their sound began to change. They'd spent much of the previous two-and-a-half years on the road and during that time had all been swamped by the excessive rock 'n' roll lifestyle so typical of the time. 'Vol 4's credits gave thanks to "the great COKE-Cola company of Los Angeles" (where it was recorded) and the song 'Snowblind' told tales of cocaine excesses that the band were enjoying. The fifth album, 'Sabbath Bloody Sabbath', took them further from their Heavy Metal roots as the sound became bathed in studio effects and overdubs. It nevertheless remains a classic, but Ozzy would later complain at length about the outcome, swearing in future never to fall into the trap of "f**king around like brain surgeons" on 32-track machines.

Black Sabbath would later look back on such times and rue their meagre financial rewards – even though they were a major act on both sides of the Atlantic and come July 1975 could headline New York's Madison Square Garden. Management wrangles plagued them to the point where, as he walked on stage in 1974,

IN THEIR OWN WORDS...

BLACK SABBATH

Ozzy was handed a belated writ from their original manager (1969-1972) which put the band out of action for over a year.

Ironically, it gave the band a much needed rest and a killer song, 'The Writ', for the next LP, 'Sabotage'. The album was altogether a more brutal affair and the last in an astonishing run of six UK Top 10, all-time masterpieces.

After it, internal friction began to grow and Ozzy in particular became less and less committed as mental and alcoholic problems mounted. Both 'Technical Ecstasy' and 'Never Say Die' were inconsistent as a result. Ozzy left on more than one occasion and was absent or unconcious for much of 'Never Say Die', when the band even announced he had been replaced by former Savoy Brown singer Dave Brown. Ozzy rejoined in time to play on the album's supporting 10th anniversary tour (when the support band was one Van Halen) but later in 1979 he quit for good and the Sabs appeared to die.

Announcing they were to continue with former Rainbow singer Ronnie James Dio brought howls of derision and horror from many diehard Sabbath fans, many of whom preferred Ozzy's new Blizzard Of Ozz venture. Few could deny, however, that Dio was technically a far superior singer and the first product of his liaison, 'Heaven And Hell', was a major success. It was far removed from the Sabs of old, but it won the band many new fans, especially in the USA. Drummer Bill Ward became ill, though, and left – to be replaced by American Vinnie Appice for the 'Mob Rules' album, tour and subsequent double-live album, 'Live Evil'. But, while fans and critics argued about the validity of Dio singing Ozzy material, an even stranger twist of fate was about to make such arguments irrelevant. Inner wrangling led Dio (and Appice) to quit and later form Dio. Then in seeming desperation, Iommi and Butler invited former Deep Purple star Ian Gillan into the fold. Their one album together (for which they persuaded Bill Ward to return) they christened 'Born Again' but in reality the project died shortly after birth. Live, Sabbath replaced Ward with Iommi's good friend, ELO drummer Bev Bevan, and took to encoring with Purple's hit 'Smoke On The Water' and it all seemed to get a little too far from the original plot. Gillan later admitted he had joined just for the money and left in 1983 to reform Deep Purple Mark II.

There followed a seven-year period that represented the lowest ebb in Sabbath's history. The original foursome reformed briefly for a one-off appearance at Live–Aid in Philadelphia on July 13, 1985, but Iommi was otherwise soldiering on with a variety of sidemen. The guitarist tells now of how he wanted to let Sabbath rest in peace and release records under his own name, but unwisely he bowed to record company pressure and both 'Seventh Star' and 'Eternal Idol' bore the band's monicker while containing little that justified such claim – although well received at the time in *Kerrang!* reviews... 'Black Sabbath' continued to record and tour, expanding to a quintet with Geoff Nichols (keyboards) plus various others like Bob Daisley then Dave Spitz (bass) and Eric Singer then Terry Chimes, ex-Clash (drums). After a false (non) start with an Italian named David Donato, the microphone went to ex-Deep Purple bassist/singer Glenn Hughes and then, mid-US tour, to Ray Gillen, before settling in the hands of Tony 'The Cat' Martin. Martin's vocals replaced Gillen's on 'Eternal Idol' and although the record was not a success and Iommi afterwards had to secure a new record deal with IRS, Martin showed enough promise to become a fully fledged member for the 'comeback' album, 'Headless Cross'. 20 years after Black Sabbath were first formed, Iommi seized on a

chance to make a fresh start. Alongside Nichols and Martin, he enlisted the respected if rather well travelled – some suggested mercenary – sidemen Cozy Powell (drums) and Neil Murray (bass), and made an album that was the band's best since 'Mob Rules'. Indeed, Martin's vocal style was close to Dio's and although purists continued to call for the return of Ozzy, 'Headless...' and to a lesser extent 'Tyr' proved there was still life left in Sabbath. But Martin's enthusiasm was poorly rewarded after Dio and Iommi conspired to recreate the line-up of 1983. Butler was keen to rejoin, having rekindled old friendships by jamming with both Dio (in Minneapolis) and Black Sabbath (in London) and Appice was not hard to persuade either. The subsequent album, 'Dehumanizer', failed to meet expectations and although Butler and Iommi did not fulfill the bassist's quip in *Kerrang!* to "open a bed and breakfast" if the album flopped, they made progress instead towards reforming the original foursome.

After years of public demand, this came about almost by accident. Ozzy Osbourne invited Black Sabbath to be special guests on his 'farewell' solo shows at the Pacific Ampitheatre in Costa Mesa, California on November 14 and 15, 1992. Iommi accepted the invitation but Dio

TONY IOMMI: the riffmeister gerneral!

declined to support the man who had spent so much of the previous 15 years deriding him in interviews. So in a bizarre twist, Black Sabbath performed with Rob Halford of Judas Priest guesting on vocals and Appice on drums. Then on the second night, as Ozzy's final encore, the original foursome played a four-song set. It went so well, despite being completely unrehearsed, that it now seems a real possibility that the band will try again... and headline the 1993 Monsters Of Rock European tour.

ALBUMS

BLACK SABBATH *(Vertigo, 1970 – KKKKK) Raw, dark, slow and evil sounding. Thunderous primeval Metal!*

PARANOID *(Vertigo, 1970 – KKKKK) As above but faster, more song-based. Essential purchase.*
MASTER OF REALITY *(Vertigo, 1971 – KKKKK) Ultra heavy riffs, archetypal "fast bits" plus ballad and acoustic instrumentals.*

VOL 4 *(Vertigo, 1972 – KKKKK) Arguably Iommi's best collection of riffs although songwriting is patchy.*

SABBATH BLOODY SABBATH *(WWA, 1973 – KKKKK) Killer songs, awesome riffs, keyboards by guest Rick Wakeman. Big production.*

SABOTAGE *(NEMS, 1975 – KKKKK) – Incredibly varied in style but uncompromising in delivery. Timeless and relentless.*

TECHNICAL ECSTASY *(Vertigo, 1976 – KKK) Many outstanding moments but lacks consistency of earlier works.*

NEVER SAY DIE *(Vertigo, 1978 – KKK) Struggling in most departments. Defiant but headed downhill.*

HEAVEN AND HELL *(Vertigo, 1980 – KKKKK) Major change of style, Dio's voice give Iommi's thunderous riffs new majesty.*

MOB RULES *(Vertigo, 1981 – KKKK) As above but more bombastic. Slightly inferior in terms of material.*

LIVE EVIL *(Vertigo, 1983 – KKKK) Best of new Dio material but sounding less confident on old Ozzy numbers. Beware of solos.*

BORN AGAIN *(Vertigo, 1983 – KKK) – "A fascinating hybrid of two of Britain's greatest heavy rock institutions... the meanest LP since 'Sabotage'." – Kerrang! 51, September 22-October 5, 1983*

SEVENTH STAR *(Vertigo, 1986 – KK) – "A monstrous work that gives Iommi a definite edge on old colleagues Ozzy and Dio" – Kerrang! 113, February 6-19, 1986*

THE ETERNAL IDOL *(Vertigo, 1987 – KK) "Forget the mistakes of yore and enjoy the rekindled glory" Kerrang! 162, November 14, 1987*

HEADLESS CROSS *(IRS, 1990 – KKK) "Iommi writes giant powerchords anthems, and Martin wraps a colossal vocal around them" Kerrang! 234, April 15, 1989*

TYR *(IRS, 1990 – KKK) "A big step towards reclamation of the status their name really demands" Kerrang! 303, August 18, 1990*

DEHUMANIZER *(IRS, 1992 – KKK) "Dinosaur Metal in a non-derogatory way. It's huge and crushing..." Kerrang! 397, June 20, 1992*

Compilations etc:

LIVE AT LAST *(NEMS, 1980 – KK) Badly recorded live collection. Disowned by band.*
WE SOLD OUR SOUL FOR ROCK 'N' ROLL *(NEMS, 1976 – KKKK) Double best of with one previously unreleased track 'Wicked Ways'.*
GREATEST HITS *(NEMS, 1980 – KKK) Pointless single compilation album.*
BLACKEST SABBATH *(Vertigo, 1989 – KKK) Mixed bag sampling LPs up to 1987.*
THE OZZY OSBOURNE YEARS *(Essential – KKKK) Triple-CD box of first six albums: ignores post 1975 Ozzy LPs omits some tracks for*

BLACKFOOT

USA, four-piece (1968-1990)
SOUTHERN BOOGIE outfit from Jacksonville, Florida who were heavier and less country than most. First LP released in 1975, but their career really took only off in 1979 with their third, best-selling, 'Strikes'. Soon after, to promote the excellent 'Tomcattin'' ('80) and 'Marauder' ('81) albums, the band came to Europe to tour. For a few years, in the UK especially, they could do no wrong. Crowds were instantly won over by the charismatic Rick Medlocke (guitar/vocals) who was superbly backed by Charlie Hargrett (guitar), Greg T Walker (bass) and Jakson Spires (drums). But after a live album released in 1982 the band bowed to record company pressure and tried to write more commercial material. Subsequent records flopped badly and the band fell apart. Medlocke tried to keep the name going with new personnel, but after a brief comeback in 1990 appears to have laid the ghost to rest.
Recommended albums:
TOMCATTIN' *(Atco, 1980 – KKKK)*
HIGHWAY SONG – LIVE! *(Atco, 1982 – KKKKK)*

BLOODGOOD

USA, four-piece (1986-present)
WHITE METAL band who have recently softened their Maiden-esque approach in to something more mainstream. One of the best on the Christian rock scene but making little impact in secular markets.
Recommended album:
HOTTER THAN HELL LIVE *(Roadracer, 1990 – KKK)*

BLUE CHEER

USA, three-piece (1968-1971, etc)
CAN JUSTIFIABLY lay claim to have invented Heavy Metal as their 1968 debut, 'Vincebus Eruptum', predated Black Sabbath, Led Zeppelin and just about everyone except Jimi Hendrix, The Who and Cream. San Franciscans Blue Cheer – Leigh Stephens (guitar, vocals), Dick Peterson (bass) Paul Whaley (drums) – were bikers who did lots of acid and played very loud. Enjoyed a hit single with their version of Eddie Cochrane's 'Summertime Blues' (building on the style of The Who's version) then guaranteed themselves a place in this book by recording their second album 'Outside Inside' ('68) outdoors, as their playing was so earth-shatteringly loud, their chosen studio couldn"t accommodate them. Made four more albums before splitting in '71, reforming for 'The Beast Is Back' ('85) and again in 1989 when they even visited the UK. Unfortunately, by that time, no one remembered who Blue Cheer once were...
Recommended album:
VINCEBUS ERUPTUM *(Philips, 1968 – KKKK)*

BLUE MURDER

UK/USA, three-piece (1988-1990)
HIGH PROFILE, low impact, band put together by ex-Thin Lizzy and Whitesnake guitarist John Sykes. Their sole record reflected his contribution to the latter's hugely successful '1987'. Sykes handled all vocals after Ray Gillen declined the offer to join. Appice took the drumstool after initial trials with Cozy Powell. Bassist was former Firm man Tony Franklin.
The one album:
BLUE MURDER *(Geffen, 1989 – KKKK)*

BLUE ÖYSTER CULT

USA, five-piece (1969-present)
LEGEND HAS it that Eric Bloom formed Blue Öyster Cult to exact his revenge on the '60s! Bloom was small, but no hippy. The classic line-up was, in fact, an extra-terrestrial strike force, a stun guitar showdown and heavier than the whole planet. The liberal gurus on the West Coast worried about the New Yorkers' symbolism and humourously-intended menace on such early albums as 'Secret Treaties' and 'Tyranny And Mutation'. Undeterred, Blue Öyster Cult revelled in their image as the Grateful Dead's worst nightmare. Throughout the '70s the band came

IN THEIR OWN WORDS...

"Every record we do we think, 'Right, this is gonna be it'! So far that hasn't quite happened!" – Eric Bloom, Kerrang! 56, December 1-14, 1983

"I guess if rock 'n' roll can be construed as a pie, then BÖC has got a small portion - but a tasty one!" – Eric Bloom, Kerrang! 56, December 1-14, 1983

"Are you familiar with the album Spinal Tap? It's a bit like that. In fact we're practically living Spinal Tap!"
– Eric Bloom, Kerrang! 112, January 23-February 5, 1986

"The thing is that people seem to LIKE live albums from Blue Öyster Cult!"
– Buck Dharma, Kerrang! 19, July 1-15, 1982

"That's fine with me, as long as they buy 'em first. Our back catalogue could do with a boost!" Eric Bloom on hearing the news that US evangelical groups plan to start burning BÖC records, Kerrang! 3, September 1981

"(Albert Bouchard) should wake up and smell the coffin! Hell, I'd like to puff a little on his pipe – the guy's obviously getting real high these days!" – Eric Bloom, Kerrang! 56, December 1-14, 1983

"I met Gene Simmons not so long ago and he said to me, 'The kids don't wanna hear fucking poetry. They wanna rock 'n' roll!'"
– Eric Bloom, Kerrang! 56, December 1-14, 1983

BLUE ÖYSTER CULT

to glorify the power, volume and wit of music that would eventually become known universally as Heavy Metal.

Originally travelling under the monikers of Soft White Underbelly and the Stalk Forest Group (recording one unreleased album for Columbia as the latter and still using the former for secret gigs and one-off projects to this day), Blue Öyster Cult rapidly established an art rock and biker following on the back of frequent support tours with Alice Cooper. Their customised Pagan logo for Chaos can still be seen on numerous road hogs worldwide.

Throughout the '70s and under the guidance of writer/producer Sandy Pearlman, the band crossed the bridge from underground to mainstream success. Eventually admired as much by the East Coast opium fiends as by West Coast surfers and European headbangers, Blue Öyster Cult were melodic, moody and the cranium-crunching alternative to the likes of Aerosmith and The Eagles. At their height they were a cartoon acid tab for the masses, a tongue-in-cheek riff monster and an intelligent powerhouse.

The band's earliest recorded output for the Columbia label could not match their live reputation. Although the eponymous debut was a hotch-potch of crashing guitars and cosmic imagery, the potential was hard to ignore. Diehard fans, however, would rather remember 1974's 'Secret Treaties' as an album to cherish.

With its cover drawing of a ME262 bomber and appropriately relentless musical muscle, 'Secret Treaties' is also unusual for its lyrical contribution from New York's priestess of punk poetry, Patti Smith. She contributed several lyrics to the album and could be seen around town in the arms of keyboard player Allen Lanier. It was a lasting relationship, both musically and romantically. In 1984 Patti Smith contributed a song ('Shooting Shark') to the band's 'Revolution By Night' album, and her involvement endeared Blue Öyster Cult to a whole new circle of fans worldwide.

In 1975 the band recorded the first of their three live albums. Although 'On Your Feet On Your Knees' was produced in a bucket of sand, the double live set contained the cream of Blue Öyster Cult's material, such as 'The Last Days Of May', 'Seven Screaming Dizbusters', 'Hot Rails To Hell' and 'The Red & The Black'. Even the cover artwork – a gleaming stretch limousine parked outside a shrouded chapel – was as powerful a statement as any in the field of Heavy Metal.

Off stage, the five members of Blue Öyster Cult were unassuming and quiet. There are no great stories of drug or stimulant abuse. All are softly-spoken and well-informed, character trends that didn't really prepare the band for their massive success in 1976.

Rumour has it that Donald 'Buck Dharma' Roesier wrote the three chords to '(Don't Fear) The Reaper' as a direct tribute to The Byrds. It became an immediate hard rock classic and is still the centre-point of any live show, the spiralling riff always played on Roesier's pre-set Gibson SG and Bloom supplying the song's massive sustain with the help of the then-revolutionary E-Bow. The song was an instant hit in America but didn't chart in the UK until 1978. It was taken from the album 'Agents Of Fortune' which could also boast another live favourite in the shape of 'E.T.I.', as well as Patti Smith on backing vocals again.

The band were finally an international attraction and toured any venue that could accomodate their pyros and lasers. Although underrated by critics, 1978's live album ('Some Enchanted Evening') was a high-energy celebration of Blue Öyster Cult. From the opening rush of 'R.U.Ready To Rock' and 'Godzilla' to the climatic rollercoaster of 'Astronomy' and '...The Reaper' itself, it's essential listening for any fan of genuinely live albums.

The release of 'Mirrors' in 1979 saw the band growing slicker. It was a move that worried long-term fans of the more familiar bludgeon and bombast. 'Cultosaurus Erectus' ('80) and 'Fire Of Unknown Origin' ('81) continued to disappoint, and when drummer Albert Bouchard quit after the band's appearance at Castle Donington festival, many feared the worst. The show was not a great success and Bloom managed to offend almost everyone he encountered backstage.

It was not a comfortable time for the band. 1982's third live album ('Extraterrestrial Live') was a stodgy affair, featuring the band's drum roadie standing in for Bouchard! That year Roesier also cut a solo album ('Flat Out') whilst Bloom could be heard as a DJ on a New York radio station.

The band's career continued to wane throughout the '80s until the release of 'Imaginos' in 1988. The album, despite hinting at the band's former glories, was received with massed critical confusion. Eventually it transpired that it was originally recorded as a solo album by Albert Bouchard, but partially re-recorded by the band and released under the name of Blue Öyster Cult. It was not a move to calm the stormy waters, although sales and general interest were relatively healthy.

After writing 90 per cent of the material on 1992's soundtrack album for the 'Bad Channels' movie, the '90s have witnessed one of the world's greatest and strangest Heavy Metal bands of all time return to the live arena with a vengeance. Still armed, still dangerous and still refusing to grow old peacefully!

ALBUMS:
BLUE ÖYSTER CULT (Columbia, 1971 – KKK)
Energetic if slightly muddled debut that nonetheless was a strong indicator of the mayhem to follow...

BLUE ÖYSTER CULT: an extra-terrestrial strike force?!?

*TYRANNY AND MUTATION (Columbia, 1973 –
KKK) Consistent with their debut's blueprint but
yet to deliver any knockout punch.*
*SECRET TREATIES (Columbia, 1974 – KKKKK)
A veritable classic and one that finally
emcompassed the band's power and menace.
Also notable for the lyrical involvement of Patti
Smith.*
*ON YOUR FEET ON YOUR KNEES (Columbia,
1975 – KKKK) Shakily produced but still a
suitably sinister live experience.*
*AGENTS OF FORTUNE (Columbia, 1976 –
KKKKK) Compulsory listening for any aspiring
rock star and not just for the biggie, '(Don't
Fear) The Reaper'.*
*SPECTRES (Columbia, 1977 – KKK) Safe but
reliable follow-up.*
*SOME ENCHANTED EVENING (Columbia,
1978 – KKKKK) Classic live album featuring the
strongest material on offer at the time.*
*MIRRORS (Columbia, 1978 – KKK) Slicker than
expected but worth hearing for 'The Vigil' and
'I Am The Storm' alone.*
*CULTOSAURUS ERECTUS (Columbia, 1980 –
KK) Weak but successful-selling set of dodgy
sci-fi, aided by novelist Michael Moorcock.*
*FIRE OF UNKNOWN ORIGIN (Columbia, 1981 –
KKKK) Most notable for unexpected hit in the
shape of the bizarrely-titled 'Joan Crawford Has
Risen From The Grave'!*
*EXTRATERRESTRIAL LIVE (Columbia, 1982 –
K) "Do we really need ANOTHER live
recording?" – Kerrang! 17, June 3-16, 1982*
*THE REVOLUTION BY NIGHT (Columbia, 1983
– KKK) "Sure, most of the songs are good but
there is little 'Cult cohesion." – Kerrang! 55,
November 17-30, 1983*
*CLUB NINJA (Columbia, 1985 – KK) "Why, you
can even rebel in your own living room by
chanting 'Rock Not War'!" – Kerrang! 110,
December 26-Jan 8, 1985*
*IMAGINOS (Columbia, 1988 – KKKK) "What the
bloody hell is it?" – Kerrang! 200, August 13,
1988*
*BAD CHANNELS (Moonstone, 1992 – KKK)
Movie soundtrack, two new 'Cult songs.*

BODY COUNT

USA, five-piece (1991-present)
OUTSTANDING LA street outfit lead by Rap star
Ice T. Infamous for the controversial track 'Cop
Killer', which was dropped from their album
after death threats to the band and record
company personnel.
Recommended album:
*BODY COUNT (Sire/Warner Bros, 1992 –
KKKKK)*

Tommy BOLIN

USA, guitar/vocalist
(April 18, 1951-December 4, 1976)
OUTRAGEOUSLY TALENTED guitarist killed in
1976, aged 25, by drug abuse. Began his
professional career as a 17-year-old in his
native Colorado with jazzy rock bands like
Zephyr and Energy. Bolin's playing was so
special he was invited to play on sessions with
Jazz Rock masters like Alphonse Mouzon and
drummer Billy Cobham – Cobham's 1973 LP
'Spectrum' is widely viewed as a classic of the
genre thanks largely to Bolin's contribution.

But Bolin could play rock with equal dexterity
and was happy to replace Joe Walsh 1973-'74
in the James Gang for two of their best albums
– 'Bang' ('73) and 'Miami' ('74). His biggest
break came, however, when Deep Purple asked
him to step into Ritchie Blackmore's shoes for
the Mark IV album 'Come Taste The Band'
(Purple, 1975). Its release coincided with Bolin's
own solo debut, 'Teaser' (Atlantic, 1975) and
although he had to work hard to convince
Blackmore fans when Purple toured, Bolin was
always impressive on record. Purple though,
decided it was time to call it a day.

Meanwhile, Bolin's drug habits got the better
of him. His second solo album 'Private Eyes'
(Columbia, 1976) was restricted to a single disc
and a new band bearing his name never got the
chance to shine like he did.
Recommended albums:
TEASER (Atlantic, 1975 – KKKKK)
*THE ULTIMATE (Geffen, 1990 – KKKKK)
Superb double-CD career retrospective.*

BOLT THROWER

UK, five-piece, (1985-present)

WAR-OBSESSED Grindsters from Birmingham whose first radio session for BBC1 DJ John Peel spurred Vinyl Solution to sign them for one record; the primitive 'In Battle There Is No Law'.

Their second collection of warped riffage was strikingly packaged by Games Workshop, and released by Earache Records. After disappointing somewhat with 'War Master', the band went on to record their finest work...

Recommended album:
THE FOURTH CRUSADE (Earache, 1992 - KKKK)

Michael BOLTON

USA, singer (1982-present)

ALMOST PEERLESS vocalist now banned from the pages of *Kerrang!* after abandoning AOR for Soul and the adoration of millions of housewives. Before he lost it, he cut – in a genre grossly distorted by superlatives – one of the truly greatest, quasi-perfect, AOR records of all time...

Consummate concoction:
EVERYBODY'S CRAZY (CBS, 1975 – KKKKK)

BON JOVI

USA, five-piece (1983-present)

FORMED BY singer Jon Bon Jovi (born John Bongiovi, in Sayreville, New Jersey, March 2, 1962). In 1983 he recruited schoolfriend David Bryan (keyboards, born David Rashbaum, February 7, 1962) after stints in a number of New Jersey club bands, Richie Sambora (guitar, born July 11, 1959), Alec John Such (bass, born November 14, 1956) and Tico Torres (drums, born October 7, 1953).

They recorded a demo at the Record Plant in New York, the studio where Jon's cousin and recording engineer Tony Bongiovi worked and Jon had previously swept the floors whilst trying to launch a solo career. A solo JBJ demo track 'Runaway' had earlier featured on a radio station compilation album of unsigned talent and this helped the two-month -old band to a

BON JOVI 1993

deal in July 1983 with Phonogram's Mercury label. The re-recorded 'Runaway' was the band's first release (and a USA Top 40 hit) closely followed by the eponymous debut album in April 1984.

It was well received all over the world and the band soon made their first European visit, supporting Kiss. Their combination of youthful good looks and hook-laden, radio-friendly, rock songs turned them into stars very quickly but the potential was not realised by the disappointing (if healthy selling) second LP '7800° Fahrenheit'.

Much more significant was the time spent at Vancouver's Little Mountain studios with producer Bruce Fairbairn during the spring of 1986. Whilst there, the combination of the band's growing maturity, Fairbairn's talents and contributions from outside songwriters (most notably Desmond Child) turned the subsequent album, 'Slippery When Wet', into a watershed not just for Bon Jovi but for rock music as a whole. Although it never reached the unparalleled sales figures of AC/DC's 1980 album 'Back In Black', 'Slippery...' still went on to sell a staggering eight million copies. It inspired a generation of would-be emulators and opened the eyes of many contemporaries to the importance of studio sounds and songwriting abilities.

BON JOVI

With monster worldwide hits in the form of 'You Give Love A Bad Name', 'Livin' On A Prayer' and 'Wanted Dead Or Alive', Bon Jovi headlined all over the globe to promote 'Slippery...', culminating in a headline appearance at the 1987 Castle Donington Monsters Of Rock show, confirming Bon Jovi's status as the biggest rock band in the world that year. The 130 date 'Tour Without End' tour grossed over $28million but took its toll on the band, mentally and physically.

While the band took a much needed break, their manager 'Doc' McGhee was convicted on drugs charges after 40,000lb of marijuana were seized *en route* from Columbia to North Carolina. McGhee was given a five-year

suspended prison sentence but fined just $15,000. He also set up the Make A Difference Foundation to raise funds for fighting drug/alcohol abuse as part of his community service order. (Relations with him are strained thereafter and a couple of years later the band dismissed him, although he continues to represent Richie Sambora as a solo artist.)

The band bounced back quickly enough with their fourth album, 'New Jersey' and another major tour that began in Dublin in October 1988. It would prove to be even more of a marathon trek than its predecessor, lasting 16 months and totalling 237 dates when it ended in January 1990. The 'NJ' album mirrored 'Slippery...' in style but in a more mature style. Predictably, its sales never emulated those of its predecessor. Nevertheless, the tour was Bon Jovi's biggest yet with a number of high-profile prestige shows along the way. First of these were two nights headlining the Moscow Music Peace Festival at the city's Olympic Lenin Stadium on August 12 and 13, over a bill featuring Ozzy Osbourne, Scorpions and Mötley Crüe amongst others. The following weekend Bon Jovi headlined before 55,000 at the UK's Milton Keynes Bowl. At the end of the tour the band played a special charity show at London's Hammersmith Odeon when they were joined onstage by former Led Zeppelin guitarist Jimmy Page.

Offstage, however, all was not going well. Sambora in particular had become disenchanted with the band and wanted to make a solo record. (The record, 'Stranger In This Town', ultimately got delayed until September 1991). Before that, the group effectively disbanded with JBJ making time for a 16 second (!) cameo appearance in 'Blaze Of Glory: Young Guns II', a movie for which he was also commissioned to write a soundtrack in the style of 'Wanted Dead Or Alive'. Despite his protests, the soundtrack, when released by Vertigo in August 1990, was widely interpreted as his debut solo album. Doubts about the band's future began to circulate. These weren't helped by a phonecall to *Kerrang!* from an irate

BON JOVI

Sebastian Bach of former Bon Jovi protégés Skid Row. In his impromptu outburst (issue 313, October 23, 1990) he revealed disagreements between JBJ and Sambora over their share of Skid Row publishing royalties, paid to a Bon Jovi company called The Underground in return for help given to Skid Row in their fledgling days. Although Bon Jovi regrouped for a 15 date tour beginning in Tokyo on December 31, 1990, rumours of a split persisted.

Bon Jovi crushed them in September 1992 with a new single, 'Keep The Faith', a subsequent album of the same name and a series of new publicity photos capturing Jon sporting a radically shorter haircut. The new 'grown up' image presented was in keeping with much – though not all – of the music on the album which, although it received only mixed critical acclaim, sold well in Europe. In the States, initially, it looked as if tastes had changed but few would write off the band's chances of recapturing the lion's share of former glories.

ALBUMS

BON JOVI (Vertigo, 1984 – KKKK) *"Truly an excellent package... already in the running for Album Of The Year." – Kerrang! 63, March 8-21, 1984*

7800° FAHRENHEIT (Vertigo, 1985 – KKK) *"A pale imitation of the Bon Jovi we have got to know and learnt to love." – Kerrang! 93, May 2-15, 1985*

SLIPPERY WHEN WET (Vertigo, 1986 – KKKKK) *"I've run out of space and superlatives... perfect AOR for the late '80s." – Kerrang! 127, August 21-September 3, 1986*

NEW JERSEY (Vertigo, 1988 – KKKKK) *"Willingness and confidence to take long shots as well as those aimed at the target from point-blank range." – Kerrang! 206, September 24, 1988*

KEEP THE FAITH (Jambco/Phonogram, 1992 – KKKK) *"Perhaps the ultimate mainstream American rock record." – Kerrang! 416, October 31, 1992*

Solo albums:

JON BON JOVI: **BLAZE OF GLORY** (Vertigo, 1990 – KKK) *"Not so much a blaze of glory as a damp squib of mediocrity." – Kerrang! 301, August 4, 1990*

RICHIE SAMBORA: **STRANGER IN THIS TOWN** (Mercury, 1991 – KKKK) *"In many ways a lot better (though not as calculatedly commercial) than any Bon Jovi album." – Kerrang! 356, August 31, 1991*

Beki BOND(AGE)

UK, vocalist (late '80s-present)
ONE TIME princess of Punk and frontwoman of
Herbert Oi! Oi! Punk-sters Vice Squad, later to
form the more rocky Ligotage, and currently
selling out her roots completely in AOR act, the
Bombshells.
Recommended album:
NO CAUSE FOR CONCERN *(Zonophone/EMI -
KKK) – with VICE SQUAD*

BONFIRE

Germany, five-piece (1987-1993)
MILDLY AMUSING but unadventurous melodic
rockers fronted by would-be rock god and
better than decent singer, Claus Lessmann.
In 1993 he opted for a bizarre change in
direction and split the band... to form a Folk
Rock/'Heavy Schlager' duet with Hans Ziller,
playing numbers sung in his native tongue!
Mildly amusing but unadventurous album:
FIREWORKS *(BMG, 1977 – KKK)*

BONHAM

UK/Canada, four-piece (1988-present)
POWERFUL QUARTET delivering grandiose
rock with several touches of latter day Led
Zeppelin. Not surprising, really, considering the
band takes its name from drummer Jason, son
of legendary Zep drummer John. Sceptics may
scoff, but most of the material is thoughtfully
constructed and convincingly delivered.
   Jason had previously enjoyed limited success
in more AOR-type groups Airrace and Virginia
Wolf, but a shift in style and, especially, the
presence of Robert Plant-soundalike Canadian
singer Daniel MacMaster proved to be a good
move, especially for the US market.
Recommended album:
THE DISREGARD OF TIMEKEEPING
(WTG/Epic, 1989 – KKKK)

Graham BONNET

UK, singer (1988-present)
SKEGNESS-BORN frontman whose beltin'
vocals graced the Marbles' 1968 Number Five
hit single 'Only One Woman' and lodged in the
memory of one Ritchie Blackmore who 11 years
later hunted him down (in Australia) to replace
Ronnie James Dio in Rainbow. Bonnet then
found himself in the charts again on Rainbow's
hit singles 'Since You Been Gone' and 'All Night
Long'. Lasted just one tour and album
(Blackmore grew tired of his Hawaiian shirts and
onstage whistling) after which he made a
mediocre solo album, 'Line Up', in 1981. In '82
he replaced Gary Barden in MSG but lasted only
one album ('Assault Attack') before, to all
intents and purposes, going mad at a gig in
Sheffield. That night he exposed himself and
alleged that Schenker's roadie played additional
guitar out of sight of the audience. In disgrace
he fled to the West Coast and formed Alcatrazz.
In due time he returned to Oz. In 1993 formed
'supergroup' Blackthorne with Bob Kulick *et al.*
Recommended album:
DOWN TO EARTH *(Polydor, 1979 – KKKK) with
Rainbow*

BOSTON

USA, five-piece, (1976-1986)
LESS THAN prolific multi-Platinum act put
together by melodic rock maestro Tom Scholtz
(guitar/vocals). With their multi-layered, fuzzed
guitars, Boston took the rock world (especially
the USA) by storm with their
eponymous debut and the
single 'More Than A Feeling'.
The weaker follow-ups 'Don't
Look Back' (LP and single) did
almost as well, but the next
record was something Schultz
almost never got around to. In

*TOM SCHOLTZ :
get on with it!*

1980 his fellow guitarist Barry Goudreau got
tired of waiting and made an eponymous solo
album. In 1983 Epic Records got tired of waiting
and sued Scholtz. In 1984 Goudreau gave up
altogether and formed Orion. Then come 1986,
when 'Third Stage' finally appeared, almost
nobody cared...
Recommended album:
BOSTON *(Epic, 1976 – KKKK)*

BRICK OUTHOUSE

UK, four-piece (1970-present)
VERY OLD (but with good make-up) pub/club rockers now immortalised in Kevin B Flannery's *Kerrang!* cartoon strip. With a style falling halfway between Motörhead, Black Sabbath (both of whom have ripped them off) and the London Philharmonic Orchestra, they have enjoyed little commercial success since their debut LP, 'Blood, Guts And Chainsaws' hit Number One in Yugoslavia in 1980. Bogthorpe Working Mens Club crowds – up to 50 (10 payers) – have long since forgiven their roadie his past panda-culling activities.
Recommended album:
BLOOD, GUTS AND CHAINSAWS *(Breznyev, 1980 – K) Ed's note: all the early LPs are very valuable, especially to Mormons who like to burn them without hesitation.*

BRIGHTON ROCK

Canada, five-piece (1984-1992)
TYPICALLY CANADIAN in their approach towards melodic AOR, Brighton Rock had the added attraction of a Helium-gargling vocalist in Gerry McGhee, a man whose voice didn't appeal to the masses – possibly why they never really broke outside of their home country, despite a few UK dates in 1989. Snapped up by WEA on the strength of a self-financed EP, Brighton Rock's anthemic style eventually led to a tougher sound by the time their last album, 'Love Machine', was released in 1991, but faced with record label and public indifference decided to pursue separate projects in '92.
Recommended album:
TAKE A DEEP BREATH *(WEA, 1988 – KKKK)*

BRITNY FOX

USA, four-piece (1985-1993)
WEANED ON a healthy diet of Slade, Nazareth and Kiss, Britny Fox – put together by former Cinderella pair Michael Kelly Smith (guitar) and Tony Destra (drums) with 'Dizzy' Dean Davidson (vocals/guitar) and Billy Childs (bass) – continued in Cinderella's footsteps bringing the Philadelphia Heavy Metal sound to the world with an 'Amadeus meets Kiss' image and a truckload of rabble-rousing anthems.

Despite the tragic loss of Destra in a car accident, Britny had snared Johnny Dee from Waysted by the time Columbia Records signed them in 1987, and thanks to high profile tours with Poison and Ratt their self-titled debut album went Gold in the wake of MTV-approved hits like 'Girlschool'. Sadly the band's decision to tone down their frilly shirts and make-up, combined with the overlong, Neil Kernon-produced second album, 'Boys In Heat', took a toll on Britny's popularity. Davidson's decision to quit the band in 1990 (and immediately form Blackeyed Susan) after a bust-up in a hotel corridor with Kelly Smith didn't help either.

Britny Fox recruited Tommy Paris for third album 'Bite Down Hard' on new label EastWest but the band found it harder than most to survive the American music industry recession and the general switch in trends. Perhaps unsurprisingly, the band split up early in '93...
Recommended album:
BRITNY FOX *(Columbia, 1988 – KKKKK)*

BROKEN BONES

UK, four-piece (1983-1992)
ORIGINALLY A ferocious Hardcore Punk band formed by ex-Discharge guitarist Bones. Unfortunately a far more Metal approach saw both the music and the fan base decline faster than a concrete parachute.
Recommended album:
DEM BONES *(Fall Out, 1984 – KKKK)*

BROKEN HOMES

USA, five-piece (1985-1991)
ROCK 'N' rollers who wrote a damn good song, thanks mostly to singer Michael Doman. Also introduced Izzy Stradlin's bassist Jimmy Ashhurst (aka, James H Ashhurst IV!).
Recommended album:
ON A WING AND A PRAYER, *(MCA, 1990 – KKKK)*

BUDGIE

Wales, three-piece (1968-1983)
SEMINAL PRIMEVAL Metal outfit from Cardiff
led by bespectacled bassist Burke Shelley. He
was partnered on seven of their 10 albums by
guitarist Tony Bourge and a variety of
drummers. Budgie are recognised
today as having written some of
Metal's most abiding songs (Metallica
and Soundgarden have covered
'Breadfan' and 'Homicidal Suicidal'
respectively) but sadly, they were
always too low-key in their
presentation to amount to the giants they
should have been. Nevertheless, consistent
touring built a massive cult following on the
large club/small theatre circuit.

After signing to MCA, Budgie repeated Black
Sabbath's first two album formula of producer
Rodger Bain and studio at Rockfield in Wales.
The resulting records – the eponymous debut
('71) and 'Squawk' ('72) – were packed full of
raw, fuzzy and brutally heavy riffs interspersed
with numbers of almost comic gentility, a
pattern they stuck to throughout their career.
They also featured another trademark: some of
the most bizarre titles known to man or beast
(or budgie). Among these, 'Nude Disintegrating
Parachutist Woman' was probably the most
insane but 'Hot As A Docker's Armpit' could
never be far behind. Third album 'Never Turn
Your Back On A Friend' ('73) was the last to
feature drummer Ray Phillips. He was replaced
briefly by one Pete Boot for their first charting
album, 'In For The Kill' ('74), then by Steve
Williams until their demise.

Fifth LP 'Bandolier' was their best selling and
probably most consistent, but marked the end
of the classic era as Budgie moved to A&M and
softened their full-on Metal approach in an
attempt to woo US audiences. First attempt, 'If I
Were Britannia I'd Waive The Rules' (! – '75) was
patchy. The follow-up 'Impeckable ('77) was
probably their weakest and in 1978 Bourge quit.
The group spent a couple of years in the US
touring with some-time Trapeze guitarist Rob
Kendrick. They met with some success but
returned to the UK in 1980 and replaced
Kendrick with ex-George Hatcher Band man
'Big' John Thomas. With him, they enjoyed
something of a renaissance after a magnificent
indie EP, 'If Swallowed Do Not
Induce Vomiting', and a storming
appearance at the Reading Festival.
They then signed to RCA and made
'Power Supply' ('80), 'Night Flight'
('81) and 'Deliver Us From Evil' ('82)
before splintering. Hugely
underrated, very sadly missed...
All MCA albums recommended, or sample:
BEST OF BUDGIE *(MCA, 1976 – KKKKK)*

BULLETBOYS

USA, four-piece (1986-present)
UNIVERSALLY REGARDED as a Van Halen
copy band – mainly because of vocalist Marq
Torien's onstage theatrics and also the fact that
they used Ted Templeman as producer on both
their albums to date – BulletBoys nevertheless
made their mark on the Metal scene after
touring the USA supporting Bon Jovi and
Cinderella, and making a visit to the UK.

All went quiet after their second album,
'Freakshow' ('91) – either because tours in
recession-hit America were hard to get, or due
to the 'Boys well-documented dalliances with
drugs – but they returned in '93 with third LP
'Zaza', promising more poke than a cabinet
minister visiting a hooker...
Recommended album:
BULLETBOYS *(Warner Bros, 1988 – KKKKK)*

BURNING TREE

USA, three-piece (1989-1991)
FORMED BY ace guitarist Marc Ford after he
moved to LA from Georgia. Their laid-back style
featured '60s guitar sounds and occasional
Hendrix-styled songs. But the band met with
little success and had split even before Ford
replaced Jeff Cease in The Black Crowes.
Only, but recommended, album:
BURNING TREE *(Epic, 1990 – KKKK)*

CACOPHONY

USA, twin guitar project (1987-1989)
OCCASIONAL PAIRING of hyperspeed widdlers Marty Friedman (now of Megadeth) and Jason Becker, with various backing musicians – and vocals. First LP, 'Speed Metal Symphony', was released in 1987, 'Go Off' followed in '89. Slight risk of follow-ups...
Recommended album:
SPEED METAL SYMPHONY *(Roadrunner, 1987 – KKK)*

CANCER

UK, four-piece (1988-present)
TELFORD TERRORS obsessed with all things sick, Cancer began life as a trio, mugging the public with their 'To The Gory End' debut. It was nasty Death Metal, done the Floridian way, and Cancer went on to recruit James Murphy, from that very US state, to weave some of his six-string lead magic on their 'Death Shall Rise' follow-up.

The alliance was to be short-lived, and 1992 saw Murphy replaced with Englishman Barry Savage for 'The Sins Of Mankind'. That Savage is his real name remains unproven...
Recommended album:
THE SINS OF MANKIND *(Vinyl Solution, 1993 - KKKK)*

CANDLEMASS

Sweden, five-piece (1985-present)
'EPICUS DOOMICUS Metallicus' was the title of Candlemass' first album, and hardly difficult to translate. This was lumbering Doom Metal in one of its more notable forms, and Candlemass went on to record a highly acclaimed second dose entitled 'Nightfall', having recruited

Messiah Marcolin – a rotund lungsman – favouring a monk's habit on stage. The following two records failed to create anything like the same buzz, and Candlemass then issued a live affair, before Marcolin called it a day and was replaced with ex-Talk Of The Town man Thomas Wilkstrom in 1991.
Recommended album:
NIGHTFALL *(Axis, 1987 – KKKK)*

MESSIAH MARCOLIN (Candlemass): praise the loud!

CANNIBAL CORPSE

UK,USA, five-piece (1988-present)
CANNIBAL CORPSE are unspeakably offensive purveyors of sonic butchery. Their 'Tomb Of The Mutilated' album sleeve, depicting oral sex between two decaying corpses, caused extreme upset among retail chains in 1992, and had to be replaced with a more subtly macabre creation.

With song titles like 'Hammer Smashed Face'

(their US single!), 'I Cum Blood', and the notorious 'Entrails Ripped From A Virgin's Cunt', Cannibal Corpse may never play TV's 'Pebble Mill', but they certainly get healthily homicidal juices raging...

Recommended album:

TOMB OF THE MUTILATED (1992, Metal Blade – KKKK)

CARCASS

UK, four-piece (1985-present)
HARDCORE GORE was the name of Carcass' tongue-in-cheek game from the off; their 1988 'Reek Of Putrefaction' debut harboured lyrics that might turn a pathologist's stomach, while their splashy musical din painted equally red pictures in the mind. Guitarist Bill Steer continued to lead a double-life in Napalm Death, but was singly devoted to Carcass by the time their third and best album was released. The Liverpudlian trio then recruited a second axe-hand in Mike Amott, ex-Carnage, leading to an increasingly complex, unique sound.

Recommended album:

NECROTICISM: DESCANTING THE INSALUBRIOUS (Earache, 1991 – KKKK)

CATHEDRAL

UK, five-piece (1991-present)
THE RELEASE of Cathedral's 'Forest Of Equilibrium' album saw vocalist Lee Dorrian's Sabbath worship manifesting itself in a far more blatant manner than had ever been the case with Napalm Death, his former endeavour. The line-up boasts three former members of Acid Reign, and serves up Doom 'n' gloom by the casket-load.

Recommended release:

GODS OF GRIND EP (Earache Records, 1991 – KKKK)

CATS IN BOOTS

USA/Japan, four-piece (1988-1990)
LED BY self-styled baron of Bonk Rock Joel Ellis, Cats In Boots were a short-lived half-American/half-Japanese trashy hard rock band who never really got the breaks they deserved –

Ellis disbanding the group in the face of mass apathy and then putting the musically more adept Heavy Bones together. Four songs on the band's only album, 'Kicked And Klawed', were re-recorded versions of tracks that appeared on the Japanese released 'Demonstration (East Meets West)' mini-album issued in 1988.

Recommended album.

KICKED AND KLAWED (EMI-USA, 1989 – KKK)

CELTIC FROST

Switzerland, four-piece (1984-present)
RISING FROM the ashes of Hellhammer, an almost universally deplauded Gothic Doom Metal outfit, Celtic Frost evolved into something almost as weird. Avant-garde Jazz and Thrash were never going to mix comfortably, but the Frosties often managed it brilliantly.

Founder members were Tom G – for Gabriel – Warrior (vocals/guitar), Martin Eric Ain (bass) and Stephen Priestly (drums). This line-up signed to Noise and recorded the Death grunt-laden debut 'Morbid Tales' ('84) and 'To Mega Therion' ('85) wearing robes and make-up but Celtic Frost had refined the image and expanded to a four-piece come the watershed and rather more accessible 'Into The Pandemonium' ('87) with new recruits Reed St Mark (drums) and second guitarist Ron Marks.

There then followed a period of internal conflict with personnel changes eventually leading to the controversial 'Cold Lake' ('88). For it, the weirdo Warrior enforced a new and almost Glam/cock rock musical stance and alienated all but a handful of their original fans – selling very few copies as a result. They tried to revert with 'Vanity/Nemesis' ('90) but much damage to their underground credibility had already been done.

St Mark spent time with Mind Funk during this period so was innocent of blame when he rejoined Warrior early in '93 for an album

promised to once again be very avant-garde and in the style of their classic third album...

Recommended albums:

INTO THE PANDEMONIUM (Noise, 1987 – KKKKK)

PARCHED WITH THIRST AM I AND DYING (Noise, 1992 – KKKK) *Compilation album worth it for the title at least.*

CEREBRAL FIX

UK, five-piece (1988-present)

EMERGING AT roughly the same time as fellow Birmingham bruisers Napalm Death and Bolt Thrower, with an album entitled 'Life Sucks... Then You Die', Cerebral Fix specialise in good, heavily Celtic Frost-inspired material.

They've nevertheless remained underdogs in terms of real achievement...

Recommended album:

TOWER OF SPITE (Roadrunner, 1990 – KKKK)

David T CHASTIAN

USA, guitarist (1985-present)

CINCINATTI GUITAR widdler who released no less than nine albums in the '80s after he was introduced on Mike Varney's Shrapnel label in 1985. All but the first are on Roadrunner, some were solo, some had a backing band, CJSS, and some featured the enticingly-monickered but banshee-voiced female vocalist, Leather.

Cautiously recommended album:

MYSTERY OF ILLUSION (Shrapnel, 1985 – KKK)

CHEAP TRICK

US, four-piece (1973-present)

THROUGH HIGHS and lows in their careers, there are certain bands who transcend mere success by achieving a 'pinnacle of cool' tag from their peers. Bands such as the Ramones, Motörhead... and Cheap Trick. With an image that was part bozo – Rick Nielsen (guitar) plus Bun E Carlos (drums) – and part dreamboat – Robin Zander (vocals) and Tom Petersson (bass), the zany yet hard-rockin' Chicago-based quartet pretty much had it sewn-up for a while Stateside at the tail end of the '70s. With their

CHEAP TRICK's Rick Nielsen: if I'm such a bozo how come I can play three at once?!?

second album 'In Color' ('77), the Cheap Trick phenomenon gained momentum and sky-rocketed with subsequent releases 'Heaven Tonight' ('78) through to their sixth elpee, 'All Shook Up' ('80). Then, alas, before the release of the aforementioned, the Cheap Trick missile returned to earth with a bump; bassist Petersson quit. Pete Comita took on tourin' duties, but come the release of 'One On One' ('82) it was the fresh visage of Jon Brant who graced the cover.

For the next few years, and despite a trio of truly fine releases, in terms of dosh-in-the-bank/bums-on-seats success the Cheap Trick hit machine was gaggin' for fuel (they were even reduced to opening for whippersnapper bands like Ratt and Mötley Crüe).

Epic Records, understandably, put their foot down. Outside 'big ballad' songwriter types were enlisted in the quest for chart action and Petersson returned. The result was the super-safe 'Lap Of Luxury' ('88), which boasted their first ever Numero Uno US single 'The Flame'. 'Busted' ('90) was of a similar formula, but with the title-track and 'You Drive, I'll Steer' reeking of eccentric golden-era stormers like 'Surrender' and 'Dream Police', one can only hope that Cheap Trick are groping in the right direction.

Recommended albums:

HEAVEN TONIGHT (Epic, 1978 – KKKKK)

LIVE AT BUDOKAN (Epic, 1979 – KKK)

CHEETAH

Australian, sister act (1981-1983)
T&A TOUTIN', Whitesnake-coverin', outfit led by blonde Chrissie and Lyndsay Hammond.
Recommended album:
ROCK 'N' ROLL WOMEN *(Epic, 1982 – K)*

CHERRY BOMBZ

Finland/UK, five-piece (1985-1986)
COMMERCIAL ROCK band formed by ex-Hanoi Rocks guitarists Andy McCoy and Nasty Suicide, interestingly opting for a female vocalist in the shape of Anita Chellemah – one –time member of horrendous pop act Toto Coelo. Ultimately, the ghost of Hanoi Rocks overshadowed this valiant effort.
Recommended album:
COMING DOWN SLOW *(High Dragon, 1987 – KKK)*

CHROME MOLLY

UK, four-piece (1984-1990)
LEICESTER MOB once tipped for the top but who lost their way. Probably best known for their sterling live show, when vocalist Steve Hawkins, never backward in coming forward, would shove a cordless microphone down his very tight cycling shorts. But the Mollies also had no shortage of decent songs, augmented by their cover of Squeeze's 'Take Me I'm Yours'.

At the height of their success they supported Alice Cooper, including a gig at Wembley Arena...
Recommended album:
YOU CAN'T HAVE IT ALL *(Powerstation, 1985 – KKK)*

CINDERELLA

USA, four-piece (1984-present)
WORKED HARD in the Philadelphia area before one Jon Bon Jovi 'discovered' them. After that, they were soon signed to Vertigo and released their debut album, 'Night Songs'. Fronted by gravel-voiced singer/guitarist Tom Keifer, their music was hard driving bluesy rock 'n' roll that, if not exactly inventive, was highly popular when

they supported on Bon Jovi and David Lee Roth tours.

Their second album, 'Long Cold Winter', sold a million in the USA and the band looked on the verge of a big breakthrough. However, 1990's 'Heartbreak Station' took a bluesier turn and the band have faded rapidly ever since.
Recommended album:
LONG COLD WINTER *(Vertigo, 1988 – KKKK)*

CIRCUS OF POWER

US, five-piece (1986-present)
TATTOOED BIKER band who were expected to take the place of Zodiac Mindwarp And The Love Reaction as bad-ass cycle riders with attitude. In keeping with this they are reported to have played several gigs for the New York Hell's Angels, but as with most bands of their ilk there are rumours that the whole image was contrived to gain publicity.

Live performances showed real class, much of the band's appeal revolved around vocalist Alex Mitchell having biceps like Popeye. Due to poor record sales Circus of Power were dropped by RCA in 1991 but have since revamped the line-up, relocated to LA and signed to Columbia.
Recommended album:
CIRCUS OF POWER *(RCA, 1989 – KKKK)*
ALEX MITCHELL (Circus Of Power): pass the spinach, please!

CLOVEN HOOF

UK, four-piece (1983-1990)
METAL MANIACS who adopted Kiss-style
make-up and costumes to complement the
elemental names of Earth, Fire, Air and Water.
Although this would have looked spectacular on
a stage in Detroit given a Kiss-style budget, in
Digbeth on a wet Wednesday evening it was a
bit crap. Dropping the make-up and employing
a Paul Stanley-lookalike vocalist in the late '80s
was just as crap and the band folded.
Good idea but shame about the album:
CLOVEN HOOF *(Neat, 1984 – KKK)*

CORROSION OF CONFORMITY

USA, five-piece (1982-present)
LIKE MANY early Hardcore bands, COC's
history is a difficult one to trace. They have
changed line-up more times than a crustie
changes underpants. The only original members
still in the band are Woody Weatherman (guitar)
and Reed Mullin (drums). Throughout the years
their musical style has changed considerably
and albums have been put out featuring three
different vocalists, Eric Eycke, Mike and and
current frontman Karl Agell. But although some
fans claim they sold out by opting for a more
Metal-orientated sound instead of the full on in-
your-face Hardcore approach, there is no
denying that their popularity has grown since
the release of 'Blind' in 1991 and subsequent
support tour with Soundgarden.
Recommended albums:
EYE FOR AN EYE *(Caroline, 1988 – KKKK)*
...with Eric
SIX SONGS WITH MIKE: 1985 *(Caroline, 1988
– KKKK) ...with Mike*
BLIND *(Relativity, 1991 – KKKKK) ...with Karl*

COCKNEY REJECTS

UK, four-piece (1979-present)
SNOTTY 'ERBERTS turned Metalheads with
their Pete Way (UFO)-produced and heavily
AC/DC and Aerosmith-influenced '82 elpee.
That recommended album:
THE WILD ONES *(A.K.A, 82 - KKKK)*

COMPANY OF WOLVES

USA, four-piece (1990-1991)
SHORTLIVED BUT promising outfit led by singer
Kyf Brewer. Their stock-in-trade was no-frills
rock 'n' roll similar in style to the Quireboys or
as heard on the first Black Crowes album. But
their sole release sold poorly and they were
dropped...
Recommended album:
COMPANY OF WOLVES *(Mercury, 1990 –
KKKK)*

CONEY HATCH

Canada, four-piece (1981-1986)
EXTREMELY UNDER-RATED outfit whose
debut (produced by Kim Mitchell of Max
Webster) was something of a hard-hitting hook-
laden classic. Vocals were shared by bassist
Andy Curran and guitarist Carl Dixon and when
backed by Steve Shelski's lead, Coney Hatch
(whose name is a corruption of a once infamous
North London lunatic asylum) made a
formidable noise. Their second album, 'Outa
Hand' ('83), had weaker material and the band
faded quickly despite 1986's 'Friction'. Still gig
occasionally in Canada but their story remains
one of potential that was never fulfilled.
Recommended album:
CONEY HATCH *(Mercury, 1982 – KKKKK)*

Alice COOPER

USA, five-piece and solo (1968-present)
''ALICE COOPER,'' rejoiced the man who
adopted the name as his own, "single-handedly
drove the stake through the heart of the love
generation!"

Despite rumours that his birthday is Christmas
Day, he was born Vincent Furnier in Detroit,
Michigan on February 4, 1948. He was raised in
Phoenix, Arizona, the son of a
preacher (!), he formed a
Stones/Beatles-esque
outfit with fellow high
school miscreants Glen
Buxton (guitar), Michael
Bruce (guitar), Dennis

ALICE COOPER's Billion Dollar Babies band

Dunaway (bass), and Neal Smith (drums). Wading through such Fab Four-inspired monickers as The Spiders, The Earwigs, and The Nazz, by the time the original do-anything-for-attention terrors hit Hollywood in '68 the band had settled on the name Alice Cooper – a handle the Coop' troupe at the time liked people

to believe was bestowed upon them by a spirit summoned at a seance! Their freak-show antics and treasured 'Worst Band In LA' tag led to management from one Shep Gordon, a Cooper associate to this day, and two, um... 'experimental' albums 'Pretties For You' ('69) and 'Easy Action' ('70) being released on top wacko Frank Zappa's Straight label. The Alice Cooper band eventualy signed to Warner Bros, and the debut for that label 'Love It To Death' ('71) – which under the guidance of producer supreme Bob Ezrin displayed an astonishing leap in every facet of creativity – is generally considered to be the band's first true album.

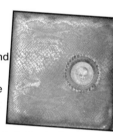

Then came the consecutive releases of further Ezrin-produced masterpieces 'Killer' ('72), and 'School's Out' ('72), and the phenomenally successful 'Billion Dollar Babies' ('73), Alice Cooper were undisputed Shock Rock kings.

But the bubble burst with the deviation to the production team of Jack Richardson and Jack Douglas on the largely insubstantial (especially as a follow-up to the hit heavy '...Babies'!) 'Muscle Of Love' ('74) – even the cardboard box packaging seemed triumphantly uninspired after its predecessor's lavish wallet concept. The album's shifting vibe obviously paralleled the Cooper outfit's frame of mind, as the band *per se* dissolved over differences in future direction with Alice Cooper (the frontman) left to cop the name in a solo situation. Incidentally, Smith, Dunaway, and Bruce later formed a band called Billion Dollar Babies for one instantly bargain-binned elpee 'Battle Axe' ('77).

Originally the horror of Alice Cooper was the greed, depravity, and decadence of our cultural surrounds, yet with 'Welcome To My Nightmre' ('75) – which, sensibly, saw the return of Ezrin as producer – Alice opted for a blatant fantasy/horror conceptual slant. Backed by top, but characterless, session musos, Alice's solo excursion has never since quite matched the promising and successful launch it had with '...Nightmare'.

IN HIS OWN WORDS...

"I think that I assume the character of Alice. I have a big mirror in my dressing room before I go on, and I stare at Alice for about 15 or 20 minutes before I go out. It's not a possession or anything like that, it's as though it's self-hypnosis."
– Kerrang! 181, April 2, 1988

"Oh, Ozzy... I wish I could say that he's done something original, but I can't think of anything that he's done that is."
– Kerrang! 69, May 31-June 13, 1984

"I've always said Alice has a love affair with the audience. But where most entertainers pet their audience – Alice rapes them." – Kerrang! 159, October 24, 1987

"When I was in Axl's position I re-wrote the rules too. In fact, the rules that I re-wrote are still intact."
– Kerrang! 362, October 12, 1991

ALICE COOPER

Over the next 10 years (and eight varied and interesting albums) Alice battled both his alcohol addiction, and worse, the claims that the former anti-hero personified had become little more than a media pet with his appearances on trashy US TV game shows and his rounds of golf with the dreaded mainstream celebrity elite – to say nothing of his string of hit ballads!!!

A lean, mean – and sober – Alice returned to prominence with the inevitably Metal-ised 'Constrictor' ('86) elpee, which displayed a distinctly Crüe/Ratt-type edge to it, along with his not-worn-for-some-seven-years (besides a cameo appearance in Twisted Sister's 1985 'Be Chrool To Your Scuel' vid) trademark whiplash mascara. 'Raise Your Fist And Yell' ('87) was in a similar vein but infinitely more brutal. Which could explain why with his first offering for new label Epic – 'Trash' ('89) – songwriter/producer/career salvage expert Desmond Child was enlisted, as the emphasis was without doubt on 'hits'. Opening cut 'Poison' did the trick. The album was bloated with guest stars (Aerosmith and Bon Jovi members etc), as was Alice's second release for the label 'Hey Stoopid', which featured hired guns Slash, Joe Satriani, Steve Vai, Ozzy, and members of Mötley Crüe! The album faired okay, but Alice's too cool appearance in the Wayne's World movie, along with its performance footage of 'Feed My Frankenstein' from 'Hey Stoopid', turned out to be the saving grace on this one...

ALBUMS

PRETTIES FOR YOU (Straight, 1969 – KKK) Abstract yet enthusiastic free-form weirdness.
EASY ACTION (Straight, 1970 – KKK) Um, wouldja believe... more abstract yet enthusiastic free-form weirdness?
LOVE IT TO DEATH (Warner Bros, 1971 – KKKKK) Dark, brooding, twisted... and beautiful.
KILLER (Warner Bros, 1972 – KKKKK) The Cooper band evolve in leaps and bounds, and display an ability to link three-minute hook-laden tunes alongside dramatic epics.
SCHOOL'S OUT (Warner Bros, 1972 – KKKKK) Both street tough/cool and passionate as the Coops wax lyrical about their school days.
BILLION DOLLAR BABIES (Warner Bros, 1973 – KKKKK) Masterfully executed US hard rock, gloriously glossy in its offensiveness.
MUSCLE OF LOVE (Warner Bros, 1974 – KKKK) Conspicuously un-structured in comparison to previous Cooper classics yet daring with its courting of styles.
WELCOME TO MY NIGHTMARE (Anchor 1975 – KKKKK) Classy and conceptual horror romp, the utilising of pacing and atmospherics unsurpassed.

ALICE COOPER GOES TO HELL *(Warner Bros, 1976 – KKKK) Loose and oft humorous follow-up to '...Nightmare', boasting some strong material.*

LACE AND WHISKEY *(Warner Bros, 1977 – KKK) Alice decked out as two-bit private eye on sleeve, but losing the plot somewhat in musical direction with this hotchpotch collection.*

THE ALICE COOPER SHOW *(Warner Bros, 1978 – KKKK) Jam-packed with goodies live offering that shoulda been a double!*

FROM THE INSIDE *(Warner Bros, 1979 – KKKK) Vibrant album from the Coop with lyrical collaborations from Elton John writer Bernie Taupin, based very loosely on Alice's spell in the loony bin...*

FLUSH THE FASHION *(Warner Bros, 1980 – KKKK) Very slight flirtations with techno-rock, but basically a breezy collection of quicky tongue-in-cheek rockers.*

SPECIAL FORCES *(Warner Bros, 1981 – KKKK) Kind of a 'Flush The Fashion' sequel; short, sharp, and black humoured.*

ZIPPER CATCHES SKIN *(Warner Bros, 1982 – KKKK) Off-the-wall (even for Alice!) lightweight rock, which appears to be our favourite ghoul's tribute to filmland.*

DA DA *(Warner Bros, 1983 – KKKK) "This record has Alice continuing through his third vinyl decade as gracefully yet tastelessly, as his terminally twisted mind will allow." – Kerrang! 57, December 15-28, 1983*

CONSTRICTOR *(MCA, 1986 - KKKK) "Vicious, aggressive rock 'n' roll Alice style with a razor-sharp production..." – Kerrang! 131, October 16-29, 1986*

RAISE YOUR FIST AND YELL *(MCA, 1987 – KKKK) "Fiendisly clever stuff." – Kerrang! 158, October 17, 1987*

TRASH *(Epic, 1989 – KKKK) "10 songs of solid sex! Less gore, more whore! Less red, more bed!" – Kerrang! 250, August 5, 1989*

HEY STOOPID *(Epic, 1991 – KKKK) " 'Hey Stoopid' isn't the greatest, but it's great enough." – Kerrang! 347, June 29, 1991*

CORONER

Switzerland, three-piece (1985-present)

COMBINING RABID aggression with guitar hero-style widdlings, and interesting arrangements, Coroner are one of the more individual Thrash bands around, if not quite one of the best.

The death-obsessed Zurich trio made good progress through four albums, but have never been renowned for their 'tour-dog' qualities, thus knackering their climb up Metal's ladder... *Recommended album:*

NO MORE COLOR *(Noise, 1990 – KKKK)*

David COVERDALE

UK, singer (1974-present)

WORKED IN gent's boutique in Redcar, North Yorkshire until 1973 when Deep Purple called him to an audition to replace Ian Gillan. Coverdale (born Saltburn, Cleveland, September 22, 1949) had sung in band's around

the North East, often mimicking the style of his (and the local) hero Paul Rodgers of Free/Bad Company. Coverdale made three studio LPs with Purple, then was tied up by contractual hassles when the band split. It was a year before he could legally sing on stage, after which time he released his first solo LP 'White Snake' ('77), a fine collection of Blues, Soul and good-time rock songs. The follow-up, 'Northwinds', was even stronger and led to the formation of the band Whitesnake, and material in a rockier vein. Recorded briefly as a solo artist for track 'The Last Note Of Freedom' on the 1990 soundtrack to Tom Cruise's movie, 'Days Of Thunder', before joining forces with Jimmy Page (see Coverdale Page, below).
Recommended solo album:
NORTHWINDS *(Purple, 1978 – KKKKK)*

COVERDALE • PAGE

UK, four-piece (1991-present)

STILL EMERGING supergroup reputedly formed by ex-Led Zeppelin guitarist Jimmy Page after Robert Plant declined his suggestion to reform Zep. Page then invited David Coverdale to sing/write lyrics for material being recorded with Ricky Phillips (bass, ex-Bad English, Babys) and Denny Carmassi (drums, ex-Heart, Montrose) plus others. Band was once to be called Legends, the album originally titled 'North-South'. The future is anybody's guess...

Recommended album:
COVERDALE PAGE *(EMI, 1993 – KKKK)*

CREAM

UK, three-piece (1966-1970)

CREAM'S CAREER was short – just four albums and seven UK Top 40 singles, but they have always enjoyed legendary status as innovators. The band comprised Eric Clapton (guitar), Jack Bruce (bass/vocals) and Ginger Baker (drums, now in Masters Of Reality). Clapton was an ex-Yardbird and many considered him to be Britain's finest rock guitarist.

The debate became academic after a young American named Jimi Hendrix came to the UK and put together a band called Experience, but Cream succeeded anyway. Hendrix even covered their 'Sunshine Of Your Love' – especially in the States, on the strength of their live shows and songs like 'Strange Brew', 'Sunshine...', 'White Room' and 'Badge'.

Drugs took their toll but Cream were sensible enough to quit while they were ahead, recording the farewell album 'Goodbye' in 1969. Two posthumous live albums followed, capturing much of the fury of the band's heavy and often improvisational blues material.

The subsequent formation of Led Zeppelin was almost exactly coincident with Cream's demise and some of Zep's early style can be traced to Cream's foundations.

Recommended, if slightly dated, albums:
LIVE CREAM *(Polydor, 1970 – KKK)*
THE VERY BEST OF CREAM *(Polydor, 1984 – KKKK)*

CRIMSON GLORY

USA, five-piece (1986-present)

TECHNO METALLERS from Florida with a sound close to Queensrÿche's, not least due to the vocals of the enigmatically-named Midnight. Lyrically, they often displayed quasi-religious leanings but stopped short of being a true White Metal act. Instead, Crimson Glory were known best for the shiny silver masks they used to wear. Over the years, as the band became better known, the masks got smaller. Then, for the third album 'Strange And Beautiful' ('91), they removed them altogether and have since plummeted to obscurity.

Recommended second album:
TRANSCENDENCE *(Roadrunner, 1989 – KKKK)*

CRIMSON GLORY: who were those masked men?

CRO-MAGS

USA, five-piece (1986–present)

NEW YORK Hardcore merchants fronted by the tattooed madman, bassist and some-time singer, Harley Flanagan. A self-confessed violent person who looks like he eats raw babies for breakfast – but in actual fact claims to be a Hare Krishna devotee! – Flanagan got into Punk when aged 10 and was playing drums two years later. Cro-Mags members have come, gone and returned again over their three albums – 'The Age of Quarrel', 'Best Wishes' (featuring Flan' on lead vocals) and '92's more Metallised 'Alpha-Omega' – but the menace has only increased. What else would you expect from a band whose now reinstated singer rejoices in the name of John 'Bloodclot' Joseph. Not for wimps.

Recommended album:
ALPHA-OMEGA *(Century Media, 1992 – KKKKK)*

CROWFORCE

UK, four-piece (1990-present)

'DANCECORE' IS only one term for this fine amalgam of Techno-Rave music and good ol' Metal; if anyone can get rock-minded folk on that dancefloor with a bottle of Vick, it's Crowforce.

Recommended debut album:
CROWFORCE *(Devotion, 1992 – KKKK)*

The CULT

UK, four-piece (1985-present)

NOT SO much a band as the schizophrenic lovechild of singer Ian Astbury and guitarist Billy Duffy. The pair have not always seen eye-to-eye, but using a number of sidemen – including Matt Sorum now of Guns N' Roses – they have set about a joint mission of creating the ultimate Heavy Metal album. Their problem was, having told everybody that, they set themselves up...

Many were loathe to take them seriously to begin with because of roots in their previous Goth-cum-Punk guises as the Southern Death Cult and Death Cult. First record as The Cult was 'Love' ('85), which produced the 'She Sells Sanctuary' hit and genuinely widened the boundaries of Metal. Its successor, 'Electric' ('87), convinced many more diehard Metal fans to take the band seriously, being less psychedelic and more AC/DC in style, but it was to be 1989's 'Sonic Temple', produced by Bob Rock, that came closest to Astbury and Duffy's stated ambition. With thundering rhythms from Sorum and bassist Jamie Stewart beneath huge Zeppelin-esque arrangements, the band came up with a true classic. Sadly, the tour to promote it was marred by some less than convincing performances often the result of Astbury and Duffy battling for supremacy.

The follow-up, 'Ceremony' ('92), saw Astbury regain supremacy but too much of the material sounded like weaker echoes of 'Sonic Temple's glories. They'll be back...

Recommended (almost ultimate) album:
SONIC TEMPLE *(Beggars Banquet, 1989 – KKKKK)*

THE CULT (Billy Duffy and Ian Astbury):
fathers of a schizophrenic lovechild

D*A*D

Denmark, four-piece (1986-present)
AFTER FOUR albums for the Danish Melody label, the bizarrely commercial rockers finally lucked out with a million dollar deal in 1989. Renowned for their surreal stage show involving exploding helmets, rocket basses and giant sofas, the quartet wrote such immediate songs with irrestable hooks that European rock clubs seemed to survive on nothing but 'Point Of View' and 'Sleeping My Day Away'.

Problems with the taxman and an unsuccessful launch in America has shrouded the band's future, but their songwriting strength should see them triumph again.
Recommended albums:
NO FUEL LEFT FOR THE PILGRIMS *(WEA, 1989 – KKKKK)*

DANGEROUS TOYS

USA, five-piece (1989-present)
YANKEE FUN rockers best known for their remarkable song titles. Heading the list is 'Sport'n A Woody'. (Runner-up... 'Ten Boots (Stompin')'.)
Recommended (for a laugh) album:
DANGEROUS TOYS *(Columbia, 1989 – KK)*

DANZIG

USA, four-piece (1988-present)
BAND FORMED by Glenn Danzig, the diminutive muscle-man who once fronted underground Hardcore/Punk heroes, The Misfits and Samhain. Danzig the band are signed to Def American, a label happy to indulge Mr Danzig's penchant for doomy Sabbath-y riffs, Satanic imagery and '50s crooner-style vocals, all produced by Rick Rubin. It's an odd mix that works very well on occasions on the three albums to date – 'Danzig' ('88), 'Danzig II: Lucifuge' ('90) and 'Danzig III: How the Gods Kill' ('92). When it doesn't, you can always take solace in the knowledge that Eerie Von is the bassist, the guitarist goes by the name of John Christ and the drummer is called Chuck Biscuits...
Recommended album:
DANZIG *(Def American, 1988 – KKKK)*

GLENN DANZIG is on the right

DARE

UK, five-piece (1988-1991)
LAUNCHED BY 1988's melodic monster of a debut album, Manchester-based Dare won mass critical acclaim and some seriously skillful songwriting – but never reached the expected commercial heights. No one has yet managed to explain this, least of all the ex-Thin Lizzy keyboard player and founder member, Darren Dean Wharton. Blame it on Britain's general inability to sell heroic melodic rock, and weep. Dare left behind two timeless albums, the second of which, 'Blood From Stone', boasted a rockier, tougher, Lizzy-er direction. File under Tragically Unfulfilled.
Recommended debut album:
OUT OF THE SILENCE *(A&M, 1988 – KKKK)*

DARK ANGEL

USA, five-piece (1981-1992)
SELF-PROCLAIMED Caffeine Metallers famed for super-speedy Thrash epics; bloodied,

breakneck insanity which hit a peak with the dizzying 'Darkness Descends' in 1986, and never really faltered on their subsequent releases. Technical obsessions climaxed in the 'Time Does Not Heal' opus, advertised as containing 246 riffs, although it seemed like more. Drummer Gene Hoglan's intellectually twisted lyrics were more plentiful than ever, discussing extremes of human behaviour and making singer Ron Rinehart's job unenviable. *Recommended album:*
TIME DOES NOT HEAL (Under One Flag, 1991 – KKKK)

DARK STAR

UK, five-piece (1979-1987)
CLASSIC MIDLANDS-based NWOBHM act (ie famous for one song only). Dark Star's was 'Lady Of Mars' as featured on 'Metal For Muthas Volume 2' compilation. Made two albums but never surpassed that sole 'hit'. Ex-singer Rick Staines now works for Magnum. *Recommended* – for one song – *album:*
DARK STAR (Avatar, 1981 – KK)

DEATH

USA, four-piece (1983-present)
DEATH IS the most minimally stark name that a Death Metal band could select for itself. Luckily, the monicker was bagged early on by a true originator, in the shape of bassist/vocalist Chuck Schuldiner.

For a few months in late '83, Death were known as Mantas, with the line-up comprising Schuldiner, Rick Rozz and drummer Kam Lee. They churned out rehearsal, demo and live tapes aplenty, although the quality left a great deal to be desired.

Eventually parting ways with his companions, Schuldiner struck out on his own, relocating from Florida to San Francisco. There, he teamed up with drummer Chris Reifert, and the duo recorded Death's seminal 'Scream Bloody Gore'. It saw Schuldiner handle

bass, guitar and vocals, which were more gruesomely guttural than anything previously heard. A whole new trend was born, there and then.

The music was relentless, thundering brutally away; the perfect accompaniment for Schuldiner's ultra-violent utterances. Song-titles included 'Mutilation', 'Torn To Pieces' and 'Baptized In Blood'...

'Scream...'s shocking extremity inspired a virtual sub-genre; Gore Metal. Literally hundreds of bands, underground or otherwise, began using the most gratuitously nasty imagery they could dream up. Among the best examples of this has been the anatomically correct Carcass. Among the worst has been anything emanating from Greece. 1988 saw the release of Death's second and most striking album, 'Leprosy'. By then, Schuldiner was banging out the mayhem with Rick Rozz (guitar), Terry Butler (bass) and Bill Andrews (drums). Retaining all of the debut's intensity, while introducing a sense of warped melody that Schuldiner was destined to push further with each release, 'Leprosy' was an awesome display.

Schuldiner proved unable to keep one line-up afloat. When 1990's 'Spiritual Healing' emerged, not only had Rozz been replaced by James Murphy, but the musical direction had veered towards more progressive playing. Despite being hailed as the biggest selling Death Metal album to date, the band almost certainly lost some hardcore fans to outfits who were staying more faithful to the original gameplan.

In addition, Schuldiner himself pulled out of a European tour at the 11th hour, leaving Bill Andrews and Terry Butler to soldier on under the name of Death, making use of replacement musos, and garnering poor reviews wherever they went.

Schuldiner, of course, subsequently returned to the driver's seat, splitting up with the Andrews-Butler rhythm section, and assembling yet another Death model. 'Human' was the 1992 album featuring Paul Masvidal on guitar, Skott Carino on bass and the highly technical Sean Reinert behind the kit. This time, they actually made it over to Europe...

In early '93, Schuldiner hooked up with drummer Gene Hoglan, ex-Dark Angel. It's done nothing to dispel the man's reputation of being a dictator surrounded by hired hands, but promises to result in more Deathly delights...

MR DEATH: Chuck Schuldiner himself, for it is he...

SPIRITUAL HEALING (Under One Flag, 1990 – KKKK) "A brilliant intro to the '90s for Death Metal." Kerrang! 272, January 13, 1990
HUMAN (Roadrunner, 1992 – KKKK) "Schuldiner's at long last struck upon the sort of Techno-Gore bludgeon Death have been tinkering around with for years." Kerrang! 367, November 16, 1991
FATE: THE BEST OF DEATH (Under One Flag, 1992 – KKKK) "Takes you all over their scene-moulding history... recommended." Kerrang! 406, August 22, 1992
INDIVIDUAL THOUGHT PATTERNS (Roadrunner, 1993 – KKKK) "Best offering since the gore-normous 'Leprosy'... more than enough substance and weighty riffage..." – Kerrang! 447, June 14, 1993

DEATH ANGEL

USA, five-piece (1982-1991)
AFTER 1987's hyper-Thrashy and much-lauded debut, Death Angel never really took off, despite producing good music with fair consistency. With its successors, 'Frolic Through The Park' and 'Act III' (their first and last for Geffen), the youthful San Francisco pushed their sound into more subtle areas, and this was perhaps their undoing. Ex-members currently appear in The Organization.

Recommended-but-now-dated debut album:
THE ULTRA-VIOLENCE (Under One Flag, 1987 – KKK)

ALBUMS

SCREAM BLOODY GORE (Under One Flag, 1987 – KKKKK) "Lots of bluster, lots of mad Thrashing, but nothing that leaves an impression." Kerrang! 148, June 11-24, 1987 (Receiving a solitary K from a self-proclaimed Thrash-hater...)
LEPROSY (Under One Flag, 1988 – KKKK) "If raw Death Metal is what you crave, then this is a feast." Kerrang! 199, August 5, 1988

DEATHROW

Germany, five-piece (1985-present)
NEVER THE most high-profile act, even during the great late-'80s German Thrash wave, Deathrow progressed from early tirades of pure aggression to an altogether more advanced brand of techno-Metal. Early 1993 saw them release an eponymous comeback album, but on a label so obscure that almost no-one noticed.
Recommended album:
DECEPTION IGNORED *(Noise, 1989 – KKKK)*

DECIMATOR

UK, five-piece (1988-present)
GROWLING, SNARLING, and suprisingly good Mad Max/Biker Thrash band with a vocalist called Lord Mad Dog who comes on stage with a large, heavily skulled machine gun. Destined to be huge after the apocalypse.
Recommended album:
DIRTY, HOT AND HUNGRY *(Neat, 1993 – KKKKK)*

DEDRINGER

UK, five-piece (1977-1984)
LEEDS BOOGIE outfit who supported Gillan and Triumph on UK tours but failed to make their fine club act transfer to bigger stages; perhaps because singer JJ Hoyle was a Phil Collins lookalike whilst one of the guitarists, Neil Hudson, resembled Captain Pugwash. Revamped line-up released 'Second Arising', their final album, on Neat in 1983.
Recommended album:
DIRECT LINE *(DinDisc, 1980 – KKKK)*

DEEP PURPLE

UK, five-piece (1968-present)
DURING THE early '70s, Deep Purple were unquestionably one of the biggest bands in the world, making great records and playing live shows that walked the razor's edge between triumph and disaster as individual members fought (sometimes almost literally) duels on their respective instruments. Guitarist Ritchie Blackmore usually reigned supreme as the band won a huge following that refused to let the band die, even after 1975 when they had fallen apart. Sadly, time has proved that while the first results of the 1983 reformation were credible enough, the band quickly lost their impetus and, soon after, much of their credibility.

Deep Purple's heritage dates all the way back to 1967, when former Searchers drummer Chris Curtis enlisted Blackmore (born April 14, 1945) and Jon Lord (keyboards, born June 9, 1941) to a band called Roundabout. Rehearsals didn't go well, so he quit and in came new men Ian Paice (drums, born June 29, 1948), Rod Evans (vocals) and Nick Simper (bass). The quintet passed on 'Concrete God' and opted to call themselves Deep Purple. They made their live debut in Tastrup, Denmark, on April 20, 1968 and signed to EMI in the UK and Tetragrammaton in the States. This line-up – later known as Mark I after a 1974 compilation called 'Mark I & II' which featured the first two line-ups – made three albums which today sound very dated. Evans was a crooner in the Neil Diamond style and the band even covered one of his songs. They also reworked Cream and Hendrix hits, but their biggest break was with Joe South's 'Hush'. Purple's version (on their '68 debut 'Shades Of Deep Purple' album) went Top Five in the States but fared less well at home. The band were never able to repeat their success and '69's second and third albums – 'The Book Of Taliesyn' and 'Deep Purple' – found the band losing their way commercially whilst experimenting with Blackmore and (especially) Lord's classical music leanings.

These came to a head with 1970's 'Concerto For Group And Orchestra' recorded just after the recruitment of new guys Ian Gillan (vocals, born August 19, 1945) and Roger Glover (bass, born November 30, 1945). Gillan in particular hardly featured on the record – a conceptual 'duel' between Mark II and the Royal Philharmonic Orchestra recorded live in London's Royal Albert Hall. The

DEEP PURPLE: the classic 1969-1973 Mark II line-up.
A fashionable look at the time, honest...

line-up later condemned it as a false start and were much more fired-up come the recording of their seminal 'In Rock' album.

It introduced Gillan's trademark – piercing screams and a soaring range (most noticeably on 'Child In Time') that worked equally well when he played the lead in the Tim Rice/Andrew Lloyd Webber production of 'Jesus Christ Superstar' – along with the band's newly adopted uncompromising hard rock style. This was refined slightly for 'Fireball' ('71), then perfected for the watershed 'Machine Head' ('72) which contained such classics as 'Highway Star', 'Space Truckin'' and the legendary 'Smoke On The Water'. All these songs turned up in even more powerful form on the double in-concert album 'Made In Japan' ('73). It captured Purple close to their best and in retrospect marked the peak of the band's career, being recorded at the end of almost three years of non-stop touring worldwide – schedules which bands in the '90s would never even consider. These strained relationships between members, in particular, the notoriously 'moody' Blackmore, Gillan and Glover. The latter pair therefore quit after a show in Osaka, Japan on June 29, 1973 – three months after 'Who Do We

Think We Are' was released.

The band immediately advertised for replacements, and come September had recruited them in the form of David Coverdale (vocals) and Glenn Hughes (bass and vocals). Coverdale had been in a number of semi-pro bands and once even supported Purple in 1972. Hughes had a more pro pedigree as a member of Trapeze. The first album to feature them was 'Burn' ('74).

Despite a slightly bluesier feel, and the doubts about Coverdale's ability to sing Gillan-era songs, the album and tour did well, especially in the States. However, Blackmore grew dissatisfied with the two new member's Soul/Funk leanings and instead of fighting – as he would have done in the past – sat back and lost interest. This was very clear on 'Stormbringer' ('75) where he could hardly be heard and also, perversely, on the single-live 'Made In Europe' ('76) where his Stratocaster is rampant – the difference being when the latter was recorded he had made up his mind to quit the band and had apparently opted to go out with a bang! His last gig was in Paris on April 7, 1975.

Blackmore's replacement was the uniquely gifted American Tommy Bolin; a guitarist Blackmore himself recommended. He made just one studio album with Mark IV, 'Come Taste The Band' ('76) – although he can also be heard on the live 'Last Concert In Japan' ('77) – because his heroin habit, alongside ego clashes between others in the band at the time of his joining, combined to engineer Purple's demise. After a relatively disastrous UK tour, the band played their last gig at the Liverpool Empire on July 19, 1976.

By then, Blackmore was fronting his own band Rainbow, Gillan was playing Jazz Rock in the Ian Gillan Band, Lord and Glover had solo albums in the racks. Paice and Lord would soon team up again in Paice, Ashton & Lord, whilst Coverdale would form Whitesnake and Hughes would launch a solo career. From 1977 to 1983, all enjoyed varying degrees of success, but throughout that period the clamour for them to reform never abated. In the States in 1980, Simper and Evans even got together a bunch of Mark II lookalikes and toured as 'Deep Purple' – until the lawyers stepped in. Meanwhile in the UK, their back catalogue continued to sell, in original and repackaged 'best of' formats. The legend grew to the point where the five members of the Mark II, line-up could resist the idea (or possibly the money) no longer, and reformed to record 'Perfect Strangers' ('84). It was well received and, enthused, the band took to the road then made 'House Of Blue Light' ('87). This sold poorly in comparison and the subsequent 'Nobody's Perfect' double-live ('88) smacked of contractual obligations. The band denied it – but they never recorded again for Polydor, and Gillan was sacked a year later. That should have been the end, but foolishly, Blackmore tried to keep it alive by re-employing former Rainbow singer Joe Lynn Turner for the album 'Slaves And Masters' ('90). Live shows were, er... different, but had little to do with the legend. As 1993 dawned, Turner had departed so that Gillan could return for a planned one-off 25th anniversary album and world tour...

ALBUMS

SHADES OF DEEP PURPLE (Parlophone, 1968 – KKK)
THE BOOK OF TALIESYN (Harvest, 1969 – KK)
DEEP PURPLE (Harvest, 1969 – KK)
All the above are Mark I and pretty average – but ace if you've a penchant for '60s pop rock laced with bursts of guitar/Hammond organ.
CONCERTO FOR GROUP AND ORCHESTRA (Harvest, 1970 – K) *Pretty godawful, really.*
IN ROCK (Harvest, 1970 – KKKKK) *Indispensible primeval Metal klassik. Raw production but superb songs. Blackmore and Lord dominant.*

FIREBALL (Harvest, 1971 – KKKK) *More refined and off-the-wall, strongly Gillan influenced.*
MACHINE HEAD (Purple, 1972 – KKKKK) *Brilliant songwriting, superb performances from every member. Packed with stage faves.*
MADE IN JAPAN (Purple, 1973 – KKKKK) *One of greatest live albums of all time. Unbelievably, the original plan was to release it in Japan only!*
WHO DO WE THINK WE ARE (Purple, 1973 – KKKK) *Features 'Woman From Tokyo' and many underrated gems.*
BURN (Purple, 1974 – KKKKK) *Storming debut by Mark III. Blackmore's work is A1 whilst Coverdale and Hughes sing brilliantly.*
STORMBRINGER (Purple, 1975 – KK) *Very lightweight. Half-hearted rockers outnumbered by soul/funky numbers.*
COME TASTE THE BAND (Purple, 1975 – KKKK) *Mark IV and Tommy Bolin's debut. Bold, funky and very classy new direction. ...but the band split until:*

PERFECT STRANGERS (Polydor, 1984 – KKKK) *Mark II comeback album. As good as some of their early '70s work.*
HOUSE OF BLUE LIGHT (Polydor, 1987 – KKK) *Some good songs but generally weaker than above.*
NOBODY'S PERFECT (Polydor, 1988 – KKK) *Double-live that pales badly in comparison to 'Made In Japan'.*
SLAVES AND MASTERS (BMG, 1990 – KK) *Joe Lynn Turner's debut. Competent, but sounding more like latter era Rainbow.*

BEST POSTHUMOUS RELEASES
MADE IN EUROPE (Purple, 1976 – KKKKK) *Ultra powerful in-concert single album. Mark III at their live best.*
DEEPEST PURPLE (EMI, 1980 – KKKK) *Strong single album compilation.*
THE ANTHOLOGY (EMI Harvest, 1985 – KKKK) *Double vinyl set. Best of plus rarities.*

IN THEIR OWN WORDS...

Ed's note: Deep Purple are so bollock-achingly ancient that they had undergone four line-ups and been split for five years before Kerrang!'s first issue ever came out. But here, because we love and respect 'em, is what they've told the Big K! since reforming in 1983...

"We had to invent something. We took from jazz, we took from old fashioned rock 'n' roll, we took from the classics; we took from here, there and everywhere. We were musical magpies..."
– Jon Lord, Kerrang! 81, November 15-28, 1984

"There's an amazing magic and chemistry that makes Deep Purple work better in this sphere of music than anyone else. Don't ask us why, it just does..."
– Ian Paice, Kerrang! 81, November 15-28, 1984

"One day I'll figure out why I'm so moody... I often say to myself, I wish I wasn't so sensitive... I think that uptight feeling, that feeling of being on the edge, can be very frustrating... I just need the slightest provocation and I'll be off."
– Ritchie Blackmore, Kerrang! 82, November 29-December 12, 1984

"This so-called 'legend' crap just makes me sick... I've always been very wary of a Deep Purple reunion. I thought the 'legend' had grown far bigger than the band ever was."
– Roger Glover, Kerrang! 82, November 29-December 12, 1984

"There was great reticence, doubt and uncertainty about reforming. It was only when we got together and started rehearsing that the smiles started picking up and the confidence started returning." – Ian Gillan, Kerrang! 194, July 2, 1988

"When Joe Lynn Turner's name came up I immediately said, 'No way! Absolutely not!'... I thought that would be a great loss of credibility for Deep Purple..." – Roger Glover, Kerrang! 312, October 20, 1990

"If I hear 'Deep Rainbow' again I think I'm gonna puke." – Joe Lynn Turner, Kerrang! 312, October 20, 1990

"There's nothing wrong with nostalgia – as long as it's not ALL nostalgia..." – Roger Glover, Kerrang! 312, October 20, 1990

DEEP PURPLE

DEF LEPPARD

UK, five-piece (1977-present)

WITHOUT DOUBT one of the most successful rock bands ever, Def Leppard nonetheless came from very humble beginnings. Britain's former steel industry capital, Sheffield, was the spawning ground for this truly remarkable band who, despite their glories, have faced more problems and heartbreak than most.

In 1977, current bassist Rick Savage (born December 2, 1960) formed a band called Atomic Mass with guitarist Pete Willis and drummer Tony Kenning. The trio spent all their spare time rehearsing at Tapton Comprehensive School. Later that year they were joined by vocalist Joe Elliott (born August 1, 1959). Rehearsals moved to an insalubrious former spoon factory and the band changed their name to Deaf Leopard, a spelling soon corrupted to give the name we all know today.

A Christmas gig for their friends convinced the band they needed a second guitarist, and Steve Clark (born April 23, 1960) was recruited on January 29, 1978 after a chance meeting with Willis in a college library. At this point, Elliott worked for a tool company, Savage and Kenning for British Rail, Clark was a lathe operator and Willis was employed by British Oxygen Company. Def Leppard's first real gig was at Westfield School, Sheffield on July 18, 1978. They were paid £5 and had to smuggle their own beer in. From then on, the band got regular gigs in and around the city, then decided to cut an EP at Hull's cheap 'n' cheerful Fairview Studios. The EP was self-financed and recorded over two days in November. However, just days before that momentous occasion, Kenning was fired for lack of enthusiasm and Sheffield sticksman Frank Noon stepped in as temporary replacement for the session. The result was the 'Def Leppard EP', more commonly known as 'Getcha Rocks Off'. Following a deal done in the gents toilet at the Sheffield Limit Club, the band acquired a permanent drummer called Richard Allen (born November 1, 1963), a baby thundergod just 15 years old.

The EP's initial 1,000 copies sold fast, as did the reprint, and sessions on Radio Hallam and for John Peel's Radio One show followed. The UK music press, most notably *Sounds*, championed the band as one of the frontrunners of the so-called New Wave Of British Heavy Metal, and a deal with Phonogram's Vertigo label was inked on August 5, 1979 at Rick Allen's parents' house. By the end of 1979, Def Leppard had made a whirlwind start to their professional career: they had seen Phonogram re-press and sell 15,000 copies of their EP (the record went on to sell around 24,000); had a debut single, 'Wasted', become a Number 61 hit; and had recorded their debut album, 'On Through The Night' with Judas Priest producer Tom Allom.

That album, accurately capturing the band's adolescent spark, was released in March 1980, after which they toured with Sammy Hagar and AC/DC in the UK, then visited America to open for Pat Travers, Ted Nugent and Judas Priest. Audiences there loved them and no one was more surprised than the band at the amount of female screaming!

Their homecoming gig at August's Reading Festival should have been triumphant but instead they were canned. Much of their UK audience simply believed the band had 'sold out' their raw NWOBHM roots to crack America. The band returned to Sheffield sore and depressed.

In March 1981, pre-production began on 'High 'N' Dry', the Leps' second album. In the chair this time was super-producer Robert John 'Mutt' Lange, who is now to production what Heinz are to baked beans. The album was released in July of that year and promptly nipped in to the US Top 40, helped by MTV picking up on the album's classic ballad, 'Bringin' On The Heartbreak'. The band played European and US tours but remained largely unloved in England, playing live dates to half-empty halls. Under pressure of this constant touring, both Willis and Clark began to hit the bottle in earnest, causing much friction within the band.

Def Leppard started work in early '82 on what was to prove their big break – 'Pyromania' – once again with 'Mutt' Lange. Recording was exhausting and fraught, as Lange's perfectionism continually pushed the band to the edge. Willis' excessive drinking continued to be a problem and he eventually became unable to play to Lange's standards so was sent home in disgrace. Finally, on July 11, 1982, Willis was sacked. In his place, the band brought in the chipper Cockney, Phil Collen (born December 8, 1957), ex- of Glam queens the Dumb Blondes and Girl.

Collen added a few last minute touches to 'Pyromania' which was finally released in February 1983. While in Britain response was still cool, on American radio, its lead-off single, 'Photograph', took off like a frenzied Cruise missile as the band set out on a tour there opening for Billy Squier. Soon they were able to headline their own dates and Lep-mania was truly taking off. The band were being mobbed at in-store appearances and screaming girls were everywhere.

After the 'Pyromania' tour ended in Bangkok at the end of the year, 'Pyromania' had sold over four million copies – but it eventually sold half as many again in the USA alone. There it spent 92 weeks on the chart, once kept from the top slot only by Michael Jackson's 'Thriller'.

In January 1984 the band took a break, reconvening in Dublin in August to prepare for the next LP, 'Hysteria'. But with 'Mutt' Lange declaring himself overworked after producing the Cars and Foreigner without a break, Def Leppard were forced to work without their mentor, instead choosing the former Meat Loaf svengali Jim Steinman to produce, at Wisseloord Studios in Hilversum, Holland. The relationship was a disaster, and within four months Steinman was out of the picture. Former 'High 'N' Dry' engineer Nigel Green was drafted in to keep things moving.

The band took a break for Christmas 1984, then on New Year's Eve, disaster struck. Drummer Rick Allen was involved in a motor accident on the outskirts of Sheffield. His car left the road, ploughed through a wall and overturned. His left arm was severed at the shoulder.

Through sheer spirit, he was out of Sheffield's Hallamshire Hospital within a month and told the band by telephone of his determination to drum again. In February he rejoined them in Holland. Meanwhile Allen went to Paris to get to grips with a new electronic drum kit, mainly pedal-operated, produced by synthesiser company Simmons.

After Lange's return, a break from recording came in August 1986. Following a couple of very low-key shows in Ireland, the band joined the bill of three European Monsters Of Rock shows. Allen's full return to the spotlight came at Castle Donington where the response was overwhelming. The whole band were bowled over by the crowd's fanatical support. Britain finally loved Def Leppard.

'Hysteria' finally came out in August 1987, with a full 'Mutt' Lange production credit, and went on to sell 15 million copies worldwide, reaching Number One in the USA after 49 weeks. The tour in support of it lasted until November 1988, with Clark's drinking and substance abuse still causing tension in the band. Work began on what would become 'Adrenalize', with Clark periodically in rehabilitation units. Writing and recording continued through 1990, then Def Leppard were struck by the harsh hand of fate once more...

Clark was found dead at his Chelsea flat early on the morning of January 8, 1991, having overdosed on "an excess of alcohol mixed with anti-depressants and painkillers". Valium and morphine were also found in his blood. The band were saddened but not surprised. Clark had put himself in a coma before, this time he never woke up. It was the worst possible start to the year, but Def Leppard, as ever, triumphed over adversity and continued with their music.

Throughout 1991 and the completion of 'Adrenalize', hotly rumoured replacements for Clark were ex-Whitesnake guitarst John Sykes and Collen's old mate from Girl, Gerry Laffy. But while the press debated, the Leps beavered away with Mike Shipley at the production helm. Shipley had mixed or engineered the last three LPs, so with Lange working with Bryan Adams, he was the obvious choice.

'Adrenalize' was released in March 1992 and in April it was announced that ex-Sweet Savage, Dio, Whitesnake, River Dogs and Lou Gramm/Shadow King guitarist Vivian Campbell had joined the band. Campbell (born August 25, 1962) made a low-key live debut at Dublin McGonagles on April 15, before stepping out in front of the whole world at the Freddie Mercury Tribute Show at Wembley Stadium three days later. Throughout Def Leppard's 1992/93 touring schedule, Campbell has slotted in like a well-oiled cog. The Def Leppard Platinum success story looks set to run and run...

DEF LEPPARD

ALBUMS

ON THROUGH THE NIGHT (Vertigo, 1980 – KKK) Rather too polished for most familiar with the EP and their rough 'n' ready early shows...
HIGH 'N' DRY (Vertigo, 1981 – KKKK) Hard hitting rock, with more than a hint of AC/DC-style rifferama!
PYROMANIA (Vertigo, 1983 – KKKKK) "Each cut has the rasping, shimmering hallmark of 'master-blaster'. These aren't just songs, but the birth of a legend." – Kerrang! 35 February 10-23, 1983

HYSTERIA (Bludgeon Riffola/Phonogram, 1987 – KKKKK) "Without doubt, THE album to set the standards in both musical style and production for the remainder of the decade." Kerrang! 153, August 20-September 2, 1987

ADRENALIZE (Bludgeon Riffola/Phonogram, 1992 – KKKK) "Def Leppard are the ultimate radio rock band and 'Adrenalize' is the state of the art." – Kerrang! 385, March 28, 1992

DEICIDE

USA, four-piece (1987-present)
TAKING BOTH the musical and lyrical bombast of early Venom to new extremes, Deicide (briefly Amon) wasted little time in becoming synonomous with Satanic Metal, brutal diatribes against the Christian faith, and remarkable press controversy.

Bassist/singer Glen Benton was their obvious focal point, right from the start. He is, after all,

GLEN BENTON: promises to be dead by 33

the man with an inverted cross branded into his forehead. The man who clearly seeks confrontational mischief wherever he goes, claiming that he will kill himself on reaching the age of 33...

An instant hit with Death Metal fans, as well as giving the media something to get their descriptive teeth into, Deicide's major piece of news-infiltration came in December '92. Benton provocatively commented on his torture of small animals, which had Britain's Animal Militia up in arms, issuing death threats.

Deicide played their two pre-Christmas gigs as planned, suffering no casualties. Clearly, Benton is smiled favourably upon by the dark forces lurking below...

Most recommended album:
LEGION *(Roadracer, 1992 – KKKK)*

DEMON

UK, five-piece (1980-present)
CAME TO prominence during the NWOBHM glory years, but were never really a part of it. Instead Demon, led by singer Dave Hill, boasted the unlikely combination of Black Metal lyrics and a melodic approach. After their 'Night Of The Demon' debut in 1981 they turned in a minor classic in the shape of 'The Unexpected Guest' ('82), with its terror-packed title-track. Real commercial success always eluded the

band, however, and live gigs were often hard to come by in the UK. Original guitarist Mal Spooner died in 1984, days after final sessions for 'British Standard Approved' ('85), but the band bravely soldiered on, finally achieving recognition on the Continent, notably Germany, where the double live 'One Helluva Night' ('89) was made. Since then, they have made one more studio album, their eighth, 'Hold On To The Dream' ('91) and look unlikely to ever go away...

Recommended album:
THE UNEXPECTED GUEST *(Carrere, 1982 – KKKK)*

DESTRUCTION

Germany, four-piece (1983-1991
ONE-TIME joint flag-holders with Kreator during the late 1980s German Thrash explosion, Destruction were a band ultimately brought down by several factors, including personal differences that led frontman Schmier to step out and form his own band, Headhunter. Destruction were noted for extremely proficient guitar work, a song called 'Mad Butcher', and such unexpected pieces as the 'Pink Panther' theme and Glen Miller's 'In The Mood'.
Particularly recommended album:
ETERNAL DEVASTATION *(1986, Noise – KKKK)*
Not-in-the-least recommended album:
CRACKED BRAIN *(Their Schmier-less tragedy, 1991, Noise – K)*

DETECTIVE

USA, five-piece (1977-1979)
SHORTLIVED 'SUPERGROUP' signed to Led Zeppelin's Swan Song label under the tutelage of Jimmy Page. Eponymous debut was the better of their two hard rock albums featuring singer Michael des Barres (ex-Silverhead and later of Chequered Past and Power Station), plus Tony Kaye (original and latter era Yes keyboard player) and guitarist Michael Monarch who went on to join Meat Loaf's touring band.
Recommended album:
DETECTIVE *(Swan Song, 1978 – KKKK)*

Paul DI'ANNO

UK, vocalist (1976-present)

PAUL DI'ANNO has never been very nice to look at. The pit-bull frontman was, however, part-responsible for defining the sound of the NWOBHM in the early days of Iron Maiden. Although his career has never reached the same heights since he quit Maiden with 'road-fatigue' in 1981 after two albums and countless, much sought-after demos, the outspoken vocalist has long been a champion of classic British Metal. He survived the '80s with Battlezone but finally secured a major deal with Killers, a band he formed in 1990 with ex-members of Passion, Jagged Edge and Tank. He is currently a proud, Harley-owning slaphead residing in California and not missing Essex at all.

Recommended albums:

KILLERS *(with Iron Maiden) (EMI, 1981 – KKKKK)*

MURDER ONE *(with Killers) (Zoo, 1992 – KKK)*

DIAMOND HEAD

UK, four-piece (1977-present)

RECENTLY REFORMED after years in limbo when the clamour of acclaim hardly faltered. Diamond Head were arguably the best of all the NWOBHM era groups but only ever realised a fraction of their potential. The major label that finally signed them, MCA, must take much of the blame but ultimately the band were also at fault for being naive enough to let themselves be mis-managed or easily and poorly led.

The original line-up of Sean Harris (vocals), Brian Tatler (guitar), Colin Kimberly (bass) and Duncan Scott (drums) came together as schoolfriends. Legend has it that Tatler asked Harris to join he and Scott after hearing reports of the singer's rendition of 'Be Bop A Lula' on a school outing. Harris auditioned with the two in Tatler's bedroom on June 25, 1976 and signed the contract the following day in an English lesson! After a few months of rehearsals in that same bedroom, Kimberley completed the fledgling line-up. Diamond Head then rose to national rock heroes through a combination of electrifying live shows and a series of rough and ready, but highly original, independent releases sold mail order and direct to fans at gigs. The first of these was 'Shoot Out The Lights'/'Helpless', released early in 1980. Like all the subsequent others, it sold out on the strength of good reviews, word of mouth and weeks on end spent in the Sounds Heavy Metal chart – the indispensable guide to HM during that period. Second single was July 1980's 'Sweet And Innocent'/'Streets Of Gold' produced by Robin George and followed it late in 1980 by an untitled, white label, plain sleeve 'promo' album. Accompanied by their first full-scale national tour, the LP was called 'Lightning To The Nations'.

This has become an incredibly collectable record which many believe to be their finest. Unfortunately for Diamond Head, it was a limited edition of 11,000 which although it sold out very quickly, it meant far too few people ever heard it. (More copies did resurface in subsequent repressings.) The band were to put out two more independent releases: the more commercial sounding 'Waited Too Long' single (backed with 'Play It Loud') in February '81; and June 1981's four-song EP, 'Diamond Lights'. At this point, MCA stepped in and secured the band's signatures on what looked like the deal to turn them in to the band everybody said they would inevitably become. Behind them they had a string of releases, Radio One sessions, enough material for two albums, and enough press and media support to set up a plan for world domination. Up to this point, their only real mistakes had been to make brash comments in interviews. They once declared "we are the natural successors to Led Zeppelin" which, when reproduced as a speech bubble headline in *Sounds* did make them look like arrogant bastards – another headline used in an early issue of *Kerrang!*... But in fairness, many reviewers had suggested they were the former, and with Harris' voice and stage moves, and Tatler's awesome guitar it was easy to understand why. The band had an understanding of dynamics that few of their contemporaries even came close to. They knew that power in music often came from the spaces between powerchords, and incredible heaviness could be produced without resorting to all-out noise or breakneck speed.

This they took to MCA. In return, MCA tried to introduce Diamond Head with another EP, 'Four Cuts' in the spring of 1982, and another single 'In The Heat Of The Night' in the autumn – failing to realise that the band no longer needed any introduction. As good as they were, all the releases achieved was to further dilute the impact of the subsequent 'debut' album (the band were quick to discount the white label as a poorly-produced false start).

When it was released in October 1982, 'Borrowed Time' was already very late in Diamond Head's career. They had been together as a working band over five years and NWOBHM contemporaries like Iron Maiden, Saxon and Samson each already had three or four albums under their belts. This then, had to be a real corker. In was, but it contained many old songs re-recorded, and did suffer from a sense of anti-climax.

Diamond Head toured the UK in October/November '82 then spent much of '83 working on the follow-up, 'Canterbury'. Sessions were fraught, and speaking at the time, Harris admitted that the band were still very naive in the studio. As the pressure mounted from MCA and producer Mike Shipley, both Kimberley (to be replaced by Merv Goldsworthy, now of FM) and Scott (to be replaced by Robbie France) left the band. When released, 'Canterbury' was received as a bold experiment – albeit one which some thought had taken them to far from their HM roots. In reality, Diamond Head were only doing what they always set out to do: to be creative and original. The record was years ahead of its time.

With it and the collective buzz around the band, Diamond Head were invited to open the '83 Donington festival where they appeared as a five-piece with Goldsworthy, France and a keyboard player called, er... Bob. Sadly, their performance was a poor one and the band soon began to slide. The subsequent tour, with Josh Phillips-Gorse on keyboards, was undersold. In 1984 the band began work on a new album, tentatively titled 'Flight East' but this was never completed as MCA lost faith in the band and dropped them. Come January '85 the band lost faith in themselves and split.

Tatler formed Radio Moscow who made some encouraging demos but failed to secure a deal until after the guitarist had left. Harris worked with guitarist Robin George, which ultimately led to a 'project' called Notorious who made one eponymous but quickly withdrawn album for Bronze.

Involved in both these sabbaticals were a bassist called Eddie Chaos and a drummer, Karl Wilcox – so in 1990 when Tatler and Harris started working together again, they were the natural rhythm section to employ. They first gigged together (billed as Dead Reckoning) in Reading in early 1991, then in July undertook a

DIAMOND HEAD original line-up: Duncan Scott, Sean Harris, Colin Kimberly, Brian Tatler

IN THEIR OWN WORDS...

"What Zeppelin did in the '70s we want to do in the '80s. We want to cause the stir they caused and be as innovative as they were. We don't want to be a good band, we want to be a great band."
– Sean Harris, Kerrang! 13,
April 8-21, 1982

"We never copied any particular band. We don't put the notes in a different order like most people do. We try to create a mood. Once we come up with a riff or idea for a song, we spend a long time trying to structure it so it flows."
– Sean Harris, Kerrang! 26,
October 7-20, 1982

"We recorded the 'Borrowed Time' album in three weeks but (with 'Canterbury') there was none of this one or two take stuff purely and simply because we weren't good enough to do it that way... It had become so much more than four people pissing about..."
– Sean Harris, Kerrang! 51, September
22-October 5, 1983

"The new record is the album we always should have made. In some senses it's the follow-on from 'Canterbury', but harder, tougher, meaner. 'Canterbury' was a bit flabby. The new one has the spirit of 'Lightning To The Nations' – the power of the dark side – and the epic feel and ambition of 'Canterbury'."
– Sean Harris, Kerrang! 426,
January 16, 1993

DIAMOND HEAD

short club tour under the Diamond Head name. Following these dates they entered the studio to work on a mini-album, subsequently shelved, opting for the full-length work, 'Death And Progress' released June 1993. As well as new bassist Pete, the LP featured numerous Metal megastars queueing up to help out Diamond Head: men like Tony Iommi of Black Sabbath, Megadeth's Dave Mustaine and long-time Diamond Head champion Lars Ulrich of Metallica.

The involvement of such names brings Diamond Head full circle from young pretenders to contemporary heroes: Megadeth having previously paid tribute to Harris when he led them in an encore rendition of the DH classic 'It's Electric' at Wembley in 1990; Metallica long since having recorded 'Helpless' and sworn to play 'Am I Evil?' at every gig. No greater tribute needed...

ALBUMS

LIGHTNING TO THE NATIONS *(DHM, 1980 KKKKK) Raw recordings of some all-time HM classics. Beg, steal or borrow!*

BORROWED TIME *(MCA, 1982 – KKKKK) "If genius is pain then Diamond Head must be the world's greatest masochists." – Kerrang! 28, November 4-17, 1982*

CANTERBURY *(MCA, 1983 – KKKKK) "Not since the days of Queen has a band successfully combined such energy with dynamic production." – Kerrang! 51, September 22-October 5, 1983*

DEATH AND PROGRESS *(Bronze, 1993 – KKKKK) A stunning return laden with Diamond Head hallmarks and still sounding fresher than almost all of its contemporaries...*

Bruce DICKINSON

UK, singer (1979-present)
FORMER IRON Maiden vocalist who first came to public attention as the moustachioed frontman in NWOBHM act Samson. He made three albums with them 1979-1981 before being poached by Steve Harris to replace Paul Di'Anno. Before he quit in '93, Dickinson made seven studio plus three live albums with Maiden since. His air-raid siren vocals can also be heard on a (since injuncted) single by Xero and, more recently, on his 1990 solo album 'Tattooed Millionaire' (a second is due late in '93).

He has also found time to write two vaguely
Tom Sharpe-styled novels so – as he
completely murdered Mott The Hoople's 'All
The Young Dudes' on that first solo album –
here, instead, is some...

Recommended light reading:
LORD IFFY BOATRACE (Sidgwick & Jackson,
1990)
THE MISSIONARY POSITION (Sidgwick &
Jackson, 1992)

The DICTATORS

US, five-piece (1972-present)
THE MISSING link betwen the New York Dolls
and the Ramones, New York's outrageously
ignored (except in cool circles, natch) Dictators
were (are?) a Punk/Metal hybrid with lyrics that
carry a health warning, and a 'secret weapon' in
roadie-turned-frontman 'Handsome' Dick
Manitoba. Changed their name to Manitoba's
Wild Kingdom on the return of guitarist Ross
The Boss (who'd been wielding his axe with
Manowar) for the virtual reformation album
'...And You?' ('90). But more recently have been
playing occassional gigs for kicks under original
'Tators banner.

Recommended album:
GO GIRL CRAZY (Epic, 1975 – KKKKK)

DIE KRUPPS

Germany, five-piece (1981-present)
DIE KRUPPS issued several obscure,
Industrially-geared, releases over the years;
becoming increasingly electronic and
danceable. 1992 saw them bring full-blooded
Metallica-styled guitars into the equation, with
riveting consequences.

Recommended album:
I (Our Choice, 1992 – KKKKK)

DIO

USA, five-piece (1983-1992)
WHEN RONNIE James Dio parted ways with
'Heaven And Hell'/'Mob Rules'/'Live Evil'-era
Black Sabbath, in less than amicable
circumstances, the singer wasted little time in
forming his own outfit – a band which went on

RONNIE JAMES DIO: ongoing fantasy-obsession problem

to do better business than the subsequently
floundering Sabs.

'Holy Diver' was their debut, receiving almost
unanimous praise for such classics-to-be as
'Rainbow In The Dark', 'Don't Talk To Strangers'
and the marching 'Holy Diver' itself. Vivian
Campbell was the resident six-string conjurer,
and continued in that role for 'The Last In Line'
and 'Sacred Heart', before being replaced with
Craig Goldie for 1987's 'Dream Evil'.

In general, each new Dio album took more
critical knocks; particularly because it was felt
that the singer's fantasy-obsessed lyrics had
become repetitive. 1990's 'Lock Up The Wolves'
was their least successful record, featuring 17-
year-old Rowan Robertson from Cambridge.
After the accompanying tour, Dio himself
decided to rejoin his 'old muckers' in Sabbath...

Most recommended album:
HOLY DIVER (Vertigo, 1983 – KKKKK)

DIRTY LOOKS

USA, four-piece (1984-present)
FORMED BY singer Henrik Ostergaard and
survived on a variety of small label deals before
signing to Atlantic in 1987 for their fourth and
heavily AC/DC-influenced 'Cool From The Wire'.
The deal lasted for just one more LP and by
1991's 'Bootlegs' they were back with an indie
(Shrapnel/Roadrunner).

Recommended album:
COOL FROM THE WIRE (Atlantic, 1987 –
KKKK)

DISCHARGE

UK, four-piece (1978-present)

PERHAPS THE most influential Punk band since the Sex Pistols, Discharge were known for Hell On Earth vocals (supplied by frontman Cal) and a policy of "noise not music" in their approach to recording and gigging!

Recommended album:

HEAR NOTHING, SEE NOTHING, SAY NOTHING *(Clay, 1982-KKKKK)*

DIVING FOR PEARLS

USA, five-piece (1989-1990)

"AN AMAZING amalgam of such AOR luminaries as 707, Starcastle, Orphan and Hotel Hunger," claimed the *K!* review of Diving For Pearls' debut, and, sadly, only album, back in October 1989. With a stunning vocal peformance from Danny Malone and a fine line in tear-jerking lyricism, Diving For Pearls were the ultimate AOR band. Surely they'd be huge?

A year later, with not even a whiff of a UK release, Diving For Pearls were history. When last heard of, Malone was making a living as a singing waiter in New York. Tragic.

Recommended album:

DIVING FOR PEARLS *(Epic, 1989 – KKKKK)*

D.O.A.

Canada, three-piece (1978-present)

LEAD BY vocalist/guitarist Joe 'Shithead' Keithley, D.O.A. are one of those heads-down three-chord Punk bands who thankfully refuse to lie down and die. Both their music and their fan base have stayed pretty constant, and almost, but not quite predictable, over the years and throughout their long career they have remained fiercely political. They even, almost unbelievably, played a gig with fellow Vancouver resident Bryan Adams under the heading 'A Night For The Environment', with proceeds going to groups like Greenpeace thus backing up the bands 'Talk-Action=0' motto.

Recomended albums:

BLOODIED BUT UNBOWED *(Alternative Tentacles, 1984 – KKKK)*

LAST SCREAM OF THE MISSING NEIGHBOURS *(Alternative Tentacles,1989 – KKKKK) with Jello Biafra.*

DOGS D'AMOUR

UK, four-piece (1983-present)

EVERYBODY'S FAVOURITE debauchery desperados! Formed in the London pub-land of '83 when current frontman/guitarist Tyla was just a string-slinger and American stringbean Ned Christie took care of the howlin'. This five-strong incarnation of the Dogs appear on the mish-mashy 'Trash On Delivery' compilation (Flicknife, '83).

Christie bailed out early in the band's career leaving Tyla as top Doggie. With their Stones-y sound and gloriously shambolic live shows, the Dogs D'Amour achieved a modicum of notoriety in the Hanoi Rocks-dominated Glam scene of the mid-'80s, even managing to release the blatantly autobiographically-titled LP, 'The State We're In'. Bugger all was then heard of Tyla's gang until a couple of years later in '87, when they had a freak minor hit single with 'How Come It Never Rains' on EMI/Supertrack. This remarkable development led to a deal with China Records, and eventually media overkill alongside 'rivals' (sic) the Quireboys, as bandannas and cowboy boots became regulation rock 'n' roll issue.

The Dogs dissolved for a while in the early '90s, members flirting with various projects (bassist Steve James put together the Last Bandits, drummer Bam joined the Wildhearts), but reformed in '93 with Crybabys guitarist Darrell Barth replacing a disinterested Jo Dog, to record once more on China.

Recommended album:

THE DYNAMITE JET SALOON *(China, 1988 – KKKK)*

DOOM

UK, four-piece (1987-present)
BRUMMIE DISCHARGE clones, favoured by
John Peel, who once included ex-Napalm Death
drummer Mick Harris. They recorded one
album, along with several bits and pieces, and
still churn out tunes like 'Police Bastard' to this
very day. Ice-T would most definitely approve.
Recommended (and only) album:
WAR CRIMES: INHUMAN BEINGS *(Peaceville,
1988 – KKK)*

DOKKEN

USA, five-piece (1982-1988)
BAND FORMED by singer/guitarist Don Dokken
after his Dieter 'Scorpions' Dierks-produced
solo album 'Breaking The Chains' on Carrere, in
'82. (Dokken had recorded (unused) vocals for
the Scorpions' 'Blackout' album, whilst Klaus
Meine overcame vocal node problems.)

Launching Dokken as a band, Don hired the
guitarist George Lynch – a move he lived to
regret after some serious personality clashes
between the two of them. Broke through in 1985
with 'Under Lock And Key' which made the
USA's *Billboard* Top 40. Its successor, 'Back
From The Attack', did even better, then 1988's
double live 'Beast From The East' went
platinum. It was all pretty unadventurous
melodic Metal, though, so few were upset when
the Dokken v Lynch feud finally split the band.

Original bassist Juan Croucier later joined
Ratt. George Lynch formed Lynch Mob. Dokken
had a shortlived band called The Don Dokken
Band (Lynch was still suing for the rights to the
name 'Dokken'!) which included drummer
Mikkey Dee (ex-King Diamond, now
Motörhead), bassist Peter Baltes (ex-Accept)
and ex-Europe guitarist John Norum.
Recommended feud-filled album:
BACK FOR THE ATTACK *(Elektra, 1987 –
KKKK)*

DREAD ZEPPELIN

USA, six-piece (1989-present)
LEGEND HAS it that when Elvis died he left a
son in his own image.
Tortelvis (right) was a
karaoke crooner from
Vegas who joined a
club band plundering
the Zeppelin back
catalogue and turning
in spirited Hawaiian
renditions of assorted

rock classics to the great amusement of the
general public. Live shows in Europe united
squat punks and train-spotters, as Tortelvis
skillfully parodied both Zeppelin and the legacy
of Elvis with no small amount of skill and sharp
observation. Even Tortelvis' stage helper – the
unfortunate Charlie Hodge – was used in the
extravaganza that could not last forever. Fears
that Dread Zeppelin could not continue without
Tortelvis were discounted only by the band
when the Rhinestone Ringmaster quit in 1992.
Recommended album (if pissed):
UN-LED-ED *(IRS, 1990 – KKKKK)*

DREAM THEATER

USA, five-piece (1988-present)
TECHNO METALLERS who have drawn
comparisons with anyone from Queensrÿche to
Yes, Metallica to Deep Purple. All the members
are highly talented musicians who deliver
progressive rock with a modern Metal edge,
much refined since their early days in New York
(1985) when they called themselves Majesty.
Signed to Mechanic for their debut, 'When
Dream And Day Unite' ('89), but bigger things
are predicted for them now they've been picked
up by Iron Maiden's management company and
Atlantic Records for their second and...
Recommended album:
IMAGES AND WORDS *(Atlantic, 1992 – KKKK)*

D.R.I.

USA, four-piece (1981-present)
DIRTY ROTTEN Imbeciles by name, and
conceivably by nature, these Texans eventually
abandoned their violently abrupt brand of
Hardcore, in favour of a far more Metallised
strategy. Their 'Crossover' LP of '86 was aptly

named, combining Punk with crunchy guitars as it did.

Recommended album:
CROSSOVER *(Roadrunner, 1987 – KKKK)*

DRIVE, SHE SAID

USA, two-piece (1989-present)
THE BABY of former Valhalla, American Tears and Touch keyboard player Mark Mangold in conjuction with vocalist Al Fritsch. Drive, She Said's eponymous debut initially appeared on the CBS label until Mangold, disturbed at a distinct lack of interest in his band, bought the record from them and promptly licensed it to Music For Nations.

The duo's music is basically an extention of Mangold's work in Touch and his co-writing with Michael Bolton; big, bold and beautiful AOR tunes with monster chorus lines. The second album, 'Drivin' Wheel', contained more of the same, but was a less outstanding release. Toured the UK with FM in 1992 and a new album was on the cards for late '93.

Recommended album:
DRIVE, SHE SAID *(CBS, 1989 – KKKKK)*

DUMPY'S RUSTY NUTS

UK, four-piece (1845-present)
ENDURING ROCKERS led by the rather rotund Dumpy Dunnel. Despite appearances, they're not at all bad and in between moments of drunken stupidity and jokes about bottoms, they occasionally play some shit-kicking blues.

Recommended album:
ER, DON'T BOTHER *(Go see 'em live instead!)*

DUMPY: nuts

ELECTRIC BOYS

Sweden, four-piece (1987-present)
THEIR '89 debut album, 'Funk-O-Metal Carpet Ride', is perhaps the best example of Funk Metal this side of Dan Reed – and saw the band perfectly placed to ride the crest of that wave. Unfortunately, although the band promised much, they delivered less live. PolyGram appeared not to notice this, as they signed the band to a worldwide deal and hired Bob Rock to remix the first album and produce a few new

ELECTRIC BOYS: set to transcend fashion

numbers for it. Purists suggest the original Swedish version was superior. Whatever, either were certainly better than 1992's second album, 'Groovus Maximus', which found them toning down their psychedelic image as well as their songwriting skills. Moreover, Funk Metal was, by then, more than a little passé. Nevertheless, mainman Conny Bloom is too talented to let a little thing like fashion stop his career.
Highly recommended album:
FUNK-O-METAL CARPET RIDE *(Mercury, 1989 – KKKKK)*

ELECTRIC SUN

Germany, three-piece (1979-1983)
FORMED BY perhaps the world's only Hendrix-fixated, astral-hippy guitar star (Uli Jon Roth), Electric Sun nonetheless explored some dramatic rock sonics. The ex-Scorpions' guitarist revelled in his role as the messiah of free-formed widdle, but the band's two largely-instrumental albums were rich in surprisingly tuneful experimentation. Roth himself cut a solo album in 1985, and has gone classical since.
Recommended album:
FIREWIND *(Brain, 1981 – KKKK)*

ELIXIR

UK, five-piece (1987-90)
DESPERATELY UNSUCCESSFUL, NWOBHM-style wannabes whose sole claim to fame was persuading former Iron Maiden drummer Clive Burr to play on one, quickly forgotten LP.
(Not) recommended album:
LETHAL POTION *(Sonic, 1990 – K)*

E.L.P.

UK, three-piece (1970-present)
DINOSAUR, NEO-CLASSICAL Prog rockers featuring Keith Emerson (keyboards/dagger), Greg Lake (bass/vocals) and Carl Palmer (drums). Best known for their 'Fanfare For The Common Man'. Extinct for a whole decade (the '80s) save when Cozy Powell became the 'P'. Sometimes very heavy, which is remarkable considering they're the only band in this book not to feature a guitarist...
Recommended album:
WELCOME BACK MY FRIENDS TO THE SHOW THAT NEVER ENDS *(Manticore, 1974 – KKKK)*

ENTOMBED

Sweden, five-piece (1989-present)
RESPONSIBLE FOR a horde of Swedish copyists, Entombed specialise in a tightly grungy sound which bears little relation to the style made famous by a certain Seattle scene.

Death Metal all the way, with a discernible Punk influence, Entombed released a promising debut in the shape of 'Left Hand Path', then followed it up with an even better album titled 'Clandestine', having replaced singer LG Petrov with the stronger Johnny Dordevic.

1993 saw the release of Entombed's third album, featuring Petrov back at the microphone, with the Danzig-esque name 'Wolverine Blues'...
Recommended album:
CLANDESTINE *(Earache, 1991 – KKKK)*

ENUFF ZNUFF

USA, four-piece (1987-present)
ENUFF ZNUFF had already recorded – and dumped – an entire, self-financed album with a line-up that differed from that which signed to Atco Records and released the Pop Rock-tastic 'Enuff ZNuff' album in 1989. Drummer Vikki Foxx had taken up the drumstool and former Le Mans man Derek Frigo had been recruited on bass, to complement main-men Donnie Vie (vocals/guitar) and Chip ZNuff (bass).

Founded on a healthy diet of Cheap Trick and The Beatles Enuff ZNuff arrived in a hail of cheap lipstick and hip clothes via the video for Cheap Trick-ish first single 'New Thing'. Enuff ZNuff have since let their music do the talking with two more quality albums, 'Strength' and the more recent 'Animals With Human Intelligence', the latter appearing on Arista following a split with Atco. Drummer Foxx was replaced shortly after the third album was completed, following his defection to former Mötley Crüe singer Vince Neil's band, by ex-War And Peace man Ricky Parent.
Recommended albums:
ENUFF Z'NUFF *(Atco, 1989 – KKKKK)*
ANIMALS WITH HUMAN INTELLIGENCE
(Arista, 1993 – KKKKK)

EUROPE

Five-piece, Sweden (1982-present)
EUROPE ARE universally known for that parp-tastic Number One single of '86, 'The Final Countdown', featuring some of the most gargantuan drum and keyboard sounds in rock history. But the band, fronted by permed girlie-favourite Joey Tempest, have found it difficult to follow up the success of the album, which achieved Triple Platinum status.

Nevertheless, they've progressed a long way since their origins as winners of a national rock competition in Sweden. The prize was a record contract; the subsequent debut album was self-titled, and made the country's Top 10.

In '85, Europe signed to Epic Records, and released the 'Wings Of Tomorrow' album. After the following success of 'The Final Countdown', the next two disappointments were the inappropriately-titled 'Out Of This World' and 1992's 'Prisoners In Paradise'...
Recommended parp-mungous album:
THE FINAL COUNTDOWN *(Epic, 1986 – KKKK)*

JOEY TEMPEST of Europe: nice perm

EVERY MOTHER'S NIGHTMARE

USA, five-piece (1990-present)
YOUNG QUINTET from Nashville who caused a

few hearts to flutter when
they appeared in 1990
with their debut release
comprised of MTV-
friendly, anthemic, fist-
punching rock 'n' roll,
with distinct Glam
overtones. Sadly by the
time the band returned
with their sophomore release in 1989 the image,
like that of their contempories, had followed a
more 'Street' path, with the music a tad
crunchier.
Recommended album:
EVERY MOTHER'S NIGHTMARE *(Arista, 1990
- KKKK)*

EVILDEAD

USA, five-piece (1988-present)
STRAIGHT THRASHERS formed by guitarman
Juan Garcia when he walked out of Agent Steel,
Evildead turned out to be more intense than
John Cyriss' outfit. On the scale of worldwide
popularity, however, the band's done little
better...
Strongest album:
ANNIHILATION OF CIVILIZATION
(Steamhammer, 1989 – KKK)

EXCITER

Canada, three-piece, (1979-present)
PROBABLY THE first of many bands to name
themselves after the classic Judas Priest track.
Er, and that's about it, really. Leather, studs and
Thrash in almost equal proportion as you might
expect.
Recommended album (for the title):
HEAVY METAL MANIAC *(Roadrunner, 1989 –
KK)*

EXHORDER

USA, five-piece (1985-present)
ORIGINALLY NAMED Sabotage, purveying a

musical style far lighter than the overwhelmingly
weighty muscle of their latter-day recordings.
Iron-throated Kyle Thomas is said to have
influenced Pantera's Phil Anselmo, and the
state-of-the-art guitar-team of Jay Ceravolo and
Vinnie LaBella rarely falls short of the awesome
mark. Heavy-duty Thrash to say the least.
Recommended albums
SLAUGHTER IN THE VATICAN *(RC Records,
1990 – KKKK)*
THE LAW *(RC Records, 1991 – KKKK)*

EXODUS

US, five-piece (1982-1993)
EXODUS FEATURED Kirk Hammett in their first
ever line-up, although he never appeared on
record. An early member who did was singer
Paul Baloff; he only lasted for one album, but a
great one, entitled 'Bonded By Blood'.

Surfacing in 1985, it was one of the first
examples of severely muted guitar chopping,
and abused the ears of thousands with
aggressive songs like '...And Then There Were
None' (recognised as a minor classic to this
day), 'Pirahna' and 'Lesson In Violence'.

After that, Baloff went off to form his own
band, named Pirahna, and got absolutely
nowhere with it. Neither did Exodus find
superstardom, exactly, with their new vocalist
Steve 'Zetro' Souza; as the '80s died, they
remained among the bands poised to achieve
the same status as Thrash's Big Four, but never
quite managed it.

Three major label albums (for Capitol who
hoped they could mirror Metallica's success)
saw them make little real progress, and 'Force
Of Habit' became their swansong...
*Most recommended
albums:*
BONDED BY BLOOD
*(Under One Flag, 1985
– KKKK)*
FABULOUS DISASTER
(Capitol, 1988 – KKKK)
**THE BEST OF
EXODUS: LESSONS IN VIOLENCE** *(Music For
Nations, 1992 – KKKK)*

EXTREME

USA, four-piece (1985-present)

ALTHOUGH FREQUENTLY panned for their squeaky clean image and success with ballads, people forget that this Boston, Massachusetts group are – when they put their minds to it – a spanking good rock band. Evidence for this was sporadic on their '89 debut LP, wrapped in a well dodgy sleeve bearing photos of even dodgier haircuts. Major redeeming factor was the guitar work of Nuno Bettencourt (above), stamping his authority all over the songs.

Vocalist Gary Cherone and drummer Paul Geary had previously played together in Boston band the Dream (who issued a six-track EP in '83) then launched Extreme in 1985. The orginal line-up secured MTV airplay in 1985 with their clip for 'Mutha (Don't Wanna Go To School Today)' as part of an indie band contest, but the line-up was going nowhere until the arrival of Bettencourt around 1986, and bassist Pat Badger a year later. They made their vinyl debut with the track 'Play With Me' on the 'Bill And Ted's Excellent Adventure' movie soundtrack.

For Extreme, however, their most excellent adventure began in 1990 with the release of their second album, 'Pornograffitti'. This 'funked-up fairytale' was a heady blend of hard rock and softer melodies striking a near perfect balance and hence selling by the cartload worldwide. Most successful song was 'More Than Words', which helped the band cross over into Mass Appealsville, and to attract a shower of awards and TV appearances.

Following the massive tour to promote it, the band set about making 'III Sides To Every Story'. This they interrupted to play at the Freddie Mercury Tribute at Wembley Stadium on April 13, 1992, where they turned in a stunning medley of Queen classics. The band were obviously major Queen fans and that band's influence was obvious by the time the third album hit the streets. It was an ambitious project that instead of mixing their songwriting styles, cordoned them off into distinct sections. The jury remains undecided as to whether this was a work of genius or lunacy. Live, the same technique looked much closer to the latter as they came on as a no-holds- barred hard rock act, did a few ballads, then appeared to go completely barking mad by introducing a horn section and some almost pantomime- like choreographed routines. What Extreme do next is anybody's guess...

Recommended album:
PORNOGRAFFITTI *(A&M, 1990 – KKKKK)*

EXTREME NOISE TERROR

UK, five-piece (1986-present)

SURPRISE, SURPRISE... this East Anglian-based mob sound exactly like their name suggests. Every track is played as fast and as loud as humanly possible in a style very much inspired by Punk stars Discharge. Over the top (of the noise) vocalists Phil and Dean bellow like buffalos on heat. ENT were one of the first bands of their kind to feature two vocalists, and the result is particularly startling...

Although the band have never really gained a large UK following, their fiercely political barrage has proved successful just about everywhere else in the world. Undoubtedly their finest moment on home turf was appearing live at the 1992 Brit Awards with KLF, playing a hideous and almost unrecogniseable rendition of the latter's '3am Eternal', much to the horror of the invited audience and most watching at home on TV.

Recommended and startling album:
PHONOPHOBIA *(Discipline, 1992 – KKKKK)*

FAITH NO MORE

USA, five-piece (1980-present)

FAITH NO MORE stick out like a happy face at a funeral. They are perverse, provocative, stupid, sick and probably one of the two most influential rock bands from the barren late-1980s. Faith No More's formula is simple.

"Subtlety is for old people," guitarist Jim Martin told *Mega Metal Kerrang!*, issue 8, in 1988. "Subtlety is for people who blow their noses into handkerchieves in the bathroom."

The West Coast quintet have been blowing their snot onto the sidewalk for years. Their massive mainstream breakthrough with 'The Real Thing' album was a lifetime away; way over there beyond their weirdest, wildest dreams. And it really was weird.

The seeds of success were first sewn in 1980 when Chuck Mosely met bassist Bill Gould on the LA drop-out circuit. They were the products of the city's rotten underbelly and skatecore clubs rather than the Cock Rock palaces up on Sunset Strip and Hollywood Boulevard. It is ironic, then, that Faith No More were discovered and largely championed by the Metal press, years before they achieved the status of pin-up pop icons.

Keyboard player Roddy Bottum had attended school with Bould, and drummer Mike Bordin was plucked from Berkeley University where he was studying tribal rhythm. Finally, 'Big Sick Ugly' Jim Martin replaced a short-lived guitarist on a recommendation from Metallica's Cliff Burton. Faith No More looked daft. It was a cult-crazy cartoon of

brightly-coloured misfits, reared on the chaos of Punk and tempered by a musical proficiency that was the envy of their peers. Faith No More reckoned they had a chance.

Packing their belongings into a battered truck and U-Haul trailer, the embryonic bastard prodigies took on the flea-pits, toilets and broom cupboards of North America. In the very first live review from the British press (the aforementioned *MMK!* 8), Faith No More were praised to the rooftops: 'Feel the Faith before the masses latch on!' The oddball bunch toured like epileptics in support of their debut album. 'Faith No More' is a little-recognised but much-sought after record, released in 1984 on the tiny Mordam label. It wasn't, however, until 'Introduce Yourself' came out in 1987 that Faith No More suddenly ignited.

The song which is widely regarded as Faith No More's pivotal masterpiece, 'We Care A Lot', was typical of the band's combination of crunching riffs and deceptively sweet melody. The song was part-responsible for the sudden emergence of Funk Metal, but in reality was only one facet of Faith No More's multi-headmelting repertoire.

Behind-the-scenes, Faith No More's provocative personal chemistry was going way too far. The band who ideally wanted to blow out all the bullshit by any possible means, had taken to winding up each other in a bid to combat road boredom. "Mike The Goat Boy, eh?" Jim Martin once said to *Kerrang!*, "The Goat Boy who would look far better with ram-horns mounted upon his forehead!"

The situation and personal antagonism was so bad at one time that every individual member walked out of the band over a four-week period. Ultimately, it was Chuck Mosely who quit, after a punch-up.

Replacement for the dread-locked, psycho-Rasta was Mike Patton, just 21 when he got the job. His first few months in Faith No More turned out to be something of a baptism by fire. His first task? Write some lyrics for what would become one of rock's greatest albums of all time!

'The Real Thing' was released in June 1989. After years spent consolidating their steadily-growing fan base in Europe and North America, Faith No More suddenly found themselves in every pop chart worldwide with the 'Epic' single. To this day, it is a song that still features heavily on jukebox and club playlists around the globe, alongside such subsequent singles as 'From Out Of Nowhere' and 'Falling To Pieces' The album was unquestionably a stroke of genius. It was sinister and macabre, air-brushed to perfection and peppered with all the FNM trademarks of humour, guitar slab-riffs and spine-chilling drumming. It was an album which grabbed the seperate strands of Thrash Metal, dub-Funk and Tribal Punk by the balls. It was finally the perfect album to smash down the walls of Metal after a decade of generally average banality. Faith No More had made Metal something great again.

The band toured the album non-stop around the world for three years. It was an exhausting schedule and one that caused no amount of friction between the five members. Faith No More sought solace in drink, sex, arguments and good old wind-ups. But despite all their efforts to the contrary, Faith No More were Pop Stars.

"We're signed up for a long time," Bill Gould told *Kerrang!* at the height of touring. "It's like there's a limited amount of oxygen and you're in a small tank... if somebody panics, it'll take everybody's oxygen away from them."

Faith No More finally came off the road with just enough oxygen left in the tank to breathe. 'The Real Thing' had been toured into the ground, to the point where Patton was blatantly taking the piss out of 'Epic' and the band's legendary cover of Sabbath's 'War Pigs' on stage. Everybody needed a rest from the beast. Mike Patton immediately went to work with Mr Bungle, the band from which he had been plucked to join Faith No More and who still held his affections. Consequently the rumours that Faith No More were finished began to snowball.

"You're waiting to do the exact same thing that you did last night," Patton explained to *Kerrang!*. "Sometimes you even say the exact same things. It's just disgusting!"

Mr Bungle released one album to massed critical confusion before Patton put the strange, dischordant rat-pack back in the box. Faith No More were back in business.

The obvious problems of recording the follow-up to such a successful album as 'The Real Thing' were negated by the band themselves. Faith No More simply recorded something completely disimilar and sat back to lap up the critical flak. In fact 'Angel Dust' was received with standing ovations. It was by no means as accessible as 'The Real Thing', but perhaps far closer to the band's chaotic roots. It was not a pop album. Faith No More were no longer a simple pop band. They took guns out on the road with Guns 'N' Roses and kept themselves amused by bickering constantly. 'Angel Dust' sold steadily, although without the constant stream of hit singles that dogged 'The Real Thing'. They even crossed over to day-time easy-listening stations with a deadpan cover of The Commodores' 'I'm Easy'!

Faith No More are probably bigger now than they ever wanted to be. They have more than proved their point.

ALBUMS

FAITH NO MORE (Mordam, 1984 – KKK) The reclusive first album that first introduced the North American clubs and college stations to the band's mess of brutal hardcore fusion. Hit

single-free, remarkably!

INTRODUCE YOURSELF (London, 1987 – KKKKK) *"How many different ways can I impress the brilliance of this album upon you? This has no peer. This is totally itself without a smattering of anyone." – Kerrang! 158, October 17, 1987*

THE REAL THING (London, 1989 – KKKKK) *"An album that jerks you to life with menace and aggression. It's the Real Thing and it takes some beating." – Kerrang! 242, June 10, 1989*

LIVE AT BRIXTON ACADEMY (London, 1991 – KKKK) *"Everybody knows FNM shows are an event, to be chewed on for 90 minutes and then spat out and forgotten." – Kerrang! 326, February 2, 1991*

ANGEL DUST (London, 1992 – KKKK) *"The album is possessed of a personality disorder, of sorts, which undermines its potential greatness. Nevertheless, even the groundbreakers hit rough spots." – Kerrang! 395, June 6, 1992*

FASTER PUSSYCAT

USA, five-piece (1986-present)
FASTER PUSSYCAT took their name from the
Russ Meyer movie 'Faster Pussycat! Kill! Kill!',
and were one of the leading lights of the '80s
American Metal invasion – a flurry of glitter and
hairspray, including the likes of Bon Jovi and
Mötley Crüe, as well as the slightly less
memorable Dokken and Quiet Riot.

   Beach-blond vocalist Taime Downe was
originally better known for his co-ownership
(with MTV presenter Riki Rachtman) of an LA
club called The Cathouse, but once Faster
Pussycat's self-titled debut LP was released,
Downe was much more in demand as a star in
his own right.

   Popular opinion suggests they've never

matched the
shag appeal of
that first LP with
its more mature
follow-ups,
'Wake Me When
It's Over' ('89),
and 'Whipped!'
('92). Certainly
early tunes like
'Don't Change
That Song',
'Bathroom Wall'
and 'Babylon'
will be dance-
floor classics forever, and make the Pussies'
claim to legendary fame as strong as anyone's –
although early 1993 found them without a
record deal.
Sleazily recommended album:
FASTER PUSSYCAT *(Elektra, 1987 – KKKKK)*

FASTWAY

UK, four-piece (1982-1990)
AS THE name hints, Fastway were a band put
together by guitarist 'Fast' Eddie Clarke and
bassist Pete Way after the pair of hellraisers left
their long term gigs at Motörhead and UFO
respectively. Way quit to form Waysted before

the band recorded, being replaced by Charlie
McCracken. Drums were by ex-Humble Pie man
turned French polisher, Jerry Shirley. Robert
Plant-esque vocals by unknown Dublin
youngster Dave King gave the earthy blues rock
a timeless (some said dated!) sound on the
eponymous debut but the first tour sold poorly
and subsequent albums did worse.

   In 1987, after four LPs, Clarke was the only
original member left as the band had taken an
unpleasant sideways swerve towards American
radio rock. New vocalist Lea Hart lifted the
band's profile again, but after two more albums,
Fastway appeared to vaporise.
Recommended (debut) album:
FASTWAY *(CBS, 1983 – KKK)*

FATES WARNING

USA, five-piece (1983-1990)
CINCINATTI TECHNO outfit, formerly Misfit,
who released five albums for Metal Blade after
debuting on that label's 'Metal Massacre V'
compilation. Their final LP, 'Perfect Symmetry'
('89) rather worryingly featured Dream Theatre's
keyboard player and a small string section...
Recommended, Max Norman-produced, album:
NO EXIT *(Metal Blade, 1988 – KKK)*

FEAR

USA, four-piece (1978-present)
LEGENDARY LA Hardcore outfit led by
frontman Lee Ving and famed for their
thoroughly offensive lyrics... and quite a few
other things. Like the fact that Red Hot Chili
Peppers bassist Flea was once in their ranks. Or
that Metallica's James Hetfield has 'Fear'
emblazoned on one of his guitars, also the
legend 'More Beer' after one of their songs. Or
that Guns N' Roses and Soundgarden are
among those who have covered Fear songs. Or
like being discovered by late great actor and
cocaine fiend John Belushi – who insisted on
buying them studio time, alcohol and illegal
substances for them to record their finest
album, which is...
Highly recommended:
MORE BEER *(Restless, 1979 – KKKKK)*

FEMME FATALE

USA, five-piece (1988-1990)
FEMME FATALE blasted out of LA in a blaze of cleavage-assisted publicity with lead vocalist Lorraine Lewis the wet dream focal point. This led instantly to a *Kerrang!* cover appearance. Yet despite this and a fairly respectable album released on MCA, featuring such innuendo-ridden songs like 'Waiting For The Big One' and 'My Baby's Gun', Femme Fatale were a disappointment as a live band, touring the UK in 1989, and the band disintegrated upon their return to the US.

In the past few years Lorraine has resurfaced from time to time; more recently teamed up with former Blackeyed Susan bassist Erik Levy in an Alabama-based duo called Mercy.
Recommended album:
FEMME FATALE *(MCA, 1988 – KKK)*

FIFTH ANGEL

USA, five-piece (1985-1989)
SEATTLE GUITAR terrorists known for just that – and the fact that they featured wonder drummer Ken Mary, later to join Alice Cooper's band and House Of Lords. Eponymous debut album on Shrapnel ('86) later remixed and re-released by Epic who released their only other LP: 'Time Will Tell'.
Recommended album:
TIME WILL TELL *(Epic, 1989, – KKK)*

FIGHT

UK/USA, five-piece (1992-present)
FORMED IN a storm of controversy by Judas Priest singer Rob Halford and inspired by his oft-stated love of Pantera. Fight's formation split the Priest as Halford broke off communication with them, then sued their label, Sony, for restrictive practices (he won) then negotiated a deal for what was initially supposed to be only a parallel project to his former band.

Early indicator of their style came in the form of debut solo number 'Light Comes Out Of The Black' on the soundtrack of *'Buffy The Vampire Slayer'* (Columbia, 1992)...

FIONA

USA, solo artist (1985-present)
KERRANG! WENT a little overboard with Fiona back in '85, the girl from New Jersey supposedly displacing Lita Ford, Lee Aaron *et al* as the ultimate hard rock queen. On a purely musical basis, despite the presence of session heavyweights, her albums have been extremely average, only the second album, 'Beyond The Pale', making any real impression, with its smooth AOR lines and an improved vocal performance over the debut. Switched from Atlantic to Geffen in recent years for her fifth album, but this didn't help the product being any less dire.
Recommended album:
BEYOND THE PALE *(Atlantic, 1986 - KKK)*

FIREHOUSE

US, four piece (1988-present)
ONE OF the few typically American Arena Rock bands to remain successful in the States, as the music industry recession gripped the nation ,and the sound of Seattle took the record stores by surprise.

Featuring ex-Maxx Warrior vocalist CJ Snare and bassist Perry Richardson, Firehouse have enjoyed seeing both of their albums hit the Platinum sales mark, thanks to consistent touring and radio support, and have more recently set their sights on Europe and other territories as word spreads, managing a brief foray here with Status Quo in December 1992.
Recommended album:
FIREHOUSE *(Epic, 1989 – KKKK)*

The FIRM

UK, four-piece (1985-1987)
WITH A line-up featuring Jimmy Page (guitar, ex-Led Zeppelin), Paul Rodgers (vocals, ex-Free and Bad Company), Tony Franklin (bass, later of Blue Murder) and Chris Slade drums (later of AC/DC) The Firm were a band that could not fail – but sadly did. After two albums and one (sell-out) tour the band realised this too...
Recommended debut album:
THE FIRM *(Atlantic, 1984 – KKK)*

FISH

Scotland, solo singer (1989-present)
FISH IS the giant – heavy but not Metal – former Marillion frontman forced to sink or swim when he and the band parted company in 1989. Launched his career with the Marillion-esque debut 'Vigil In The Wilderness Of Mirrors', but has never been able to match the success he enjoyed with his former band.
Recommended album:
VIGIL IN THE WILDERNESS OF MIRRORS *(Polydor, 1990 – KKK)*

FLOTSAM AND JETSAM

USA, five-piece (1984-present)
FLOTSAM AND Jetsam are Arizona men, famed mostly for losing their bassist, Jason Newsted, to Metallica in 1987. Combining melody with Eric AK's unorthodox voice and some hard riffs, Flotsam have nevertheless found it difficult to break through into Thrash stardom.

'Doomsday For The Deceiver' was their first release, introducing the band's ridiculous Flotzilla mascot, which was long gone by the time 'Cuatro' came out in '93. The band's future appears limited.
Recommended album:
NO PLACE FOR DISGRACE *(Roadrunner, 1988 – KKKK)*

FM

UK, five/four-piece (1986-present)
FEATURING EX-WILDLIFE members Steve and Chris Overland (vocals/guitar and lead guitar respectively) alongside drummer Pete Jupp (formerly with Samson), FM's initial line-up was completed by one-time Diamond Head bassist Merv Goldsworthy and the somewhat enigmatic keyboardist Didge Digital.

Working themselves solidly in the clubs and on several major support tours on the back of the brilliant debut album, 'Indiscreet', problems with management and label politics prevented band development, compounded by the failure of the second album, 'Tough It Out', and the eventual loss of their record deal.

Refusing to admit defeat, FM, now with ASaP guitarist Andy Barnett in place of the departed Chris Overland, returned in 1991 on Music For Nations and, after finally giving problem child Didge Digital his cards, have worked themselves back into the public eye with successful bouts of domestic touring and an excellent fourth album in 'Aphrodisiac', which displays to the max FM's more blusier, harder style as opposed to the pop-flavoured AOR of old.
Recommended albums:
INDISCREET *(Portrait, 1986 – KKKKK)*
APHRODISIAC *(Music For Nations, 1992 – KKKKK)*

FORBIDDEN

USA, five-piece (1985-present)
RIDING IN on the second wave of Bay Area Thrash alongside Vio-lence, Testament and Death Angel, Forbidden unleashed their first album in 1988; a self-titled collection of quasi-Thrash, taking obvious cues from traditional Metal on such tunes as 'Chalice Of Blood' and 'Follow Me'.

After a perfectly gratuitous live EP from Holland's Dynamo Festival, featuring the band's rendition of Priest's 'Victim Of Changes', Forbidden came out with their rather fine 'Twisted Into Form' LP. Unfortunately, they then became embroiled in a split between Megaforce Records and Atlantic, and were consigned to record release limbo.

Nowadays, they're reportedly pursuing a sound more in tune with Soundgarden...
Recommended album:
TWISTED INTO FORM *(Music For Nations, 1990 – KKKK)*

Lita FORD

USA, solo artist (1982-present)
THERE'S NOTHING sweeter than our Lita! First picked up the guitar at the tender age of 11, joining the legendary Runaways at 15. She's led a typical rock 'n' roll lifestyle ever since.

After leaving The Runaways as that band began to fall apart, Lita worked as a beautician by day to pay the bills as she took the time to develop her singing voice to the point where labels would listen to what she had to offer, eventually resigning with the Mercury label (who had issued most Runaways product) and releasing the fairly impressive 'Out For Blood' in 1983, which left no one in any doubt as to her prowess as a guitar player.

Following the rather disappointing follow-up, 'Dancin' On The Edge' in 1984, however, Ford parted ways with Mercury, despite taking some considerable time recording a third album for the company, 'The Bride Wore Black', that has never been released.

Lita's career did take an upward turn once RCA picked her up, enjoying a good deal of success with the 'Lita' and 'Stiletto' albums, whilst 'enjoying' a brief marriage to W.A.S.P. guitarist Chris Holmes. She has since not only left Holmes far behind but is also now negotiating a new record deal, after leaving RCA in the wake of the disapointing 'Dangerous Curves' album, issued in 1991, but still remains as popular as ever in the K! end of year polls.
Recommended albums
OUT FOR BLOOD (Mercury, 1983 – KKK)
LITA (RCA, 1988 – KKKK)

LOVELY LITA : ain't no one sweeta!

FOREIGNER

UK/US, four-piece (1976-present)

A BAND whose mere name is enough to get many HM fans reaching for the sick bag, but who have nonetheless been hugely successful in finding a way to take rock music to an audience that wouldn't normally give it the time of day. Foreigner are the epitomy of AOR music and American rock: in that territory alone they have sold over 30 million albums. This they have achieved with a very simple formula: they write songs. Sometimes, they write incredibly slushy and sentimental songs but with these, they have the knack of writing lyrics that millions can identify with. They have also released any number of rock tracks as singles too – it's just that fewer people have bought them. Any who have seen the band live know that for every lighter-in-the-air singalong ballad, Foreigner kick back with three or four riff-fuelled belters. If you choose to hate the former and ignore the latter, the band couldn't care less, as they sell albums by the truckload.

They were formed in 1976 by guitarist Mick Jones (born London, December 27, 1944). Jones cut his musical teeth during a six year apprenticeship in Paris in the '60s. He was a member of 'The French Elvis' Johnny Hallyday's backing band and spent three weeks supporting The Beatles in 1964. Later in the '60s he worked with Soul legend Otis Redding, Jimi Hendrix when he was assembling his Experience, Humble Pie as they evolved out of the Small Faces, and Jimmy Page prior to the formation of Led Zeppelin. He was also a member of the Leslie West Band and Spooky Tooth. Ultimately, though, he was destined to put his own band together. Come February '76, by which time he had emigrated to the New York area, he did just that. He recruited two other Englishmen – Ian McDonald (a multi-instrumentalist, ex-King Crimson) and Dennis Elliott (drums, ex-Ian Hunter's Overnight Angels)

– plus three Americans – Ed Gagliardi (bass), Al Greenwood (keyboards) and Lou Gramm (vocals). The split nationality of the band pretty much dictated the choice of name for the band, but it was the choice of the diminutive former Black Sheep singer, Gramm, that dictated their blueprint for success. His vocal talents are of the very highest calibre and when married to Jones' crafted songwriting skills, made for a sound that radio stations the world over found impossible to ignore.

The band worked hard in rehearsals, signed to Atlantic and released their eponymous debut album a year after forming, in February '77. First single 'Feels Like The First Time' was a hit both sides of the Atlantic Ocean, as was its follow-up 'Cold As Ice'. But both singles did better in the States, setting a pattern that would be repeated throughout Foreigner's career. The album, for example entered the Top Five in the USA, but did not chart in the UK...

1978 saw the band reach bigger audiences thanks to a couple of major festival appearances. In the States in March they played 'California Jam II' alongside Aerosmith and Ted Nugent before a six-figure audience, then in August they did themselves the power of good with a sterling performance (in front of rather less) at the Reading Festival in England. At the show they premiered material from their forthcoming tougher sounding second album, 'Double Vision' ('78), which included the hit title-track and 'Hot Blooded'.

Its successor, 'Head Games' ('79), was tougher still and the first to feature new bassist Rick Wills (ex-Roxy Music and Small Faces). The by-then expected string of three hit singles were topped by the title-track and 'Dirty White Boy'. In September '80, Greenwood and McDonald departed and the group reduced to a four-piece for their fourth album, titled simply '4' ('81). Produced at great length by Robert John 'Mutt' Lange, it broke the band worldwide on a massive scale. The hits from it took the band to new heights: 'Urgent', featuring Junior Walker's rasping sax; 'Juke Box Hero'; and the monster ballad 'Waiting For A Girl Like You'. The latter gave Foreigner their first UK Top 10 placing and in the States spent an unprecedented 10 weeks at Number Two. The album went one better

FOREIGNER circa 1981: juke box heroes

FOREIGNER

there and eventually peaked at Number Five in the UK during its impressive 62 week run on the chart. After the world tour to promote '4', when the band were augmented by session musicians including Mark Riviera on guitar and saxophone, the band laid low for a while. Meanwhile, to capitalise on the success, Atlantic issued a compilation album, 'Records' ('82). Reports of friction between Jones and Gramm about the direction of the next album filtered out. Gramm complained that Foreigner were drifting away from their roots as a hard rock band, whilst Jones would later deny this defend his occasional dalliances with the Big Ballad...

Whatever, the line-up was still intact come the next LP, 'Agent Provocateur' ('84), featuring many more keyboards than earlier works. It also featured the New Jersey Mass Choir singing backing vocals on the gospel-flavoured 'I Want To Know What Love Is'. When released as a single, it soared to Number One in the USA and the UK – so destroying much of Foreigner's rock credibility! Although it failed to match the sales of '4', 'Agent Provocateur' sold very well. But the cracks in were beginning to show when, after it, Lou Gramm made his first solo album, 'Ready Or Not' ('87). The record even gave him a Top 10 hit with 'Midnight Blue', but it couldn't match Foreigner's success and he was back in the fold for 'Inside Information', their sixth album, released in 1988. The record saw the usual chart action but has since been written off by both Gramm and Jones as the band's weakest. Following it, both of them made solo albums: Jones a very weak eponymous set (September '89) followed two months later by Gramm's 'Long Hard Look'. Gramm enjoyed a hit ('Just Between You And Me') whilst Jones tried his hand at producing (Billy Joel) and co-writing (Eric Clapton's 'Bad Love'). In effect, Foreigner had ground to a halt.

They made a false restart with Kentucky-born Gramm-soundalike Johnny Edwards on vocals for the proficient but lacklustre 'Unusual Heat' ('91). Simultaneously, Gramm formed a new outfit, Shadow King featuring Vivian Campbell on guitar, who released an eponymous album in late '91. Edwards was a fine singer but Foreigner had lost their magic 'X' factor. In '92, they also lost bassist Wills (who joined Bad Company) and drummer Elliott...

But when Shadow King split after just one show (in London), because drummer Kevin Valentine quit and Campbell joined Def

Leppard, it was inevitable that Gramm should join forces once again with the guitarist who made his name. He and Jones appeared to reconcile their differences and wrote three new songs that were added to a revamped version of a '92 'Greatest Hits' compilation, retitled 'The Very Best... And Beyond'.

This latest incarnation – basically a two-some backed by session musicians – made their live debut in the States late in '92 and although just like all the other line-ups they'll never make headlines for anything as exciting as destroying a hotel room, as long as Gramm and Jones are working together, you can guarantee songs about heartache and pain...

ALBUMS

FOREIGNER (Atlantic, 1977 – KKK) Some weak tracks let down this melodic rock masterpiece.
DOUBLE VISION (Atlantic, 1978 – KKKK) Heavier than debut. Stronger in most departments. Singles sold better too!
HEAD GAMES (Atlantic, 1979 – KKKK) As heavy as Foreigner got! Blistering first side but second half lets it down.

4 (Atlantic, 1981) An AOR monster! All-time classic, dripping with hooklines... Classy ballads and kick-ass rockers.
RECORDS (Atlantic, 1983 – KKKKK) "A live treat in 'Hot Blooded'... 100 per cent correcto... A 'Best Of' album that is totally, utterly justified." – Kerrang! 32, December 30, 1982-January 12, 1983
AGENT PROVOCATEUR (Atlantic, 1984 – KKKK) "Foreigner have made a good record when we've all been waiting for a great one." – Kerrang! 84, December 27, 1984-January 9, 1985
INSIDE INFORMATION (Atlantic, 1987 – KKK) "Yet another Platinum disc to hang on Mick Jones' loo wall!" – Kerrang! 166, December 12, 1977
UNUSUAL HEAT (Atlantic, 1991– KKK) "The

return of the heavier side of Foreigner... The most accessible since '4'..." – Kerrang! 349, July 13, 1991
THE VERY BEST OF FOREIGNER (Atlantic, 1992 – KKKKK) "Gramm and Foreigner were truly touched by the Gods when lamenting their lack of luck with the ladies..." – Kerrang! 388, April 18, 1992
THE VERY BEST... AND BEYOND (Atlantic, 1992 – KKKK) As above but with three new songs not quite up to classic Foreigner status. (Reviewed Kerrang! 415, October 24, 1992)

FREAK OF NATURE

USA/Denmark, five-piece (1992-present)
BAND FORMED by Danish-born singer Mike Tramp after the demise of White Lion. Freak Of Nature boast a much tougher sound and image than his previous outfit, where Tramp wouldn't have been seen dead wearing a 'Noddy' hat. Debut album:
FREAK OF NATURE (Music For Nations, 1993 – KKKK)

FREE

UK, four-piece (1968-1973)
STUNNING AND beautifully simple blues rock outfit, who debuted with 'Tons Of Sobs' (Island, 1968) when all were still teenagers. Although fronted by Paul Rodgers (vocals) and Paul Kossoff (guitar), Free were a band that had astonishing talent in every department thanks to Andy Fraser (bass) and Simon Kirke (drums).

Second LP 'Free' ('69) and constant touring saw them build a substantial following before their classic third, 'Fire And Water' ('70) and its single, 'All Right Now' (ultimately a UK hit five times in three different decades!) turned them into household names.

They hated the fame and pressure this brought and fourth LP, 'Highway' ('70), they made as uncommercial as possible. Free then split to pursue various side projects whilst Island released 'Free Live' ('71). The band reformed for the lacklustre 'Free At Last' ('72) then bassist Fraser quit to be replaced by

Japanese bassist Tetsu and keyboard player John 'Rabbit' Bundrick for 'Heartbreaker' ('73). By that stage, Kossoff's reliance on heroin was getting the better of him and the band were forced to quit, after completing a US tour with stand-in guitarist Wendell Richardson (of Osibisa). A sad end to a brilliant band, but at least they left a seven album legacy of mellow rockers and passion-packed blues.

Try all the above or sample compilations:
THE FREE STORY *(Island, 1974 – KKKKK)*
THE BEST OF FREE *(Island, 1991 – KKKK)*
...Originals remixed by Bob Clearmountain

FREHLEY'S COMET

US four-piece (1984-present)
AFTER REASONABLE ballyhoo over the so-so 'Frehley's Comet' ('87) – later to become band's handle – along with his 'Ace Is Back' slogan, former Kiss guitarist, Ace Frehley, went on to achieve a quite unremarkable solo career. Strange, considering what was technically Frehley's debut – his offering of the cunningly marketed simultaneously released '78 Kiss solos – was a sonic delight and the most successful of the batch.

Recommended album:
FREHLEY'S COMET *(Megaforce, 1987 – KKK)*

Marty FRIEDMAN

USA, guitarist (1987-present)
MEGADETH SHREDDER who came to first came to the spotlight alongside Jason Becker in Cacophony in 1987, although was previously in a Honolulu-based band called Vixen (!). Made his first solo LP, 'Dragon's Kiss', for Roadrunner in 1988. A second, 'Scenes', came four years later. Both were instrumental, mellow, quasi-New Age affairs.

Recommended album:
SCENES *(Roadrunner, 1992 – KKK)*

FRIDAY ROCK SHOW

UK, radio show (1978-present)
AS THE sole national radio outlet for hard rock in the UK, the BBC's Friday Rock Show has long been vital listening for the country's Metal-starved fans. For 15 years the show was fronted by the near legendary Tommy Vance, a man whose voice came to symbolise the power of the music he so passionately championed.

In April '93 he handed over the show to 26-year-old Claire Sturgess, whose fresh approach it is hoped will herald a new era of contemporary rock on the radio. The show's format has consistently merged album tracks, live concerts and sessions as well as providing a much-needed outlet for struggling unsigned talent. Although criticised by some for its relatively conservative tastes, the Friday Rock Show still remains the backbone of rock exposure. Not 'arf!

FUCK OFF

Spain, four-piece (1988-who cares)
CRAP BAND, interesting name.
Strangely unsuccessful album:
ANOTHER SACRIFICE *(Claxon, 1989 – K)*

FUDGE TUNNEL

UK, trio (1989-present)
NOTTINGHAM GRUNGERS with some of the cooler T-shirt designs around, Fudge Tunnel recorded two singles for Pigboy Records, before defecting to Earache and recording their first long-player, 'Hate Songs In E Minor'. Some compared it to Nirvana's 'Bleach', Sepultura loved it enough to make them their opening act. After 1992's 'Teeth' EP, the trio have recorded a new album, entitled 'Creep Diets'. More unholy noise and great T-shirts are sure to follow.

Recommended album:
HATE SONGS IN E MINOR *(Earache, 1991 – KKKK)*

GAMMA RAY

Germany, two-piece (1990-present)
HISTRIONIC AND average 'solo' unit formed by ex-Helloween guitarist Kai Hansen with Ralf Scheepers (ex-Tyron Pace) on vocals.
Recommended (only to upset neighbours):
HEADING FOR TOMORROW *(Noise, 1990 – K)*

GANG GREEN

USA, four-piece (1981-1991)
BOSTON BAND, originally a Hardcore/Punk trio, famous mainly for their obsession with Budweiser beer. Led by Chris Doherty, they also recorded a mean cover of Led Zeppelin's 'Livin' Lovin' Maid' and took the piss out of Van Halen's 'OU812' album by naming one of their own 'I81B4U'. Fast and drunk.
Recommended (with an ice-cold Bud) album:
CAN'T LIVE WITHOUT IT *(Roadrunner, 1990 – KKKK)*

GBH

UK, four-piece (1980-present)
ENDURING BIRMINGHAM-based Hardcore Punk outfit. Perhaps the first to make the crossover to Thrash even though they still consider themselves Punk. Same three chords, anyway!
Recommended 12":
LEATHER, BRISTLES, STUDS AND ACNE *(Clay, 1982 – KKKKK) under the name Charged GBH*

GEDDES AXE

UK, five-piece (1980-1983)
MADE A big splash in *Sounds* on the release of their debut EP 'Return Of The Gods'. The EP was superb and topped UK HM charts, but the Axe never made an album and disappeared into the smog of Sheffield.

GEORDIE

UK, four-piece (1972-1984)
GLAM/YOB rockers from the North East in the style of Slade. Had four UK hit singles but would have been long since forgotten if singer Brian Johnson hadn't joined AC/DC in 1980. Geordie reformed without him two years later then changed their name to Powerhouse.
Recommended album:
DON'T BE FOOLED BY THE NAME *(EMI, 1973 – KKK)*
Or any of the myriad compilations available...

Robin GEORGE

UK, solo artist (1983-present)
GRACED THE cover of *Kerrang!* 51 in 1983 – then promptly disappeared into obscurity. He remained, however, a hotly-tipped and talented guitarist/singer/songwriter/arranger. Resurfaced briefly alongside Sean Harris in Notorious who (dis)graced page 23 of *Kerrang!* 316 in 1990 – then disappeared again...
Recommended album:
DANGEROUS MUSIC *(Bronze, 1984 – KKKK)*

GEORGIA SATELLITES

USA, four-piece (1984-1990)
NO FRILLS, shit-kickin' Southern rock 'n' rollers fronted by Dan Baird (vocals/guitar) and Rick Richards (guitar/vocals). Debuted with 'Keep the Faith' EP (Making Waves, '85), but were soon snapped up by Elektra for whom they made three full-length albums. The records were usually very good but could never hope to match their blistering live shows which were

never less than stunning. Other than that, they will always be remembered for the classic rocker 'Battleship Chains' (co-written by Baird's friend Terry Anderson, with whom he worked again when launching his solo career in 1992) and for their short-but-sweet cover of 'Hippy Hippy Shake' which featured in the otherwise godawful Tom Cruise movie 'Cocktail'. Rick Richards went on to join Izzy Stradlin's Ju Ju Hounds.

Recommended albums:
GEORGIA SATELLITES *(Elektra, 1986 – KKKKK)*
LET IT ROCK *(Elektra, 1993 – KKKK)*
Posthumous compilation

GIANT

USA, four-piece (1989-present)
CONSIDERED TO be something of an AOR supergroup, given the individuals involved, the sheer quality of the music actually surprised even the most cynical of observers.

Brothers Dann (guitar/vocals) and David Huff (drums) had begun their careers in the Christian outfit White Heart but had subsequently found themselves much in demand as session players, particularly Dann who, with keyboardist Alan Pasqua (who departed Giant shortly before second album 'Time To Burn' was released) had been key men in Van Stephenson's recording band, the pair actually going on to contribute to Whitesnake's hallmark '1987' album.

But, regardless of the classic status of the band's two albums now behind them, the future looks a little bleak, as no sooner were the band signed by Epic from their former home at A&M than Giant have been dropped. A very sad state of affairs.

Highly recommended albums:
LAND OF THE RUNAWAYS *(A&M, 1989 – KKKKK)*
TIME TO BURN *(Epic, 1992 – KKKKK)*

Ian GILLAN

UK, singer (1966-present)
ALONGSIDE ROBERT Plant and Paul Rodgers, Gillan can justifiably claim to be one of the UK's most influential singers. Musically, his career is long and chequered, but his distinctive vocals have rarely been less than excellent.

First evidence for that can be heard with Episode Six (1966-1968), a sometimes psychedelic pop outfit which also featured Roger Glover on bass, or on a 'Jesus Christ Superstar' soundtrack album (MCA, '71), but rock fans will appreciate Deep Purple far more. 1993 saw him rejoin for his third spell with the band, having fronted them from 1969-1973 and 1983-1989.

Aside from the that band, however, Gillan's recorded works are many and varied. He made a jazzy solo album 'Child In Time' (Polydor, 1975) which led to the formation of the Ian Gillan Band (featuring guitarist Ray Fenwick, with Colin Towns on keyboards) and two further studio albums in a similar vein: 'Clear Air Turbulence (Island, '76) and 'Scarabus' (Island, '77). Various live recordings from Tokyo's Budokan theatre of this era also exist.

The singer grew tired of the style, however, and returned to a heavier vein with another solo album (originally available in Japan only), 'Gillan' (East World, '79). This excellent comeback led to the formation of the band known as Gillan which – after a few personnel changes – also included Towns, alongside Bernie Tormé (guitar), John McCoy (bass) and Mick Underwood (ex-Episode Six, drums). This line-up made 'Mr Universe' (Acrobat '79 – although a version with a different tracklist was released in the Far East), 'Glory Road' (Virgin, '80) and 'Future Shock' (Virgin '81) before ex-White Spirit (now Iron Maiden) guitarist Janick Gers replaced Tormé for 'Double Trouble' (Virgin, '81) and their final album 'Magic' (Virgin '82).

The band fell apart acrimoniously and Gillan (the man) then surprised everyone by joining Black Sabbath for one tour and album; 'Born Again' (Vertigo, '83).

Whilst back in Deep Purple, he took advantage of their casual schedule to make 'Accidentally On Purpose' (Virgin, '87), a joint album with Glover, and tour UK clubs as Garth Rocket And The Moonshiners (who did not

IAN GILLAN

record).
He also
made
'South
Africa', a
1988
single
with
Bernie
Marsden,
before
getting
fired from
Purple
and
going
solo
once
again with 'Naked Thunder' (Teldec/EastWest,
'90) and 'Toolbox' (Teldec/EastWest, '91).

Recent works have not sold well, but Gillan
doesn't care. He'll continue doing exactly what
he wants until the cows come home – and
anyone who can sing like he does on 'Child In
Time' is perfectly entitled to do so. (Even if he
does wear naff trousers...)

Recommended (Gillan band) albums:
GILLAN (RPM, 1993 re-issue – KKKK)
GLORY ROAD (Virgin, 1980 – KKKK)
FUTURE SHOCK (Virgin, 1981 – KKKK)

GIRL

UK, five-piece (1979-1982)
PASSIONATELY LOATHED out-of-vogue pretty
boys fronted by prima donna vocalist Phil Lewis
(later to join LA Guns), who also included one
Phil Collen, now guitarin' it with Def Leppard.
Girl are most remembered for Lewis' much-
publicised dalliance with Britt Eckland, film star
and ex-wife of Rod Stewart... but their debut
album 'Sheer Greed' was a killer. Come their '82
follow-up 'Wasted Youth', Girl were trying to cut
it as a regular macho-posin' rock act – but they
sold themselves short and neither the press nor
the public fell for it.

Recommended album:
SHEER GREED (Jet, 1980 – KKKK)

GIRLSCHOOL

UK, four piece (1978-present, but only just!)
THE MID-'80s nearly killed Girlschool. By their
own admission, the South London hooligans
were adrift from any serious direction and
floundering in the ever-shifting Metal climate.
No one, however, could argue with Girlschool's
past achievements since forming at school as
Painted Lady.

Loved by the predominantly male rock
audience and tolerated by Punk, Girlschool
were tough and brazen long before it was
fashionable. The natural charm and cheek of
vocalist Kim McAuliffe and drummer Denise
Dufort saw the band through their three-chord
smash-a-bout of tomboy Power Metal, and their
collaboration with Motörhead in 1980 (for the
'St Valentine's Day Massacre' EP) saw them
gain a real foothold within the rock hierachy.

In 1992 the band reassembled for a
surprisingly gritty album ('Girlschool') and
announced in 1993 that they would be touring
with original guitarist Kelly Johnson (now a US
citizen) to the delight of the loyal fanbase. Their
days may be numbered, but one hell of a
swansong is assured.

Recommended albums:
DEMOLITION (Bronze, 1980 – KKKK)
SCREAMING BLUE MURDER (Bronze, 1982 –
KKKKK)
CHEERS YOU LOT (Razor compilation, 1988 –
KKKKK)
GIRLSCHOOL (Communique, 1992 – KKK)

GIUFFRIA

USA, five-piece (1984- 1987)
THE RE-EMERGENCE of former Angel keyboard
player Gregg Giuffria caused a bit of a stir in K!
circles. Initially, Giuffria's comeback was to
have been under the Angel banner, creating an
instant cover story, much to the annoyance of
his former colleagues who advised him to use
his own name for the new outfit's monicker. And
so it came to pass...

Comprised of Giuffria, vocalist David Glenn
Eisley, ex-Rough Cutt guitarist Craig Goldy,

former Quiet Riot bassist Chuck Wright (who had replaced ex-Sabu man Rick Bozzo before recording commenced) and Alan Krigger on drums, this band concocted an almost inch-perfect debut album ("A release so pompous, so ballsy, so full of 'twiddly bits' that it cracks yer nuts while caressing yer cheeks", ran the *Kerrang!* review) that was met with almost overnight success in America and a brief tour opening for the reformed Deep Purple.

By the time second album 'Silk And Steel' was issued, both Goldy and Wright had been ousted (replaced by Lanny Cordola and David Sikes respectively) and the magic and momentum had all but died.

Seeking a new challenge Giuffria disbanded the group and formed House Of Lords.
Recommended album:
GIUFFRIA (MCA/Camel, 1984 – KKKKK)

GODFLESH

UK, two-piece (1988-present)
IT BEGAN when guitarist Justin Broadrick (who played on Side One of Napalm Death's 'Scum' bombshell) left Head Of David, and started working with both G Christian Green and a drum machine.

The result was Godflesh, the pretentious critic's dream, and their eponymous debut EP was a massive Industrial nightmare.

The excellent 'Streetcleaner' remains their least indulgent album, thus making the biggest impression. Later releases, such as the 'Pure' album, saw the duo stretch their lumbering, bleak compositions out to questionable lengths...
Recommended album:
STREETCLEANER (Earache, 1989 – KKKK)

GODZ

USA, four-piece (1975-present)
WITH A 'Z' – don'tcha just love it?! Biker-boogie raunch 'n' rollers replete with the shattered windscreen vocals of mainman Eric Moore. Released just two albums in the '70s, then Moore gave the Godz handle another rev in '85 along with ex-Outlaw Freddie Salem. A 1987

album 'Mongolians' also featured journeyman drummer Kevin Valentine. Latest rumours suggest Eric Moore (and what's left of his liver) is still out there somewhere, occasionally flying the Godz flag. Rock till you drop? Believe it!
Recommended album:
I'LL GET YOU ROCKIN' (Heavy Metal America, 1985 – KKKKK)

GOLDEN EARRING

Holland, four-piece (1964-present)
CRIMINALLY UNDERRATED everywhere except at home – and famous everywhere else in the world for just one song, 'Radar Love', a huge hit in 1973. What Earring should be famous for, however, is a string of quality albums – especially from '73 onwards – that would have made them international superstars if only they could be bothered to go out and tour their asses off like so many lesser bands have done. They tried it sporadically – with The Who in '72, and with Rush *et al* in '82 when they enjoyed a second international hit with 'Twilight Zone' – but always got too homesick to make it a full-time occupation! Although they have occasionally expanded to a five-piece, the ever-present unit of Barry Hay (vocals/guitar), George Kooymans (guitar/vocals), Rinus Gerritsen (bass) and Cesar Zuiderwijk represent the longest working band in rock – notwithstanding the varying Kinks line-ups and the now sporadically active Rolling Stones. Today, their one hope of shifting their impressive back catalogue is this entry and the fact that Steve Harris of Iron Maiden will tell anybody who asks that they are his favourite band in the whole world. Good, on ya Steve!
(Most) recommended albums:
MOONTAN (Track, 1973 – KKKKK)
CUT (21 Records, 1982 – KKKKK)

GORKY PARK

Russia, four-piece (1987-present)
WOEFULLY BEHIND the times heavy rockers who came to international attention when Bon Jovi manager Doc McGhee enlisted them for the bill of 1990's Make A Difference Foundation

album ('Stairway To Heaven – Highway To Hell' on Vertigo) and festival, in Moscow. They claim to be a supergroup whose members' previous bands have combined sales of 40 million... But then again, their drummer and singer/bassist rejoice in the respective handles of Little Sasha and Big Sasha.

Recommended album (only for the very Russian cover of The Who's 'My Generation'):
GORKY PARK (Phonogram, 1989 – K)

Lou GRAMM

USA, singer (1974-present)
FOREIGNER SINGER with solo aspirations. Listed under his real name of Louis Grammatico on the two acid blues-flavoured Black Sheep albums ('Black Sheep' and 'Encouraging Words', both on Capitol, both 1975) before Mick Jones picked him up to make history with Foreigner as the only serious rival to Steve Perry of Journey as THE voice of AOR. Gramm fell out with Jones periodically and made two solo albums for Atlantic 'Ready Or Not' ('87) and 'Long Hard Look' ('89) before formally quitting to form the shortlived Shadow King, who released just one eponymous album. With him throughout all the above solo ventures was bassist and sometime songwriting partner, Bruce Turgon.

Recommended albums:
READY OR NOT (Atlantic, 1987 – KKKK)
SHADOW KING (Atlantic, 1991 – KKKK)

GRAND FUNK RAILROAD

USA, three-piece (1969-1983)
OFTEN CITED AS the American equivalent to Black Sabbath – but in the States that was usually spoken as an insult rather than a compliment because the band – Mark Farner (guitar/vocals), Mel Schacher (bass) and Don Brewer (drums) – played so loud and so relentlessly. Their profile was hyped mercilessly by manager and former Detroit DJ Terry Knight, who became almost as well known as the band. Come 1971 (when they released their fifth album, just two years after their first!) they noticed he was probably richer, too, and

so tried (successfully) to sue his ass off...

Their best music is sporadically spread over their 15 album legacy, but tends to be more in evidence on their rawer early work. They added a keyboard player and enlisted the help of Todd Rundgren in 1974, then on 'Good Singing, Good Playing' ('76) Frank Zappa produced, but they split soon after only to reform, rather ineffectually, with a different bassist, Dennis Bellinger 1981-83.

Much better to recall tracks such as 'We're An American Band' (since covered live by Bon Jovi *et al*) and especially 'Closer To Home' or over-the-top covers of 'The Locomotion' or 'Gimme Shelter'.

Recommended (if rather dated) albums:
CLOSER TO HOME (Capitol, 1970 – KKKK)
E PLURIBUS FUNK (Capitol, 1972 – KKKK)

GREAT WHITE

USA, five-piece (1982-present)
LA BAND who quickly grew in to seasoned road-warriors playing blues rock and covers – including a particularly fine line in Led Zeppelin numbers. On stage, fronted by singer Jack Russell – once the brunt of unconfirmed reports that he had served time for manslaughter while under then influence of the drug PCP – Great White are the archetypal good-time bar band. On vinyl, however, this is now a matter of some debate, as the last few years have seen the band (depending on your point of view) deteriorate/mature into a more bland/radio-friendly melodic outfit.

They debuted with a Don Dokken-produced EP, 'Out Of The Night' (Aegan, '82). This helped win them a deal with EMI but the resultant eponymous album ('84) sold poorly so they and the label parted company. Manager Alan Niven, later to co-manage Guns N' Roses, suggested the band make another independent EP, 'Shot In The Dark' (Telegraph, '86), and this helped win them a deal with Capitol who released 'Once Bitten...' in '87. The following year, Enigma (an offshoot of EMI) demanded a release, due to outstanding contractual obligations of one more record. Knowing their strengths, Great White opted to give them a pair of old concert recordings (the US version differed to that put out in Europe) as 'Recovery... Live' in '88. The next studio album was '...Twice Shy' ('89) featuring their hit cover of Ian Hunter's 'Once Bitten, Twice Shy'. In 1990, a 'Live In London' CD emerged in Japan (of a BBC recorded Whitesnake support slot in '89) but since then both 'Hooked' ('91) and' 'Psycho City' ('92) have seen them drift from their roots.

Recommended album:
RECOVERY... LIVE (Enigma, 1988 – KKKK)
...TWICE SHY (Capitol, 1989 – KKKK)

GREEN JELLŸ

USA, nine-piece (1992-present)
FORMERLY GREEN Jellö until Kraft Foods objected. Started as the world's first video band then got (kinda) real with '93 debut hit single and video, 'Three Little Pigs'. Sounding like Lawnmower Death whilst claiming to be untalented bozos seems like a good career move...

Recommended album:
CEREAL KILLER (Zoo/BMG, 1993 – KKKK)
video soundtrack

GREEN RIVER

USA, five-piece (1987-1989)
ONE OF the instigators of the 'Seattle/SubPop sound' whose line-up included Mark Arm (vocals) and Steve Turner (guitar) – both later of Mudhoney – and future Mother Love Bone/Pearl Jam members Stone Gossard (guitar) and Jeff Ament (bass).

Recommended:
REHAB DOLL (eight song EP) (SubPop, 1988 – KKKK)

GRIM REAPER

UK, four-piece (1979-1988)
AIR-RAID SIREN vocals from Steve Grimmett over a very traditional British Metal backing was Grim Reaper's stock-in-trade. It earned them a respectable cult following but no major deal until 1987 (for their third LP 'Rock You To Hell' on MCA), by which time it was too late.

Grimmett moved on to join Onslaught.
Recommended album:
SEE YOU IN HELL (Ebony, 1983 – KKK)

GRINGOS LOCOS

Finland, five-piece (1987-1992)
SOUTHERN STYLE boogie merchants who really should have been raised on long balmy days of Georgia sunshine rather than the long frozen nights of Scandinavian twilight.

Undeterred, they drank Jack Daniel's and wore cowboys boots. Made damn fine music too, especially on their first album, although they lost their way on the next two – 'Punch Drunk' ('89) and 'Raw Deal' ('91) – and have not been heard of since.

Recommended album:
GRINGOS LOCOS (Mercury, 1988 – KKKK)

The GRIP

UK, four-piece (1984-1990)
ORIGINALLY, AND most probably remembered as, a trio. Led by the immeasurably talented Willie on vocals and guitar, the Grip were weavers of sublime pop/rock who spent most of their career being propelled by critical acclaim. But alas, they were never propelled as far as the big time.

Recommended album:
BE YOURSELF (Razor, 1988 – KKKKK)

GUARDIAN

USA, four-piece (1986-present)
LA-BASED Christians signed initially to Engima as Stryper-soundalikes and sporting the 'Armour Of God'. But by their second album, 'Love And War', Guardian underwent a transformation which showed the band pursuing a healthier, bluesier, direction. Since then, have toured on-and-off on the continent and planned a concept album for 1993.

Highly recommended album:
LOVE AND WAR (Pakaderm, 1990 – KKKKK)

GUN

Scotland, five-piece (1988-present)
VERY CLASSY hard rock act who write songs

with irresistable melodies superbly married to in-yer-face guitars. If anything, this Glasgow outfit has been hidden from much of the Heavy Metal audience by an image much less 'rock' than their music. They should worry: their debut album, 'Taking On The World' (A&M, '89) – made when they were still teenagers – drew them to a more mainstream audience and spawned three UK Top 40 singles – 'Better Days', 'Shame On You' and 'Money'. It also went a long way to winning them the chance to support the Rolling Stones on the European leg of their 1990 'Urban Jungle' European tour. The tour was the icing on the cake, after 18 months spent on the road playing over 200 shows. However, the sight of those last two-and-a-half million Stones fans took its toll on livewire guitarist 'Baby' Stafford, who left to go solo thinking he could never top supporting his heroes. His replacement was Alex Dixon (formerly of Midnight Blue, and if anything, even more animated on stage than his predecessor!) – who completed a line-up fronted by Mark Rankin (vocals) and featuring Gizzi brothers Giuliano 'Joolz' (guitar) and Dante (bass), plus Scott Shields (drums).

That line-up laid low in '91 whilst they made the second album, 'Gallus' ('92), an altogether tougher record. Songs from it sounded great live when they supported Def Leppard and suggested that for Gun, the best is yet to come. *Recommended album:*
GALLUS *(A&M, 1992 – KKKKK)*

GUNS N' ROSES

USA, six-piece (1985-present)
THE MOST Dangerous Band In The World? Maybe... The most notorious? Certainly... If nothing else, Guns N' Roses have seen more, done more, played more and sold more than most bands even dream of. Their figureheads W Axl Rose and Slash have become household names the world over and icons for a whole generation. Test the theory, ask your milkman to name a world famous rock band: if he doesn't say Guns N' Roses, cancel that extra pinta...

Axl (vocals, piano) was born William Bailey, February 6, 1962; a surname he dropped after learning that he lived with a stepfather: his mother having remarried after his natural father (Rose) left home when he was a baby. 'Axl' was the name of a band he once sang for in Indiana. He sowed the seeds of Guns N' Roses when he left home for LA in 1982. There he met up with Izzy Stradlin' (real name, Jeffrey Isabell) who had spent the previous couple of years playing the LA club circuit with little success. They had been friends and fellow juvenile delinquents back in Lafayette, Indiana. Of the pair, Axl was probably the most notorious, and actually spent three months in jail after being too broke to pay a fine. His poverty would soon change, his volatile character perhaps couldn't...

In 1985, he and Stradlin' enlisted guitarist Tracii Guns, and with others they gigged under the name of Rose, then Hollywood Rose, before changing to Guns N' Roses – the latter deemed a better choice than both Heads Of Amazon and AIDS... Tracii Guns left, eventually to form LA Guns, and the the band settled on a five-piece line-up completed by Slash (guitar, born Saul Hudson, July 23, 1965, in Stoke on Trent), Steven Adler (drums) and Michael 'Duff' McKagan (bass, born February 5, 1964). Slash and Adler had played together in Road Crew (a name Adler would resurrect years later when he tried to start again, with ex-Vain members). McKagan (formerly of Seattle band Ten Minute Warning) they met when he travelled from south to audition for Road Crew.

First gigs on 'The Hell Tour '85' (beginning in June, mainly in California) were sparsely attended, but word of mouth later brought many more, keen to be hit in the face by an adrenaline/booze/drug-fuelled cocktail of Punk and Metal. Come May '86, GN'R offered the world a taster in the form of 10,000 copies of the 'Live ?!*@ Like A Suicide' on the Uzi/Suicide label. Two months later, the record and gigs had caused enough of a stir for Geffen to sign the band. The singer also legally adopted his stage name.

In August they began recording 'Appetite For Destruction' with producer Mike Clink. It was released in August '87, but before then Geffen re-issued '...Like A Suicide' (January '87) and put the band out on tour with Iron Maiden in the States (April). The band's early publicity made much of their over-indulgences with drugs and alcohol, and so it was of little surprise when they had to leave the tour halfway through – Axl having lost his voice, Slash being ordered into a centre for chemical detox in Hawaii. Although the band don't now like to talk about their indulgences, their lyrics were more candid.

Whether the debut record would have been better or weaker without that kind of influence is a matter for debate, but there is no doubt that it was absolutely in the right place at the right time. It was perfect for Europe – where the band had made their debut at London's Marquee June 28, '87 – and the States – where they'd

opened for Mötley Crüe in July. In a little over a year, 'Appetite...' had been certified as sextuple Platinum. Today it has sold more than double that: 12 million and counting...

In November 1987 the band played their first proper UK tour, supported by Faster Pussycat, dates and a bill that were once to have been topped by Aerosmith. Aerosmith couldn't make it – and neither could Adler who was replaced by Cinderella's Fred Coury after breaking a hand in a fight.

Six months later Guns N' Roses had got it together enough to be supporting Aerosmith in the States, then playing major venues and riding the crest of a wave with their 'Pump' album. The tour contract insisted GN'R, if using chemicals, went nowhere near the newly cleaned-up headliners... The tour stretched all the way into November marking the end of 14 months' road action for Guns N' Roses interrupted briefly in August for an ill-fated visit to the UK to play the ninth Castle Donington Monsters Of Rock

AXL and SLASH at the London Marquee in June '87

festival on a bill topped by Iron Maiden. Wet weather, slippery conditions underfoot and over-enthusiasm in some sections of the crowd whilst the band were on stage combined to sour the day. From the stage, the band could see fans being pushed and three times stopped their set to ask for calm. Tragically, Axl's impassioned pleas came too late for Alan Dick and Landon Peter Siggers who both fell and died as a result of the crush.

With 'Appetite For Destruction' having finally made it to the US Number One slot, the band returned to finish the Aerosmith tour and await the release of some much-requested new material, after a steady stream of singles taken from the debut album and issued in a huge variety of formats. The new material was 'GN'R Lies', released December 1988, not strictly an album but described officially as an EP. In fact, it was an album-length repackaging of live material from the long-since deleted '...Like A Suicide' EP backed with four acoustic numbers (one a reworking of 'You're Crazy' from 'Appetite...'). The EP's sub-title, '...The Sex, The Drugs, The Violence, The Shocking Truth' was the band's ironic response to the increasingly sensational coverage of themselves and their private lives in some sections of the press – coverage which, predictably, got even more extreme and distorted following the EP's release! The record eventually sold six million copies, due in no small way to the success of one track, 'Patience' – featuring some fine whistling from Axl! – which became a Top 10 hit both sides of the Atlantic in June '89. Another track, 'One In A Million', however, got the band into some very hot water...

In March '89, they were due to play the (later cancelled) 'Rock And A Hard Place' AIDS benefit in New York but were pulled from the bill after gay activists objected to use of the word 'faggots' in the lyrics of 'One In A Million'. Black representatives, including Living Colour and the Black Rock Coalition, had previously branded the band as racists due to references to 'immigrants' and 'niggers' in the same song. The lyrics, Axl has always insisted, were about

his first visit to LA and never meant to cause offence – only reflect the tensions on the streets of downtown Los Angeles.

More controversy followed on August 30 when Stradlin' was arrested, primarily for urinating on the floor, after stepping off a US Air jetliner. On October 18, Guns N' Roses were special guests on the bill of the Rolling Stones' LA Coliseum shows. Mid-show, Axl announced he would quit if certain members (ie Slash) didn't stop 'Dancing with Mr Brownstone, (ie heroin). At the next day's gig, Axl apologised and Guns N' Roses continued, although rumours of their demise continued to circulate for months. Much of this was fuelled by the lack of progress on their new studio album. Work had begun in June '89 but was constantly interrupted as the band struggled to get itself together – mentally and physically. Ill health caused by overindulgences was much to blame and predictably, when the band did regroup for a charity gig in Indianapolis on April 7, 1990, it was viewed as something of a minor triumph (the feat, not the performance). They performed two songs: a cover of the UK Subs' 'Down On The Farm' and 'Civil War', a number they would soon record for inclusion on the Romanian Angel Appeal charity album.

Although he didn't play at Farm-Aid, keyboardist Dizzy Reed was by then working with the band on the forthcoming album. His recruitment heralded a period of major upheaval which many thought signalled the end of the band. First, in October, Steven Adler left the band, reportedly after failing to stop his reliance on drugs and alcohol. Martin Chambers (ex-Pretenders) and Adam Maples (ex-Sea Hags) worked with the band before they appointed Matt Sorum, formerly of The Cult. Sorum made his live debut with the band on January 20, '91, in front of 120,000 people in Rio de Janiero's Maracana soccer stadium, at the second all-star Rock In Rio festival. Presumably none off the giant crowd were aware that the drum solo he played that night was completely improvised, after the band didn't get around to suggesting he played until they walked to the stage.

"It's new to us, this business, and we meet these people and they say, 'Do this, do that'. And we go, 'Fuck it, fuck you!', because it's just not us. We do whatever we want to..."
– Axel (sic) Rose, Kerrang! 148, June 11-24, 1987

"Originally I wanted to be the only guitarist in the band... It's not that I didn't like Izzy's playing, I did. But I was very into my own thing and it had never worked before between me and another guitar player." – Slash, Kerrang! 229, March 11, 1989

"Look at me – T-shirt, jeans, boots, that's me, that's all there is, that's all there's gonna be... Gimme a roof over my head and something to drink and I've got everything I need. What difference is this money going to make?" – Slash, Kerrang! 198, July 30, 1988

"Some funny shit went down on that Aerosmith tour. We were so similar, and yet we made such a contrast... Their whole operation runs like clockwork... Which is exactly the opposite from the way we usually get things done!"
– Slash, Kerrang! 218, December 17, 1988

"I trust everybody until they fuck me over. When they do, I don't trust them any more, but I like to give everyone a fair chance at that trust." – Axl Rose, Kerrang! 242, June 10, 1989

"(I prefer the) studio. Live is fun, live is interesting and live is a blast but, you know, the live thing is like a one night stand – which is great, but the things that last are the songs." – Axl Rose, Kerrang! 242, June 10, 1989

"Vince Neil took a pot-shot at Izzy as he was walkin' off stage at the MTV Awards, after jammin' with Tom Petty, because Vince's wife has got a bug up her ass about Izzy... I tell ya, Vince Neil's gonna get a good ass-whippin', and I'm the boy to give it to him... I wanna see that plastic face of his cave in when I hit him!" – Axl Rose, Kerrang! 286, April 21, 1990

"I thank God for it, that I've managed to succeed at what I love doing... (And) I'd like to continue being good at it. You can't let the hype justify the whole band's existence... You don't even know how hard it is once you get here, to keep it together..." – Slash, Kerrang! 439, April 17, 1993

GUNS N' ROSES

Debuted that night were more songs from the, by then, long overdue studio product, to be called 'Use Your Illusion'. The title was taken from the painting which Axl chose for the cover artwork. Originally, the record was due to be a double, then followed a year later by a second record – containing the remainder of the 35 songs the band had recorded – with an EP of punk covers also somewhere in the pipeline. In the end, 'Use Your Illusion' became two double albums (containing 30 songs in all) released simultaneously on September 16, 1991. Final delays, while Bill Price mixed the tapes and Axl added finishing touches, led to at least nine official but postponed release dates, plus what in retrospect was the pure wishful thinking of plans like 'Spring 1991'...

Whatever, when finally unleashed, the albums displayed a much-matured Guns N' Roses with songs spanning a kaleidoscope of styles and textures. Axl in particular had apparently worked hard on developing his piano playing and the band's slower, balladic, abilities. Not everyone liked it, but they all seemed to buy it as, come 1993 – despite initial assurances that the two records were separate entities – Geffen could boast a combined worldwide sales total of 17 million units for the pair.

To promote the albums, the band began the major arena 'Get In The Ring Motherfucker' tour in the USA in May, with a line-up expanded to include a three-piece horn-section, two girl backing singers and a second keyboard player. When GN'R headlined Wembley Stadium on

August 31, '91, many considered this bloated cast to have moved to far from their raw rock 'n' roll roots. Foremost among them was Izzy Stradlin', who quit the band shortly after the Wembley date. (Izzy laid low for about a year, then re-emerged in 1992 fronting the Ju-Ju Hounds). He also said he had grown tired of Axl's unpredictable nature – arriving late for shows and sometimes leaving early. The latter trend had sparked riots in St Louis in July '91 and would again in Montreal in August '92, whilst the band toured with Metallica.

Dave Navarro of Jane's Addiction was the first rumoured replacement for Stradlin', with Rose Tattoo men Mick Cocks and Peter Wells also rumoured, but the final choice was Gilby Clarke, formerly of LA band Kill For Thrills. Initially hired as a touring guitarist, he eventually appeared to be more of a permanent member, although whether he would write and record with the band remains to be seen.

As the mammoth world tour wound to an end in the summer of 1993, Guns N' Roses dispensed with the sidemen and stripped their line-up down to the bone once again. Whether it restored their status as The Most Dangerous Band In The World was open to debate, but few would contest their status as the biggest.

ALBUMS/EPS

LIVE ?!*@ LIKE A SUICIDE (Uzi Suicide, 1986 – KKKK) *"The sleaziest record to come out of Smog Angeles since Mötley Crüe's 'Too Fast For Love'... What a scorcher..."* – Kerrang! 138, January 22-February 4, 1987

APPETITE FOR DESTRUCTION (Geffen, 1987 – KKKKK) *"Rock 'n' roll is being wrestled from the hands of the bland, the jaded, the tired, the worn, and thrust back into the hands of the real raunch rebels."* – Kerrang! 151, July 23-August 5, 1987

GN'R LIES (Geffen, 1988 – KKKK) *"The live numbers... hit home hard and low. We're talking down in the gutter... The change of mood, four acoustically dominated numbers owe one hell of a lot to those original bad boys, the Stones."* – Kerrang! 216, December 3, 1988

USE YOUR ILLUSION I/USE YOUR ILLUSION II *(Geffen, 1991 – KKKKK) "Comparable, but not equal to the Rolling Stones' classic double 'Exile On Main Street'. Too many songs isn't such a bad thing, but were the best of these two albums put into one double set, Guns N' Roses might just have wound up with the greatest rock 'n' roll album ever made." – Kerrang! 359, September 21, 1991*

GWAR

USA, eight-(at least!)-piece
(eight million BC-present)

SOONER OR later, GWAR were bound to happen. Led by Oderus Urungus, they claim to have come from another planet though their abode on earth is Antarctica. Live, they decapitate politicians, sever limbs, eat brains, sodomise a priest with a large crucifix, shoot a

GRATUITOUSLY LARGE pic of GWAR (note gratuitously large fish between legs of gentleman in foreground)

policeman in the face, cover their audience in blood and torrents of green semen... In short, GWAR are very badly behaved and their first UK tour ground to a halt after just three dates as they were banned from everywhere else!

In actual fact, GWAR (apparently short for God What A Racket) are a bunch of art students who since 1984 have displayed an unhealthy interest in stage blood, gunge and making gruesome costumes. They also have a magnificent sense of humour as when taken to court in the States over their alledged use of a large (working) penis stage-prop, they claimed the offending item was in fact a fish! Somewhat astonishingly, some of their Splatter Rock tunes are remarkably good.

Recommended album:
SCUMDOGS OF THE UNIVERSE *(Master, 1990 – KKK)*

USA, six-piece (1987-1990)

FORMED IN Florida and originally featuring a line-up which included former Pat Travers bassist Mars Cowling, Gypsy Queen was purely a vehicle for the talents of identical twin sisters, Pam and Paula Mattioli, who, prior to appearing at the Reading Festival and at the Marquee in August of 1987, had the distinction of appearing topless in an issue of Playboy, although the duo had actually turned down the opportunity of a full frontal centrefold!

Signed to the French independent Loop label, media hype gave them more than the usual 15 minutes of fame. Having replaced the entire band by 1988, legal battles ensued which kept the Mattioli twins well and truly out of the picture, the pair not popping up again until 1992, although going under the handle of Cell Mates and signed to Scotti Brothers.

Recommended album:
GYPSY QUEEN *(Loop, 1987 – KKKK)*

Sammy HAGAR

USA, solo artist (1975-1987)

BEFORE HE ever turned his tonsils to titivate Van Halen's 'Jump' *et al* (1985-present), Sammy Hagar was a solo star in his own right. Quite rightly too: whilst with Montrose he had made one of the best HM records ever, and without them he was a Bay Area big noise who had a mouth that could sing as well as it could slag his rivals (ironically, Dave Lee Roth was his favourite target).

Prior to stepping into the latter's shoes in '85, curly-topped Hagar made eight studio albums under his own name beginning with the unusually modest 'Nine On A Ten Scale' (Capitol '76). Live shows, including some Montrose classics, were much stronger. As long ago as 1977, when he released his second album, 'Red', Hagar admitted his penchant for all things, er... red. He's always been in love with fast cars, too, particularly his Trans-Am, which he once wrote a song about.

In 1981, he sang the title-track to the animated sci-fi/fantasy movie 'Heavy Metal'; ironic, considering on record his music was often more Soul than HM – f'rinstance, Hagar covered Otis Redding's '(Sittin' On) The Dock Of The Bay' when Michael Bolton still had hair. In 1984 he made 'Through The Fire' with the aborted supergroup, HSAS (Hagar plus Neal Schon of Journey; Kenny Aaronson, ex-Billy Squier bass; and Michael Shrieve, ex-Santana, drums)... but it was not until a year later and his move into the ranks of Van Halen that his name became famous on an international scale. Since then, Hagar has released one more record, an eponymous affair on Geffen in '87 and further solo outings cannot be ruled out.

Recommended albums:
ALL NIGHT LONG *(Capitol, 1978 – KKKKK) live LP*
LOUD AND CLEAR *(Capitol, 1980 – KKKKK) ...re-release of 'All Night Long' with extra track*
DANGER ZONE *(Capitol, 1980 – KKKK)*

HANDSOME BEASTS

UK, four-piece, (1980-1987)

IRONICALLY NAMED, lower division NWOBHM act from Wolverhampton fronted by the original fat bastard, Garry Dalloway.
Recommended album (for fans of cellulite only):
BESTIALITY *(Heavy Metal Records, 1981 – KK)*

HANOI ROCKS

Finland, five-piece (1980-1985)

STRANGE BOYS. 'Hanoi', as one would affectionately refer to 'em, were a buncha fun-lovin', life-livin' punks from Finland, with an epileptic sound which encapsulated the Stones, Damned, Japan, Clash, Alice Cooper and the New York Dolls (etc!). Fronted by the

MICHAEL MONROE in Hanoi Rocks days: impossibly beautiful...

'impossibly beautiful' Mike Monroe, and with Frankenstein tunes stitched together by flashin' psychedelic axe-slinger Andy McCoy, Hanoi Rocks were an almost too perfect glam-sleaze-rock 'n' roll dream. A dream that a lovable rogue hailing from the Isle Of Wight called Razzle craved a slice of after seeing 'em open a bill headlined by the Lords Of The New Church at a London gig in '82. That dream, of course, turned into a nightmare. Razzle blagged his way onto the Hanoi drumstool, his thug personality and designer lingo completely rubbin' off on his band-mates, but during their ill-fated US tour of '84 Razzle lost his life. Razzle (real name Nicholas Dingley) was a passenger in a car driven by the then Mötley Crüe frontman Vince Neil which was involved in an accident caused by an intoxicated Neil.

It was a sobering awakening for the band who revelled in living on the edge. Hanoi Rocks limped on listlessly for a while after the tragedy, but it was testament to the importance of Razzle as a band member and character, along with reported in-band bickering and restlesssness, that the hotly-tipped band eventually went their separate ways after just four studio albums. Like the 'Dolls, a place in the annals of rock notoriety remains Hanoi Rocks' sole reward.

Recommended albums:
BACK TO MYSTERY CITY *(Lick, 1983 –*
KKKKK)
TWO STEPS FROM THE MOVE *(CBS, 1984 –*
KKKKK)

Randy HANSEN

USA, guitarist, (1980-present)
JIMI HENDRIX copyist who once impressed Ritchie Blackmore but annoyed the shit out of everyone else. Hansen doesn't appear to have an original thought in his head but can reproduce 'Axis: Bold As Love' at the drop of a hat, and better than most.
Recommended in the event of all Jimi Hendrix albums mysteriously disappearing from Earth:
RANDY HANSEN *(EMI, 1980 – KKK)*

HARD-ONS

Australia, three-piece (1984-present)
A BASICALLY good bunch of Summer-lovin' melodic hardcore rock 'n' rollers, hampered

only by continually dodgy production jobs, the Hard-Ons certainly know a tuneful song when they sing one. Unfortunately, the last thing heard of them was a rather pointless cover of 'Let There Be Rock' with Henry Rollins.
Recommended album:
YUMMY! *(Vinyl Solution, 1991 – KKKK)*

HARLOW

USA, five-piece (1988-1990)
STUDIO PROJECT turned short-lived band based around the stunning vocals of Teresa Straley. Touring band featured AOR journeymen Kevin Valentine (drums), Tommy Thayer (guitar), Todd Jensen (bass) and Tommy Rude (keyboards), the one LP featured stunningly powerful Heart-meets-Led Zeppelin style rock.
Recommended:
HARLOW *(Reprise, 1990 – KKKK)*

HAWKWIND

UK, anything up to 10-piece (1969-present)
THE ORIGINAL psychedelic space cadets who since 1970's eponymous debut, have been touching down on planet earth to put out more albums than you could ever possibly listen to! I mean, these people have a bigger back catalogue than Freemans...

Hawkwind's music varies from being dismal hippy nonsense to being really quite splendid, and as a result their live shows can either be tedious beyond belief or totally awe inspiring. Probably the only person who hasn't been in the band is your mum (although they did feature a buxom, scantily-clad young dancing wench called Stacia in the mid-'70s). Most notable ex-Hawklords include: Lemmy, who was thrown out in 1975 having been caught at US customs in possession of amphetamine sulphate and went on to form Motörhead; Robert Calvert, who wrote many a classic Hawktune and had a memorable solo career before his untimely death in 1988; and Nik Turner, who was barking mad, occasionally dressed up like a frog and later went on to form Inner City Unit. For best results witness Hawkwind at a free festival whilst completely out of your mind...

Recommended Hawkwind albums:
SPACE RITUAL *(United Artists, 1973 – KKKK)*
Or any of the other four LPs 1971-1975 with Lemmy on 'em. Just ask an old hippy...

Dokken, Quiet Riot, Night Ranger, Spinal Tap, Rough Cutt etc...
Recommended album:
HEAR 'N AID *(Vertigo, 1986 – KKK)*

HEADBANGERS BALL

UK, satellite rock show (1988-present)
ORIGINALLY BASED on the massive American MTV show of the same name, the weekly two-and-a-half hour programme has become a firm favourite with European rock fans. The show has been produced and presented by Vanessa Warwick since going on-line five years ago, and the show is now beamed into 46 million homes across 29 European territories.

The show's format is obviously led by rock videos but also features tour dates, general news and lifestyle soundbites. In 1993 the main theme music and advertising idents were written by two young British bands – New England and Tarrasque – underlining MTV's claims to support young talent wherever possible.

HEADGIRL

UK, seven-piece (1987)
THE AMALGAMATED members of Motörhead and Girlschool – no surprises there! The surprise was they had a Number Five UK hit with their cover of Johnny Kid And The Pirates' 'Please Don't Touch', and appeared on 'Top Of The Pops' in full gangster gear to promote it. The hit was the A-side of their sole recording, the 'St Valentines Day Massacre' EP.

HEAR 'N AID

Global, 40-piece (1986)
CHARITY FOUNDATION set up in the wake of Live-Aid by Ronnie James Dio to raise funds for African famine relief.

A compilation album was preceeded by a single, 'Stars', which featured Dio plus Rob Halford, Ted Nugent, Yngwie Malmsteen, Neal Schon, Tommy Aldridge, Rudy Sarzo, Carmine Apice, Craig Goldy, assorted members of Mötley Crüe, W.A.S.P., Blue Öyster Cult, Queensrÿche, Iron Maiden, Y&T, Twisted Sister,

HEART

USA, five-piece (1974-present)
HEART'S REBIRTH in the mid-'80s was a spectacular affair. Some might argue that the glossy, folk-tinged arena colossus was a calculated stab at mainstream chart sales, but Heart had already endured a decade of enormous cult success around the globe. No one could possibly begrudge Heart their eventual stardom.

The band's story is a tale of grace under pressure. No one could predict that the small, Vancouver-based bar band would blossom so productively over the years. At first, they survived for one week on a sack of rice and some eggs. It was not a glamorous existence. At the same time, however, it was an existence that toughened Heart and prepared them for the years of gruelling roadwork they would later undertake without one word of complaint.

Heart are undoubtedly led from the front by Ann Wilson. Over the years the raven-haired and happily-spoken singer has come to be regarded as the finest rock vocalist since the heyday of Robert Plant. At the band's inception, Ann's younger sister, Nancy, was dating guitarist Roger Fisher. Over the years Nancy's own guitar virtuosity has become legendary. No one, it is said by many, can hold a candle to Nancy's mandolin expertise!

Early photos of Heart are hilarious. Their Folk Rock image of cheesecloth, tambourines and big acoustic guitars looks dated, but Heart's attention to style was largely constructed by a new record label in the mid-'80s.

Instead, Heart concentrated on their live show and some veritable rock masterpieces. The appeal of their sensual, husky undertow eclipsed the music's occasional flaws, and word

ANN and NANCY WILSON:
setting hearts a-pounding

spread like wildfire. It wasn't long before North America fell in love with the two Heart sisters.

The band's early albums for the Portrait label were bold and imaginative affairs. Just as able to pen such mighty riffs as 'Crazy On You' and 'Barracuda' as they were to incoporate the more melancholic moments, Heart's music painted a rich, ethereal tapestry.

Constantly tagged a 'relationship band', Ann and Nancy kept the sentiments sharp and simple. They were traditional craftswomen, raised on The Beatles and Led Zeppelin, and to this day are unafraid to belt out their own versions of 'Helter Skelter' and 'Rock And Roll'. In the early days of Heart, it was the uplifting acoustic refrains of 'Dreamboat Annie' and 'Mistral Wind' which convinced the crowds of Ann Wilson's vocal magic.

Friends of both Queen and Fleetwood Mac, the band rapidly came to embody the heaviness of the former and the latter's smouldering emotion. By the very early '80s, with their seemingly tireless touring schedules igniting arenas and stadiums around the globe, Heart were as big as they were ever going to get in their current state. After two relatively tame records for Epic, however, in 1984 Heart were about to be drastically re-invented.

Constantly dogged by personnel and legal wrangles, Heart finally switched to the Capitol label with only Ann and Nancy remaining from the early days up in the Vancouver bars. They signed, by their own admission, at an all-time low.

"We were basically in Death Valley!" Ann remembered. "It was a case of fight on or die, so we rolled up our sleeves and said, 'Okay!'."

The eponymous album for Capitol would rapidly become Heart's most successful. With the help of outside songwriters (Holly Knight, Bernie Taupin, Sue Ennis, Jim Vallance, uncle Tom Cobley and all) and an updated image to set teenage hearts a-pounding, the band became the proverbial Overnight Sensation!

'Heart' was less folky, more polished and punchier than ever before. Again, it joined Ann's consummate genius as a rock balladeer to the band's love of classic hard rock, creating an album that quickly found a home on MTV and daytime rock radio. It was undeniably a commercial masterstroke.

Since the album's release, Heart have continued to rework the formula with varying degrees of success. The band's Platinum status, some might argue, has sapped the band of their original diversity and gentle good nature. On the European 'Bad Animals' tour, the press were perturbed at the band's no-photo policy and took it as a sign of growing paranoia within the band's close-knit camp. Similarly, there were reports of friction in Ann and Nancy's private lives, but Heart continue to present one of rock's most endearing live shows nonetheless.

Off-stage, Ann and Nancy are quiet, endearing and genial. Romantics at heart despite the turmoil of several unhappy relationships, both sisters enjoy the solitude of their success. They are not showbiz party vultures in any way, but respected throughout the industry for their longevity and talent.

The '90s will prove a tough decade for Heart. Whether they re-invent themselves again to accommodate the passing of time, or revert to their traditional origins remains to be seen. Whatever the decision, however, Heart have already left a legacy of supreme soft rock.

ALBUMS

DREAMBOAT ANNIE (Mushroom, 1976 – KKKKK) A deceptively gentle debut with moments of inspired melodic riffing. Worth buying for 'Crazy On You' and 'Magic Man' alone.

LITTLE QUEEN (Portrait, 1977 – KKK) An underwhelming successor to their debut, but the album's standout track – 'Barracuda' – was an immediate classic.

MAGAZINE (Mushroom, 1978 – KKK) A record released despite Heart's legal action against the label. It was issued with a disclaimer from the band. Part live, it was a commercial success nonetheless.

DOG AND BUTTERFLY (Portrait, 1979 – KKKKK) A landmark record that finally captured the band's myriad of moods and textures. A classic.

BEBE LE STRANGE (Portrait, 1980 – KKK) Hastily recorded but still a million-plus seller. The first album to be toured without guitarist Roger Fisher.

GREATEST HITS/LIVE (Portrait, 1981 – KKKK) Patchy record of the band's career to date, but the weaker moments are completely negated with such stunning vocal showcases as the live versions of 'Mistral Wind' and 'Unchained Melody'.

PRIVATE AUDITION (Portrait, 1982 – KKKK) "Off with the jeans and on with the party frocks! This is not a Heavy Metal album but definitely a fine rock record." – Kerrang! 18, June 17-30, 1982)

PASSION WORKS (Epic, 1983 – KKKK) "Finds the band leaning firmly back towards their older hard rock direction." – Kerrang! 52, October 6-19, 1983

HEART (Capitol, 1985 – KKKKK) "The real excitement lies in the fact that Heart haven't forgotten how to rock out. Considering that their last great rock song was 'Barracuda', it's been a long time." – Kerrang! 96, June 13-26, 1985

BAD ANIMALS (Capitol, 1987 – KKKKK) "Heart have delivered another 10 tracks of lathered luxury. Ann's spine-tingling vocals help to weave every song into a joyous, wholesome bag stuffed with brittle beauty" – Kerrang! 148, June 11-24, 1987

BRIGADE (Captiol, 1990 – KKK) "Genuinely, unashamedly soft, and as close a representation of female fragility as anything Kate Bush has produced. Delightfully feminine." – Kerrang! 283, March 31, 1990

ROCK THE HOUSE LIVE (Capitol, 1991 – KKK) "Hurt me! Hurt me! Hurt me! Yep, I'm still stuck on Ann – an' maybe my underpants too!" – Kerrang! 360, September 28, 1991

IN THEIR OWN WORDS...

"When the '80s began, record companies were looking for fresh young bands. They told us, 'You pay our light bills!'." – Nancy Wilson, Kerrang! 281, March 17, 1990

"Actually, some of the new kids are so young they really don't identify with the old stuff at all. They go out and buy a beer when we play those songs!" – Ann Wilson, Kerrang! 176, February 27, 1988

"When you're on the road, travelling from town to town, and you check into a new hotel, all the fresh, perky guests start staring at you as if you were a creature from another planet..." – Ann Wilson, Kerrang! 149, June 25-July 8, 1987

"Am I a pin-up?" – Nancy Wilson, Kerrang! 124, July 10-23, 1986

"Hey, rock 'n' fuckin' roll! It keeps us on our toes and makes things interesting!" –- Ann Wilson, Kerrang! 108, November 28-December 11, 1985

"C'mon, let's face it... Heart are a safe band, kids!" – Ann Wilson, Kerrang! Mega Metal 14, 1989

"Personally, I think there's something about being fashionable that is pathetic!" – Ann Wilson, Kerrang! Mega Metal 14, 1989

"In a way, Heart had nothing to do with public opinion." – Ann Wilson, Kerrang! Mega Metal 14, 1989

HEART

HEAVY BONES

USA, four-piece (1990-present)
BORN FROM the ashes of the sadly ignored Cats In Boots, HB's debut featured Booties' singer Joel Ellis as well as journeyman drummer Frankie Banali. After a semi-frantic first wave of interest, the band seemed to disappear faster than free beer...
Recommended album:
HEAVY BONES *(Reprise, 1992 – KKK)*

HEAVY METAL KIDS

UK, five-piece (1974-1978)
NEVER REALLY lived up to their name, purveying instead rather raucous yob rock. Star of the band was jack-the-lad singer Gary Holton (later to find fame as Wayne in the 'Auf Wiedersehen Pet' TV series), who died in '85. Other members included keysmen Danny Peyronel (later in UFO) and John Sinclair (his replacement, later in Uriah Heep).
Recommended album:
ANVIL CHORUS *(Atlantic, 1975 – KKK)*

HEAVY PETTIN'

Scotland, five-piece (1981-1988)
PERHAPS THE most memorable thing about this Glasgow mob is the very thing most of you would like to forget... That once their HM career began to wane, they entered the Eurovision Song Contest with a ditty called 'Romeo'. HARGH! No Bucks Fizz-style triumph for the boys, thank God, but it really did end their career with a wet fart.

Waaaay back in the early '80s, however, HP were being bandied about by all and sundry as The Next Very Big Thing. After one single on Neat in '82, Polydor signed 'em up, and released their spiffo Mack-produced debut LP 'Lettin' Loose' ('83). Testosterone-loaded Heavy Pettin's featured trademark was Hamie's squeaky voice, which had a habit of

HAMIE: heavy poutin'?!

rising alarmingly at the end of every line like somebody had just pulled his zip up a bit too quickly. But their follow-up LP 'Rock Ain't Dead' ('85) strayed little from the path of the first but is most memorable for the line, *'Throw a party/Throw it my way!'*. They don't write 'em like that any more... And neither did HP come their farewell album 'The Big Band' (FM/Revolver, '89).
Recommended album:
LETTIN' LOOSE *(Polydor, 1983 – KKKK)*

HELIX

Canada, five-piece (1978-present)
HELIX WERE virtually unknown outside of Canadian bar-rooms, save for a couple of average albums on the H&S label, until signing to Capitol and unleashing 'No Rest For The Wicked' on an unsuspecting public. Thereafter they became a party band for all seasons, with vocalist Brian Vollmer the court jester.

But Helix failed to really capitilise on their success. Dropped by Capitol after two further albums they returned to indie labels and Canadian bars only to suffer more wretched luck, with the tragic loss of guitarist Paul Hackman in a horrific tour bus accident during 1992.
Wickedly recommended:
NO REST FOR THE WICKED *(Capitol, 1983 – KKKK)*

HELLBASTARD

UK, four-piece (1984-present)
THE SUPERBLY named Hellbastard began life as bringers of Metalpunk filth, with a riffy debut album called 'Heading For Eternal Darkness', and some appreciation from John Peel.

After their highly limited 'They Brought Death' EP, this Newcastle upon Tyne band moved to Earache Records and produced the unremarkable 'Natural Order'; an album closer to clean Thrash, and further from what you might call interesting.
Recommended album:
HEADING FOR ETERNAL DARKNESS *(Meantime, 1988 – KKKK)*

HELLHAMMER

Switzerland, three-piece (1982-1984)
EVOLVED INTO Celtic Frost. Led by Satanic
Slaughter (aka Tom G Warrior, vocals) with
Savage Damage (aka Martin Ain, bass) and
Bloodhunter (aka Bruce Day, drums) plus a
guitarist as sideman only. With demonic vocals
and bass-heavy sound, they practically invented
Death Metal – or sounded like shit, depending
on your point of view. Best known for some very
collectable demos, but did make one EP...
Recommended EP:
APOCALYPTIC RAIDS *(Noise, 1984 – K or
KKKKK)*

HELLION

USA, five-piece (1982-1988)
TRADITIONAL STYLED Metal whose first demo
was produced by Ronnie Dio. Varying line-ups
all led by vocalist Ann Boleyn, one time publicist
and DJ who made only one album and has
since become head of New Renaissance
records.
Recommended EP:
HELLION *(Music For Nations, 1984 – KKK)*

HELLOWEEN

Germany, five-piece (1984-present)
SMILEY PUMPKINS were Helloween's chosen
brand of imagery by the time they came to their
second and best album, 'Keeper Of The Seven
Keys Part One' in 1987. Before that, was 'Walls
Of Jericho' – a Speed/Thrash opus which the
band soon grew away from.
'Keeper Of The Seven Keys Part Two' saw the
band achieve fair success – such as winning the
opening slot at Donington in 1988, coinciding
with their 'Dr Stein' single. But after that,
guitarist Kai Hansen went off to form his own
band, Gamma Ray, while his former mates lost
ground with 'Pink Bubbles Go Ape', then went a
bit more pop-meets-Queensrÿche with the 1993
studio album, 'Chameleon'.
Recommended album:
KEEPER OF THE SEVEN KEYS PART ONE
(Noise, 1987 – KKKK)

HELMET

US, four-piece (1990-present)
COLLEGE BOY nice-guys with a penchant for
high-discipline grind-rock, Helmet issued their
first album, saucily entitled 'Strap It On', in
1991, through Amphetamine Reptile Records.
'Meantime' was the far superior follow-up for
a major label, rippling with precise power and a
certain alternative edge.
Recommended album:
MEANTIME *(Interscope, 1992 – KKKK)*

Jimi HENDRIX

*USA, guitarist (November 27, 1942
-September 18, 1970)*
WORLD'S GREATEST. Invented techniques few
today are able even to copy. Nuff said.
Essential albums:
ARE YOU EXPERIENCED *(Track/Polydor, 1967
– KKKKK)*
AXIS: BOLD AS LOVE *(Track/Polydor, 1968 –
KKKKK)*
ELECTRIC LADYLAND *(Track/Polydor, 1968 –
KKKKK)*
SMASH HITS *(Track/Polydor, 1969 – KKKKK)*
BAND OF GYPSYS *(Track/Polydor, 1970 –
KKKKK)*

JIMI HENDRIX

HOLLYWOOD BRATS

UK, five-piece (1973-1975)
BRITAIN'S ANSWER to the New York Dolls? The should-be-legendary Brats were likewise dishing out souped-up Stonesy rock 'n' roll. Their eponymous debut album (originally titled 'Grown Up Wrong'), was not released in Britain until after their demise, and a reunion elpee 'What Ever Happened To...' ('86) only achieved a European release.
Recommended album:
HOLLYWOOD BRATS *(Cherry Red, 1980 – KKKKK)*

HONEYMOON SUITE

Canada, five-piece (1982-present)
WITH ALBUM cover concepts that played on their Niagara Falls roots (the Canadian side being North America's answer to Gretna Green), Honeymoon Suite swept to cult stardom with a kind of New Wave-tinged AOR, that got progressively heavier with each outing but peaked with the sophomore release, 'The Big Prize'. This band never sounded as classy on the brace of records since.
Recommended with wedding bells attached:
THE BIG PRIZE *(WEA, 1986 – KKKKK)*

HORSE (LONDON)

UK, four-piece (1988-1990)
SUPER-BASIC post-Zodiac Grebo Blues outfit which collapsed under the weight of just one too many Harley Davidson clichés. Despite early pub promise, they eventually lost out to The Almighty and could never regain a foothold.
Highly recommended for bozos only:
DIESEL POWER *(Wild West, 1989 – KKK)*

HOUSE OF LORDS

USA, five-piece (1988-1992)
GRAND AND ambitious outfit formed from the ashes of Giuffria, House Of Lords represented the first signing to Gene Simmons' custom record label. Mainman Gregg Giuffria, along with one-time LA Rocks vocalist James Christian, often struggled to keep the band together yet still managed to record three perfectly respectable Pomp Rock albums in their time. The debut is a classic of the genre, more grandiose than Giuffria *or* Angel.

Following the band's demise, Giuffria reportedly cut his hair and went to work in the A&R department of RCA/BMG in LA.
Majestically recommended debut:
HOUSE OF LORDS *(Simmons/BMG, 1988 – KKKKK)*

HUGHES/THRALL

USA/UK, two-piece (1982)
MAGNIFICENT PAIRING of Glenn Hughes (ex-Deep Purple, bass/vocals) and Pat Thrall (ex-Pat Travers, guitar) backed by Frankie Banali (drums). Clash of egos of the two stars prevented a second album ever being made but the one they did make was an absolute corker.
Highly recommended album:
HUGHES-THRALL *(Epic, 1982 – KKKKK)*

Ian HUNTER

UK, solo artist (1975-present)
THE DUDE in the shades! 'Untah an' Ronno (that's the late great one-time Bowie guitarist Mick Ronson, to you!) ejected their considerable talents from Mott The Hoople in late '74 and worked together on Ian's '75 eponymous solo, which contained Hunter's only British hit to date 'Once Bitten Twice Shy' (since covered by Great White). Ronson teamed-up on-and-off with Hunter since then, in a career which for Hunter has been decidedly hit and miss – the only real (and well deserved) success since his debut being for the lyrical masterpiece 'All American Alien Boy' ('76), and the well balanced rock of 'You're Never Alone With A Schizophrenic' ('79). Hunter's 1988 release 'YUI Orta' saw his ol' mate Ronson's return (with equal billing too!), yet despite a UK tour, the record did zilch.
Recommended albums:
IAN HUNTER *(CBS, 1975 – KKKK)*
WELCOME TO THE CLUB *(Chrysalis, 1980 – KKKK) Live double!*

HURRICANE

USA, four-piece (1986-1991)
LA BRAT pack Power Metal band formed by
Robert Sarzo and Tony Cavazo – kid brothers of
Rudi (ex-Whitesnake) and Carlos (ex-Quiet Riot)
respectively. Made a mini LP ('86) and two full
length ones of unadventurous but entertaining
rock with good haircuts. One for the ladies...
Recommended album:
OVER THE EDGE *(Enigma, 1988 – KKKK)*

HUSKER DU

USA, three-piece (1979-1986)
WITH HINDSIGHT, Bob Mould (vocals/guitar),
Grant Hart (drums) and Greg Norton (bass),
have been called the Godfathers Of Grunge.
Signed to US Hardcore label SST, their mix of
heavy guitars, pop melodies and vocal
harmonies was certainly a blueprint for legions
of bands throughout the '80s. Amazingly prolifc,
Hüsker Dü released eight albums – two of those
doubles – in their seven year career. Early
releases, such as aptly-titled 'Land Speed
Record', consisted of 100mph Hardcore but
Hüsker Dü mellowed with each release resulting
in a major deal with Warners for their last two
LPs. Split in '86, one of the reasons being Hart's
heroin addiction. Mould eventually returned with
Sugar.
Recommended album:
FLIP YOUR WIG *(SST, 1985 – KKKK)*

ICON

USA, five-piece (1983-1990)

TAKEN UNDER the wing of Shrapnel Records boss Mike Varney under their original monicker of The Schoolboys, the Phoenix-based quintet were snapped up by Capitol thanks to Varney's enthusiasm and, whilst the debut album was above average, the follow-up was even better: perfect radio rock. Sadly, despite a change of vocalist and record label, Icon just didn't do it for the most record buyers who must have had more money than sense.

Criminally ignored and underrated album:
NIGHT OF THE CRIME *(Capitol, 1985 – KKKKK)*

Chris IMPELLITERI

USA, guitarist (1986-present)

BETTER THAN average, Connecticut-born classically-trained widdler whose band once included Graham Bonnet (vocals) and Pat Torpey (now Mr Big, drums).

Recommended album:
STAND IN LINE *(Music For Nations, 1988 – KKK)*

INFECTIOUS GROOVES

USA, five-piece (1992-present)

SLOPPY FUNKY side project led by Suicidal Tendencies' Mike Muir (vocals) and Robert Trujillo (bass). Originally featured Jane's Addiction drummer Stephen Perkins too, but the band had lost him – and their way – come second album 'Sarsippius' Ark' (Epic, '93).

Recommended album:
THE PLAGUE THAT MAKES YOUR BOOTY MOVE... IT'S THE INFECTIOUS GROOVES *(Epic, 1992 – KKK)*

IRON BUTTERFLY

USA, five-piece (1967-1975)

OFTEN TOUTED as the original American Heavy Metal band. But although their debut album was even called 'Heavy' (Atlantic '67), the emphasis was usually more on organ than guitar. Finest hour was undoubtedly the 17 minute title-track of second LP 'In-A-Gadda-Da-Vida' – covered by Slayer in a happily more truncated form on the 'Less Than Zero' movie soundtrack.

Recommended album:
IN-A-GADDA-DA-VIDA *(Atlantic, 1968 – KKKK)*

IRON MAIDEN

UK, five-piece (1976-present)

TAKING HIS cue from childhood heroes like UFO and, especially, Judas Priest, in 1976, bassist Steve Harris set about making a HM legend of his own. Starting at the very height of the Punk explosion, when most of the spiky-topped, safety-pin totin' upstarts were going out of their way to kill off heavy rock, launching Iron Maiden looked like a suicide mission – but the first line-up shared an honest, street-level attitude with their Punk counterparts, and that attitude won them respect from the media and a fan-base of youngsters often not much younger than the band. Ultimately, it earned Iron Maiden the status of HM giants with success and fame all over the world.

The roots of Iron Maiden lie in pub bands called Gypsy's Kiss and Smiler, both featuring a young Harris (born Leytonstone, East London, March 12, 1957) perhaps still wondering whether to pursue his dream of becoming a professional footballer with West Ham United. Maiden actually debuted at the Cart & Horses pub in Stratford in May '76, but with the first of many shortlived line-ups that only began in earnest when Harris enlisted guitarist Dave Murray (born December 23, 1958), singer Paul Di'Anno (born May 17, 1959) and drummer Doug Sampson. Gigging mainly around London, they gained a sizeable following, but no real record company interest. On December 30, '78, they recorded a demo featuring 'Iron Maiden', 'Prowler' and 'Strange World'. This they sent to DJ Neal Kay who played it at his (by then) legendary North London HM disco, the Kingsbury Bandwagon Soundhouse. The tapes were an instant hit and came to the attention of

the rest of the UK through the club's charts, which were published regularly in *Sounds* magazine. *Sounds* championed Punk, but also identified a groundswell movement, which it christened the New Wave Of British Heavy Metal, of bands attempting just what Maiden were doing. Maiden typified the independent spirit of the movement when they pressed up their demo themselves as a seven inch EP called 'The Soundhouse Tapes', released November 1979. By that time, former agent Rod Smallwood had become their manager.

Smallwood, a bold-as-brass Yorkshireman who says what he likes and likes what he says, would eventually become almost as famous as the band themselves, and certainly as big a part of the set-up as their slightly less handsome

STEVE HARRIS: the trooper in full flight

mascot, Eddie. After featuring on numerous pieces of artwork, Eddie (at first a roadie wearing a false head) first joined the band on stage in 1980. Originally, his face was part of the logo, mounted behind the drumkit on stage, and nicknamed Eddie The 'Ead. But we digress...

The EP, sold mainly through mail order, plus the band's growing media profile finally attracted the attention of EMI. Before they signed to the label proper, EMI released two Maiden tracks, featuring additional guitarist Tony Parsons, on the 'Metal For Muthas' compilation. By the time the now five-piece line-up recorded their debut single and eponymous album for the label, Parsons had been replaced by Dennis Stratton, and Sampson by Clive Burr. The single, 'Running Free', reached Number 34 in the UK charts and earned the band a slot on 'Top Of The Pops' in February '80, where Maiden became the first band to play live on the then still very influential show since The Who in '73. From this point on, the band took off very quickly. Their eponymous debut came out in

April and in that same year, they went on to support Kiss in Europe and Judas Priest in the UK, headline their own show at the now-closed 4,000-plus capacity Rainbow Theatre, and appear at the Reading Festival.

In October, Stratton was fired and replaced by Adrian Smith (born February 27, 1957), a long-term friend of Murray's. By the end of '80, Maiden had three Top 40 singles under their belts and were well fired up to make their second album, 'Killers'. This record made a dent on the American charts and also opened up the Japanese market. Whilst there, they recorded tracks for the live 'Maiden Japan' EP, released in November '81. But before its release, in August '81, the band finally grew tired of Di'Anno's enthusiasm for artificial stimulants and opted to replace him with Samson singer Bruce Dickinson. In that band he had adopted

BRUCE DICKINSON

the moniker Bruce Bruce, although his real name was Paul Bruce Dickinson (born August 7, 1958).

With Dickinson in the band, the group were able to step up a gear, his first two albums with them being arguably their finest – given production (by former Deep Purple producer Martin Birch) that was infinitely stronger than on their debut. These were 'Number Of The Beast' (released May '82) and 'Piece Of Mind' (May '83) – the latter featuring former Pat Travers and Trust drummer Nicko McBrain (born June 5, 1954) replacing Burr. 'Run To The Hills' (February '82, from '...Beast') began an uninterrupted string of UK Top 40 hits that continues to this day and couldn't solely be explained away by shrewd marketing – although Maiden have always led the field in terms of bonus cuts and multi-formats when it comes to such releases.

The next couple of studio albums – 'Powerslave' (November '84) and 'Somewhere In Time' (September '86) – didn't quite match the previous pair for consistency, but between them, the live double 'Live After Death' (October '85), was powerful enough. In retrospect,

IN THEIR OWN WORDS...

"Everyone seems to forget that Maiden were going for ages before we got a deal. We must have had 15 line-up changes before we signed with EMI because people... I mean, how many people realise that Thunderstick (of Samson) used to be our drummer?" – Steve Harris, Kerrang! 3, September, 1981

"(American radio's) taste in music is very puerile... People keep coming up to us and asking: 'When are you going to release a radio track?' and we say: 'We're not!'. We won't compromise, we'll just have to change the airplay." – Bruce Dickinson, Kerrang! 25, September 23-October 6, 1982

"We're really proud of the way we've built our success because there aren't many bands who've broken it in the way we have... Our punters are hard-core so we do what we do and if other people don't like it, then it's tough shit!' – Steve Harris, Kerrang! 76, September 6-19, 1984

"With a tour as long as that, we were all pretty knackered. To be honest, I didn't

pick up a guitar for four months after we got off tour..." – Steve Harris, Kerrang! 130, October 2-15, 1986

"There's probably nothing that Bruce couldn't sing if he put his mind to it, which enables me to write songs in any key, any style, any style, any rhythm..." –Steve Harris, Kerrang! 183, April 16, 1988

"If 'Number Of The Beast' brought HM properly into the 1980s, which I believe it did, then with 'Seventh Son Of A Seventh Son' I think we've shown the way for HM in the 1990's..." – Bruce Dickinson, Kerrang! 183, April 16, 1988

" 'Seventh Son...' has no story. It's about good and evil, Heaven and Hell, but isn't every Iron Maiden record?! What the fuck is the difference?!" – Bruce Dickinson

"If he can't give Maiden 100 per cent, then we don't want him in the band... In fact, if he backtracked now and said he wanted to stay, we probably wouldn't let him!" – Steve Harris, Kerrang! 441, May 1, 1993

IRON MAIDEN

though, the uniterrupted pattern of recording an album and then undertaking a massive world tour to promote it put the band under a strain that seemed reflected in their creative output. Such strains had, according to mainman Harris, been overcome by the time of 1988's 'Seventh Son Of A Seventh Son' opus, but many critics were less convinced by the album's conceptual leanings and started to write the band off as tired and outmoded. Four Top 10 UK singles from it, a record 107,000 attending Castle Donington's Monsters Of Rock Festival, and thousands more at Monsters shows on the Continent, begged to differ – and although the Donington day was overshadowed by the death of two fans, in terms of mass recognition it was a triumph for Maiden. A happier footnote to the day's tragedies came in October, when Maiden fan Gary Dobson, in a coma since being crushed at the festival, finally awoke after being

played a tape of his heroes...

A month later, the UK and European dates that followed turned out to be the last to feature Adrian Smith. In 1989, Maiden took a break. Smith made the ASaP album 'Silver And Gold', and Dickinson found time out to achieve a seventh ranking in Great Britain's domestic fencing rankings, write a book – 'Lord Iffy Boatrace' (published May '90) and write 'Bring Your Daughter To The Slaughter' for the soundtrack of 'Nightmare On Elm Street 5: The Dream Child'. The track later won a Golden Raspberry Award for the Worst Original Song but Harris was impressed enough to insist Dickinson not to include it on his April '90 solo album, 'Tattooed Millionaire', but save it for Maiden's forthcoming album.

Around that time, Smith – having had a taste of doing things his way with ASaP – decided not to continue with Maiden. A replacement was not difficult to find. His name was Janick Gers, formerly of White Spirit and Gillan, but most recently and significantly of Dickinson's own solo touring band. Gers made his unofficial live debut with the band when the rest of Maiden joined him and Bruce for an encore of 'The Trooper' at Dickinson's London's Astoria gig on June 27, 1990, but his first date proper with Maiden was at Southampton Mayflower September 20.

In October, Iron Maiden released their eighth studio album, 'No Prayer For The Dying'. On it, and the tour (with Wolfsbane opening) which followed, the band appeared to toughen their sound, apparently recharged by Gers' fresh input and enthusiasm. Extra dates at larger venues, when the band were supported by Anthrax, were slotted in before Christmas and Maiden looked to be fast returning to old form. The trend continued with the release of 'Fear Of The Dark'. Musically, times had changed, however, and in terms of tickets sales Maiden weren't able to match earlier glories. In the US, two or three night stints in single cities were a thing of the past. And, when the band headlined Donington for a second time in August '92, they pulled just 65,000 (admittedly with a weaker supporting bill than '88).

Nevertheless, the band were playing as well as at any time in their career and in March '93, on the eve of the release of the in-concert album 'A Real Live One', nothing could have shocked the faithful more than the announcement that Bruce Dickinson was to quit the band to pursue his solo career full-time and that the May UK dates would be his last with the band. The rest of Maiden were less than pleased but vowed to replace him and continue...

ALBUMS

IRON MAIDEN *(EMI, 1980 – KKKKK) Packed to the gills with Maiden klassiks, even though, as Harris often complains, it lacks a killer production.*
KILLERS *(EMI, 1981 – KKKK) Production was better, but sadly the songs weren't...*

THE NUMBER OF THE BEAST *(EMI, 1982 – KKKKK) "Polished but exciting... A thunderous set of performances..." – Kerrang! 13, April 8-21, 1982*

PIECE OF MIND *(EMI, 1983 – KKKK) "Generally good, sometimes great, though marred once or twice by an almost perverse pursuit of the downright mediocre." – Kerrang! 42, May 19-June 2, 1983*

POWERSLAVE *(EMI, 1984 – KKKK) "May one day be recognised as Iron Maiden's greatest phonographic achievement. It's a grower..." – Kerrang! 76, September 6-19, 1984*

LIVE AFTER DEATH *(EMI, 1985 – KKKKK) "The nearest that any person could get to being on an Iron Maiden world tour without actually leaving town." – Kerrang! 104, October 3-16, 1985*

SOMEWHERE IN TIME *(EMI, 1986 – KKK) "A very UP album. Two sides of pure energy that crackle and spit like a bonfire." – Kerrang! 129, September 18-October 1, 1986*

SEVENTH SON OF A SEVENTH SON *(EMI, 1988 – KKKK) "...Unified with a dramatic and engrossing theme, delivered with a confidence and enthusiasm often sought after and rarely achieved." – Kerrang! 183, April 16, 1988*

NO PRAYER FOR THE DYING *(EMI, 1990 – KKKK) "Maiden returning to their roots, getting heavier, rawer and tougher than at any time since (1983)..." – Kerrang! 309, September 29, 1990*

FEAR OF THE DARK *(EMI, 1992 – KKKK) "There's some who feel Maiden have passed their prime; have no such fear." – Kerrang! 391, May 9, 1992*

A REAL LIVE ONE *(EMI, 1993 – KKK) "A far better idea would have been one single gathering of the band's best tunes... It's ironic that (the forthcoming oldies set) 'A Real Dead One' will almost certainly exhibit more life.." – Kerrang! 433, March 6,1993*

JAGGED EDGE

UK, four-piece (1986-1991)

BAND FORMED by guitarist Myke Gray whose early line-ups had a revolving door policy. Signed to Polydor and Sanctuary Management (home of Iron Maiden) in 1990 with a line-up led by the excellent vocals of Swedish-born Matti Alfonzetti. But after a mini album, 'Trouble' ('90), and one full-length affair, Jagged Edge never achieved the success so many had tipped them for. Gray and drummer Fabio Del Rio went on to work with Bruce Dickinson.

Only album:
FUEL FOR YOUR SOUL *(Polydor, 1990 – KKK)*

JANE'S ADDICTION

USA, four-piece (1986-1991)

THE '80s were pretty dull until Jane's Addiction turned up. Nothing much was happening. Trad Metal was dying on its feet, having been replaced by Thrash Metal. Thrash was just as Trad but had dropped all the pose. Jane's Addiction were bright, colourful, confused... and just plain fucked. They were never meant to be a viable commercial alternative, but Europe saw Perry Farrell and found a leader.

Jane's Addiction was Farrell's band. The androgynous frontman was a spooky clown, a Metal Iggy Pop for the new generation. The tag of Art Rock was immediate.

The press loved Jane's Addiction as soon as the band's debut album appeared on the budding Triple X label. The press loved Jane's Addiction because they could use lots of interesting adjectives that were, frankly, inappropriate for the Trad Thrash scene.

The media tried to understand the incomprehensible, adding to the enigma that Farrell relished.

It wasn't, however, until 1988's major label debut, 'Nothing's Shocking', that Jane's Addiction found true greatness. It was an eerie, frazzled record, with cover art depicting siamese twins naked, their heads ablaze. The LP turned Gold.

The band's live shows became notorious. Attracting an audience of disillusioned travellers and rebellious middle-class drop-outs, Jane's Addiction were an accepted alternative.

Tall tales of drug and sex binges dogged the band, just like tall tales are *supposed* to dog a bunch of crusading individuals. Rumours suggested: Farrell was an avid collector of dead seagulls and suffering from AIDS, guitarist David Navarro was close to death through heroin abuse. Only one of the above is true.

In 1990, the band released 'Ritual De Lo Habitual' to enormous acclaim. It too, had a controversial cover: a photo of Farrell's lifesize sculpture of him, his girlfriend Casey and a.n. other innocently naked. It was banned. Instead, Farrell designed an alternative: a plain brown

PERRY FARRELL: androgynous frontman and spooky clown

wrapper with the First Amendment of the US Constitution (the bit about freedom of speech) printed on the front and a statement about Adolf Hitler on the back. There was an uneasy truce between Jane's Addiction and the corporate mainstream. They scored a major hit with the typically perverse 'Been Caught Stealing' single. There was happy talk of great things to come.

Then Farrell played his artistic ace. "In all likelihood, this is gonna be the last Jane's Addiction album. I've got ideas in my head about places I want to go and things I want to do, and they don't include Jane's Addiction."

The band dutifully toured 'Ritual De Lo Habitual' throughout 1990. In 1991 they split up. The enormous gap in the market was soon being plugged by the tiny Grunge labels of the Midwest. Jane's Addiction had made it okay to be a fuck-up.

Farrell's immediate plans for films, books and exhibitions were eclipsed by his talk of a cross-cultural touring festival. His aim was to unite rock cultures in the spirit of Woodstock, incorporating information stalls and fringe politics. It was an extraordinary gamble for Farrell, but caught the imagination of the world's media, nonetheless. Lollapalooza was a great idea. After two years the magic has soured considerably.

"The whole Lollapalooza tour is entertainment for the leisure class," sighed Soundgarden's Kim Thayil, during the second annual circus tour. "There's no pretending about that. All it is, is a guilt release for the establishment's kids. I'm tired of the lie that alternative music somehow offers something that's anti-corporate."

It was predominantly a white, male, alternative rock festival. Soundgarden's Chris Cornell summed up the feelings of many when he announced on stage: "I'd like to apologise for all of us. My penis would also like to apologise."

Perry Farrell's Lollapalooza, despite those critics who might look back and blame their disappointment on his naivety, has been one of the few successful summer tours. Farrell himself has recently launched his own solo project, typically titled Porno For Pyros, and he continues to plough his eclectic furrow to the delight of his many fans.

ALBUMS
JANE'S ADDICTION *(Triple X, 1987 – KKKK)* *"A more curious and mysterious bunch of fellas you will not find... check 'em out right now before the whole world joins in." – Kerrang! 152, August 6-19, 1987*
NOTHING'S SHOCKING *(Warner Bros, 1988 – KKKKK) "They discovered and understood – it'll be our turn soon. This is the second coming, don't sleep." – Kerrang! 202, August 27, 1988*
RITUAL DE LO HABITUAL *(Warner Brothers, 1990 – KKKK) "Less a work of Metallic velocity, the mood here is lucid and dream-like, an eerie Chinese puzzle that moves with ease from orchestral semantics to skewed Arabic configurations." – Kerrang! 340, May 11, 1991*

IN THEIR OWN WORDS...

"If you do see me next to Tiffany on the MTV playlist, it's really not my fault!" – Perry Farrell, Kerrang! 304, August 25, 1990

"There's so many things I want to do and dying isn't one of them." – Perry Farrell, Kerrang! 338, April 27, 1991

"I have gone to rallies. They haven't done much, man. You just listen to some people and then you go home." – Perry Farrell, Kerrang! 338, April 27, 1991

"Vanilla Ice sold a lot more records than we did but that doesn't mean it's good music." – Perry Farrell, Kerrang! 338, April 27, 1991

"I need, at this time in my life, to get away so I can think and dream a little bit and then creep back into the system, somewhere unexpected,and observe again." – Perry Farrell, Kerrang! 338, April 27, 1991

JANE'S ADDICTION

JETHRO TULL

UK, five-piece (1968-present)
25 YEARS is a long time to spend standing on one leg whilst playing the flute, ask Tull frontman Ian Anderson. To while away some of the years, he has led this archetypal English Folk Rock band into more Metallic territory, but away from the stage, it hasn't happened often...
Recommended quasi-Metal album:
AQUALUNG *(Island, 1971 – KKKK)*

Joan JETT

USA, solo artist (1979-present)
VOTED MOST likely to permanently reside in the has-been limbo after the break-up of jailbait rockers the Runaways, feisty femme Joanie, all panda eyes and black leather, raised a stiff middle pinky to the majors who turned down her solo debut 'Bad Reputation' ('80), and released the album independently on her invented Blackhearts label (a slightly altered version was eventually released in '81 on Epic). But justice was really hers when she and her band the Blackhearts covered 'I Love Rock 'N' Roll' (B-side of a single by '70s TV show nightmares the Arrows). Taken from her '81 LP of the same name, it was, as they say, a chart smash. Her taste for anthemic bubblegum, as opposed to the Heavy Metal of her notorious former act, paid off big time. The trouble is, it's a formula that to this day, despite maybe even a slight mellowing (!), she has rarely deviated from. Still, nobody can say our Joanie isn't consistent...
Recommended (and not just cos Ms Jett looks particularly yummy on the sleeve) album:
GLORIOUS RESULTS OF A MISSPENT YOUTH *(Epic, 1984 – KKKK)*

David JOHANSEN

USA, solo artist (1977-present)
CURRENTLY DOIN' movie work in preference to sporadic solo albums, the charismatic ex-New York Dolls frontman/mouth took a far less punky route with his solo career than one would have expected. His eponymous debut in '78 was a guitar-fuelled frenzy of power rock, which, on a coupla tracks, boasted the added sonic addition of Aerosmith guitarist Joe Perry!
Recommended album:
DAVID JOHANSEN *(Blue Sky, 1978 – KKKKK)*

Johnny CRASH

USA/UK, five-piece (1990)
LA-BASED AC/DC soundalike act formed by Brit emigré Vicki James Wright, ex-Tokyo Blade singer who had a girl's name before Glam and wore a kilt before Axl Rose.
Only album:
NEIGHBORHOOD THREAT *(WTG, 1990 – KKK)*

Steve JONES

UK, guitarist (1978-present)
EX-SEX PISTOLS, now LA-based, bully-boy guitarist. Along with that somewhat infamous band's drummer, Paul Cook, he formed the Professionals some time after the Pistol's gloriously patchy disbanding in 1978. Yet, after two punchy power-riffed n' light hearted singles ('Join The Professionals' and '1-2-3'), the band's fully-fledged debut album, 'I Didn't See It Coming' ('81) was disappointingly 'muso'! He played at supergroup-dom as a member of Chequered Past in 1984, but it wasn't till '89, after Jonesy had conquered his addiction to substance abuse, that he resurfaced with the Very Metal 'Fire And Gasoline' – which featured GN'R screamer Axl Rose on an updatin' of the Pistols tune 'I Did U No Wrong'.
Recommended album:
FIRE AND GASOLINE *(MCA, 1989 – KKKK)*

JOURNEY

USA, five-piece (1973-1987)
ALTHOUGH FREQUENTLY lauded as the greatest AOR band of all time, San Francisco's Journey started as something far less melodic and easy on the ears: instrumental jazz fusion. The band were put together by guitarist Neal Schon (born February 27, 1954) who, when aged just 16, had joined Santana in preference to an invitation from Eric Clapton to join Derek And The Dominoes!

After playing on Santana's eponymous third album (CBS, 1972), Schon formed Latin Rock band Azteca then played in what became Graham Central Station. Former Santana road manager Herbie Herbert then approached Schon in February '73 to link up with Ross Valory (bass, born February 2, 1949), George Tickner (guitar), Prairie Prince (drums, then also of The Tubes). Gregg Rolie (keyboards) joined in June and calling themselves the Golden Gate Rhythm Section offered their services as a backing band for all-comers. With Herbert as manager, the band soon decided to go it alone, however, and having adopted the far simpler name of Journey, made their live debut on December 31, 1973 at San Francisco's Winterland theatre.

Prince returned to The Tubes, ultimately to be replaced by Aynsley Dunbar (ex-David Bowie, John Mayall, Frank Zappa – also co-credited on 'The Warning' on Black Sabbath's debut album) for the eponymous Journey debut on the band's lifelong CBS/Columbia label, released April '75. Second and third LPs 'Look Into The Future' ('76) and 'Next' ('77) found the band experimenting with their own vocal capabilities but getting nowhere. CBS gave them an ultimatum: get a singer or get dropped...

In came Robert Fleischman, a man from Chicago with a voice not too dissimilar to Robert Plant's. His arrival prompted a major change in direction but he would be replaced after just four months by a man called Steve Perry (born January 22, 1953). Perry had sent in a demo of his band Alien Project that impressed Herbert enough to prompt the decision to fire Fleischman (later to join Vinnie Vincent's Invasion), allegedly for arrogance.

Perry made his live debut – dressed all in white! – singing two songs during encores at San Francisco's tiny Old Waldorf on October 28, 1977. 'Infinity', the first album to feature his

JOURNEY circa 1983: note Perry (centre) bursting into tears at the sheer AOR emotion of it all

dulcet tones, was released three months later. It was produced by Roy Thomas Baker of Queen fame, and featured the hits 'Wheel In The Sky', 'Anytime' and 'Lights' – each unlike anything the band had written before and each pointing the way to a multi-Platinum radio-friendly future. But unlike so many bands since who have simply employed this 'formula', Journey wrote music in this style quite naturally. They were all incredibly accomplished musicians, and in Perry, had a vocalist unlike anyone else in rock.

As the music evolved, so did the band. Dunbar's style was considered too complex and he was replaced by Steve Smith – who had been drumming with Ronnie Montrose, support act on the 'Infinity' tour – debuting on the next album, 'Evolution' ('79). Before its release, the band made its UK debut, co-headlining seven dates with the Pat Travers Band where they went down like a lead balloon, coming on second whilst much of the crowd filed out. Back in the States, it was a different story where the album was the second in a row to go Platinum, and spawned Journey's first Top 20 hit, 'Lovin', Touchin', Squeezin''. By then, the band were also a major concert draw, playing the World Series Of Rock festival in July in Chicago sharing top billing with Aerosmith, Ted Nugent and Thin Lizzy.

To capitalise on their success, CBS re-issued the best of the first three albums on a compilation called 'In The Beginning', in January 1980. Much more successful was 'Departure' (March '80) featuring 'Any Way You Want It' and 'Walks Like A Lady'. In Japan, in April of that year, 'Dream After Dream', a soundtrack album credited to Journey – but really mainly down to Rolie – was released, but not issued worldwide until much later as it didn't represent the band as a whole. Rolie would leave after the 'Departure' tour – and 'Captured', 1981's double live album from it – recommending they hire instead Jonathan Cain from Journey's then opening act, The Babys.

Cain (born February 26, 1950) could play guitar as well as keyboards, but more importantly could write songs. His name

IN THEIR OWN WORDS...

"I sent them some tapes and went on the road with them while they were supporting ELP. Neal and I started writing songs straight off. Next thing I know, they asked me to join the band and we went straight into the studio to do 'Infinity'..." – Steve Perry, Kerrang! 4, October, 1981

"All the things I hated (like) the ponciness... are slowly going. There's just a different attitude with the band. It's a little tougher, a little freer, more of a street sound." – Jonathan Cain, Kerrang! 4, October, 1981

"There's nothing wrong with being commercial. It's just another way of saying you're successful, getting a wider audience." – Neal Schon, Kerrang! 4, October, 1981

"I'm not hung up on this Heavy Metal thing. I enjoy playing hard rock 'n' roll but I also enjoy playing music that people appreciate – period... I must be crazy – a workaholic or something. I'm not really happy unless I'm playing music." – Neal Schon, Kerrang! 18, June 17-30, 1982

"We didn't want to leave this great big, beautiful Harley-Davidson we had customised sitting in the garage. Neal and I thought we could ride it. But we knew who had the keys..." – Jonathan Cain (referring to Steve Perry and the calls for a Journey reunion), Kerrang! 426, January 16, 1993

JOURNEY

appeared on the credits to every song on the band's next, and arguably greatest ever album, 'Escape' (August '81), which hit the US Number One spot, selling over two million copies during a 146 week tenure on the *Billboard* chart and a further three million elsewhere. One song from it, 'Don't Stop Believin'' went to Number Nine and has ever since epitomised Journey's style. A beautiful song with heart-rending lyrics, a superb arrangement and a quite stunning solo from Schon. Two other singles went Top 20 in the States and the band were officially massive – they even added a couple of tracks to the soundtrack of Disney's mega movie, 'Tron'.

Bizarrely, Schon chose that year to release 'Untold Passion', a less commercial collaboration with keyboardist Jan Hammer. (They also made 'Here To Stay' a year later.) But this was only a side-step as the 'Escape' tour rolled on into '82 and the band eventually took time out to record its heavier follow-up, their eighth proper studio LP, 'Frontiers' ('83). From it, 'Faithfully', 'After The Fall' and 'Send Her My Love' saw US singles chart action, but whilst the band toured, cracks began to appear. Perry became discontented and began to make plans for a solo record – 'Street Talk' emerged in '84 – and Schon teamed up with Sammy Hagar, Kenny Aaronson (bass) and Michael Shrieve (drums, ex-Santana) as the shortlived HSAS for the album 'Through The Fire' ('84). Cain produced an album by his wife Tane Cain, Steve Smith made his second jazz record 'Orion' ('83) after a first, 'Vital Information' ('81).

Writing for the next album didn't involve Smith or Valory and when they regrouped in '85, both were ousted. Journey vowed to continue as a three-piece, hiring a rhythm section for recording and roadwork. The fruits of that plan would be the last ever Journey album: 'Raised On Radio' released in May '86. The gigs featured session player Randy Jackson on bass and Mike Baird on drums.

The band split after that tour although regrouped for an awards ceremony in March '87, and again for a benefit gig in November '91 after the death of legendary San Francisco promoter Bill Graham. Schon and Cain went on to form Bad English. Perry has yet to releae his second, long-expected solo LP.

A 'Greatest Hits' compilation released in 1988 went Top 10 Stateside and 'Time³', '92's triple-CD box set of hits and out-takes plus rarities, proved hugely popular... But despite reformation rumours and popular demand, it seems unlikely Journey will ever work together formally again...

ALBUMS
JOURNEY (CBS, 1975 – K)
LOOK INTO THE FUTURE (CBS, 1976 – KK)
NEXT (CBS, 1977 – K)
IN THE BEGINNING (CBS, 1980 – KK) 'Best of' the above three: all the above are pre-Perry. Kinda rock 'n' roll meets fusion jazz. For students of complex arrangements and chord progressions only...
INFINITY (CBS, 1978 – KKKK) "Perry's soothing vocals grab you every time. Just listen to him go..." – Mega Metal Kerrang! 14, April 1989
EVOLUTION (CBS, 1979 – KKK) "Roy Thomas Baker was once again at the dials... gave the band a much harder edge." – Mega Metal Kerrang! 14, April 1989
DEPARTURE (CBS, 1980 – KKK) "Records like this make you realise how dull and predictable AOR has become." – Mega Metal Kerrang! 14, April 1989
DREAM AFTER DREAM (CBS Japan, 1980 – KK) "This (soundtrack) rubbish really is for die-hard Journey fans only." – Mega Metal Kerrang! 14, April 1989
CAPTURED (CBS, 1981 – KKKK) "Beautifully packaged (double live)... Remixed – so even a polished act like Journey can get a bit rough round the edges." – Mega Metal Kerrang! 14, April 1989
ESCAPE (CBS, 1981 – KKKKK) "The greatest AOR record of all time... Still sounds as fresh and new today as when I first played it." Mega Metal Kerrang! 14, April 1989
FRONTIERS (CBS, 1983 – KKKK) "Steve Perry dropped an octave or two but the music was pure Journey..." Mega Metal Kerrang! 14, April 1989
RAISED ON RADIO (CBS, 1986 – KKKKK) "Second best album after 'Escape'... a more mature and thoughtful Journey." Mega Metal Kerrang! 14, April 1989
GREATEST HITS (CBS, 1988 – KKKK) All the hits plus soundtrack-only rarities from 'Vision Quest' and 'Two Of A Kind'.
TIME³ (Columbia, 1992 – KKKKK) "The definitive package from the greatest AOR band in history..." Kerrang! 426, January 16, 1993

JUDAS PRIEST

UK, five-piece (1973-present)

STUDS AND leather. Motorbikes. Screams worthy of The One With Horns. These are all things that personify traditional Heavy Metal in most people's eyes, and all things embodied by rugged Rock vets Judas Priest.

Based amid the industrial smoke of Birmingham, the band's first release came in 1974 with 'Rocka Rolla' – an album much more Blues-based (and certainly many times worse) than Priest's 13 subsequent LPs.

It was the beginning of a career that was to take many a musical swerve, and face some disgraceful legal nonsense in the Reno courts, where the band were accused of leading teenagers to commit suicide. Strangely, the Priest album that was alleged to contain harmful backwards messages and suchlike, had been available for 12 years. It was 'Stained Class' from '78.

The quintet have always been renowned for the awesome stage presence, character, and vocal intensity of Rob Halford; the man who rides onto stages astride a Harley-Davidson, before ripping into one of the band's countless Heavy Metal anthems, 'Hell Bent For Leather'. Halford's image has become progressively harder over the years, leading up to his ultra-tough appearance during the 'Painkiller' tour of '91, befitting the album of that name, which is Priest's heaviest release.

One of the band's additional strengths has always been the duelling guitars of Glenn Tipton and KK Downing. They're one of the great duos of Metal string-scalding, priding themselves on their fine, highly inventive lead work, as well as some classic riffs. Ironically, before Tipton joined, the band were to have been a four-piece. Backing them and Halford in the 'Rocka Rolla' line-up were Ian Hill on bass and drummer John Hinch.

When it comes to classic Priest, their 'Sad

JUDAS PRIEST on stage:
Downing, Halford, Tipton
making their Full Metal Racket

Wings Of Destiny' album of '76 is one release that most people are in agreement about. Containing the standard-to-be 'Victim Of Changes', plus 'The Ripper', which is also one of their all-time best, featuring a marvellous Jack impersonation from Halford, and such classic spine-tingling lines as, *'I'm a nasty surprise/A devil in disguise...'*. John Hinch had by then been replaced by Alan Moore, who was in turn replaced by session drummer Simon Phillips on the 'Sin After Sin' LP.

Unfortunately, Priest's label at the time, Gull Records, didn't have the power to really break 'Sad Wings...'. But '77 saw CBS Records step into the fray, and sign the band. As a result, the next albums, 'Sin After Sin' and 'Stained Class', did much better business, particularly in the States. Judas Priest were now seen as one of the British Heavy Metal bands, partly due to some serious touring.

Halford's onstage S&M imagery was developing steadily. By the October-November UK tour of '78, the man was brandishing a bull-whip. Aptly enough, Priest's next album was entitled 'Hell Bent For Leather' in America

(showcasing yet another new drummer, Les Binks), although it appeared in Europe as 'Killing Machine', minus the Stateside extra track, 'Green Manalishi'.

'Take On The World' was the single that infiltrated the British Top 10, and 'Evening Star' did the same a few months later. Priest were expanding all the time, and their 'Hell Bent...'/'Killing Machine' album managed to triple the sales of 'Stained Class'.

'Unleashed In The East' was the next step; a live album often dubbed 'Unleashed In The Studio', for fairly obvious reasons. Halford began his Harley-Davidson entrances during the subsequent tour, building on what were to become the great Heavy Metal clichés, to dramatic effect.

The turn of the decade heralded 'British Steel'. As well as spawning another British Top 10 single in 'Living After Midnight', the album contained such monsters as 'Breaking The Law' and 'Grinder', and led to *Rolling Stone* magazine describing the band as defining "the Heavy Metal genre at the outset of the 1980s". It also introduced Priest's longest staying

IN THEIR OWN WORDS...

"Because we were there at the very beginning, I suppose we've been looked upon as sort of mentors, which has meant we've grown and expanded over the years...to the point where we look like this, with studs, leather and chains!"
– Rob Halford, Kerrang! 59, Jan 12-25, 1984

"What we'll be looking for in the long-term is to be considered legendary, or at least semi-legendary. For being the foremost in what we do, Heavy Metal"
– KK Downing, Kerrang! 148, June 11-24, 1987

"The whole horizon of the Heavy Metal world needs to be expanded, and 'Turbo' was an attempt to do something about it. We wanted to make a statement and push those margins out a little bit further..." – Glenn Tipton, Kerrang! 148, June 11-24, 1987

"We're at the point really, where I think what our fans want is more of a failure than a success. They want a record that's gonna fail, but they're gonna love it to death!" – KK Downing, Kerrang! 308, September 22, 1990

"The (prosecution lawyers in the 'teen suicide' court case) expected us to come into court in leather and chains, with lasers and fucking smoke bombs going off. But into the court came four adult, respectful, intelligent Englishmen and it knocked them for six, I tell ya!"
– Rob Halford, Kerrang! 318, December 1, 1990

"We were informed of Rob Halford leaving the band by fax, and to date have had no satisfactory explanation for his actions, nor any direct contact with him" – the three remaining members of Judas Priest, Kerrang! 422, December 12, 1992

JUDAS PRIEST

sticksman Dave Holland.

'Point Of Entry' ('81) was disappointingly laid-back in comparison, but the Priest machine continued to roll on and grow. And 'Screaming For Vengeance' surfaced the next year, ranking as another career stand-out. The opening combination of the 'Hellion' intro, leading into 'Electric Eye' and 'Riding On The Wind', was quite magnificent.

Almost as effective was one of Priest's faster tracks, 'Freewheel Burning', which opened 1984's 'Defenders Of The Faith'; an album which some felt was merely 'Screaming...' Part Two, but nevertheless packed a similar punch.

'Turbo', however, didn't live up to its name. 1986 was the year when Priest took a musical turn and introduced guitar synthesizers to their sound. For many people, the likes of 'Wild Nights (Hot And Crazy Days)' worked, but the subsequent 'Priest... Live!' album was more of an obvious treat for the band's following.

1988's 'Ram It Down' was much more like it, and the 'Painkiller' album (released after a delay caused by the Reno court case, which the band won) truly found Priest screeching back into 1990 with a remarkable new drummer, Scott Travis (ex-Racer X), and a batch of intense compositions.

After the tour, crisis struck, when Rob Halford and Scott Travis began another band, Fight. A messy legal battle ensued, resulting in Priest facing an uncertain future while a retrospective double compilation sits on the shop racks. A nasty surprise...

ALBUMS

ROCKA ROLLA (Decca, 1974 – K) Pretty ropey stuff, actually, unadventurous Heavy Metal at best...

SAD WINGS OF DESTINY (Decca, 1976 – KKKKK) Totally awesome. As crucial to Metal as many of the early Sabbath albums. All-time classic...

SIN AFTER SIN (CBS, 1977 – KKK) Some great songs but Roger Glover's production lacks the punch they deserved...

STAINED CLASS (CBS, 1978 – KKK) Very Not as Heavy as it could have been. Songs moving away from earlier Gothic imagery...

KILLING MACHINE (CBS, 1979 – KKKK) Style now honed to short, sharp shock Metal. Introduced the now familiar leather and studs image with one or two S&M-styled lyrics...

UNLEASHED IN THE EAST (CBS, 1979 –

KKKKK) Superb summary of their career to date. Included in-concert staple cover of Fleetwood Mac's 'Green Manalishi'...

BRITISH STEEL (CBS, 1980 – KKKK) Broke Priest to a more mainstream audience with its succesion of hit singles..

POINT OF ENTRY (CBS, 1981 – KK) Some strong tracks but relatively lightweight by Priest's standards...

SCREAMING FOR VENGEANCE (CBS, 1982 – KKKKK) "Not only Judas Priest's best LP, but one of the finest to emerge this century!" – Kerrang! 19, July 1-15, 1982

DEFENDERS OF FAITH (CBS, 1984 – KKKK) "An unstoppable album; Priest's finest hour, and a Heavy Metal album to make most troupes down tools in exasperation" – Kerrang! 60, January 26-February 8, 1984

TURBO (CBS, 1986 – KKK) "The kings of Heavy Metal are back at their greatest, earth-splintering, toe-nail removing BEST!" – Kerrang! 117, April 3-16, 1986

PRIEST...LIVE! (CBS, 1987 – KKKK) "This is as close to any live album I've ever heard, capturing the live experience to the full. The fact that it's an official release and not a bootleg makes it all the more surprising" – Kerrang! 147, May 28-June 10, 1987

RAM IT DOWN (Columbia, 1988 – KKKK) "A welcome return to form for Judas Priest, although it's still a little short of the killer we all wanted..." – Kerrang! 185, April 30, 1988

PAINKILLER (Columbia, 1990 – KKKKK) "Just when you thought the Priest machine couldn't get heavier, the hammer hits the anvil with even more earth-shattering might... Metal album of the year!" – Kerrang! 307, September 15, 1990

JUNKYARD

USA, five-piece (1988-present)
SOLDIERING ON despite being dropped by Geffen in '92, Junkyard are a gritty and down-to-earth outfit who at best come close to reviving the spirit of Lynyrd Skynyrd's early hell-raisin' days/daze.
Recommended album:
JUNKYARD (Geffen, 1988 – KKKK)

KANSAS

USA, six-piece (1983-present)
TAKING THEIR name from their home state, Kansas (from the town Topeka) made over a dozen albums, taking Pomp Rock to places even Styx were afraid to visit, and Get Religion (not necessarily in that order). They are now a shadow of the band that made the classic freak 1976 hit single 'Carry On My Wayward Son', having lost their way after their extraordinarily-named singer John Elephante and guitarist Kenny Livgren left in '82. Now officially "too heavy" for James Hetfield. Possibly...
Recommended album (but not by James Hetfield):
POINT OF KNOW RETURN *(Kirshner, 1977 – KKK)*

The Great KAT

USA, three-piece (born in Hell, a millenium ago, Kat has eternal life)
KAT IS a fiery Goddess of CLASSICAL HEAVY METAL, wielding a guitar as skilfully as she did her violin on such ultra-speed delights as 'Satan Says' and 'Worship Me Or Die'.

The dangerous vixen will go down in history for her run-in with *K!* journo Chris Watts, at whom she hurled obscenities from behind a

KAT: a dangerous vixen

locked hotel room door. Watts had not heard her 'masterpiece' of the time, 'Beethoven On Speed', and was therefore an IGNORANT MOTHERFUCKER.

Unfortunately for Kat, 99 per cent of the Heavy Metal community were IGNORANT MOTHERFUCKERS too...
Most amusing album:
WORSHIP ME OR DIE *(Roadrunner, 1988 – KKK)*

KEEL

USA, five-piece (1984-1990)
MADE FIVE albums but little impact. Guitarist Marc Ferrari dyed a shock of his hair blond in tribute to Joe Perry (although Keith Richards did it first). Singer Ron Keel moved on to front Fair Game with an all-girl backing band.
Recommended Gene Simmons-produced second album:
THE RIGHT TO ROCK *(Vertigo, 1985 – KKKK)*

KERBDOG

Ireland, four-piece (1991-present)
KILKENNY QUARTET aiming to follow in Doc Marten-ed footsteps of fellow countrymen Therapy?. Formed from the more indie-flavoured Christian Brothers, who turned kinda Thrashier with the recruitment of second guitarist Billy Dalton. Fronted by the splendidly monikered Cormac Battle.
Recommended debut EP:
EARTHWORKS *(Vertigo, 1993 – KKKK)*

KERRANG!

UK, weekly magazine (1981-present)
ORIGINALLY THE onomatopoeic representation of a powerchord struck on a heavily amplified electric guitar. The first useage of the word (spelt *Kerraaannngg*) headlined a photo-spread in *Sounds* magazine of Rainbow's Ritchie Blackmore smashing a Stratocaster (later a bootleg cover and title), Motörhead used it at Hammy O, too, but has ever since been spelt

with an exclamation mark! *Kerrang!* the mag was originally a black-and-white A3 supplement to *Sounds*. Then launched as a one-off in June 1981. A second issue followed in August and came out monthly until 1982 when two issues in February saw it turn fortnightly. In October 1987 (issue 156) it went weekly. 1993 saw rumours of a book, even...

Recommended reading:
MOST DEFINITELY *(Every Week)*

KILLER DWARVES

Canada, four-piece (1981-present)
CANUCK QUARTET who have enjoyed more than 15 minutes of fame because for years, the members of the band all claimed to share 'Dwarf' as their surname!

Although fronted by the pint-sized Russ Graham, the other 75 per cent of the Dwarves are actually quite tall. Together, they ply a melody-friendly strain of hard rock that has sadly failed to propel them to superstardom. Despite being a killer live act, they were dropped by Epic Records after the most recent album failed to sell in huge quantities.

Small in stature but recommended nonetheless:
STAND TALL *(Maze, 1986 – KKKK)*
BIG DEAL *(Epic, 1988 – KKKK)*

KILLING JOKE

UK, four-piece (1979-1991)
YET ANOTHER of those bands whose influence was far more appreciated after they'd split up, Killing Joke were perhaps the first band to emerge from Punk Rock with what would now be described as an Industrial sound.

They were also greatly helped by the fact that they were all barking mad! Bassist Youth, in particular, went completely off his trolley and was eventually admitted for psychiatric treatment after taking enough acid to kill a small army and then wandering naked down London's King's Road burning wads of cash. Vocalist Jaz Coleman went one step further and after a brief spell in Iceland (because he thought the end of the world had come), was last reported to have been trying to buy a small army (perhaps the same one) with Killing Joke royalties. *Woof woof!!*

Recommended album:
KILLING JOKE *(Malicious Damage, 1979 – KKKKK)*

KING CRIMSON

UK, five/four-piece (1969-present)
ANTI-COMMERCIAL muso outfit who have at times – notably on the original '69 version of '21st Century Schizoid Man' – been as heavy as Slayer. Such times are rare, however, so King Crimson can usually be filed under avant garde jazz...

Recommended (debut) album:
IN THE COURT OF THE CRIMSON KING *(Island, 1969 – KKKK)*

KING DIAMOND

Denmark, five-piece (1985-present)
GOTHIC HORROR is something that King 'Billy' Diamond simply can't get enough of. He loves it! Listen to any of the heavily-made-up Satanist's solo albums, and that fact will come across instantly.

'Abigail' is his best; a concept album which actually tells a (tame) horror story from start to finish, and gives it a decent Metal soundtrack. In contrast, the similarly conceptual 'Them' is poor, and unbelievably features a track entitled 'Tea'.

1990's 'The Eye' didn't do particularly good business, and this surely explains the resurrection of King's original band, Mercyful Fate, in '93.

Recommended album:
ABIGAIL *(Roadrunner, 1987 – KKKK)*

KING KOBRA

USA, five-piece (1985-1988)
A SHORTLIVED act although they certainly left their mark with an excellent debut album in 'Ready To Strike'.

Formed by legendary drummer Carmine Appice, who headhunted his peroxided cohorts from the LA club scene, the band tried too hard to be different on their second record, and they'd already split up by the time 'King Kobra III' hit the shelves.

Original vocalist Mark Free went on to pursue a patchy AOR career with Signal and Unruly Child, whilst his replacements were (briefly) Marq Torien (who later formed BulletBoys) and Johnny Edwards (later of Foreigner) who sang on King Kobra's 'posthumous' third album.

Recommended album:
READY TO STRIKE (Capitol, 1985 – KKKK)

KINGDOM COME

USA, five-piece (1988-present)
BRIEFLY METAMORPHOSED into the most controversial band in Metal but was really only ever a solo venture by the Hamburg-born, ex-Stone Fury singer, Lenny Wolf. Nonetheless, their eponymous debut was credited to the band and – because it unashamedly ripped off Led Zeppelin and was topped by Wolf's Plant-esque vocals – earned them many more haters than fans (the record sold 500,000 copies). It would have sold far more, but instead of owning up to their kleptomania, guitarist Danny Stag claimed never to have even heard a Led Zeppelin record. Instantly, the band's credibility sunk lower than a Lee Marvin vocal. Second album, 'In Your Face', was less of a 'Led Clone' (a song written by Gary Moore to show his disgust), but the improvement was largely ignored. The band began to feud, then split. Only Wolf remained come third album 'Hands Of Time', with a fourth due in 1993.

Recommended album:
IN YOUR FACE (Polydor, 1989 – KKKK)

KINGOFTHEHILL

USA, four-piece (1990-present)
FROM ST LOUIS, Missouri where they were previously known as Broken Toyz. Hit the hard rock scene like Frank Bruno with a javelin in each glove. Released an eponymous debut album then toured extensively in the UK, most notably in support of Extreme.

Central to the outrageous live show is vocalist Frankie, a blond bombshell who breaks all the moulds and does it HIS way. He is backed up beautifully by Jimmy Griffin (guitar), George Potsos (bass) and Vito Bono (drums), and if KOTH never achieve the super-mega-global stardom they deserve, then at the very least they've shot a life-saving injection into the arm of an, at times, tired genre.

Recommended album:
KINGOFTHEHILL (SBK, 1991 – KKKK)

KISS

USA, four-piece (1972-present)
KISS WERE formed in New York in 1972 by the nucleus of Gene Simmons (bass/vocals) and Paul Stanley (rhythm guitar/vocals). They had become dissatisfied with the direction of their previous band Wicked Lester, who had actually recorded an album for CBS but which has, even to this day, never been released. Simmons and Stanley both shared the dream of creating the ultimate rock band, a 'Heavy Metal Beatles' in which each member had his own personality and an upfront role.

Recruiting drummer Peter Criss from the classifieds of *Rolling Stone*, then picking up lead guitarist Ace Frehley, Kiss made their live debut at the Coventry Club in Queens, New York on January 30, 1973, to an audience of four! Borrowing many ideas from the New York Glam boom of the time (and, in Simmons' case, his mother's fur coat!) it was some months before Kiss finally hit on the greasepaint and thunder concept that would take them to superstardom within two years and would hide their real 'identities' for the next 10.

'Discovered' by Bill Aucoin and Joyce Biawitz (later to become manager to disco star Donna Summer, as well as the wife of their record label boss), two TV music show producers, following a self-promoted show at the Hotel Diplomat in New York City, Kiss soon found themselves as the first signing to Casablanca, a new label set up by former Buddah Records president Neil Bogart.

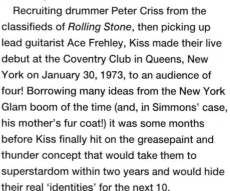

KISS: who says they're just as good without make-up?

Just over a year after their first gig, Kiss released their debut album, with the second, 'Dressed To Kill', following soon after. Then, completing a remarkable 15- month period of constant touring and recording, Kiss released their third album, 'Dressed To Kill' in February 1975. But it was the double 'Alive!', recorded at the Cobo Hall in Detroit and the year's greatest rock 'n' roll single, 'Rock And Roll All Nite' that broke the band in America once and for all.

Teaming up with producer Bob Ezrin for the ambitious and triumphant 'Destroyer' ('76) began a steady stream of album releases (including the awesome 'Alive II') increasing the band's reputation, which was cemented by unique memorabilia and solo albums.

Criss quit the band in 1980, following rows about musical direction, marking the beginning of a disastrous time for the band. Despite a successful European tour, with new drummer Eric Carr, the first LP to feature him was the curious concept album '(Music From) The Elder' ('81) which sold poorly and forced plans for a plot-revealing movie to be shelved indefinitely.

Anxious to recover ground, Kiss unleashed 'Creatures Of The Night'('82), touring on the back of it with Ace Frehley replaced by ex-Treasure guitarist Vinnie 'The Wiz' Vincent. It would be the last time the band went out with make-up, for come October 1983 and the 'Lick It Up' album, Kiss unmasked. And a year later,

touring on the back of another new album, 'Animalize', Kiss had not only replaced Vincent but had also replaced Vinnie's replacement (!), due to original choice Mark St John contracting Reiter's Syndrome. In came Bruce Kulick (ex-Blackjack/Goodrats and brother of long-time Kiss associate Bob Kulick) who has since been part of a resurgence in Kiss' popularity. Since his arrival, they have enjoyed a string of successful albums and singles, even breaking into the UK Top Three with 1987's 'Crazy Crazy Nights'. Although Gene Simmons has been distracted in recent years, his re-commitment to the Kiss cause led to the impressive 'Revenge' in 1992 (sadly, a record without Eric Carr, who succumbed to cancer in December 1991, and has been replaced by ex-Badlands man Eric Singer). 1993 heralded 20th anniversary celebrations marked by the release of the long-awaited 'Alive III' set...

ALBUMS

KISS (Casablanca, 1974 – KKKK) *Stands up to the test of time like a true classic...*
HOTTER THAN HELL (Casablanca, 1974 – KKKK) *Piledriving Heavy Metal rock with intense amounts of flair and originality...*
DRESSED TO KILL (Casablanca, 1975 – KKKK) *A riotous rock 'n' roll celebration...*
ALIVE! (Casablanca, 1975 – KKKKK) *Probably the greatest live album of all time...*
DESTROYER (Casablanca, 1976 – KKKKK) *An essential purchase. Classic studio album...*
ROCK AND ROLL OVER (Casablanca, 1976 – KKKK) *Sex, drugs and rock 'n' roll has always been a winning formula...*
LOVE GUN (Casablanca, 1977 – KKKK) *Bang bang! More of the above...*
ALIVE II (Casablanca, 1977 – KKKKK) *Probably the greatest live album of all-time (again)...*
DOUBLE PLATINUM (Casablanca, 1978 – KKKKK) *Where Casablanca honours Kiss' achievements. Fully remixed, hits and more...*
DYNASTY (Casablanca, 1979 – KKKK) *Showed Kiss turning its focus to the world market...*

IN THEIR OWN WORDS...

"This album ('Creatures Of The Night') is meant to tell everyone: no more fooling around, no more artistic self panderings, and that's in no way apologising for anything we've done because we're really proud of 'The Elder'. But this is right between the eyes..."
– Gene Simmons, Kerrang! 21, July 29-August 11, 1982

"Kiss is much bigger than anybody in the band, because it's a philosophy and a commitment to a certain attitude."
– Paul Stanley, Kerrang! 32, December 30-January 12, 1983

"I think our fans are gonna see that we're still the same band, prepared to go out and give 110 per cent. I've probably seen Kiss play more without make-up than with and I've never been too let down."
– Paul Stanley, Kerrang! 53, October 20-November 2, 1983

"I'm sure that Bruce will be with us now until the band no longer exists."
– Paul Stanley, Kerrang! 137, January 8-21, 1987

"There's always somebody asking me when I'm gonna do another solo album, but to me Kiss is a solo album, it's everybody's solo album." – Paul Stanley, Kerrang! 201, August 20, 1988

"The first time we played together was a real disaster. We first played the Wicked Lester stuff, but I couldn't get into that at all. But when we played 'Strutter' for the first time I really felt we had something."
– Peter Criss, Kerrang! 226, February 18, 1989

"The day the group becomes a machine is the day it's over" – Gene Simmons, Kerrang! 377, February 1, 1992

KISS

UNMASKED (Casablanca, 1980 – KKK) Reasonable attempt at exploring further pop rock avenues, but not what Kiss is about...

(MUSIC FROM) THE ELDER (Casablanca, 1981 – KKK) Lambasted by critics and greeted with astonishment by the Kiss Army...

KILLERS (Casablanca, 1982 – KKK) Run of the mill compilation with four new songs...

CREATURES OF THE NIGHT (Casablanca, 1982 – KKKK) The band retapping their early hunger and aggression...

LICK IT UP (Vertigo, 1983 – KKKK) "Gargantuan heap of thoughtful rock power, primed to explode on aural impact." – Kerrang! 53, October 20-November 2, 1983

ANIMALIZE (Vertigo, 1984 – KKK) "A good album, but is it good enough?" – Kerrang! 77 September 20-October 3, 1984

ASYLUM (Vertigo, 1985 – KKKK) "All the songs are about sex, and if they aren't they sound like they are!" – Kerrang! 103, September 19-October 2, 1985

CRAZY NIGHTS (Vertigo, 1987 – KKK) "Not so much a change in style but a consolidation." – Kerrang! 156, October 3, 1987

SMASHES, THRASHES & HITS (Vertigo, 1988 – KKKK) 15-track, remixed compilation...

HOT IN THE SHADE (Vertigo, 1989 – KKKK) "Where the former kings of the night-time world have become masters of the cornball HM innuendo." – Kerrang! 261, October 21, 1989

REVENGE (1992 – KKKK) "A good nostalgia trip." – Kerrang! 391, May 9, 1992

ALIVE III (1993 – KKKKK) "Simply awesome!" – Kerrang! 443, May 15, 1993

KIX

USA, five-piece (1979-present)
ARGUABLY AMERICA'S best party rock 'n' roll band, although it took them almost 10 years to approach big time success, after being huge in their native West Virginia and bordering states.

With a succession of AC/DC-ish tunes penned by bassist Donnie Purnell and topped with a cartoon worthy vocal from Steve Whiteman, Kix are actually even better live in concert.

Guaranteed to blow your fuse:
MIDNIGHT DYNAMITE (Atlantic, 1985 – KKKK)
BLOW MY FUSE (Atlantic, 1988 – KKKK)

Paul KOSSOFF

UK, guitarist (June 14, 1950-March 19, 1976)
STUPENDOUSLY GIFTED guitarist who rose to
fame as part of Free. One of only a handful of
truly original white Blues guitarists, Koss – as he
was affectionately known – also recorded solo,
as part of Kossoff, Kirke, Tetsu And Rabbit, for
Back Street Crawler and on various other
sessions. Tragically, his drug addiction caused
his health to plummet and ultimately took his
life. Never fulfilled his enormous potential but
has at least left us with some beautiful music.
Recommended albums (other than Free):
BACK STREET CRAWLER *(Island, 1973 –
KKKKK) solo album*
BLUE SOUL *(Island, 1986 – KKKKK)
posthumous compilation*

Richie KOTZEN

USA, guitarist (1989-present)
BEFORE HE replaced CC Deville in Poison,
Kotzen (whose surname, incidentally, means 'to
puke' in German) had made three solo LPs and
played around 500 club dates by the time he
turned 21 (in 1991).
Recommended (third) LP:
ELECTRIC JOY *(Roadrunner, 1991 – KKK)*

KREATOR

Germany, four-piece (1982-present)
LONE SURVIVORS (almost) of the Great German
Thrash Explosion, Kreator have progressed well
beyond the mayhemic Thrash leanings of their
first two albums, 'Endless Pain' and the
enjoyably painful 'Pleasure To Kill'.

Originally called Tormentor, the lads set
about carving through PAs with the fastest,
most vicious noise they could muster. But by
the fourth album, Kreator were showing signs of
breaking out of their own poisonous bubble,
and 1992's 'Renewal' saw them embracing
more influences; a bit of Industrial here, some
Pink Floyd there...

A positive reaction has left Kreator quite
comfortably on the map. The map of Europe,
that is.

Recommended albums:
PLEASURE TO KILL *(Noise, 1986 – KKKK)*
RENEWAL *(Noise, 1992 – KKKK)*

KROKUS

Switzerland, five-piece (1974-1990)
STRUGGLED FOR years then broke through
with fourth album 'Metal Rendez-Vous' (Ariola,
'80) which featured Maltese-born singer Marc
Storace (ex-Tea) belting out histrionic classics
like 'Heatstrokes' and 'Bedside Radio'. Follow-
up albums, 'Hardware' ('81) and 'One Vice At A
Time' ('82), also achieved some success but
gradually the band's penchant for recycling
AC/DC riffs ran out of steam and favour. They
battled on doggedly to 12th album 'Stampede'
(back on Ariola, their fifth recording deal), but
are now remembered chiefly for having a
bandanna'-d madman (Fernando Von Arb) on
lead guitar, upsetting Def Leppard when they
supported them in the States on the
'Pyromania' tour, and having a drummer called
Freddy Steady. Oh... and for silly song titles like
'Smelly Nelly', 'Mad Racket' and 'Long Stick
Goes Boom'...
Recommended album:
ONE VICE AT A TIME *(Ariola, 1982 – KKKK)*

KYUSS

USA, four-piece (1991-present)
ONE MINUTE you're four nobodies from Palm
Springs playing third on the bill to The Dwarves
at a San Francisco Punk club, the next you're
doing huge tours with Danzig and Faith No
More; the rock business is weird like that. The
Kyuss bomb has really exploded in the past
year, and rightly so!

After a fairly naff debut album that was pretty
much second rate Punk Rock, Kyuss teamed up
with Masters Of Reality genius Chris Goss and
came up with an awesome mixture of Punk,
Blues and aggression called 'Blues For The Red
Sun'. The rest, as they say, is history... or it will
be when they've been around a bit longer.
Recommended album:
BLUES FOR THE RED SUN *(Chameleon/Dali,
1992 – KKKKK)*

L7

USA, four-piece (1986-present)
NON-DIETING, make-up smearing, jeans an'
party frock-tearin' LA gals who fuzz their guitars
and rock harder than just about everyone
except the Ramones and Motörhead – two
bands who would probably sound exactly like
L7 if *they* were gals.

The line-up of Jennifer Finch (bass/vocals),
Suzi Gardner (guitar/vocals), Dee Plakas (drums)
and Donita Sparks (guitar/vocals) like to be
listed alphabetically and remind people that
they made a debut album for Epitaph as long
ago as 1987. In 1990 they recorded the 'Smell
The Magic' EP for SubPop, but it was not until
they signed to Slash/London and recorded
'Bricks Are Heavy' that they really broke
through...
Recommended album:
***BRICKS ARE HEAVY** (Slash/London, 1992 –
KKKKK)*

LA GUNS

USA/UK, five-piece (1986-1992)
PUT TOGETHER by Tracii Guns after he left the
primeval Guns N' Roses line-up. Original singer,

LA GUNS: flawed... but exciting

Paul Black, was replaced by English emigré,
Phil Lewis (ex-Girl and Bernie Tormé) when he
moved to Los Angeles in 1987. LA Guns signed
to PolyGram and made three flawed but
exciting albums, never achieving the initial
impact of contemporaries Faster Pussycat, and
poor ol' Tracii could only wonder about what
might have been as Axl's mob took his name to
unparalleled heights... Tracii, a top geezer,
deserved much better, and looked to be on the
verge of it when he finally brought the band to
Europe to open for Skid Row in 1991. The gigs
were great and their third album, 'Hollywood
Vampires', earned encouraging reviews. But
sadly, internal tension saw the band splinter
with Tracii concentrating on his punkier side-
project, Killing Machine, whilst Lewis looked to
start again with an outfit named Filthy Lucre. LA
Guns' Japanese label released two posthumous
titles: 'Live Vampires' and 'Cuts', an EP of
covers plus two bonus tracks...
Take your pick of all three albums:
***LA GUNS** (PolyGram, 1988 – KKKK)*
***COCKED AND LOADED** (PolyGram, 1989 –
KKKK)*
***HOLLYWOOD VAMPIRES** (PolyGram, 1991 –
KKKK)*

LAST CRACK

USA, five-piece (1986-present)
UNCATEGORISABLE MINNEAPOLIS outfit
fronted by Buddo Buddo (also known as, er...
Buddo), self-confessed psychotic whose other
claim to fame is posing naked for publicity
shots. Weird, left-of-centre, unsuccessful etc...
Recommended (debut) album:
***SINISTER FUNKHOUSE #17** (Roadracer, 1989
– KKKK)*

LAWNMOWER DETH

UK, five-piece (1987-present)
WACKY FUNSTERS from Nottingham way, the Deth have always been the self-confessed "most pointless band of all time". Very silly indeed, the funky, ska-ridden, crunchy Thrashers have revelled in such ridiculous song titles as 'Seventh Church Of The Apocalyptic Lawnmower', and 'Spook Perv Happenings In The Snooker Hall'.

Perhaps if we all ignore them for long enough, they'll go away.
Most ludicrous album:
RETURN OF THE FABULOUS METAL BOZO CLOWNS *(Earache, 1992 – KKKK)*

LEATHERFACE

UK, four-piece (1989-present)
WITH GRAVEL throats, stubble chins and big fuck-off boots, Leatherface make a surprisingly melodic Hardcore noise that takes in the likes of Hüsker Dü, Stiff Little Fingers and early Motörhead. Frontman Frankie Stubbs leans towards articulate and poignant lyrics with songs like 'Bowl Of Flies' and 'Winning', but is quite happy to round off a set with a rowdy rendition of 'You Are My Sunshine' or a 300mph version of Elton John's 'Candle In The Wind'. He is also noted for a quite abysmal dance known as the Serious Shuffle. Probably the best band of their ilk in the UK.
Recommended albums:
FILL YOUR BOOTS *(Roughneck, 1990 – KKKKK)*
MUSH *(Roughneck, 1991 – KKKKK)*

LED ZEPPELIN

UK, four-piece (1968-1980)
WITH OVER 60 million albums sold worldwide, none can dispute Led Zeppelin's stature as the biggest hard rock band of all time. It should be noted also that Zeppelin's massive success was achieved in the days before MTV and the video age – and before marketing became as much an art as recording. Zeppelin's strengths were as obvious then as they are today – when time has

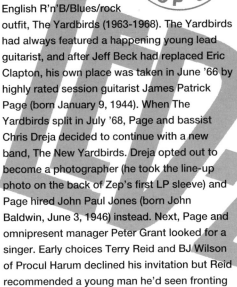

dulled barely a note they recorded: they could write, they could play, and in Jimmy Page, they had a producer par excellence.

The band rose out of the ashes of legendary English R'n'B/Blues/rock outfit, The Yardbirds (1963-1968). The Yardbirds had always featured a happening young lead guitarist, and after Jeff Beck had replaced Eric Clapton, his own place was taken in June '66 by highly rated session guitarist James Patrick Page (born January 9, 1944). When The Yardbirds split in July '68, Page and bassist Chris Dreja decided to continue with a new band, The New Yardbirds. Dreja opted out to become a photographer (he took the line-up photo on the back of Zep's first LP sleeve) and Page hired John Paul Jones (born John Baldwin, June 3, 1946) instead. Next, Page and omnipresent manager Peter Grant looked for a singer. Early choices Terry Reid and BJ Wilson of Procul Harum declined his invitation but Reid recommended a young man he'd seen fronting a Midlands outfit called The Band Of Joy: one Robert Plant. When Page and Grant caught up with Plant (born August 20, 1948) he was singing in a band called Hobbstweedle. Plant accepted the invitation and soon recommended Band Of Joy drummer John Henry Bonham (born May 31, 1948) to complete a line-up that never changed.

In September '68 – after Grant had negotiated an unprecedentedly large and generous deal with Atlantic Records – the quartet recorded their debut album then flew to Scandinavia to fulfil a contract for gigs booked as The New Yardbirds, but they first played together as Led Zeppelin at Surrey University on October 15. Is there anybody out there that doesn't know that the name came from Who drummer Keith Moon's oft-repeated phrase: "Going down like a lead Zeppelin"? Well, there isn't now...

Christmas '68 was a hurried affair for the band as on December 26 they made their US debut in Boston, Massachusetts, opening for

Vanilla Fudge and the MC5. The Yardbirds connection earned them much attention. The live performance earned them rave reviews. Come January 31, 1969, the audience response was enough to persuade headliners Iron Butterfly to cut their losses and not take the stage...

Instantly, Led Zeppelin's live reputation turned them into superstars in the States. Their eponymous debut was rush-released there in February '69 and went Top 10. The UK release was two months later, and, when they returned home to play, critical acclaim was similarly lagging behind the American counterpart. Audience reaction wasn't, however, and Zep fans sent 'Led Zeppelin II' to Number One both sides of the Atlantic when it was released towards the end of '69.

The record stayed on the UK chart for 138 weeks, and 98 weeks in the States. Come December, they had sold so many records that *The Financial Times* reported the fact and asked why – unlike the Beatles – Zep had not been awarded MBEs for their export achievements... The reported $5 million earned in US sales to that point was not the first in a long line of record-breaking statistics that could be used to sum up the band's career. But to do that would be to overlook the band's greatest achievement: their music. Zeppelin's only detractors in the early days were purists who attacked the band for 'stealing' phrases and melodies from blues artists. Lyrics in their second album's 'Lemon Song', for example, can certainly be traced back to 1920s Blues legend Robert Johnson, but in these days of wholesale repetition and sampling, such misdemeanours seem trivial. In any case, such analysis missed the point: Zeppelin were musical *fanatics* who listened to as much as they could, always working backwards trying to find out where ideas came from. Having listened, they learned, then took the influences as far *forward* as they could. Even when they covered Johnson's 'Travelling Riverside Blues' (a tribute not released until 1991) it sounded like a Led Zeppelin original.

In February '70, coming towards the end of

almost 18 months on the road, Led Zeppelin performed a gig in Copenhagen as 'The Nobs', after one Eva von Zeppelin – a relative of the airship designer – threatened to sue if the band used her family name. Legend has it she took advantage of her free tickets and was very impressed by the show, however... Which wasn't exactly the reaction 'Led Zeppelin III' met with when it was released in October of that year. Again, it hit Number One in the UK and USA, but because it was so different to its predecessors – being almost entirely acoustic – many felt confused by the abrupt change of style. The band were unrepentant, insisting that their music would remain unconfined by others' preconceptions. In many ways, the chosen style was a deliberate attempt to escape the term Heavy Metal, which many were branding the band with. Zeppelin hated the term and accused those who directed it at them of confusing power and volume with a form of music they had nothing to do with.

Nevertheless, Zeppelin have always been hugely popular with HM fans, a link cemented forever by the twin opening salvo of 'Rock And Roll' and 'Black Dog' on their untitled fourth album, released in November '71. The album also featured 'Stairway To Heaven', a song which has been played more times on FM radio than any other by any other band and played a huge part in making 'Four Symbols' (as the LP is widely known) into the group's best seller: around 12 million worldwide.

Its follow-up, 'Houses Of The Holy', was a further musical departure for the band, relying more heavily on the keyboards of John Paul Jones than ever before. In July, whilst playing New York's massive Madison Square Garden venue, three months after its release, the band were filmed for what eventually became the movie 'The Song Remains The Same' (not released until October '76).

Their next album, 'Physical Graffiti', was a double made after a lengthy break. It was released on their own newly formed label Swan Song in March '75 and remains probably their finest work, spanning the whole spectrum of

their styles. Following its release, the band began to wind down the touring process.

In the UK, they played just five shows – all at West London's Earl's Court in May, where they sold all 85,000 tickets in just four hours: just minutes more than the length of the shows themselves.

In August, Plant and his wife were badly hurt in a car accident on the Greek island of Rhodes. Plant's leg injuries were severe enough to mean that he was still in a wheelchair during sessions for Zep's sixth album, 'Presence'. One track on that record, the slow Blues of 'Tea For One', documents the mental anguish caused by his slow recovery...

The band toured the States with 'Presence' but didn't play any European shows until July 1979 when they did two nights in Copenhagen's Falconer Theatre as warm-ups for the following weekend's Knebworth Festival in the UK. The first show, on August 4, attracted an estimated 200,000 people – although around 80,000 got in without paying. The second show, a week later, attracted 90,000 more and proved to be Zeppelin's last UK date. Their final studio album, 'In Through The Out Door', was released in September 1979 and in the States re-activated the band's entire back catalogue... for one week, the *Billboard* Hot 100 featured every Led Zeppelin album!

June/July saw Zep play their first full-scale Continental tour for seven years. The final show on July 7 in West Berlin was to be their last ever.

They regrouped in September to rehearse for a forthcoming American tour, but on September

25, after a night of heavy drinking, Bonham was found dead in bed. On December 4, the remaining members of the group issued a short statement that they felt unable to continue as Led Zeppelin after "the loss of our dear friend" and the greatest rock band in history were officially no more.

Since then, rumours have frequently suggested they would reform with a different drummer. These names have included Cozy Powell, Bonham's son Jason, as well as Phil Collins and Tony Thompson (who both backed the other three for the one-off performance at Live-Aid on July 13, '85), but not even the vast sums of money reportedly being offered have persuaded the group that it would work. Plant has forged a successful solo career, Page enjoyed mixed fortunes with solo records and The Firm, whilst Jones' excursions onto record have been altogether more sporadic.

If you need more details, most bookshops' music shelves are positively groaning under the weight of books on the band. But all you really need is the music...

IN THEIR OWN WORDS...

"I think that the first album had so many firsts on it, as far as the content goes... Even though we were heavily involved in a sort of Progressive Blues thing, one of the most important parts was the acoustic input." – Jimmy Page, Kerrang! 313, October 27, 1990

"One of the most surprising times... must have been about 1974, and we did two open air festivals, one after another. These were the first two dates on the tour and there were, well, 50,000 people at each one. And that was just the band on its own, because we didn't have a support act. We thought, hey, what's going on!?!" – Jimmy Page, Kerrang! 193, June 25, 1988

"Musically, the whole Zeppelin thing came into full bloom at the beginning of 'Zep III' when we went up into the Welsh Mountains and I started taking Page around these places. We were on the trail of the Holy Grail for a bit!" – Robert Plant, Kerrang! 441, May 1, 1993

"Once we'd recorded the numbers and then started playing them live we were pushing them more and more, making the numbers work for us. Like on 'The Song Remains The Same' album, you hear all this energy roaring through it. That energy and intensity there's no escape from... It could be almost trance-like some nights..." – Jimmy Page, Kerrang! 313, October 27, 1990

"One of the most courageous things about Zep (was) – 'Fuck the mistakes...'. 'Physical Graffiti' has got quite a few errors but we were just going for it... The magic of Zep was its sheer chance factor, total lack of professionalism, the shit or bust phenomenon that won those nights it worked, against all odds." – Robert Plant, Kerrang! 293, June 9, 1990

"(Compiling the box set), it was evident what a brilliant textbook Zeppelin was. Especially in the different areas we approached. We went boldly where few men had been before, let's put it that way." – Jimmy Page, Kerrang! 313, October 27, 1990

"If Soundgarden and Mudhoney and Mother Love Bone and... Nirvana and Pearl Jam questions the whole pompous Hard Rock/Heavy Metal shit, then that's great! That's all I've ever wanted because I think that the majority of Heavy Metal is a farce." – Robert Plant, Kerrang! 441, May 1, 1993

"The real Led Zeppelin would have blown any band sky high – apart from Whitesnake. That powerhouse, that thundering entity could never reform, because there's one bloke missing..." – Robert Plant, Kerrang! 293, June 9, 1990

LED ZEPPELIN

STUDIO ALBUMS

LED ZEPPELIN *(Atlantic, 1968 – KKKK)* Earthy and raw Blues, recorded in just 30 hours of studio time. Features 'Babe I'm Gonna Leave You' and 'Dazed And Confused'...

LED ZEPPELIN II *(Atlantic, 1969 – KKKKK)* Indispensable! Zep's heaviest and most riff-laden album. But contrast 'Whole Lotta Love' with the sublimely gentle 'Thank You'...

LED ZEPPELIN III *(Atlantic, 1970 – KKKK)* A mellower record made after time spent in the Welsh mountains. Almost half acoustic plus the electric Blues of 'Since I've Been Loving You' and the full-on rock of 'Immigrant Song'...

'FOUR SYMBOLS' *(Atlantic, 1971 – KKKKK)* Indispensable! Even the lesser known tracks are awesome, with the whole gelling together as one of rock music's most celebrated works...

HOUSES OF THE HOLY *(Atlantic, 1973 – KKKK)* Plant's lyrical and musical input at its strongest. Includes John Paul Jones' showpiece 'No Quarter' and the wacky reggae of 'D'Yer Maker' which later inspired Dread Zeppelin...

PHYSICAL GRAFFITI *(Swan Song, 1975 – KKKKK)* Indispensable! Four sides that capture every side of Led Zeppelin. Some of the material was left over from the previous LP but none of it ever sounds less than masterful. Probably Zep's greatest album...

PRESENCE *(Swan Song, 1976 – KKKK)* Extremely intense and initially quite one-dimensional compared to earlier works, but given time, its power is unrelenting – especially on the classic 'Achilles Last Stand'.

IN THROUGH THE OUT DOOR *(Swan Song, 1979 – KKKK)* Relatively mellow. Showed Zeppelin branching out into new musical territories, using keyboards more than before...

OTHER ALBUMS

THE SONG REMAINS THE SAME *(Swan Song, 1976 – KKKK)* 1973 live soundtrack to the film of the same name. Better produced but weaker in performance than many of the bootlegs from this – or any other tour!

CODA *(Swan Song, 1982 – KKK)* Collection of out-takes and miscellany spanning Zep's whole career. An interesting curio that, although asembled by Page, fails to do justice to the legend...

LED ZEPPELIN *(Swan Song, 1991 – KKKKK)* Four-CD, 54-track box-set compilation remastered by Page after his dissatisfaction with the earlier transfer of the back catalogue to CD. Includes previously unreleased rarities...

REMASTERS *(Swan Song, 1991 – KKKK)* Double CD truncated version of the above...

REMASTERS II *(Swan Song, 1993)* Scheduled follow-up to the box-set which includes all tracks it omitted – plus extra rarities...

LEGS DIAMOND

USA, five-piece (1976-present)

ONE OF the most enduring of all American hard rock bands although still commanding only cult appreciation worldwide. The band's first three albums sold well on import and are now much prized by collectors.

The band have endured a variety of line-up changes – even splitting up to try again under the name of Rag Doll for a short period. Since 1984, signed to the Music For Nations label, Legs Diamond has revolved around original members Rick Sandford (vocals) and Michael Prince (keys/guitar). The pair's devotion to the act knows no bounds continuing a tradition of finely tuned melodic hard rock well into the 1990s.

Struttingly recommended

LEGS DIAMOND *(Mercury, 1977- KKKKK)*

LAND OF THE GUN *(Music For Nations, 1986-KKKK)*

LIFE, SEX AND DEATH

USA, four-piece (1989-present)

FORMING A band around the central figure of an alleged street bum has provoked extreme opinions. The official story goes that Stanley was a garbage-scavenging fuck-up, who was discovered and nurtured by the three musicians in the band and then let loose on an unsuspecting world. Cynics have accused Stanley of being a failed Chicago Glam Rocker who merely adopts his stinking persona to shift records. The full truth about Life, Sex And Death has yet to emerge.

Anyway, despite controversial artwork and the suspected sham of Stanley, LSD's debut album failed to shock anybody.

Cautiously recommended album:
THE SILENT MAJORITY (Warner Brothers, 1992 – KKK)

LITTLE ANGELS

UK, five-piece (1985-present)
CURRENTLY ONE of Britain's Great Rock Hopes, Little Angels began life in Scarborough under the rather less salubrious name of Mr Thrud. A change of monicker was obviously in order, so they became Little Angels, signed to indie label Powerstation and put out the seven-track 'Too Posh Too Mosh' mini album in 1987.

Ever since signing to major label Polydor in June 1988, Little Angels have fought a constant battle against 'unhipness'. Despite the improvement between debut album 'Don't Pray For Me' ('89) and 'Young Gods' ('91), to many folk in the music industry, the band were just too young, too clean and too nice... Fortunately, British rock fans had no such silly reservations

LITTLE ANGELS: battling 'unhipness'

and got behind Toby Jepson (vocals), Bruce Dickinson (guitar), his brother Jimmy (keyboards), Mark Plunkett (bass) and Mark Richardson (drums, replacing Michael Lee who in turn had replaced Dave Hopper after 'Too Posh...'), with a vengeance. It was not until 1993 and their third album, 'Jam', that they finally reaped the rewards of their fans' persistence and their record company's faith. The record entered the UK chart at Number One and did much to secure them the coveted opening slot on the Van Halen tour of the UK and Europe.

Recommended albums:
YOUNG GODS (Polydor, 1991 – KKKKK)
JAM (Polydor, 1993 – KKKKK)

LITTLE CAESAR

USA, five-piece (1987-1992)
EXCELLENT LA band distinguished by the gruff but soulful vocals of frontman Ron Young. Released a mini album, 'Name Your Poison', in '89 then signed to Geffen. Second and final full album featured guitarist Earl Slick (ex-Dirty White Boy, Ian Hunter, Dirty White Boy etc), replacing the intriguingly-named Apache. Their tattooed biker image was at odds with their music – although perfectly suited their live delivery! The paradox must have contributed to their lack of progress and Geffen's decision to drop them. Young has since formed a new quintet called Dirt.

Recommended second album:
INFLUENCE (Geffen, 1992 – KKKK)

LIZZY BORDEN

USA, five-piece (1983-present)
LED BY that clown in 'The Decline And Fall Of Western Civilisation, Part II: The Metal Years', with the loud hair and tassles. The frontman is a never-say-die LA wannabe whose eponymous band have made at least six albums. They will never be successful but will always sell tickets... in LA.

Recommended (mainly for the title) double live album:
THE MURDERLESS METAL ROAD SHOW (Roadrunner, 1986 – KKK)

LONDON

USA, four-piece (1979-present)
DITTO LIZZY Borden – but sadder. London, formed by the now departed Lizzie Grey, have made just three albums but have a family tree more impressive than Deep Purple, Rainbow, Whitesnake and Gillan's combined. Early members included Nikki Sixx and Blackie Lawless.

Now fronted by the pompously-named and impossibly-coiffeured Nadir D'Priest...

Recommended debut album:
NON-STOP ROCK (ROADRUNNER, 1986 – KKK)

LONE STAR

Wales, six-piece (1975-1978)
DESPITE A years ahead of its time Roy Thomas Baker-produced debut, and a stunning lower budget follow-up, 'Firing On All Six', Lone Star imploded rather than going super nova. Lead guitarists were Paul Chapman (ex-UFO) and Tony Smith. First album vocals were by Kenny Driscoll, replaced by John Sloman (later of Uriah Heep and Gary Moore Band) on the second.
Recommended album:
LONE STAR *(Epic, 1976 – KKKK)*

LOUDNESS

Japan, four-piece (1980-present)
LOUDNESS, OFT regarded as Japan's premier Metal band, wanted American success so much that they eventually replaced their popular vocalist Minoru Nihara with an American, ex-Obsession man Mike Vescera, but have since replaced him with another Japanese singer: EZO's Masaki Yamada.

Despite a slide into commercial obscurity with their more recent albums, Loudness' earlier affairs are technically brilliant, the two live albums being (almost) indispensable.
Vely lecommended:
LIVE-LOUD-ALIVE (LIVE IN TOKYO)
(Roadrunner, 1983 – KKKKK)
8186 LIVE *(Atco Japan, 1987 – KKKKK)*

LOVE/HATE

USA, four-piece (1986-present)
AFTER TWO years of getting nowhere as Data Clan, the quartet changed style and name in '86 and dubbed themselves the 'stoopidest band in the world', then flashed onto the scene in 1990 with their debut LP 'Blackout In The Red Room'. The album impressed almost universally; their live show, however, was just total head removal.

Opening with bass player Skid brandishing a cross made from empty Budweiser cans, and rapidly followed onstage by drummer Joey Gold, guitarist Jon E Love and singer/dynamo Jizzy Pearl, only the finest of strings stopped the whole thing crashing into total acarchy.

LOVE/HATE (Jizzy Pearl): bun-shaking

Their follow-up LP, 'Wasted In America' ('92), was equally bun-shaking, but while Jizzy & Co received frenzied receptions in the UK, America was less keen to warm to their brand of psycho rock.

In 1992, Love/Hate lost their deal with Columbia and replaced Love with former Roadrunner solo widdler Darren Housholder. A comeback album is expected late '93...
Recommended albums:
BLACKOUT IN THE RED ROOM *(Columbia, 1990 – KKKKK)*
WASTED IN AMERICA *(Columbia, 1992 – KKKKK)*

LOVERBOY

Canada, five-piece (1980-present)
DESPITE THAT name and a procession of quite laughable videos, on their day, Loverboy could rock as hard as the next band. Huge in North America they fared badly in Britain, possibly more due to lack of touring than anything, the band having only played in the UK supporting Def Leppard (plus a Marquee one-off) in 1988.

Fronted by ex-Moxy singer Mike Reno and featuring the talents of guitarist Paul Dean (who later released a solo album) Loverboy were at the very pinnacle of AOR. Will they ever return?
Recommend, every minute of:
GET LUCKY *(CBS, 1981 – KKKK)*
LOVIN' EVERY MINUTE OF IT *(CBS, 1985 – KKKK)*

Phil LYNOTT

Ireland, genius
(August 20, 1951-January 4, 1986)
THE GREATEST songwriter of his generation...
The loveable rogue fronting Thin Lizzy... But
also a solo artist. Debut album 'Solo In Soho'
(Vertigo, '81) was a Lizzy-esque collection but
the following year's 'The Philip Lynott Album'
showed him stretching his musical horizons.
The following year, he featured on a single,
'Please Don't Leave Me' (on MCA), alongside
the then new Lizzy guitarist John Sykes. After
Lizzy split in '83, Lynott formed Grand Slam but
never won a deal. He had a Number Five hit with
Gary Moore on the single 'Out In The Fields' in
May 1985, then played his last gig, with Grand
Slam, at the Marquee in Wardour Street on
December 4, 1985. One month later he was
dead and the world was a much poorer place.
Recommended album:
THE PHILIP LYNOTT ALBUM *(Vertigo, 1982 –*
KKKK)

LYNYRD SKYNYRD

USA, seven-piece (1965-present)
FORMED AS a high school band called My
Backyard in Jacksonville, Florida. Later, to
antagonise their sports teacher Leonard Skinner
who habitually complained about the length of
their hair, they corrupted his name to Lynyrd
Skynyrd and adopted it as their own. For those
having trouble, they christened their '73 debut
album 'Pronounced Leh-Nerd Skin-Nerd'. By
then, however, everybody should have known
the name, as the band had worked their asses
off touring around the Southern states. They
released their debut single, 'Need All My
Friends', in Jacksonville as early as 1968, with a
second rushed out in... 1971! Two years later,
ex-Blood Sweat And Tears guitarist turned
talent scout, Al Kooper, signed them to MCA.

Skynyrd's name has become synonymous
with Southern/Dixie rock/boogie – not to
mention on-the-road drinkin' an' hell-raisin'!
Their musical style is epitomised by the three
guitar lead break in the classic 'Freebird'. Over-
exposure of this song has tended to eclipse
much of the rest of their catalogue – which is a
travesty as it is all worthy of closer inspection.

Personnel has varied over the years
(Blackfoot's Ricky Medlocke played drums in an
early incarnation) but come 1977, the line-up
had peaked at Ronnie Van Zandt (vocals), Gary
Rossington, Allen Collins and Steve Gaines
(guitars), Leon Wilkeson (bass), Billy Powell
(piano) and Artimus Pyle (drums). Tragically, this
line-up was aboard their rented plane when it
crashed into a swamp in Gillsburg, Mississippi
on October 20, 1977. The accident claimed the
lives of Van Zandt, Gaines and his sister Cassie
(one of three backing singers touring with the
band), plus personal manager Dean Kirkpatrick.

The band had just released the superb fifth
studio album 'Street Survivors', a follow-up to
the epochal double live 'One More From The
Road' (also '77) and seemed poised on the brink
of even greater success. Such plans and
dreams were all cast aside as the rest of the
band recovered from injuries and tried to come
to terms with the tragedy. In 1979, all the
survivors apart from Pyle regrouped as the
Rossington-Collins Band and made two albums
with a female singer, Dale Krantz (who would
later marry Rossington). This band split in 1982.

In September 1987, a new Lynyrd Skynyrd
played a 32-date tour featuring new men
Johnny Van Zandt (Ronnie's brother, on vocals)
and Randall Hall (guitar) plus Rossington,
Powell, Pyle, Wilkeson, King and two backing
singers. Ronnie Van Zandt's wife objected to
the use of the name, so for legal and
contractual reasons the band didn't work until
1991, when they re-emerged – originally called
'Lynyrd Skynyrd 1991'. With a drummer called
Custer, the band played gigs that were as good
as any Skynyrd fan dared hope for. The South –
as they always promised – had risen again.
Recommended albums:
SECOND HELPING *(MCA, 1974 – KKKKK)*
ONE MORE FROM THE ROAD *(MCA, 1976 –*
KKKKK)
LYNYRD SKYNYRD *(MCA, 1991 – KKKKK) 47*
track triple-CD collection of hits and rarities

MADAM X

USA, four-piece (1984-1986)

DUMBO METAL band, initially signed to Jet, only noteworthy for beginning the careers of Vixen drummer Roxy Petrucci (whose sister, Maxine, played guitar in Madam X) and much later, a young Canadian singer called Sebastian Bach (who failed to record with the act).

Good for a laugh:

WE RESERVE THE RIGHT *(Jet, 1984 – K)*

MAGNUM

UK, five-piece (1977-present)

ANYONE FROM Birmingham who decides to form a Pomp Rock band is clearly two parps short of a keyboard – but don't tell Magnum guitarist Tony Clarkin cos he's made a very sucessful career out of it. Love 'em or ignore 'em, you just can't hate Magnum – they're too quintessentially British and, er... harmless. Having supported Judas Priest in '77, then Whitesnake in '78, the band attracted a sizeable and loyal following of Metalheads. Bog knows why, because most of their music is about as heavy as gently tissued dry lettuce leaf. Frontman Bob Catley is a Very Nice Man who can sing very well and waves his arms around a lot on stage.

These days, Clarkin and he are ably backed by Mark Stanway (keyboards, ex-Phil Lynott's Grand Slam), Wally Lowe (bass) and Mickey Barker (drums). Their debut album, 'Kingdom Of Madness' (Jet, '78), has been followed by eight other studio albums, plus a handful of live sets and compilations that have slowly (and politely) drifted away from Pomp and towards AOR, notably since signing to Polydor in 1986. All jolly pleasant, really.

Recommended albums:

KINGDOM OF MADNESS *(Jet, 1978 – KKKK)*
ON A STORYTELLER'S NIGHT *(FM, 1985 – KKKK)*

MAHOGANY RUSH

Canada, three-piece (1970-1988)

LED BY weirdo guitarist Frank Marino, who took far too many drugs for an adult – when he was still a teenager – and claims to have been visited by the spirit of Jimi Hendrix whilst unconcious in hospital during a bad trip. Upon awakening he could play like Hendrix, even though he'd never even picked up a guitar before... Nah, we don't believe it either but it's a good story.

His records were uncannily close to the master's in style but lacked originality. Added a second guitarist, his brother Vince, in the early '80s but the band remained only middle league. Best remembered in the UK for a storming performance at the Heavy Metal Holocaust festival at Port Vale FC's ground in '81 – and for Frank's FX pedal board which was so long it took two roadies to carry it onto the stage.

Recommended album:

LIVE *(CBS, 1978 – KKK)*

MALEVOLENT CREATION

USA, five-piece (1987-present)

VIRTUAL MASTERS of the sonic whirlwind, Malevolent Creation hail from Buffalo, New York. Their 1991 debut, 'The Ten Commandments', was ferocious enough, but merely paved the way for one of 1992's most deadly Death Metal attacks...

Recommended album:

RETRIBUTION *(R/C Records, 1992 – KKKK)*

MALICE

USA, five-piece (1981-1988)
AT THE forefront of the so-called New Wave Of
US Heavy Metal in the early '80s, Malice
suffered greatly from both label and fan
indifference and lost their way once Thrash
began to rise to prominence, despite touting
some very good Priest-influenced Metal around
on two albums with Atlantic.

Malice fell apart not long after a UK tour
opening for Slayer, but not before an
appearance in the movie 'Vice Versa' and a third
album appeared with Paul Sabu (!) singing in
place of James Neal.
Maliciously recommended:
LICENSE TO KILL *(Atlantic, 1986 – KKKK)*

Mitch MALLOY

USA, solo artist (1990-present)
RIGHTFULLY CHRISTENED the New God Of
AOR towards the end of '92, Malloy is the pin-
up rock shag for a new generation. The
antithesis of dinosaur AOR and with enough
pulsation an' pout to cross over into chartland,
Mitch's future oughta be brighter than a
sparkler jammed in yer eyeball! Hey, you're
gonna need shades...
Recommended album:
MITCH MALLOY *(RCA/BMG, 1992 – KKKK)*

Yngwie J MALMSTEEN

Sweden, guitarist (1984-present)
KNOWN AS Yngwie J to avoid confusion with all
the other Yngwie Malmsteens out there, Mr
Malmsteen is a classical music fanatic with a
serious Ritchie Blackmore fixation.
Unquestionably brilliant as a guitarist,
Malmsteen nonetheless suffers from delusions
of grandeur even he could not hope to attain –
not to mention the fact that he can't write a
decent song to save his life.

In Sweden, he rose to fame in Powerhouse
and Rising, with whom he made demos that
ultimately reached LA guitarist fanatic Mike
Varney, who in '81 persuaded the 18-year-old
Malmsteen to move to LA, join Steeler (fronted

by Ron Keel) and record an album for Varney's
own Shrapnel label ('83). Malmsteen's stay in
Steeler was short, and after reportedly turning
down offers to join UFO, Kiss and Ozzy
Osbourne, he teamed up with ex-Rainbow
singer Graham Bonnet in Alcatraz. Next he
formed his own band, Yngwie Malmsteen's
Rising Force (featuring Jeff Scott Soto on
vocals) who recorded an eponymous album
(Polydor, '84) that owed much to Blackmore's
'Rainbow Rising'. 'Marching Out' (Polydor, '85)
and 'Trilogy' (Polydor, '86 – with new singer
Mark Boals) followed before Malmsteen
attempted to gain more commercial success by
enlisting another ex-Rainbow vocalist Joe Lynn
Turner for 'Odyssey' (Polydor, '88). It didn't
really work and ultimately the pair fell out,
Turner making his second and final appearance
on 'Trial By Fire – Live In Leningrad' (Polydor,
'89). After '90's 'Eclipse', he and Polydor ended
their commercially unremarkable liaison and he
moved to Elektra for '92's mind-numbingly
tedious 'Fire And Ice'.
Recommended (third) album:
RISING FORCE *(Polydor, '84 – KKKK)*

MAMA'S BOYS

Ireland, four-piece (1978-present)
McMANUS BROTHERS Pat (guitar), John (bass)
and Tommy (drums) had played only traditional
Irish folk until they saw Irish folk rockers the
Horslips, in concert in 1978. Swapping fiddles,
pipes and goat-skin drums for electric guitars
and a proper kit, they turned into a blues rock
power trio (with John handling vocals), retaining
Folk influences and occasionally sounding like
early Thin Lizzy. That band's Phil Lynott was
impressed enough to let Mama's Boys open the
show on the band's '83 farewell UK dates. A
couple of years later, the band added a vocalist
so their music became more AOR and less
unique. 1992's eighth album, 'Relativity' (CTM,
'92) found them mixing both styles to some
effect with new singer Mike Wilson hopefully a
more permanent feature than his predecessors.
Recommended (second) album:
PLUG IT IN *(Albion, 1982 – KKKK)*

MANIC STREET PREACHERS

UK, four-piece (1989-present)

PERHAPS THE most shameless media agitators ever, the Manics are custom-designed for these tabloid times. Educated, ruthless and informed, the Welsh designer-rebels took on the music press with a vengeance, claiming to hate pop and sex and art and everything. When asked if the band was a joke, guitarist Richie James' reply was to carve '4 Real' into his arm, a move that guaranteed further exposure.

A massive audience hung on Richie's every word and the band's uncluttered, gratuitously sloganeering pop-punk. The trash-scam worked brilliantly, despite admissions from the band that Richie had actually not played on the ensuing album due to apathy and because James was a better guitarist than he was.

Manic Street Preachers have gleefully courted controversy to fuel their brief but exhilarating career to date. Despite original assurances that their first album would definitely be their last, the band did release another in 1993. Time will tell whether the band have bitten off more than we can chew.

Highly recommended album:

GENERATION TERRORISTS *(Columbia, 1992 – KKKKK)*

MANOWAR

USA, four-piece (1980-present)

NEW YORK-based Manowar are either the epitome or the epitaph of Heavy Metal, taking the music either to a logical conclusion or the most laughable dead end. Whichever path of opinion you choose to follow, only a fool would express his or her preference for the latter within earshot of the band. You might be big and brave enough to beat all four of them to a pulp – unlikely, admittedly – but would it really be worth running the risk of being branded an unworthy non-believer and a wimpish supporter of False Metal?

The story of Manowar is laden with so much hyperbole, that it's better to believe than to question – whatever you think of the music. And shame on you if you grin whilst listening: Manowar and Heavy Metal are more serious than life itself...

The band was put together by one-time Black Sabbath roadie Joey DeMaio as a mission to become the loudest band in the world or at least, the only band that matters. Although nominally the band's bass player, DeMaio is really far more as apart from conceiving most of the songs, four strings are rarely enough for him, preferring to play his beloved instruments as if they were rhythm guitars in most instances. One particularly treasured model he has named 'The Enterprise' as it has enough knobs and switches on it to keep Captain Kirk and his whole crew busy for a series.

DeMaio first recruited a like-minded (ie completely over-the-top) guitarist in the shape of Ross The Boss, a legendary guitarist who'd made his name (actually Ross Friedman) and reputation with furious New York rockers, The Dictators. Immediately prior to joining Manowar Ross The Boss had been a member of the Sandy 'Blue Öyster Cult' Pearlman-managed French band Shakin' Street. DeMaio and Ross sowed the seeds of Manowar backstage at Newcastle City Hall where Shakin' Street were supporting Black Sabbath on a UK tour, whilst DeMaio worked for the headliners on their pyros.

When the tour was over, the two got together in New York to look for others to complete what might prove to be the last ever True Metal band. The only vocalist able to impress them was Eric Adams, a former butcher and meat cutter, who claims to have a five-and-a-half octave range. The best drummer in the world was apparently Donnie Hamzik. With the line-up complete, Manowar set about their Grail-like quest to overcome any who stood in their way.

EMI America financed a $250 demo which led to a management deal with former Kiss manager Bill Aucoin, and ultimately their debut album 'Battle Hymns' (Liberty, '82). The record featured a guest appearance by Orson Welles, who did the voiceover for the track 'Dark Avenger'. Tragically, after selling around 10,000 copies, the label committed the remarkable *faux pas* of dropping them the same year they were signed.

For its heavier follow-up, 'Into Glory Rides' ('83) the band dispensed with Aucoin (and the Dolby noise reduction system) and hired a new drummer; man-mountain Scott Columbus. Columbus was said to hit his drums so hard that conventional kits just fell apart. He therefore played a custom-built stainless steel set-up. Manowar showed off Columbus – not to mention their furry loincloths – during their sword-brandishing performance at NY's quasi-legendary 'World War III' indoor Metal festival. The band were picked up by Megaforce in the States (in Europe by the then fledgling label Music For Nations) who got *exactly* what they bargained for at the contract signing ceremony – the band dutifully opened their veins with a ceremonial dagger and signed their names in their own blood.

This record was the birthplace of the HM classic, 'All Men Play On 10' released as a single and a paean not to their lable but to the correct setting of all volume knobs. The output from DeMaio's amps is so intense that the bassist has christened the effect 'The Black Wind'. During 'All Men Play On 10' is played in concert, a member of the audience is invited on stage to share the experience...

Recorded output then ceased for three years whilst the band toured to consolidate their reputation. Although they could headline in Europe, support slots on major tours in the States were difficult to come by as apparently Motörhead were the only band in the world not afraid to share a bill with them. With Lemmy & Co, they co-headlined eight shows. Then in 1987, Manowar undertook their first US headline tour, known as 'The Spectacle Of Might' tour. During it they made it into 'The Guinness Book Of World Records' as the loudest rock 'n' roll band on the planet – peaking at 160 decibels.

The next studio album, 'Fighting The World' ('87) was released on another new label, Atco, part of the Atlantic stable to whom they are currently signed. The record was their first to be digitally recorded, enabling Manowar to reach new heights of volume. But all was not well in the Manowar camp and, unbelievably, Ross The Boss left the band in 1988.

Suitably impressed, the new label helped finance a couple of UK tours in '83 and '84 – the latter promoting 'Hail To England', an album recorded in tribute to those who turned up for the first tour – a following they have dubbed 'The Army Of The Immortals'. There weren't actually that many for either sortie, but the band won consistently good press and so Virgin affiliate 10 Records signed them for album number four, 'Sign Of The Hammer' (also '84).

Replacing him seemed a monumental task and only one man could meet the challenge... Enter the Death Dealer, known, reluctantly, to the rest of the world, as Dave Shankel.

Death Dealer made his debut on 'Kings Of Metal' (Atlantic, '88) – an opus which featured DeMaio's solo piece, 'The Sting Of The Bumble Bee', probably the fastest bass playing ever, some of which clocked an unprecedented 208 beats per minute on a metronome.

IN THEIR OWN WORDS...

"We're not scared – we just don't give a shit! It's our mission! The original buzz I got from bands like Cream and The Yardbirds was incredible. Somehow those moments have to be related to today's generation." – Ross The Boss, Kerrang! 22, August 12-25, 1982

"When we were doing those gigs in Florida, we were dropping plaster off the roofs in all the clubs. It was truly awesome... we also did great business with the ladies... We'll claim the Harems Of Allah, because the fact is, Manowar is a 'mannish' band founded on 'mannishness' – believe me!" – Ross The Boss, Kerrang! 22, August 12-25, 1982

"People have accused us of having big mouths and we have! But we're sick and tired of False Metal and we can back up everything we say." – Joey DeMaio, Kerrang! 37, March 10-23, 1983

"No tape can really hold the sound of the band, but I think we've managed to capture most of the 'Black Wind' (on 'Into Glory Rides')." – Joey DeMaio, Kerrang! 47, July 28-August 10, 1983

"We play with anger, vengeance and animal intensity, and we don't like high-gloss with nothing beneath it – we want the sound that everyone else is trying to get away from. The last thing we're concerned about is getting played on the radio." – Joey DeMaio, Kerrang! 47, July 28-August 10, 1983

"It's tough, man, when all your friends are diggin' into cheeseburgers and all you're eatin' is your tuna fish sandwich and a salad, but I love this band – and that's the commitment you have to have if you love something that much." – Eric Adams, Kerrang! 217, December 10, 1988

"It's not my fault that I happen to be in a band that has three other musicians who are the most competent in Heavy Metal. We set a standard of group performance that exceeds anything else on the market. We've set our standards to be the Led Zeppelin of the '90s." – Joey DeMaio, Kerrang! 415, October 24, 1992

"Death to False Metal!" – Manowar, Kerrang!, every available opportunity

MANOWAR

Before Manowar's most recent work, Scott Columbus was "forced to leave the band due to family commitments", an amicable split mended by the arrival of new drummer, Rhino (not his real name). As a parting gesture, Columbus donated his stainless steel kit to Rhino, a young man so overwhelmed that he set fire to his own kit and hired a photographer to record the conflagration. 'Triumph Of Steel' (Atlantic, '92) introduced Rhino to an unsuspecting world via a drum solo in the middle of the 28-minute epic 'Achilles: Agony And Ecstasy In Eight Parts': based on the ancient Greek myths of the hero Achilles. A promised 1992 European tour to promote the album failed to materialise, but when next they play here, the band have also promised to use two buses – one for themselves and one for any females that wish to join the tour and serve the band.

Other than having sex – a pleasure reserved only for their women fans – the ultimate compliment bestowed by the band on their loyal male supporters is to be given the Sacred Salute: during which the band drop to one knee with arms aloft and chanting 'Hail!' to the lucky recipient! It's a moment no other band in the world could have thought of...

ALBUMS

BATTLE HYMNS (Liberty, 1982 – KKKK) "Guaranteed to garotte the unprepared and staple the knees of the meek..." – Kerrang! 24, September 9-22, 1982

INTO GLORY RIDES (Music For Nations, 1983 – KKK) "This isn't so much a superb rock 'n' roll album as a total vindication... Manowar were born to rule." – Kerrang! 47, July 28-August 10, 1983

HAIL TO ENGLAND (Music For Nations, 1984 – KKKKK) "Gut wrenchingly heavy... An excellent album... 'Impale me on the horns of death if I lie'." – Kerrang! 61, February 9-22, 1984

SIGN OF THE HAMMER (10 Records, 1984 – KK) "Whisper the name of Manowar in the same breath as Venom... Songs spiralling into the realms of the truly epic." – Kerrang! 77, September 20-October 3, 1984

FIGHTING THE WORLD (Atco, 1987 – KKKK)
"An album that deserves to be heard if only for its sheer Herculean heaviness... Absolute savage menace..." – Kerrang! 140, February 19-March 4, 1987

KINGS OF METAL (Atlantic, 1988 – KKKK)
"Let's face it, Manowar are a bunch of cornballs. They're so serious it's hilarious... Yet not without entertainment value." – Kerrang! 213, November 12, 1988

TRIUMPH OF STEEL (Atlantic, 1992 – KKKKK)
"If 'K's could be arranged in great legions atop a bloodied battlefield, stretching back beyond the distant horizon and littered around the bones of the newly dead, only then could they begin to convey the utter Heavy Metalness..." – Kerrang! 413, October 10, 1992

MARILLION

UK, five-piece (1979-present)
"THE THING we made sure to avoid was being classed as a second Genesis," said Fish in his first interview with Kerrang! back in March 1982. Marillion were, however, dogged with this comparison for most of their early career. But it didn't stop the Prog Rockers from becoming one of the largest cult status bands the UK has ever seen. The live buzz took them overnight from the London Marquee to sell-out shows in what was to become their home-from-home, Hammersmith Odeon. As well as being entertained with music, fans were also treated to comical banter from the gigantic Fish, making each gig a unique night out.

Once signed to EMI, Marillion released the 'Market Square Heroes' EP ('82) then remained a cult band for three albums – 'Script For A Jesters Tear' ('83), 'Fugazi' ('84) and the live 'Real To Reel' (also '84). They finally broke into mainstream success and named a thousand new-born babies with the '85 single 'Kayleigh', and concept album 'Misplaced Childhood', which launched them on their way to stadium tours across the UK and Europe.

1989 saw the departure of Fish to go solo, following the tour for studio album, 'Clutching At Straws'. Few thought Marillion would survive the loss of such a prominent character – but a new frontman in the shape of Steve Hogarth took the band to greater commerical success. A third album featuring him is imminent.
Recommended albums:
SCRIPT FOR A JESTER'S TEAR (EMI, 1983 – KKKKK)
MISPLACED CHILDHOOD (EMI, 1985 – KKKK)

MARIONETTE

UK, four-piece (1981-1985)
SUB-LEGENDARY Trash Rock street urchins ripping off Aerosmith before it became fashionable.
Recommended album:
DARK SECRETS AND BLONDE BOMBSHELLS (Heavy Metal Records, 1985 – KKKKK)

MARSHALL LAW

UK, four-piece (1987-present)
ALMOST UNBELIEVABLY enduring Trad Metal stalwarts from Birmingham, Marshall Law have stuck to their Judas Priest-influenced guns despite a lethargic response from the public. Unfashionable and resolute, Marshall Law will probably be around forever.
Recommended album for Plod Metallers:
MARSHALL LAW (Heavy Metal Records, 1990 – KK)

Richard MARX

USA, singer/songwriter (1987-present)
PLATINUM-SELLING, coiffeured AOR type whose music enables any self-respecting headbanger to fill an airline sickbag at the drop of a syrupy sweet harmony. Two claims to street cred are his writing partnership with ex-Tubes frontman Fee Waybill, and the song 'Children Of The Night' which raised funds for abused children.
Recommended album:
REPEAT OFFENDER (EMI, 1989 – KKK)

MASTERS OF REALITY

USA, four/three-piece (1980-present)
FORMED BY guitarist/singer Chris Goss and bassist Googe in upstate New York, and named after a Black Sabbath album to turn off all the "Punk snobs". Played the clubs for seven years, then at a gig in New York City, caught the ear of Rick Rubin. In '87 the band signed to his Def Jam label, moving in '88 to Def American. The band released their excellent eponymous debut LP, but attempts to tour proved disastrous; at each others' throats, the band split. The LP was re-released in 1990 on Rap label Delicious Vinyl with an extra track. At about the same time, Goss and Googe met former Cream drummer Ginger Baker in LA. A new partnership was born, resulting in the Def American follow-up 'Sunrise On The Sufferbus'.
Recommended album:
MASTERS OF REALITY *(Def American, 1988 – KKKKK)*

MAX WEBSTER

Canada, four-piece (1975-1982)
TORONTO WEIRDOS led by Kim Mitchell (guitar/vocals) who had an association with lyricist Pye Dubois and fellow countrymen Rush – who they supported many times, and with whom they released the awesome joint single 'Battlescar' in '81. Mitchell wore the daftest stage-gear this side of the Bay City Rollers, and his haircut was almost as bad, but he was an engaging frontman and inspired the band to make six humorous and off-the-wall records before going solo.
Recommended album:
A MILLION VACATIONS *(Capitol, 1979 – KKKK)*

MC5

USA, five-piece (1968-71)
"KICK OUT the jams, motherfuckers!" was the phrase that said it all, from the band who did it all! Formed in Detroit, the Motor City Five were rock 'n' roll revolutionaries of the high(!)est disorder. Their debut album, 'Kick Out The Jams', recorded live in '68, is without doubt one of the most uncompromising Heavy Rock records of all time. Follow-up LP, 'Back In The USA' ('70), was once described as 'one of the greatest rock albums ever', yet due to lack of success, the MC5 dissolved after their third and final release 'High Time' ('71).
Recommended album:
KICK OUT THE JAMS *(Elektra, 1969 – KKKKK)*

MEAT LOAF

USA, singer (1971-present)
MADE HIS recording debut as early as 1971 on 'Stoney And Meat Loaf' but didn't really do anything of significance to Heavy Metal until he guested on Ted Nugent's 'Free For All' (Epic, '77). After that, Jim Steinman enlisted him to sing on 'Bat Out Of Hell' in '78 and the rest is history... The 20 stone Meat (real name: Marvin Lee Aday) played a cameo in the 'Rocky Horror Picture Show' as the biker/Rock Star Eddie, but has been unable to make a record as good – never mind as successful – as 'Bat...' in four studio attempts since. The lucky sod did get to dance very close to Cher in the video for their '81 hit 'Dead Ringer For Love', though: it sure beat getting close to John Parr for '86's 'Rock 'N' Roll Mercenaries' collaboration...
Recommended album:
BAT OUT OF HELL *(Epic, 1978 – KKKKK)*

MEGADETH

USA, four-piece (1983-present)
DAVE MUSTAINE became a man hellbent on vengeful success when he was suddenly ejected from a fledgling Metallica's companyin Jnauary '83. The lead guitarist may have covered it all up by saying that he'd been seriously considering a solo career anyway, but from that day forth, he was a venomous motormouth with a mission.

The name Megadeth is a corruption of the real word 'megadeath', meaning: "the death of a million people, esp. in a nuclear war or attack", and made Mustaine's musical intentions plain from the off. Enlisting the services of his bass-plucking pal Dave 'Junior' Ellefson, guitarist Chris Poland and drummer Gar Samuelson, he set about devising Megadeth's fiendishly quirky debut album. Probably the first song set for inclusion was 'Mechanix', which Mustaine co-wrote with Metallica; it appeared on the latter's 'Kill 'Em All' debut under the name 'The Four Horsemen'. Mustaine's own set of lyrics were little more than a painful string of garage-related puns.

'Killing Is My Business... And Business Is Good' surfaced on Music For Nations in 1985. The sound quality was none too wonderful (a emergency remix operation was subsequently performed), but it nevertheless showcased some early Megadeth aggro. One of the more striking tracks for the fans was 'Rattlehead' – the rabble-rousing equivalent of Metallica's 'Whiplash', or Exodus' 'Bonded By Blood'. 'Killing...' also contained a cover of Nancy Sinatra's 1966 Number One 'These Boots Are Made For Walking', and a grisly little bastard of a song entitled 'Skull Beneath The Skin', which detailed the birth of Megadeth's Eddie-style mascot, Vic Rattlehead.

Looking back on those days, Mustaine now sees the band as "a bunch of young kids with very snotty noses trying to save the world but not knowing how to go about it". The next step was signing to a major label (Capitol), and creating their second album – at which point the frontman explained: "the snot in our noses had changed from clear to brown, because we'd started putting heroin up it".

The album, 'Peace Sells... But Who's Buying?', came out in 1986, and twisted minds everywhere. The centre-piece was the chugging political diatribe of the title-cut, which stands as one of Metal's (not just Thrash's) finest moments.

A subsequent Hammersmith Odeon gig was plagued with problems, however, leaving bad first impressions of Megadeth in the raw. Mustaine's cordless guitar insisted on repeatedly cutting out, forcing him to leave the stage, and the whole affair had a generally doomed feel. Reviews were not charitable.

Chris Poland and Gars Samuelson had both

been replaced by the time the next Megadeth album, 'So Far, So Good... So What?', appeared in 1988. Poland went on to tour with the Circle Jerks and embark on an unproductive solo career, while Samuelson became a painter and decorator... or something like that.

'So Far, So Good...' saw Jeff Young contribute guitar and Chuck Beehler occupy the drum stool. More accessible than its predecessor, and noticeably more widdly-lead obsessed, it still packed some great punches with 'Mary Jane', the emotionally charged power-epic 'In My Darkest Hour' and the PMRC-demolishing 'Hook In Mouth'.

Further line-up changes made Mustaine look like the David Coverdale of Thrash. Beehler and Young were ousted in less-than-amiable circumstances, and replaced with Nick Menza and Marty Friedman. (The latter had carved a reasonable solo career with guitar hero antics on various albums.) More significantly, perhaps,

"I don't think too many people are into us because of Metallica, and Metallica's brainwashing the world that I was a headcase and I was a drunk. It was hard for me to win over those people again."
– Dave Mustaine, Kerrang! 127, August 21-September 3, 1986

"Hey, just 'cause we had a $4,000 piece of crap first album, it doesn't mean that our next album is gonna suck."
– Dave Mustaine, Kerrang! 127, August 21-September 3, 1986

"Look at Reagan's name: Ronald Wilson Reagan, six letters, 666... now of course I'm not stupid enough to suggest that he's the Anti-Christ, but it sure makes you think, doesn't it?"
– Dave Mustaine, Mega Metal Kerrang! 5, January, 1986

"I have sop many addictions, it's ridiculous! I'm a gambler. I take compulsive high risks because I skydive and snowboard. Right there, I'm gambling with my life..."
– Dave Mustaine, Kerrang! 444, May 22, 1993

MEGADETH

was Mustaine's rebirth following drying-out counselling to kick heroin and booze...

The new, all-clean, Megadeth line-up spawned 'Rust In Peace' ('90) – their first without three suspension dots in its title or the customary cover version! It displayed a harder, cleaner sound, with plenty of lead guitar and melody, while still supplying those Mega-riffs by the dozen. The band toured and toured after this one, including the 'Clash Of The Titans' trek with Testament and Slayer, and incredibly, none of Mustaine's minions had been fired by the time Megadeth got around to concocting 'Rust In Peace's follow-up.

1992 gave rise to the eco-friendly 'Countdown To Extinction' – even more melodic, but full of good stuff nevertheless. The lead single was 'Symphony Of Destruction', with its main riff sucking on AC/DC minimalism, and the album's shifted units aplenty.

These days, Mustaine appears to be a fully reformed, white-shirted family man; the complete opposite of his evil twin from the past. But no-one knows what lies around the corner. The snot in his nose could stir at any given moment...

ALBUMS:

KILLING IS MY BUSINESS... AND BUSINESS IS GOOD (Music For Nations, 1985 – KKK) "These Thrash units just seem to keep on getting better and better, faster and faster." – Kerrang! 94, May 16-29, 1984

PEACE SELLS...BUT WHO'S BUYING? (Capitol, 1986 – KKKKK) "Taut guitars that grind and fire like there's no tomorrow, completely wicked time changes..." – Kerrang! 132, October 30-November 12, 1986

SO FAR, SO GOOD...SO WHAT? (Capitol, 1988 – KKKK) "This record will be too much to ignore... Just as Metallica started a trend, so too will Megadeth. Their time has arrived." – Kerrang! 172, January 30, 1988

RUST IN PEACE (Capitol, 1990 – KKKK) "Listen, and you could believe that the world really does owe Mustaine a living" – Kerrang! 308, September 22, 1990

COUNTDOWN TO EXTINCTION – (Capitol, 1992 – KKKK) "A drugs-free Mustaine may be less inclined to pen evil ditties like 'Black Friday' these days, but this hasn't weakened the Mega-drive any..." – Kerrang! 399, July 4, 1992

MELVINS

USA, three-piece (1987-present)
SAN FRANCISCO mob with a preference for the kind of slow, fuzzy dirge that is currently big in Seattle. But the Melvins have one up on so many of those from Washington State: they have a sense of humour. Best evidence to date was in 1992 when all three members released eponymous solo albums on the same day in virtually identical sleeves – echoing what the four members of Kiss had done 14 years earlier. *Recommended album:*
LYSOL (Boner/Tupelo, 1993 – KKKK)

MERCYFUL FATE

Denmark, five-piece (1981-present)
INNOVATIVE BAND who introduced the world to the Danish dingbat and King Diamond. A would-be footballer, once sued by Kiss' Gene Simmons who was afraid people would confuse a man brandishing a mikestand made out of bones whilst singing Doom/Thrash/Satanic Metal in an impossible falsetto with his own good self – because he too wore black and white make-up... 'Fate had split up at the time whilst 'Diamond went solo but the band's influence, even after only a mini-LP and three studio albums, is still considerable. Certainly strong enough to prompt a '92 reunion. Whether the new live show will, like the old one, feature sacrificial altars and exploding nuns, remains to be seen...
Recommended album:
MELISSA *(Music For Nations, 1983 – KKKK)*

METAL CHURCH

USA, four-piece (1982-present)
COMIN' OUTTA Seattle long before it was fashionable has never helped Metal Church. Numerous line-up changes have plagued their career, although the arrival of vocalist Mike Howe and ex-Metallica roadie John Marshall in 1988 began to pay dividends come their fourth LP, 'The Human Factor' (Elektra, '91).
Recommended debut album:
METAL CHURCH *(Ground Zero, 1984 – KKKK)*

METALLICA

USA, four-piece (1981-present)
FROM GARAGE-CAGED NWOBHM freaks to black-clad titans of the stadium world, and one of Heavy Metal's most respectable names, Metallica have made astounding progress during their 10 years of weighty chunk-riffs and constant musical advancement.

Metallica now loathe the term 'Thrash Metal', preferring to be seen as a rock band, pure and simple. But the undeniable, and somewhat ironic, fact remains that the quartet issued the first ever example of true Thrash, with 'Kill 'Em All' in 1983. Venom and Motörhead certainly paved the way, but Metallica took them as cues, rather than mere templates. The challenge was to use those two bands, and the slightly less extreme NWOBHM outfits, as a springboard into sonic violence never suffered before.

'Kill 'Em All' overbrimmed with snarling spit and snot, but most importantly... *that* guitar sound, one which was to stoke the fires of Thrash Metal in the decade to come. The line-up then was: James Hetfield (rhythm guitar/vocals), ex-tennis player Lars Ulrich (drums), Kirk Hammett (lead guitar, briefly with Exodus) and Cliff Burton (flares-loving bassman).

Dave Mustaine had already joined and been ejected from the Metalli-ranks by the time that debut was recorded, although he did play lead guitar on their first vinyl appearance (Metal Blade's 'Metal Massacre 1' compilation) and a few demo recordings. His alcohol and attitude problems forced the band to sack him, on the eve of negotiations with Megaforce Records. Mustaine, of course, stormed on to vent his spleen with Megadeth...

After the release of 'Kill 'Em All', Metallica gained prominence by touring with England's Venom and Raven. Music For Nations started handling them in Europe, and the underground following burgeoned. At this point, Johnny Z (Megaforce entrepeneur/Metalli-manager) asked Armored Saint's John Bush to handle vocals. Bush declined, but accepted an offer from Z to join Anthrax 10 years later!

The band's second album, 'Ride The Lightning' (July '84), demonstrated a fair amount of progression. While opening with one of Metallica's most holo-caustic cuts to date ('Fight Fire With Fire'), it goes on to display many a subtle side; most notably 'Fade To Black', which arguably began a whole trend of Wishbone Ash-styled soft-heavy-soft-heavy 'power-balladry' in Metal.

Even at this early stage, Metallica had learnt a lesson which was to shape the rest of their career: speed doesn't necessarily equal power.

Having said that, the third album, 'Master Of Puppets' ('86) stands as one of Metallica's mightiest moments, beginning with 'Battery', which sounds exactly like its title, ending with 'Damage Inc', and offering a whole load of great stuff in between.

Metallica's days as an 'indie' act were now limited. The deal with Music For Nations ended, and the band's new management Q-Prime secured a deal with Phonogram. A support slot on Ozzy Osbourne's six-month tour of America gave the band a massive break. Everything seemed perfect, until tragedy cruelly struck... On the road to Copenhagen one night, Metallica's tour bus crashed, and Cliff Burton was killed outright.

After a period of trying to decide whether or not to quit, Metallica eventually forged ahead and recruited Jason Newsted, formerly with Flotsam And Jetsam. Their first release with Newsted was a light-hearted affair entitled 'The $5.98 EP – Garage Days Revisited'. It contained three ropey covers of NWOBHM tunes, plus two segued Misfits cuts, and Killing Joke's 'The Wait' on the US version. Fans lapped it all up, placing the EP at Number 20 in the UK chart.

1988 was the year when Metallica 'got serious' again, and the highly convoluted '...And Justice For All' took some fans by surprise. Lasting 65 minutes, it's an album of epic stature, and dabbles with brilliance throughout its running time. 'One' was the single that gave Metallica real crossover appeal, and prompted the band to create their first ever promo video: a harrowing clip featuring footage from the movie of Dalton Trumbo's novel 'Johnny Got His Gun.

In 1991, the none-more-black 'Metallica' album appeared, with its more commercial approach. When the first MTV track, 'Enter Sandman', had an optional five-CD holder for future singles, it was obvious that this album was

designed to make Metallica bigger, if not necessarily better.

Since 1991, Metallica have toured without end. Perhaps the highlight in terms of career-peaking achievement, was their three-song set at the Freddie Mercury Tribute gig, and there's clearly no stopping them now...

ALBUMS

KILL 'EM ALL (Music For Nations, 1983 – KKKKK) "Mirror, mirror on the wall, who's the fastest of them all? Motörhead? Venom? METALLICAaaaarrrggghh!" – Kerrang! 47, July 28-August 10, 1983

RIDE THE LIGHTNING (Music For Nations, 1984 – KKKK) "One of the greatest, most original Heavy Metal albums of all time!" – Kerrang! 73, July 26-August 8, 1984

MASTER OF PUPPETS (Music For Nations, 1986 – KKKKK) "If you like to believe that even your worst mania has at least some hidden meaning...'Master Of Puppets' is most definitely the album for you." – Kerrang! 115, March 6-19, 1986

...AND JUSTICE FOR ALL (Vertigo, 1988 – KKK) "Lars' drum sound is really odd... Will finally put Metallica into the big league..." –

Kerrang! 203, September 3, 1988
METALLICA (Vertigo, 1991 – KKKKK) "Their most accessible album since 'Ride The Lightning'. Musically, it leaves '...And Justice For All' on the scrapheap." – Kerrang! 353, August 10, 1991

IN THEIR OWN WORDS...

"We are a band with a little originality, quality songs and the ability to play our instruments, so I'm sure we'll be successful." – Lars Ulrich, Kerrang! 70, June 14-27, 1984

"Thrash Metal implies lack of arrangement, lack of ability, lack of songwriting, lack of any form of intelligence." – Lars Ulrich, Kerrang! 83, December 13-26, 1984

"I don't think success has changed us as people at all. We're still the same lunatics as we were when this band first got going and never see ourselves as being on a higher level than the fans..." – Lars Ulrich, Kerrang! 120, May 15-28, 1986

"Metallica will never sacrifice stage bullshit for the venues we wanna play, and we just aren't the type of band that you sell as a live show. We don't need 50 feet tall dragons to sell our tickets." – Lars Ulrich, Kerrang! 153, August 20-September 2, 1987

"I think a lot of people in America right now are saying that we are doing the same arena rock clichés that these other bands were doing. It doesn't affect me, because I know what we are doing is something distinctly different." – Lars Ulrich, Kerrang! 389, April 25, 1992

"It's not about money any more. It's about egos; I wanna go out there and be the biggest band in the world and sell more records than anybody else. And I'm not gonna compromise that for anything." – Lars Ulrich, Kerrang! 404, August 8, 1992

METALLICA

MIND FUNK

USA, five-piece (1989-present)
BROUGHT MELODY to the heaviest of Metals on their eponymous debut album which rammed their message home like a bunny in heat. The band really want to be called Mind Fuck originally featured Pat Dubar (vocals), Louie Svitek (guitar, ex-MOD), Jason Coppola (guitar), John Monte (bass, ex-MOD) and Reed St Mark (drums, ex-Celtic Frost). After being dropped by Epic in 1992, they replaced Coppola and St Mark, with Jason Everman (ex-Nirvana and Soundgarden) and Shawn Johnson and signed to Megaforce/Music For Nations.
Recommended albums:
MIND FUNK (Epic, 1991 – KKKKK)
DROPPED (Music For Nations, 1993 – KKKKK)

MINISTRY

USA, duo plus guests (1982-present)
AFTER A rather embarrassing start with the bland Euro-pop outing called 'With Sympathy' Ministry have since put out some seriously awesome records. The nucleus of the band consists of just Al Jourgensen and Paul Barker, their live shows are ridiculously wild affairs featuring a large band made up of such people as Murder Inc's Martin Atkins (drums, ex-Killing Joke) and Chris Connelly (vocals), guitarists Tez Roberts (ex-Broken Bones) and Louie Svitek etc: expect anyone and anything to happen...
Recommended album:
PSALM 69: THE WAY TO SUCCEED AND THE WAY TO SUCK EGGS (Sire, 1992 – KKKKK)

MISFITS

USA, four-piece (1978-1983)
THEATRICAL PUNK lunatics led by Glenn Danzig, who have recently become trendy after being covered by Metallica, Soundgarden and Guns N' Roses. Wrote magnificent songs like 'Last Caress' and 'Mommy Can I Go Out And Kill Tonight', but much of their notoriety stems from the fact that few ever saw them play.
Recommended album:
WALK AMONG US (Ruby, 1982 – KKKKK)

Kim MITCHELL

Canada, solo artist (1982-present)
THE EVER wacky Mitchell was previously leader of off-the-wall Canadian act Max Webster, but split the band up to pursue a more fulfilling AOR-tinged solo career, despite huge domestic success.

Mitchell has recorded a steady stream of solo efforts in the ten years since Max Webster but has yet to achieve anything like the kind of success outside of Canadian borders as he has inside them.
Highly recommended:
ROCKLAND *(Atlantic, 1989 – KKKKK)*

MOLLY HATCHET

USA, six-piece (1971-present)
SOUTHERN BAND that originally leant more towards the raunch 'n' boogie than country flavours of, say, Lynyrd Skynyrd and have since drifted more towards the mainstream. None of the band are what you'd call slim, and when they played the Reading Festival in '79, it was touch and go as to what would give out first: the stage or the PA as they stood line-abreast for the heads-down no-nonsense finalé of 'Boogie No More'. Vocalists have come and gone over their eight LPs, but Danny Joe Brown (who went in '80 and came back in '89 after battling with diabetes) is best remembered.
Recommended second album:
FLIRTIN' WITH DISASTER *(Epic, 1979 – KKKK)*

Michael MONROE

Finland, singer (1980-present)
IMPOSSIBLY BEAUTIFUL former Hanoi Rocks vocalist. His debut solo album, 'Nights Are So Long' (Yahoo, 1988 – KKK), was largely overlooked but he signed to PolyGram for 'Not Fakin' It' ('89). The touring band featured Sam Yaffa (ex-Hanoi Rocks) on bass. A follow-up has yet to emerge as he made the tragic error of teaming up with ex-Michael Jackson/Billy Idol/Atomic Playboys guitarist Steve Stevens in Jerusalem Slim. Stevens jumped ship to join the Vince Neil Band; ironic, considering Neil was at the wheel of the car which killed Monroe's buddy and former Hanoi Rocks drummer Razzle in '84... Hence JS had split by the time their horrible eponymous debut was released in '93. Monroe is too good not to bounce back.
Recommended album:
NOT FAKIN' IT *(PolyGram, 1989 – KKKK)*

MONSTER MAGNET

USA, four-piece (1989-present)
NEW JERSEY burn-outs whose music is like a Hunter S Thompson novel dragged kicking and screaming into life, wild hallucinations and all. The band are seriously into blotter acid and once spent $80 on the stuff in order to "dose the crowd". "They just rushed the stage and tried to kill us," recalls Charles Manson lookalike vocalist/guitarist Dave Wyndorf.

Bands who get this messed up are either appaling or manage to attain some level of twisted genius; the latter is the case with Monster Magnet, and everything they have recorded to date has been a totally mind-blowing, drug fiend frenzy! Expect at least one of them to end up with a brain more fried than Syd Barrat after a night out with Colonel Sanders!
Recommended albums:
SPINE OF GOD *(Caroline, 1991 – KKKKK)*
SUPERJUDGE *(A&M, 1993 – KKKKK)*

MONTROSE

USA, four-piece (1973-1977)
MONTROSE WERE the makers of perhaps the greatest Heavy Metal debut album of all time, a stunning eponymous affair released in 1973 which set a standard few have come close to. The record became a template for American Metal but none – with the exception of Van Halen in 1978 – has been able to rival its power and vitality.

Montrose came from San Francisco and took their name from lead guitarist Ronnie Montrose, but was a group that far exceeded the sum of

may have been to do with Hagar's aspirations as a guitar player. He's since proved himself no slouch, but whether he was not good enough – or too good – for Ronnie at the time remains a mystery... Hagar went on to forge a successful solo career before joining Van Halen in 1975.

After he left the band, Montrose its parts to begin with. Also featured were Sammy Hagar (vocals), Bill 'Electric' Church (bass) and Denny Carmassi (drums). Comparisons with Led Zeppelin were made but never really held water, although Hagar was a bit of a Robert Plant lookalike and Carmassi was strongly influenced by John Bonham. (20 years later, Carmassi, ironically, would find himself drumming with Coverdale/Page...). The album was produced by Ted Templeman (who was the natural choice for Van Halen five years later, and countless others since!) and opened with three absolute classics: 'Rock The Nation', 'Bad Motor Scooter', 'Space Station Number 5'. The fact that the other five cuts were killer tracks too is often overlooked; a testimony to the brilliance of the record. The band visited the UK at the time, appearing with The Who at their legendary gig at Charlton Athletic FC's Valley Ground.

The follow-up, 'Paper Money', released in '74, was also a superb record, but has always been overshadowed by its predecessor. It featured new bassist Alan Fitzgerald on a number of softer, more atmospheric tracks, but which still bristled with power. Behind the scenes, though, something else was bristling: a clash of egos between Hagar and Montrose. The full truth has never really emerged but some of the conflict

were never the same again. They expanded to a five-piece by adding Jim Alcivar (keyboards) for the third LP 'Warner Bros Presents' ('75) with Bob James taking over lead vocals. The record was a patchy affair, as was its follow-up, 'Jump On It' ('76), which rocked a little harder but to no greater effect. Ronnie Montrose could tell, as could the fans, that it just wasn't happening any more...

In fact, come 1976, it had all become too much for Ronnie, who was having to cope with the twin pressures of controlling the musical direction and overseeing the finances of the band. Seeing that the musical side of things could never match their amazing start, he made the decision to knock the band on the head.

Although Montrose the band were thereafter dead, the story doesn't really end there. Montrose the guitarist returned in '79 with a jazz-influenced instrumental solo album called 'Open Fire' – which confused the hell out of Montrose fans. Ronnie had succeeded in distancing himself from his past – but took a small step back towards it when he formed a new outfit, Gamma, who signed to Elektra. Included in the line-up were ex-Montrose men Alcivar and Fitzgerald, plus Davey Pattison (vocals) and Skip Gallette (drums). Their eponymous debut ('79) was unremarkable, but

MONTROSE

the follow-up, 'Gamma II' ('80), was altogether heavier with another ex-Montrose man, Carmassi replacing Gallette and Glen Letsch taking over on bass. After a US hit with the track 'Voyager', they took an about face for 'Gamma III' ('82) and synths of Mitchell Froom (replacing Alcivar) dominated over Montrose's guitar. This line-up supported Foreiegner in Europe in '83 but soon after, Gamma was put on ice.

Ronnie returned to Jazz Rock for 'Territory' (Passport '86) then switched again to rock with 'Mean' (Enigma, '87) – a record which featured Letsch, Johnny Edwards, who briefly replaced Lou Gramm in Foreigner, on vocals and Kames Kottak (later to join Kingdom Come *et al*) on drums. Both had been in Buster Brown, a band from Louisville that supported Gamma.

Since then Ronnie has made two further albums – 'The Speed Of Sound (Enigma, '88) and 'This Diva Station' (Roadrunner, '90) – but he began to look more towards production work...

Sammy Hagar, of course, has gone on to achieve the kind of success with Van Halen, that ironically would surely have been awarded to Montrose the band had he stayed with them. An odd trick of fate...

ALBUMS

MONTROSE (Warner Bros, 1973 – KKKKK) Totally essential purchase. Voted Fourth Best HM Album Of All Time by Kerrang! staff in 1989. Few have surpassed it since...

PAPER MONEY (Warner Bros, 1974 – KKKKK) A great album by any standards – except Montrose's own!

WARNER BROS PRESENTS (Warner Bros, 1975 – KKK) First without Sammy Hagar, a major disappointment...

JUMP ON IT (Warner Bros, 1976 – KKKK) A step back in the right direction but could never hope to match earlier glories, so proved to be Montrose's swan song...

(See text for Ronnie Montrose albums since 1976)

Gary MOORE

Ireland, guitarist (1970-present)

MADE TWO albums with Irish band Skid Row – 'Skid' ('70) and '34 Hours' ('71) – then made a solo effort 'Grinding Stone' in '73. But his name only really became well known when he worked with Thin Lizzy. He guested on one track on 'Night Life' ('74), then featured on 'Black Rose' ('79). This followed a Lizzy-esque solo album, 'Back On The Streets' ('78), and led to a more HM solo career – with the Gary Moore Band – kicked off in '82 with 'Corridors Of Power'.

'Rockin' Every Night' and 'Victims Of The Future' preceded '84's live LP 'We Want Moore' (cough) and 'Run For Cover' ('85) before he remembered his Gaelic roots and went a bit Big Country with 'Wild Frontier' ('87) and 'After The War' ('89). Things had all got very silly so he forgot all about Big Country and HM and remembered his Blues roots for the infinitely more palatable (not to mention successful!) 'Still Got The Blues' ('90) and 'After Hours' ('92). Now, people with Golf GTi's have Gary Moore tapes in their glove compartments and he gets to jam with old black blues legends. Not bad for a guy who Ozzy Osbourne once suggested had a face less attractive than "a welder's bench"...

Recommended album:

BACK ON THE STREETS (MCA, 1988 – KKKK)

MORBID ANGEL

USA, four-piece (1984-present)
FIRM BELIEVERS in the Anton LaVey creed of "Do what thou wilt", Morbid Angel have carved out a career of brutal Death Metal, unafraid to experiment with occasional tasteful touches.

After spending five years in the underground, releasing demos and building up an incredibly devoted following, Morbid Angel then recorded their 'Abominations Of Desolation' LP in 1988. However, this was deemed unworthy by the band themselves, and their first album to be released was 'Altars Of Madness' in 1989, through Earache Records (followed by 'Blessed Are The Sick' in 1991, and 'Covenant' in 1993).

Four years later, Morbid Angel are one of the most respected Death bands, and have also become the first band of their ilk to sign with a major – Giant Records in the States.
Most recommended album:
ALTARS OF MADNESS *(Earache, 1989 – KKKK)*

MORDRED

USA, six-piece (1988-present)
SAN FRANCISANS once mentioned in the same breath as Faith No More but who lost it by first being too Funk Metal, then too bloody weird on their third album with keyboards and samples.
Recommended second album:
IN THIS LIFE *(Noise, 1989 – KKKK)*

MORTAL SIN

Australia, five-piece (1987-1991)
AFTER CALLING their major label debut 'Every Dog Has Its Day', Mortal Sin *didn't* – because they were such unashamed Metallica clones making an unoriginal, very mortal din...
...And justice recommends:
EVERY DOG HAS ITS DAY *(Vertigo, 1991 – KK)*

MOTHER LOVE BONE

USA, five-piece (1989-1990)
THE DEATH of singer Andrew Wood has ultimately had more impact than the band's music. They made just two releases: the EP 'Shine' ('89) and the album 'Apple' ('90), both at their best in their mellower moments... but Wood's demise just before 'Apple' came out (due to heroin) led to the formation of tribute band Temple Of The Dog, and then, Pearl Jam – with ex-MLB members Stone Gossard (guitar) and Jeff Ament (bass).
Recommended album:
STARDOG CHAMPION *(Polydor, 1992 – KKKK)*
Compilation/re-issue of EP, album, plus demos.

MOTHER'S FINEST

USA, five/six-piece (1972-present)
CONSIDERED TO be the precursors of Funk Metal Mother's Finest have spent much of their 20 year career trying to dodge the endless pigeon holes record labels and the media have tried to confine them to.

Having recorded a little known and extremely uneventful album for RCA in 1972 (a follow-up for the label was never issued) the Atlanta, Georgia-based group really got their act together once signed to Epic, releasing the highly rated 'Mother's Finest', a fantastic combination of funky rhythms, crunching guitars and totally amazing vocal performances from the band's vocal team of Joyce 'Baby Jean' Kennedy and Glenn Murdock.

Building a strong following in their native Deep South and all along the East Coast of the States, MF toured with a diverse list of artists, including Black Sabbath and Lynyrd Skynyrd. They were persuaded to play in a more R'n'B style on third album, 'Mother Factor', but compensated for the mistake on the ensuing 'Live' and unforgettably heavy 'Iron Age' records. Decreasing sales, however, led them back to the R'n'B trail and a poorly received album, 'One Mother To Another', only released in Europe before the last remnants of the band (guitarist Gary 'Moses Mo' Moore and drummer BB Borden had quit after 'Iron Age', eventually forming Illusion, signed to Geffen) called it a day, Joyce Kennedy going on to record two soul albums for A&M and bassist Jerry 'Wizzard' Seay working with Rick Medlocke's Blackfoot.

Yet you can't keep a good band down and

although the comeback album, 'Looks Could Kill' ('89), was a total disappointment, once a market had been re-established in Germany with the help of a Dieter Dierks-produced live set titled 'Subluxation', MF hit back in 1992 with the Thrash Metal tinged and prophetic 'Black Radio Won't Play This Record', representing a fresh and exciting direction for Kennedy, Murdock and Seay the only remaining originals.
Funkily recommended:
MOTHER'S FINEST *(Epic, 1976 – KKKK)*
IRON AGE *(Epic, 1980 – KKKK)*
BLACK RADIO WON'T PLAY THIS RECORD
(Scotti Brothers, 1992 – KKKKK)

MÖTLEY CRÜE

USA, four-piece (1981-present)
THE PRESS hated 'em, the fans loved 'em. It was an almost too perfect rock 'n' roll romance. Back in the early '80s the bastardised Glamsters set out to give rock music a much needed shot in the arm. A seemingly indestructible hybrid of classic warpaint Kiss, the New York Dolls, and anything trashy or sleazy they could cram into their blueprint-for-decadence melting pot. The Crüe were the original Tinsel Town Terrors! The Horrors of Hollywood...

A one-time member of LA sub-legends (and self-professed 'training school for Rock Stars') London, bassist Nikki Sixx, armed with almost an album's worth of his own material, left that act to follow his deranged dream. Through a mutual acqaintance Sixx hooked up with six-foot-to-infinity drum-lord Tommy Lee. Mick Mars was discovered through an ad in local rag *The Recycler*: 'Loud, rude, aggressive guitarist', and the trio spotted blond bomber Vince Neil at The Starwood Club fronting a band with the dubious handle of Rock Candy. Within a week-and-a-half, Mars added umlauts to the original name and Mötley Crüe came into being!

The Mötleys touted a self-financed 45 which coupled 'Toast Of The Town' with 'Stick To Your Guns', followed soon after by a full album of 'demos' – 'Too Fast For Love' ('81) on their own Leathür label. Selling like red hot cakes, the Elektra label soon swooped, contract in hand, on the band that were setting LA alight. The debut album was re-mixed (and, sadly, refined) under the guidance of Roy Thomas Baker for Elektra. The new version not only found the meaty riffin' intro to the title track amputated, but 'Stick To Your Guns' missing completely! Said Sixx of the Elektra version: "I don't think it had enough nuts."

Not ones to let the moss grow under his stacks, practising visionary Sixx left his contemporaries (Ratt, W.A.S.P. *et al*) trailing, as each album found the band opting for an extreme and blatant change of direction in both image and music. Second album, 'Shout At The Devil' ('83), for example, left the perfect Pop Thrash and chrome-accessorised black leather look of their debut outing, for big Metal riffs and a post-apocalyptic glam warrior wardrobe.

But the Mötley rollercoaster came to a screeching halt on Saturday, December 5, 1984 when, in close proximity to his LA home, driving while intoxicated, Vince Neil was involved in an accident which tragically took the life of his passenger Razzle, the drummer of Hanoi Rocks. At first, the future looked grim for Mötley Crüe, but Neil eventually got off lightly with a short prison sentence and college lecturing duties. Their '85 album 'Theatre Of Pain' (the weakest to date, and at their least macho, image-wise) was dedicated to Razzle.

Through 1987 and 1988, notoriety continued to fuel the Crüe's gas tanks. The back-to-business 'Girls, Girls, Girls' album was released, and at the tail-end of the US tour (with Guns N' Roses as support) promoting said opus, Nikki Sixx OD'd on heroin and came close to being worm-bait. The planned British tour, amidst rumours, speculation and ridiculous official explanations, was cancelled. But then came the story of one Matthew Trippe, a man who elaborately claimed to have been Nikki Sixx's stand-in for a length of time during Mötley Crüe's tranquil career... *(Kontinues page 257)*

Come the release of '89s slick (by Crüe terms)

'Dr Feelgood' (and their first US Number One album), the Mötleys had 'cleaned-up' and parted company with manager Doc McGhee over disagreements which came to a head at the Moscow Music Peace Festival. More controversially, Vince Neil took a swing at (then) Guns N' Roses guitarist Izzy Stradlin backstage at the MTV awards!

1991 found the lads placed middle on the bill at Castle Donington (a festival they opened in '84). Vince Neil childishly yet humorously wore a 'No Axl' T-shirt during their set, as the Crüe's feud with their former GN'R buddies escalated. Vince later challenged Axl to a few rounds in the ring on MTV...

In '92, the hits 'n' bits 'Decade Of Decadence' package was released as the Crüe celebrated their 10th year on top, but the end of the year, unbelievably, found Sixx, Lee, and Mars ousting Neil. They later replaced the frontman – who

they considered didn't share their enthusiasm for the new material – with Scream vocalist John Corabi. Ironically and prophetically, the final lyric on record that Neil sang for Mötley Crüe, was, 'Now it's time for change'...

ALBUMS

TOO FAST FOR LOVE (Leathür Records, 1981 – KKKKK) "Chock-full of hedonistic charm and contemporary commercial appeal." – Kerrang! 10, February 25-March 10, 1982

SHOUT AT THE DEVIL (Elektra, 1983 – KKKK) "Has its own little masterpieces of fiery rock..." – Kerrang! 52, October 6-19, 1983

THEATRE OF PAIN (Elektra, 1985 – KKK) "Take a riff and stretch it further than Spandex and you're bound to leave weak spots." – Kerrang! 97, June 27-July 10, 1985

GIRLS, GIRLS, GIRLS (Elektra, 1987 – KKKKK) "This is a monster-mutie sensation, a Godzilla in glitter, genius with sharp party molars..." – Kerrang! 146, May 14-27, 1987

DR FEELGOOD (Elektra, 1989 – KKK) "Iffy album...." – Kerrang! 254, September 2, 1989

DECADE OF DECADENCE (Elektra, 1991 – KKKKK) "Fuck yeah, dude!" – Kerrang! 360, September 28, 1991

IN THEIR OWN WORDS...

"I mean we're all from the street, and every member of this band has been in and out of jail many times, yet everybody thinks we're a bunch of prissies." – Nikki Sixx, Kerrang! 30, December 2-15, 1982

"But we never were Heavy Metal. We were always like sleazy. Difference is, we could barely play in the beginning, and we've become a pretty good band now – we're not great, we're just alright." – Nikki Sixx, Kerrang! 113, February 1-19, 1986

"Nothing the other guys do could ever upset me. We're like a fist; if anyone ever left, the band would break up. There'll only be one Mötley Crüe!" – Nikki Sixx, Kerrang! 147, May 29-June10, 1987

"No, no, no! (Vince Neil) cut his hand alright, but not in a fit of temper or because he had his hand in a jar of mustard... Where do these stories come from?" – Mick Mars, Kerrang! 173, February 6, 1988

MÖTLEY CRÜE

MOTÖRHEAD

UK, three/four-piece (1975-present)

IF NOT for the diligence of a customs officer then Motörhead would probably never have existed. In May 1975, Hawkwind bassist Lemmy, (born Ian Fraiser Kilminster, December 24, 1945) was arrested at the Canadian border and spent five days in jail for drug possession. He was later released having been mistakenly charged with possession of cocaine instead of amphetamine sulphate, but by that time he had also been booted out of Hawkwind.

On returning to the UK, Lemmy announced plans to form another band initially named Bastard, but quite rapidly changed to Motörhead – the name of the last song he wrote for Hawkwind, the B-side of 'Kings Of Speed'. Motörhead then also included Lucas Fox (drums) and Larry Wallis (guitar). Their first gig was supporting Greenslade at the Roundhouse in London in July '75. In December of that year Fox was replaced by an ex-skinhead hoodlum by the name of Philthy Animal Taylor (born Philip Taylor September 21, 1954).

In January '76, Hawkwind's label United Artists rejected Motörhead's first album (it was later released as 'On Parole' in 1979). 'Fast' Eddie Clarke replaced Larry Wallis one month later. They remained unsigned for a further seven months... Motörhead were, however, beginning to build up a following mostly made up of Hell's Angels (Lemmy used to live with Angels president Tramp and co-wrote the song 'Iron Horse' with him), bikers and punk rockers.

On a tour (ironically) supporting Hawkwind, Philthy broke his hand punching someone but the tour carried on, and Chiswick released the 'Motörhead'/'City Kids' single, followed by the 'Motörhead' album which reached Number 43 in the UK charts. In August that year, while on a headlining tour, Taylor broke his hand again, this time on their own tour manager's face, and the remaining dates were cancelled....

Second album, 'Overkill' ('79), was released on their new label Bronze and confirmed Motörhead as the loudest, ugliest, heaviest and most obnoxious band on the planet. Both it and the following album, 'Bomber' (also '79), went Silver, selling in excess of 60,000 copies; before the immortal 'Ace Of Spades' ('80).

Motörhead were huge at this point: they headlined four consecutive nights at Hammersmith Odeon, played to over 15,000 people at the 'Heavy Metal Barn Dance' in Stafford Bingley Hall, their 1981 live album 'No Sleep 'Til Hammersmith' went straight in at Number One in the UK and they were regulars on 'Top Of The Pops'...

But mid-way through the US 'Iron Fist' tour in 1982, Fast Eddie quit. Lemmy had recorded an outrageously bad version of Tammy Wynette's 'Stand By Your Man' with Punk star Wendy O Williams but Eddie didn't see the funny side. For many fans this is where Motörhead should have called it a day, but instead, ex-Thin Lizzy axeman Brian Robertson stepped in on a temporary basis and ended up staying long enough to play on 'Another Perfect Day'.

Despite making some truly outstanding music, this line-up didn't fair well and when Robertson left the band, Taylor went with him. This time it really did look like the end of Motörhead, but against all odds Lemmy bounced back with a completely new line-up consisting of ex-Persian Rick guitarist Phil Campbell, ex-Saxon/Glitter Band drummer Pete Gill, and a previously unknown lunatic guitarist called Würzel (real name Michael Burston). They debuted at Hammersmith Odeon, May 7, 1984.

Legal hassles – always the bane of Motörhead's career – stopped them releasing any new material for two years, but they certainly delivered the goods when

they finally got the chance. Written in two days and recorded in three weeks, 'Orgasmatron' was a triumph of power and bludgeoning heaviness.

Sadly, although the band continued to play impressive shows and regained the much-missed Philthy Animal, their records gradually slid downhill from here on. 1987's 'Rock 'N' Roll' album contained some fine tunes – including the title-track of the Comic Strip film 'Eat The Rich' in which Lemmy stared as, er... Lemmy and Motörhead performed 'Doctor Rock' – but the production was as weak as British Rail tea.

Their second live album 'No Sleep At All' released in October '88 only reached Number 79 in the UK and Phil 'Wizzo' Campbell started wearing make-up and Spandex on stage. Ironically, it was after all this time that Motörhead finally signed their first major deal, with Epic. At the same time, both Lemmy and Philthy moved to LA. Unfortunately, their major debut couldn't match their former glories...

Philthy was thrown out and replaced by ex-King Diamond pretty boy Mikkey Dee. But the next album, 'March Or Die', was lacklustre. Nowadays, Motörhead seem back at square one: no deal, no money and far less fans than they've previously been accustomed to. A light still burns for this once magnificent beast, but without much hope or conviction...

ALBUMS

MOTÖRHEAD (Chiswick, 1977 – KKK) Garage rock 'n' roll/Punk with dreadful production...
OVERKILL (Bronze, 1978 – KKKKK) A hairs breadth away from their onstage ferocity...
BOMBER (Bronze, 1979 – KKKK) Excellent stuff, but largely a carbon copy of 'Overkill'...
ACE OF SPADES (Bronze, 1980 – KKKKK) All-time classic, and not just for the title-track...
NO SLEEP 'TIL HAMMERSMITH (Bronze ,1981 – KKKKK) Greatest live album of all time?!? Everything louder than everything else...
IRON FIST (Bronze, 1982 – KKKK) "LOUD! MAYHEMIC! DISGUSTING! SKULL-CRACKING! etc" – Kerrang! 13, April 8-21, 1982
ANOTHER PERFECT DAY (Bronze, 1983 –

KKK) "Still cracking (and croaking) the same joke..." – Kerrang! 42, May 19-June 2, 1983
NO REMORSE (Bronze, 1984 – KKKK) Strong compilation Including four brand new tracks...
ORGASMATRON (GWR, 1986 – KKKK) "Lemmy's still sweating and snorting..." – Kerrang! 124, July 10-23, 1986
ROCK 'N' ROLL (GWR, 1987 – KKK) "Tired, listless, and lacking any belief..." Kerrang 153, August 20-September 2, 1987
LIVE – NO SLEEP AT ALL (GWR, 1988 – KKKK) "No pretensions. No illusions..." – Kerrang! 207, October 1, 1988
1916 (Epic, 1991 – KKKKK) "All the expected Motörhead-isms operating at full whack..." – Kerrang! 324, January 19, 1991
MARCH OR DIE (Epic, 402 – KKK) "A capable, though far from best, collection of tunes." – Kerrang! 402, July 25, 1992
In addition to these, Motörhead's back catalogue has been plundered and repackaged on a host of compilations and rehashes...

IN THEIR OWN WORDS...

"Oh sure, I am Motörhead and Motörhead is me, but this is a very democratic band and every member has his say..." – Lemmy, Kerrang! 65, April 5-18, 1984

"We've just been doing what everybody fucking expected us to do, knock off 10 tracks a year and Bob's yer uncle!" – Lemmy, Kerrang! 322, January 5, 1991

"Maybe (Epic) felt they were getting the 'Grandfathers of Thrash', and they weren't. They were getting an extremely opinionated older guy and three younger geezers who were worse!" – Lemmy, Kerrang! 403, August 1, 1992

"Ages ago, we had the 'No Sleep 'Til Hammersmith' tour. The last gig was at the Odeon and we had KERRANG written across the top. About a year later, Kerrang! came out... I'd have thought they would have had us on the cover a bit more seeing as they stole the name..." – Lemmy, Kerrang! 207, October 1, 1988

BLACK SABBATH

MOTT THE HOOPLE

UK, five-piece (1969-1974)

GOT NOWHERE (with five raw heavy blues/rock 'n' roll albums for Island in three years) until they decided to split up in '72 – whereupon David Bowie wrote 'All The Young Dudes' for them, and they had a Number Three UK hit at the height of the Glam Rock era. A new deal, with CBS, also helped – but the band split up anyway after three LPs plus a live set from them in '74. After that, mainman Ian Hunter (vocals/keyboards/guitar) went solo whilst some of the rest continued for two LPs as a shadow of their former selves called Mott, with Nigel Benjamin on vocals. No one should ever forget that Mott The Hoople also featured Dale 'Buffin' Griffin (drums) and Overend Watts (bass), plus various guitarists including Mick Ralphs (Island albums), the ludicrously named Ariel Bender (real name: Luther Grosvenor) plus the late great Mick Ronson from David Bowie's Spiders From Mars who guested on some latter era tracks.
Recommended albums:

WALKIN' WITH A MOUNTAIN *(Island, 1990 – KKKK)* Compilation of first five albums.
MOTT *(CBS, 1973 – KKKK)* Pink cover!
THE HOOPLE *(CBS, 1974 – KKKK)* Blue cover!

MOUNTAIN

USA, four-piece (1968-1985)

HEAVYWEIGHT VEHICLE for heavyweight guitarist Leslie West. The band split in '75 but reformed some years later and appeared on the bill with Deep Purple at Knebworth in '85. Main claim to fame – apart from including Felix Pappalardi (bass) and Corky Laing (drums): names well known to anyone who ever owned an Afghan coat – was that the heaviest bit of 'Nantucket Sleighride' was used for years as the signature tune to highbrow ITV

current affairs programme 'World In Action'.
Recommended album (but only for the 'World In Action' bit):
NANTUCKET SLEIGHRIDE *(Island, 1970 – KK)*

MOURNBLADE

UK, four-piece (1980-1991)

UNDER-RATED outfit who got lumbered with a tag for sounding like Hawkwind despite changing and improving drastically over the years. Unfortunately, they are best remembered for the size of their frontman's nose and for mis-spelling Hammersmith on their T-shirts when they supported Motörhead – oops!
Recommended album:
LIVE FAST DIE YOUNG *(GI RECORDS, 1989-KKK)*

MR BIG

USA, four-piece (1989-present)

NOT TO be confused with the mid-'70s British band of the same name – although ironically, the original vision of Messrs Eric Martin (vocals), Paul Gilbert (guitar), Billy Sheehan (bass, ex-Dave Lee Roth and Talas) and Pat Torpey (drums, ex-Robert Plant US touring band) was to create a band that paid homage to mid-'70s British bands, particularly bands like Free, Humble Pie and The Who. Mr Big have since been categorised as something altogether poppier – like Extreme – as the result of having a hit ballad. But live, they kick ass. They also have a rather annoying tendency to play very long solos and (on their second tour) use Makita drills instead of plectrums. Very silly. Each member, however, is undeniably a fine musician and singer Martin has a set of pipes comparable to Aretha Franklin's.

Second album 'Lean Into It' ('91) consolidated the fine start made by '89's eponymous debut and has left them well placed for major success with the third...
Recommended album:
LEAN INTO IT *(Atlantic, 1991 – KKKK)*

MR BUNGLE

USA, five-piece (1990-present)
CHILDISH, TOILET and masturbation fixated, mask-wearing side project put together by singer Mike Patton – which for a short period of time he appeared to think were of more importance than Faith No More. And then he grew up...
Not recommended album:
MR BUNGLE *(Slash, 1991 – K)*

MSG

UK, five-piece (1980-present)
APOLOGIES TO all those who were looking under 'S'... These days, MSG stands for

McAuley-Schenker Group after Robin McAuley (vocals, ex-Grand Prix, Far Corporation) and the main man Michael Schenker. Schenker is the mad German who made his name in UFO after once playing alongside his older brother Rudi in the Scorpions. After quitting UFO in '79, he recorded 'Michael Schenker Group' ('80) then assembled the touring Michael Schenker Group featuring Gary Bardens (vocals), Paul Raymond (keyboards and guitar, ex-UFO), Chris Glen (bass, ex-Sensational Alex Harvey Band) and Cozy Powell (drums, ex-Rainbow). Bloody good they were too. Bardens was not a great singer, however, and after the confusingly-titled second Chrysalis LP 'MSG' ('81) and a live double (also '81), was replaced by Graham Bonnet (ex-Rainbow).

From then on, personnel changed from album to album and MSG records got steadily worse – although Schenker could still play guitar like nobody's business. Bardens returned but after 'Rock Will Never Die' ('84), it very nearly did. McAuley came in for 'Perfect Timing' ('87) when the band toured with Whitesnake but they've never really happened since. Have gone very quiet since '92's appaling and even more confusingly-titled 'MSG' (on EMI) with hopes

that Schenker will rejoin UFO not quashed yet...
Recommended album:
ONE NIGHT AT BUDOKAN *(Chrysalis, 1981 – KKKKK) Double live!*

MUCKY PUP

USA, four-piece (1986-present)
FAIRLY USELESS Rap/Metal/Funk/Anything-that-might-make-them-popular band, with such desperately unfunny songs as 'U-Stink', 'Hippies Hate Water' and 'Skinheads Broke My Walkman'.
Not recommended under any circumstances:
ACT OF FAITH *(Century Media, 1992 – KK)*

MUDHONEY

USA, four-piece (1988-present)
ALONG WITH Nirvana and Soundgarden one of the Seattle/Sub Pop 'big three', Mudhoney became known for their screwed-up sense of humour as much as their ragged noise. They soon developed into an excellent live act but were erratic on vinyl; debut Sub Pop LP 'Superfuzz Bigmuff' (named after guitar effects pedals) set their reputation as grunge anti-heroes, followed with eponymous follow-up in '89. Recording technique was definitely low-fi, and the third LP in '91 – 'Every Good Boy Deserves Fudge' – cost $1,000 to make! Band broke up in '91, only to reform the following year and sign to Warners. Fourth LP 'A Piece Of Cake' saw Mudhoney stick to their rough-edged grungy roots, even if it was a 24-track recording this time.
Recommended album:
EVERY GOOD BOY DESERVES FUDGE *(SubPop, 1991 – KKKK)*

MURDER INC

UK, five-piece (1990-present)
A MUCH more Industrial flavoured reincarnation of Killing Joke with both drummers Martin Atkins and Paul Ferguson, and Chris Connelly on vocals instead of Jaz Coleman. Er, but they don't actually sound like Killing Joke.
Recomended album:
MURDER INC *(Devotion, 1991 – KKK)*

MY SISTER'S MACHINE

USA, four-piece (1991-present)

ALICE IN Chains soundalikes from – you'll never guess where – Seattle. But it's still early days for the band yet and their frontman Nick Pollock was once in AIC before Layne Staley, so that's okay.

Recommended debut album:
DIVA *(Caroline, 1992 – KKK)*

MYTHRA

UK, five-piece (1978-1982)

LONG FORGOTTEN by almost everyone (but not Lars Ulrich) South Shields NWOBHM band who made the classic and very collectable 'Death Or Destiny' EP – featuring the killer track, er... 'Killer'.

Recommended, classic and very collectable EP:
DEATH OR DESTINY *(Guardian, 1979 – KKKK)*

NAKED TRUTH

USA, four-piece (1988-present)

THREE BLACK street kids who got togther in Atlanta, Georgia then set about making a difference on their arrival in this country. First they hired London bassist Kwame Boaten then set about polishing their Thrash-meets-Jazz-meets-Hardcore-meets-more-than-a-few-other-styles music. Radical lyrics help to show Naked Truth are a band with obvious conviction.

Recommended album:

FIGHT (Sony, 1993 – KKKK)

NASTY SAVAGE

USA, five-piece (1984-1990)

FLORIDIAN WEIRDOS with a professional wrestler by the name of Nasty Ronnie on vocals, Nasty Savage made three albums and a mini-album before calling it a day. Techno-Metal with bags of twisted guitar interplay, intensified in the live situation by Ron's penchant for hurting himself in bizarre fashions.

Recommended album:

PENETRATION POINT (Roadrunner, 1989 – KKKK)

NAPALM DEATH

UK, five-piece (1982-present)

NAPALM DEATH are a band that once sent frissions coursing through the veins of the music industry. The year was 1987. The album was 'Scum'. The independent chart position was Number Three.

'Scum' was an album of dizzying, primitive extremity, comparable to nothing that had gone before. It introduced the Metal/Thrash public to the concept of 'blast-snare', which is the art of drilling out the fastest beats a human being can feasibly drill out. As such, Napalm Death were ridiculed to hell and back by those who couldn't or wouldn't understand.

The band appeared on the cover of *NME* for their second album, and subsequently started embracing Death Metal values. Today, they are in the business of producing formula Grind. You know what you're getting when you buy a Napalm Death album. Total whirlwind insanity.

Recommended albums:

FROM ENSLAVEMENT TO OBLITERATION (Earache, 1988 – KKKK)

UTOPIA BANISHED (Earache, 1992 – KKKK)

NAZARETH

Scotland, four-piece (1969-present)

NEVER-SAY-die rockers from Dunfermline whose albums have rarely been able to match their sterling live shows, and who have hardly received the acclaim they deserved. Expanded to a five-piece for 'No Mean City' (Mountain, '78) by adding ex-Sensational Alex Harvey Band guitarist Zal Cleminson, and also tried it as a six-piece – as on the live double 'Snaz' (Nems, '81) featuring Billy Rankin (guitar) and John Locke (keyboards) – but were always at their best as the classic quartet of Dan McAfferty (vocals), Manny Charlton (guitars), Pete Agnew (bass) and Darrell Sweet (drums). Sadly, Charlton left in '92 (to be replaced by Rankin). Should be remembered for their whisky consumption and hit singles – eg 'Bad Bad Boy', 'Broken Down Angel' – and a neat line in cover versions such as 'This Flight Tonight', 'My White Bicycle', 'Love Hurts'. Axl Rose and Michael Monroe are among their biggest fans...

Recommended albums:

RAZAMANAZ (Mooncrest, 1973 – KKKK)

HAIR OF THE DOG (Mooncrest, 1975 – KKKK)

NELSON

USA, six-piece (1986-present)
FRONTED BY the bounteously blond and
beautiful twins Matthew and Gunnar Nelson
(sons of the late Ricky Nelson), this lot
unfortunately got themselves tagged as a bit of
a joke band. But look beyond the teenage
overkill image, and it's plain to see that Nelson
are a class or two above the AOR pack.

Their one album to date holds more
masterpieces than the Louvre and fluffy pics of
Matt an' Gunn soon had them nicknamed 'The
Timotei Twins' – much to their good-humoured
amusement. Most noticeable non-Nelson
brother in the line-up is muscle-mountain
drummer Bobby Rock.
Recommended album:
AFTER THE RAIN *(DGC, 1990 – KKKKK)*

NEW YORK DOLLS

USA, five-piece (1969-1971)
"THE DOLLS failed because they lived their rock
'n' roll fantasy. They were supposed to be
drunk, and they were." – Gene Simmons, Kiss.
They were also purveyors and undoubted
darlings of the early '70s New York Glitter/Glam
freak-scene (which, indeed, Kiss were born out
of!). David Johansen (vocals), Johnny Thunders
(guitar), Sylvain Sylvain (guitar), Arthur Kane
(bass), and Jerry Nolan (drums), were a molotov
cocktail of The Rolling Stones at their most
camp, The MC5, and The Shangri Las. Despite
their lack of commercial success, the flame of
the Dolls influence ever burns, in music and
most definitely in anarchic attitude. After their
label, Mercury, bid them good riddance, one
Malcolm McLaren took a shot at being their
manager. (He would later use them as a
blueprint for his Sex Pistols 'project'.) But by
this time, the Dolls had lost their shock impact,
and had become a sad industry joke. Their
prophetically-titled second album 'Too Much
Too Soon' ('74), continuously used as evidence
against them, really did say it all.
Recommended album
NEW YORK DOLLS *(Mercury, 1973 – KKKKK)*

NEW ENGLAND

UK, four-piece (1990-present)
STRAIGHT OUT of Deptford with no homes to
go to, New England have rapidly evolved into a
self-supporting hate machine. Formed by Atom
Seed's founding bassist, Chris Huxter, this
confrontational battle tank have smashed Metal
and Punk into a formidable hybrid of New Age
yobbism. Thanks to their stubborn refusal to
bend to any industry whim or fad, New England
arguably stand as the strongest unsigned hope
for this country.
Highly recommended album:
YOU CAN'T KEEP LIVING THIS WAY *(Street
Link, 1991 – KKKKK)*

NIGHT RANGER

USA, five piece (1982-present)
GUITARIST BRAD Gillis quit his spot with the
Ozzy Osbourne Band in 1982 to return to San
Francisco once his pet club band Ranger had
secured themselves a deal with the late ex-
Casablanca boss Neil Bogart's shortlived
Boardwalk label.

A name change to Night Ranger preceded the
debut album, 'Dawn Patrol', released in late '82,
and went hand in hand with a transformation
into a band soon considered to be at the very
pinnacle of classic, melodic hard rock. The
subsequent album, 'Midnight Madness', gained
them a Top Five US single with the ballad 'Sister
Christian'. By this time, Boardwalk had been
absorbed into MCA and Night Ranger began to
lose artistic control as the label failed to see
that first and foremost, they were a rock band
and not an endless pit of hits.

The band's fifth album, 'Man In Motion',
released in 1988 marked the end of the road,
although MCA did issue a live album recorded
in Japan in early 1991. Frustrated by label
intervention the band had decided to go their
seperate ways, with bassist/vocalist Jack
Blades going on to form Damn Yankees and
both Gillis and guitar partner recording
remarkably dull solo records.

Much to the disappointment of both Blades

and Watson, Gillis and drummer/vocalist Kelly Keagy decided to reform the band with a couple of new faces in 1992. Typically, they remain unsigned...

Hotly recommended album:
DAWN PATROL *(Boardwalk, 1982 – KKKKK)*

NINE INCH NAILS

USA, one-piece (1989-present)

TRENT REZNOR'S one-man-show has been a fascinating journey through the guts of electronic hatred. The first NIN track presented to the world was 'Head Like A Hole' on the otherwise restrained 'Pretty Hate Machine' ('90) – a colossal piece of anger ventilation, it set the tone for 1992's 'Broken' mini, and its bizarrely re-mixed brother, 'Fixed'.

Expect nothing but the finest angst from Trent Reznor.

Recommended album:
BROKEN *(Island, 1992 – KKKKK)*

NIRVANA

USA, three-piece (1988-present)

IN THE Autumn of 1991 it was impossible to tune in to MTV for more than about 20 minutes without seeing Nirvana. The album 'Nevermind' was just released and its first single, 'Smells Like Teen Spirit', was skyrocketing up the *Billboard* Hot 100. The band were clearly even hotter property than Guns N' Roses, or Michael Jackson, whose 'Dangerous' LP 'Nevermind' eventually displaced at the US Number One in January 1992 after only one week on release...

Just a few months earlier though, it was a completely different story and back in 1988 when the band (definitely not to be confused with the late '60s/early '70s act of the same name) formed, that kind of success was more a nightmare than a dream, even, for Kurt Cobain (guitar/vocals) and Chris Novoselic (bass/vocals). Cobain (born February 20, 1967) and Novoselic (born May 16, 1965, of Yugoslavian origin) were both from a town called

NIRVANA: bastard offsprings of The Beatles and Black Sabbath?!?

Aberdeen near Seattle in Washington State, but met at the Grays Harbor Institute Of North West Crafts. They formed Nirvana in 1988 along with Chad Channing (drums) after much encouragement from Buzz Osborne of The Melvins.

Cobain was heavily influenced by Black Sabbath and The Beatles (in particular) whom he began listening to in 1973 at the age of six. He reputedly didn't know The Beatles had split (in 1971) until 1976, by which time there was a burgeoning punk scene for him to immerse himself in. Four years later, in Seattle, a new label called SubPop was launched. In 1988 Nirvana signed to it and made their debut with a single, 'Love Buzz'/'Big Cheese' in October. The record was sold initially only to members of the label's 'Singles Club' in a numbered, limited edition of 1,000.

In 1989 the line-up began a period of flux. Jason Everman (guitar) came and went (later to join Soundgarden as bassist, then Mind Funk) before the band released their debut album 'Bleach' in June (on Tupelo in the UK a couple of months later). Its recording budget was around $600 yet it re-entered the charts in 1992 when re-released on the back of the success of 'Nevermind'. Later, Nirvana borrowed Dan Peters (drums) from Mudhoney and he hung around long enough to play on Nirvana's second single, 'Sliver'/'Dive', released in September 1990. Soon after, a permanent replacement for Channing (departing due to "religious differences") arrived in the shape of Dave Grohl (born January 14, 1969 in Washington DC). Grohl was formerly a member of Washington DC cult Hardcore outfit The Scream (definitely not the same outfit which spawned John Corabi, now of Mötley Crüe).

The newly consolidated three-piece signed to Geffen for a modest $250,000, promising to make an album "so diverse that we have no choice but to cross over". Cobain (soon to be married to Hole singer Courtney Love) said: "We want to try to be mainstream, too. We want to reach the Top 40." He got his wish but never seemed happy, withdrawing into a self-contained world of heroin and struggling to hold the band together on a sell-out series of unpredictable mostly club and mid-sized venue gigs around the world (the band declined opening slots on arena tours offered by Guns N' Roses, U2, Skid Row and Metallica).

As sales of 'Nevermind' rose to the six million mark, Novoselic and Grohl seemed more level-headed and eventually the band returned to something like an even keel– although rumours of a new LP *and* a split continue...

ALBUMS

BLEACH (SubPop, 1989 – KKKK) "One hell of a piss-up for berry boys."– Kerrang! 255, September 9, 1989
NEVERMIND (Geffen, 1991 – KKKKK) "Sad and beautiful. Pained and empowered." – Kerrang! 359, September 21, 1991
INCESTICIDE (Geffen, 1992 – KKKK) "A collection of singles, B-sides, compilation tracks, out-takes, sugar and bile." – Kerrang! 422, December 12, 1992

IN THEIR OWN WORDS...

"We're a very, very heavy punk band. Like if Cheap Trick were to have a lot of distortion in their guitars..."
– Kurt Cobain, Kerrang! 355, August 24, 1991

"Dave and I were sitting around watching a documentary on childbirth under water and I thought, 'Gee! That's a good image' and then I thought, 'Let's put a dollar in it as well!'." – Kurt Cobain, Kerrang! 374, January 11, 1992

"I think the idolisation of rock stars as a whole is pretty disgusting."
– David Grohl, Kerrang! 378, February 8, 1992

"All the record and DJ geeks come back and say, 'Hey, you beat out Metallica on the requests the other day!'. What am I supposed to say – 'That's exactly the reason I wrote that one song!'?"
– Kurt Cobain, Kerrang! 407, August 29, 1992

"Imagine if Black Flag sold a million records – like they should have. Imagine what kind of social value that would have!" – Chris Novoselic, Kerrang! 407, August 29, 1992

NIRVANA

NO SWEAT

Ireland, six-piece (1989-1991)
UNINSPIRING BAND briefly adopted by Def Leppard's Joe Elliott who proved his taste in new talent was almost as bad as his taste in stage gear when he tipped them to be: "The next big thing... the best new band". Apparently not. Adverts also quoted Iron Maiden's Bruce Dickinson, going equally over-the-top.

To be fair, lead singer Paul Quinn had a good set of pipes on him, and the band could deliver very well in an acoustic setting, but their one and only album never warranted the kind of support and expenditure label London Records appeared to throw at them. After tours supporting Little Angels and Thunder in 1990 they quietly disappeared.
Vaguely recommended album:
NO SWEAT (London,1990 – KK)

John NORUM

Sweden, solo artist (1989-present)

WENT SOLO after rising to fame if not notoriety or even critical acclaim as guitarist in pop-rock parpers Europe, quitting the band just after 'Final Countdown' was released...

Instead Norum teamed up with Marcel Jacob (bass, ex-Yngwie Malmsteen), Peter Hermannsson (drums, ex-220 Volt) and Goran Edman (vocals, ex-Madison) to make a solo LP. Although he claimed to be unhappy with Europe's Pop Metal direction, 'Total Control' followed a similar path. More recently, he relocated to LA and worked with ex-Trapeze, Deep Purple singer/bassist Glenn Hughes on 'Face The Truth', leaning heavily on his guest's work in Hughes-Thrall.

Recommended albums:
FACE THE TRUTH (Epic, 1992 – KKK)

Aldo NOVA

USA, solo artist (1980-present)

GUITARIST/SINGER who burst onto the scene back in 1982 with a self-titled debut of polished AOR under the guidance of Blue Öyster Cult svengali Sandy Pearlman. Nova was in no hurry to make his next two albums – 'Subject' ('84) and 'Twitch' ('85) – after which he seemed to disappear without trace. Then in 1991, Jon Bon Jovi repayed a favour (Aldo had helped on Bon Jovi's 1984 debut album) and resurrected Aldo's career by employing him on his solo album 'Blaze Of Glory', then producing Nova's own Bon Jovi-esque comeback album 'Blood On The Bricks'.

Recommended album:
ALDO NOVA (Portrait, 1982 – KKKK)

NUCLEAR ASSAULT

USA, four-piece (1983-present)

NEW YORK Thrashers put together by bassist Dan Lilker (as a side project when he was still in Anthrax) and vocalist John Connelly. Much to Connelly's annoyance, Lilker quit in early '93 to concentrate on another side project – grindcore outfit Brutal Truth. Original guitarist Anthony

Bramante was booted out around the same time, the pair being replaced by Scott Metaxas and Dave DiPietro respectively – both formerly of US cult Pomp Rockers, Prophet – joining a line-up completed by drummer Glenn Evans . Whether the new personnel were to blame for Nuclear Assault's poor showing on the subsequent 'Something Wicked' – or whether this once seminal Thrash outfit has just had its day, remains to be seen. Early albums are best...

Recommended third album:
SURVIVE (Music For Nations, 1988 – KKKK)

Ted NUGENT

USA, solo star (1958-present)

TED NUGENT hates 99 per cent of Heavy Metal. Ted Nugent is a rock 'n' roller. His music, whilst a long way from what a purist might call rock 'n' roll certainly ain't so far from what Chuck Berry would sound like if he wore earplugs and cranked his amp to the max. But that ain't the point with Ted Nugent, cos whilst he can point to the finer points of his damn fine guitar virtuosity and name any number of HM players whose asses he could whip, Ted Nugent has a Heavy Metal mouth. It is loud, uncompromising and offensive! So Ted makes it as one of the *Kerrang!* All-Time Top 50 for services to the genre despite the fact that he has joined up with an ex-Styx member in Damn Yankees and despite his insistences that Heavy Metal is usually "rock 'n' roll poorly played by inept geeks"...

Born in Detroit, Michigan on December 13, 1948, Theodore Nugent turned pro as a 10-year-old. Then as a whippersnapper schoolboy whizzkid joined bands like the Royal High Boys and Lourds. But he shot to fame – whilst still a whippersnapper schoolboy whizzkid – when he joined the Amboy Dukes, a garage band with attitude and a penchant for long guitar freak-outs. A coupla years after Nugent joined, their cult status had risen to the point where US label

TED NUGENT: *legend in a loincloth*

Mainstream offered them a recording deal. Their debut album, 'The Amboy Dukes' came out in America only in 1967, followed at intervals (in Europe also) by 'Journey To The Center Of Your Mind' (Mainstream, '68) – let that title be a warning to any who find it in a bargain bin – 'Migration' (Mainstream, '69), 'Marriage On The Rocks' (Polydor, '69), 'Survival Of The Fittest' (Polydor, '71), 'Dr Slingshot And The Best Of The Original Amboy Dukes' (Mainstream, '74), 'Call Of The Wild' (Discreet, '73) and 'Tooth, Fang And Claw' (Discreet, '74). The latter two (credited to Ted Nugent And The Amboy Dukes as he assumed control, hiring and firing at will anyone he thought wasn't good enough or was using drugs) were by far the best, and the only ones that have stood the test of time. Both featured bassist Rob Grange who would later join the Nuge's solo band. 'Tooth, Fang And Claw' included the classics 'Hibernation', 'The Great White Buffalo' and a cover of the Chuck Berry fave 'Maybelline' featuring the Reverend Atrocious Theodosius – almost certainly one of Nugent's alter egos – on 'lead

vocal and one finger guitar solo'!

The Amboy Dukes used to gig constantly, playing over 150 gigs a year, the highlight always being when Nugent got a roadie to stand a glass goldfish bowl atop his amp – replete with water and hapless fish – during the 'Hibernation' finale. When the number reached its climax in a howl of excruciating feedback, a note would be reached that would shatter the bowl. Reports that this trick was later scaled down to a wine glass or that Nugent employed a roadie who had a particularly deft aim with a slingshot are to be discounted right here and now... Our Ted also organised guitar duels with whoever happened to be up for it. Frank Marino of Mahogany Rush, Mike Pinera of Iron Butterfly, Wayne Kramer of the MC5 and Leslie West of Mountain were among those who tried to outgun the fastest six-stringer in the (mid) West...

Eventually the inevitable happened and Ted went solo, securing a deal with Epic Records in '75 and management with Leber-Krebs, who were also handling Aerosmith at the time. His first release, produced by Tom Werman, was eponymously titled and gobsmackingly good. The band was completed by Derek St Holmes (vocals/guitar), Grange and Cliff Davies (drums). In interviews at the time Nugent spoke of his brilliance completely unhindered by any trace of modesty. "If there had been any blind people at the show, they would have walked away seeing," he opined. Nugent quickly became as legendary for his talking as his guitar playing – with his unrelenting self-praise, his attacks on others in general and drug/alcohol users in particular, and his other passion in life: hunting. His onstage persona was even more over-the-top. Between-song raps like "This guitar could shoot the balls off a charging rhino at 50 paces..." would go unrivalled until (and maybe even after) Dave Lee Roth; and his stage-gear of a leather loincolth looked particularly fetching as he swung onto the stage, his beard and wild mane of hair flying in the breeze, from a trapeze rope... (The beard would eventually be shaved off, but only – as he explained – to make him even more attractive to women.)

To be perfectly honest, he never really topped his first three solo albums: that debut plus 'Free For All' ('76, his first Platinum seller, featuring Meat Loaf as guest vocalist on some other tracks) and 'Cat Scratch Fever' ('77, featuring the lyrically unprecedented 'Wang Dang Sweet Poontang'). With brilliant timing, he recorded shows on the latter tour for the brilliantly-titled 'Double Live Gonzo' ('78). After it, although he never failed on stage – where even the weakest material could sound stunning – his studio albums began to run out of ideas and sound a little like a parody of his unstoppable self.

The first of these, 'Weekend Warriors' ('78), was his fourth consecutive but last Platinum seller. Ditching vocalist St Holmes, who toured with Aerosmith's disenchanted Brad Whitford as Whitford-St Holmes in '81 – didn't help but at least the album enjoyed the ultimate honour of having its cover artwork turned into a pinball machine – repeating a feat previously achieved only by Kiss! Next up came 'Scream Dream' ('80) which continued the comic-book style imagery on its cover – and the musical decline within – was followed in '81 by a live album of mostly new material; a rather desperate idea completely vindicated by its title: 'Intensities In 10 Cities'. After that it was clear that Epic had lost patience and after 'Great Gonzos! The Best Of Ted Nugent' ('81), they let him go.

IN HIS OWN WORDS...

"I think 'Wang Dang Sweet Poontang' is one of the most wonderful songs in the history of rock 'n' roll. You write that when you've got a hard-on and three teenagers that need plunging!" – Kerrang! 405, August 15, 1992

"Anything that smelled of compromise I shot in the kneecaps and sent home to mama..."
– Kerrang! 34, January 27-February 9, 1983

"What kind of question is that?! Where is the equation saying keyboards equals safe ground?! I think there's some keyboards that sound like giant boulders being shoved up yer ass with NO lubricant and I think that's a desirable sound!"
– Kerrang! 61, February 9-22, 1984

"Over the top? You gotta be kidding me! I'm just fucking cruising. If I went over the top you'd be lying here in a pool of blood..." – Kerrang! 64, March 22-April 4, 1984

"I can't begin to tell you how good some of the songs are! 'Crazy Ladies' gives hope to the whole planet... 'Little Miss Dangerous' will probably cure AIDS single-handed..."
– Kerrang! 118, April 17-30, 1986

"Do you realise the craving for rock 'n' roll you get after having been in the woods with a bow and arrow for three months? During the hunting season, I'll blast down into Indianapolis and pick up my friend and we'll go into a club and tear people's heads off!"
– Kerrang! 177, March 5, 1988

"Rock 'n' roll is kinda like the Big Hunt... A shotgun is a lot like a guitar: a lotta wood, a little metal, loaded with Magnum ammo, a reasonable blast, an element of twang... and DAMNED if I can't get my dinner with both of them!!!" – Kerrang! 310, October 6, 1990

"I'm the most abrasive thing this side of a barbed-wire suppository!" – Kerrang! 405, August 15, 1992

TED NUGENT

Atlantic Records picked him up, apparently in the belief that he was going to start aiming more towards the mainstream. His first album for the label, 'Nugent' ('82), saw him re-recruit St Holmes and employ Carmine Appice (drums). St Holmes had gone again come 'Penetrator' ('84), to be replaced by Brian Howe, an excellent singer who would later go on to join Bad Company.

In January '85, Nugent made his TV debut in an episode of 'Miami Vice', where he was far more convincing than on 'Little Miss Dangerous' ('86) and 'If You Can't Lick 'Em... Lick 'Em' ('88). Even if the latter did show him to be back on form with his titles, it didn't sell well and proved to be his last solo LP to date.

At *Kerrang!* we live in hope that he will one day dust off his loincloth and get back to his Motor City Madman days – or at least grow a beard – and indeed, rumours of a future solo thang, with St Holmes singing, do seem to be on the cards. But in the meantime Nuge fans have to bite their lips whilst he wrestles with what can hopefully be only a temporary loss of sanity as a member of Damn Yankees – a band not listed elsewhere in this book in case he gets the idea we're taking him seriously.

The Damn Yankees are a mainstream band who were formed in 1989 to write songs for American radio. The line-up features Nugent alongside (gulp) Tommy Shaw (guitar/vocals, ex-Styx), and Jack Blades (bass/vocals, ex-Night Ranger) plus Michael Cartellone (drums). The mere sight of Ted's name in such wimpish company is an afront to all who ever played air guitar to 'Yank Me, Crank Me' – but because Ted is Ted, and because on stage he gets to do a solo spot where he fires flaming arrows into cardboard effigies of whoever has him most fired up, we'll make space to mention that Damn Yankees have made two albums for Warner Bros: 'Damn Yankees' ('90) and 'Don't Tread' ('92).

Nugent has meanwhile gained more notoriety for his extra-curricular hunting activities than his guitar playing. Bring back the goldfish bowl, Ted, and all will be forgiven...

SOLO ALBUMS

TED NUGENT (Epic, 1975 – KKKKK) As raw and precious as a great white buffalo on the hoof. The essence of Nugent will make you eyes water...

FREE FOR ALL (Epic, 1976 – KKKK) The attitude is still there but the songs are ever so slightly gentler...

CAT SCRATCH FEVER (Epic, 1977 – KKKK) Ted cranks it up to stun once again with a buncha songs that'll scratch yer eyes out...

DOUBLE LIVE GONZO (Epic, 1978 – KKKKK) The very best of his back catalogue to date – LIVE including raps!

WEEKEND WARRIORS (Epic, 1978 – KKK) Uh-oh: Ted starts to lose it. Poor songs compared to earlier works...

STATE OF SHOCK (Epic, 1979 – KKK) Great title but average material once again...

SCREAM DREAM (Epic, 1980 – KKK) Excuse me Ted, but aren't you stuck in a groove here?

INTENSITIES IN 10 CITIES (Epic, 1981 – KKKK) Live! And better (it had to be) but still not a patch on the legendary 'Double Live Gonzo'...

GREAT GONZOS! THE BEST OF TED NUGENT (Epic, 1982 KKKK) "The Motor City Madman hits hard with this neat collection of 10 of his most brain-damaging epics." – Kerrang! 9, February 11-24, 1982

NUGENT (Atlantic, 1982 K) "A marked departure from his previous work... a somewhat more subtle approach." – Kerrang! 20, July 15-28, 1982

PENETRATOR (Atlantic, 1984 KKK) "The monster Metal maverick has emerged meaner, slicker and fresher than at any time for a few years..." – Kerrang! 61, February 9-22, 1984

LITTLE MISS DANGEOUS (Atlantic, 1986 – KK) "Not a startling release... fewer genuine hell-for-leather highs than lows..." – Kerrang! 117, April 3-16, 1986

IF YOU CAN'T LICK 'EM... LICK 'EM! (Atlantic, 1988 – KKK) Not even reviewed in Kerrang! and certainly not worthy of that ace title. Ted, get it together agin, please...

(See text for Amboy Dukes/Damn Yankees...)

NUTZ

UK, five-piece (1974-1980)
SECOND DIVISION act who made four albums
for A&M then re-grouped as Rage – the UK
version. Singer David Lloyd did the vocal for an
old Crunchie ad...
Recommended 'farewell' album:
LIVE CUTZ (A&M, 1977 – KKK)

N.W.O.B.H.M.

UK, spurious generic noun (1979-present)
AFTER PUNK Rock kicked a few of the Boring
Old Fart bands in the teeth in 1977, numerous
other more refined bands broke through using
the same route to stardom as the Punks: sod
the big labels, make your own records and sell
them independently. This movement became
known as the New Wave. When a groundswell
of Metal bands decided to fight back and do the
same thing it was quite natural for *Sounds*
magazine (its champion) to christen it the New
Wave Of British Heavy Metal. Only Iron Maiden,
Def Leppard and Saxon survived. Diamond
Head were best of the lot so they've just
reformed. All you need to know these days is
that (a) nearly all the bands were crap but (b) the
records are still big in Japan, and (c) asking Lars
Ulrich about it could open such a can of worms
you'll really wish you hadn't bothered.
Cautiously recommended album:
NWOBHM – '79 REVISITED (Vertigo, 1990 –
KKK)

NYMPHS

USA, five-piece (1989-1992)
IT WAS a brief but exhilarating ride. Nymphs left
a trail of wreckage in their wake and one of the
most soul-wrenching records since Patti
Smith's 'Easter'. The comparison is an easy
one, but Nymphs put drug and suicide poetry to
a tuneful Stooges thunder, and got a mad
woman to front the band.

Inger Lorre was the band. When the boys
eventually ran out of patience with the eccentric
chanteuse and kicked her out, Geffen Records
immediately dropped the band!

She was deranged. Institutionalised twice for
her own protection, she nonetheless managed
to cause havoc. Prone to violent moodswings,
the ex-model literally fought with her band,
pissed on the desk of her A&R man in protest at
studio delays, lost her boyfriend (Sea Hags
bassist, Chris Schlosshardt) in a car crash and
at least four close friends took their own life.

Nymphs finally ground to a halt on the road in
America. The band split and Inger Lorre was
back in therapy, writing children's books and
making clay pots. Sad and damned.
Essential album:
NMPHS (Geffen, 1992 – KKKKK)

INGER LORRE: havoc-causing former model

OBITUARY

USA, five-piece (1985-present)
FORMERLY XECUTIONER, Obituary set out to
be the heaviest band on the planet, and nearly
achieved this aim. With a sound based around
re-energized Celtic Frost riffs, and John Tardy's
guttural, inhuman growls, it took no time at all
for Obituary to find a place in the dark hearts of
most Death Metal disciples. Nasty.
Recommended album:
CAUSE OF DEATH *(Roadrunner, 1991 – KKKK)*

ONLY CHILD

USA, four-piece (1988-1990)
ONLY CHILD'S one (and only!) album to date
was considered by *Kerrang!*'s Geoff Barton to
be beyond a mere K rating, so he promptly gave
it an L!

"Above and beyond the magnitude of even
the legendary Michael Bolton," he reckoned.
Actually, hype aside, the record was simply just
well-polished hard AOR from the pen of Paul
Sabu, a man with a big reputation but little to
show for it save for a string of records, mostly
under his own name, and a few production jobs
of note, including the mysterious blonde Alexa,
the gorgeous 'female Sabu'.

The son of Selar Sabu, the child actor who
starred as the original Elephant Boy, Paul is
likely to issue a comeback album sometime
during 1993 on the Now And Then label.
*Originally received an OTT review but
recommended nonetheless:*
ONLY CHILD *(Rampage, 1988 – KKKK)*

ONSLAUGHT

UK, five-piece (1983-1991)
FROM PUNK to Thrash, to commercial Power
Metal, Bristol's Onslaught never quite settled in
a niche. Part of the collection of British bands
signed and then ditched by major labels after
one album (Toranaga, Slammer...), Onslaught
were always fairly popular, but were unable to
maintain a frontman, and 'In Search Of Sanity'
was their Metallica-esque swansong.
Recommended album:
IN SEARCH OF SANITY *(London, 1990 – KKKK)*

ORAL

UK, three-piece (1987)
T&A GIRLS with bonking 'n' bondage fixation
who never gigged and made just one record,
called 'Sex'. Oral: 'Sex'. Geddit?
Smut-filled mini album:
SEX *(Conquest, 1987 – K)*

Ozzy OSBOURNE

UK, solo artist (1979-present)
JOHN MICHAEL Osbourne is a genuine nutter.
A lovely bloke and a family man –
but a nutter nonetheless. This
probably goes a long way to
explain why he has been far
more successful as a solo
artist than as a member of
Black Sabbath – that and the
fact that he's managed by his wife
Sharon. As good as his six studio solo records
have been in part, few have really been able to
hold a candle to the majority of the Sabs
records he was involved in. But as ironic as that
seems, Ozzy totally deserves every penny he's
earned because no one has worked harder, or
given more to the fans...

He was born on December 3, 1948 in Aston,
Birmingham. His youth was misspent in a

number of ways, only some of them legal. Fooling around in a slaughterhouse, shooting at his neighbours' cats and burglary earned him the sack, a bad reputation and two months in Winson Green Prison, respectively. Then one day in 1967 he crossed the road to talk to three longhairs going to a jazz-blues club – the short-haired Ozzy was probably *en route* to a white soul hop to look for girls. Tony Iommi, Geezer Butler and Bill Ward (for it was they), hired Ozzy and became Polka Tulk, then Black Sabbath. With them, Ozzy released eight albums between 1970 and 1978, consumed large amounts of drugs and alcohol, and found the need to seek psychiatric advice on more than one occasion. Eventually, the pressure of it all got too much and he quit for good (after a number of false alarms) in '78. His initial plan to form a band with Glenn Hughes and Gary Moore fell through and instead he hired Lee Kerslake (drums, ex-Uriah Heep), Bob Daisley (bass, ex-Rainbow) and a young American who played on the first two Quiet Riot albums, Rhandy Rhoads. He signed a deal with Jet Records, managed by one-time Sabbath manager Don Arden, who released the band's debut album, 'Blizzard Of Ozz', in September 1980. The title was a name Ozzy thought of years earlier when still in Sabbath and plotting a solo project. The band debuted at the Edinburgh Nite Club on August 14, 1980.

In April '81, the album began a two-year run on the US chart, fuelled by Ozzy's first solo tour there which began in May. Before the dates Kerslake returned to Uriah Heep, taking Daisley with him. But Daisley's friendship with Ozzy remained intact and the bassist featured on subsequent albums and also played a behind-the-scenes role writing lyrics for many Ozzy songs. Daisley's initial replacement was Pete Way (ex-UFO), later succeeded by American psycho Don Costa, before Ozzy settled on a new rhythm section of Tommy Aldridge (drums, ex-Pat Travers Band *et al*) and Rudi Sarzo (bass, ex-Quiet Riot). Their impact, however, paled into insignificance alongside Ozzy's at a Columbia Records executives meeting

in LA when he bit the head off a live dove...

In August, with news of Ozzy's new-found Stateside superstar status filtering back to the UK, the band themselves returned to play the Heavy Metal Holocaust festival at Port Vale FC. In November, Jet released the second album 'Diary Of A Madman' which went Top 20 both sides of the Atlantic, becoming his second Platinum-seller in the USA.

In January '92, the band began a second US tour, presenting a spectacular castle stageset, replete with a dwarf roadie who Ozzy would introduce to audiences as 'Ronnie' (after the vertically-disadvantaged Mr Dio, recently hired to replace Ozzy in Sabbath). The audience reaction (to the whole show...) was little short of hysterical and each night Ozzy's stage would be bombarded with clothing, banners and strange gifts. In Des Moines, Iowa, Ozzy picked one of these up – believing it to be a toy bat – and bit it. The bat was not a toy, or even dead, and bit Ozzy back – necessitating a rabies shot after the show. On top of the dove incident, Ozzy's place in tabloids the world over was assured for ever more...

Tragically, though, the next time he featured would be after the death of Randy Rhoads. The enormously gifted guitarist was on board the tour plane when it flew low over over the tour bus near Orlando, Florida. A wing tip clipped the

OZZY OSBOURNE: the world's most lovable nutter

bus and the plane crashed, killing the 25-year-old Rhoads, pilot Andrew Aycock and Ozzy's hairdresser Rachel Youngblood. The accident and the loss of Rhoads haunts Ozzy to this day...

Bernie Tormé (ex-Gillan) stepped in as a replacement so the tour could continue before being slightly more permanently replaced by Brad Gillis (ex-Night Ranger). Gillis, Sarzo, Aldridge and Ozzy are the line-up featured on 'Talk Of The Devil' ('82), the double live LP of 13 Sabbath covers rush-released to pre-empt the Dio-fronted Sabbath's plans to release a live LP featuring some Ozzy-era Sabs material.

In 1983, Don Arden and his daughter Sharon (whom Ozzy had married in Hawaii on July 4, '82) quarrelled over Ozzy's future direction and Sharon assumed full control of the singer, negotiating him a new deal with Epic/Columbia. This proved to be far more important than Aldridge's brief departure (replaced by Carmine Appice) and probably more significant in the long-term even than the release of the 'Bark At The Moon' album – featuring new guitarist Jake E Lee, keyboardist Don Airey (ex-Rainbow) and complete with cover and title-track video featuring Oz' in full werewolf make-up. As wife and manager, Sharon would come to give Ozzy the personal and professional guidance he had always lacking and so badly needed: enabling him to reduce his horrendous touring work-load, make albums at greater intervals, and ultimately come to terms with his drug and alcohol dependencies.

These became public in June '84 when he entered the Betty Ford Clinic. Six months later, Ozzy played the massive first Rock In Rio festival. After Live-Aid with a briefly reformed Sabbath in July 13, '85 came the next studio album – his biggest seller – 'The Ultimate Sin' album ('86). Soon after, backing Ozzy on his first full UK tour since December '83, was a band changed again – with Phil Soussan (bass, ex-Wildlife) and Randy Castillo (drums, ex-Lita Ford). In '87, Ozzy got his own back on all the preachers who had been slagging him and his music off, by playing one in the otherwise godawful movie 'Trick Or Treat'. The highlight of that year for him, though, was releasing 'Tribute' – a double set of live recordings featuring Rhandy Rhoads...

1988 saw the release of 'No Rest For The Wicked' and another new line-up featuring American guitarist Zakk Wylde (born January 14, 1967) and persuading his old Sabbath buddy Geezer Butler to rejoin his fold. He stayed almost two years – until October '90.

1989 was a black year in comparison, despite his hero's welcome over two nights at the Moscow Music Peace Festival because, still struggling with alcohol addiction, he was charged with threatening to kill Sharon. The two separate, but ultimately forgive and re-unite...

A fairly pointless live EP, 'Just Say Ozzy', was released in 1990 but after the 'No More Tears' album ('91) Ozzy shocked the rock world by announcing that he would quit touring for good after the extensive worldwide 'No More Tours' tour. The final dates were at the Costa Mesa Pacific Ampitheatre on November 14/15, '92. In an effort to smooth over previous conflicts with Dio, Ozzy invited him and the Sabbath line-up he was again fronting, to play as special guests. Dio declined but Sabbath said yes – and ex-Judas Priest singer Rob Halford took the microphone. On the second night, for his final encore, Ozzy re-united with Geezer Butler, Tony Iommi and Bill Ward for a blast of original Sabbath material – a perfect end to a stunning solo career. Whether plans to make the re-union more widespread ever come off, Ozzy can at least be certain that he's earned himself a place in the corner of the heart of everyone who ever saw him perform...

ALBUMS

BLIZZARD OF OZZ *(Jet, 1980 – KKKKK) Klassik record featuring the monsters 'Crazy Train', 'Mr Crowley' and 'Suicide Solution'...*
DIARY OF A MADMAN *(Jet, 1981 – KKKK) New American rhythm section but songs written by original line-up. Slightly weaker material...*
TALK OF THE DEVIL *(Jet, 1982 – KKKK) Double live oddity of 13 Sabbath covers*

IN HIS OWN WORDS...

"When I left Sabbath, I thought, 'Well, the best way to get your head back together is to go as far back to basics as you can without getting ridiculous... This is what rock 'n' roll is all about. We're rock 'n' rollers; not executives. I mean, is this a rock band or a bunch of donuts on the road?" – Kerrang! 6, December, 1981

"My body is telling me to cool it, cos I'm getting pains in my kidneys and I get a real severe pain on one side of my head. I've been to several doctors about it... Possible brain tumour one of them said... It's probably just a gramm o' coke lodged up there..." – Kerrang! 24, September 9-22, 1982

"(US evangelists) put me down for what I do yet they'd love to have the audiences I get... I don't consider myself a bad or evil person, but I'm in the public eye. I'm on the radio 10 times a week for something I've got up to..." – Kerrang! 54, November 3-16, 1983

"I went to those Alcoholics Anonymous meetings with Don Powell of Slade, and it was so boring you wouldn't believe it! he said to me, 'What time is it?' and I said, 'A quarter to two – there's still time for a drink'..." – Kerrang! 114, February 20-March 5, 1986

"No matter what I say, people are still convinced that I'm totally insane... (but) I don't MIND being looked upon as crazy: I mean, I make a good living at it. It's better than working in a factory..." – Kerrang! 152, August 6-19, 1987

"I mean, I don't even like drinking... Ultimately, I've got two choices: either I get it right this time, or I screw it up again. And if I don't get it right I'll either die or go insane..." – Kerrang! 262, October 28, 1989

"I miss the kids a lot and the kids miss me. I have a family that I never see grow up, y'know? And I don't really enjoy touring for 12 months at a time any more.' – Kerrang! 334, March 30, 1991

"I have no idea why I'm still here. I should have died a thousand times..." – Kerrang! 422, December 12, 1992

"Everybody go fuckin' crazy..." – 1948-present

OZZY OSBOURNE

recorded at two gigs in New York...

BARK AT THE MOON (Epic, 1983 – KKK) "It's not so much the material that lets the side down as the production." – Kerrang! 56, December 1-14, 1983

THE ULTIMATE SIN (Epic, 1986 – KKK) "Solid production and expert guitar histrionics (but) ...average and ordinary." – Kerrang! 113, February 6-19, 1986

TRIBUTE (Epic, 1987 – KKKKK) "The finest Ozzy Osbourne album ever... We shall probably never witness the like again." – Kerrang! 145, April 30-May 13, 1987

NO REST FOR THE WICKED (Epic, 1988 – KKK) – "Relatively refined and restrained... Less mayhem, more mature." – Kerrang! 207, October 1, 1988

JUST SAY OZZY (Epic, 1990 – KKK) Pointless live EP...

NO MORE TEARS (Epic, 1991 – KKKK) Big production job, two years in the making

LIVE & LOUD (Epic, 1993 – KKKK) Big farewell!

OVERKILL

USA, five-piece (1985-present)

FROM THEIR 'Feel The Fire' debut to the present day's 'I Hear Black', Overkill have kept an eagle eye on quality control. Their style has occasionally wavered, and today they flaunt much more of an updated '70s feel, but the emphasis has always been on massively crunchy riffage, spurred on by Bobby 'Blitz' Ellsworth's unique vocals. One of Metal's best. *Most recommended albums:*

UNDER THE INFLUENCE (Megaforce/Atlantic, 1988 – KKKKK)

THE YEARS OF DECAY (Megaforce/Atlantic, 1990 – KKKKK)

Jimmy PAGE

UK, guitarist (1959-present)
JOINED BLUES outfit Neil Christian And The Crusaders when aged 15 (1959!) then made such a name for himself that he became an in demand session player – adding licks to more hits of the '60s than he can remember. Replaced Jeff beck in The Yardbirds in '66, then formed Led Zeppelin in '68. After they split in 1980 he became very reclusive, failing to deliver the soundtrack to 'Lucifer Rising', but meeting the deadline for 'Death Wish II' ('82). Apart form the occasional Zep re-union/jam with Robert Plant, Page re-emerged in '88 with the 'Outrider' album and tour. He then turned his attention to remastering the Zep back catalogue for CD re-issue compilations before (apparently) trying to reform Zeppelin. Plant must have said no because in '93 came Coverdale Page...
Recommended album:
OUTRIDER *(Geffen, 1988 – KKKK)*

PANTERA

USA, four-piece (1981-present)
NOW AN unstoppable, full-force riff machine, Pantera have evolved well away from their early '80s origins as a Glammy hard rock outfit with albums like 'Metal Magic' and 'Projects In The Jungle'. It goes without saying that these modern day, cutting edge Cowboys From Hell would rather forget old song titles like 'Heavy Metal Rules!'.

Their real turn-around came in 1986, when Phil Anselmo replaced David Peacock on vocals. From this point, each successive Pantera album became more aggressive, heavy and intense. 'Power Metal' ('88) was Thrash-tinged Metal; 'Cowboys From Hell' ('90) went on to embrace that style wholeheartedly; and 'A Vulgar Display Of Power' was exactly that.

Pantera's chief strengths lie in the personality of Phil Anselmo, who manages to be an endearing hard man, avoiding muscleheaded Danzigian trappings while onstage, plus the water-tight rhythm section and the crushingly innovative guitar warps of Diamond Darrell.

They are claiming this world, piece by piece.
Most recommended albums:
COWBOYS FROM HELL *(Atco, 1990 – KKKK)*
A VULGAR DISPLAY OF POWER *(Atco, 1992 – KKKKK)*

PEARL JAM

USA, five-piece (1990-present)
"IF WARNER BROS or whoever says anything more about the Seattle scene on any billboard or ad, I'm gonna go to a state where you can buy a rifle and drive to Los Angeles and blow somebody's head off. I'll be the martyr."

When Eddie Vedder moved up to Seattle from San Diego in 1990 to join Pearl Jam, no one could forsee the massive impact of like-minded anti-heroes that the scene would soon spawn. Seattle was just a little, rainy smalltown. The city's drop-outs and liberals, punks and poets, got together because they were bored and disillusioned. As a result there was a hope in their music, a big bonding thing that would unite teenagers like never before. Pearl Jam were by no means the first, but at the time of writing they are perhaps the third most important band in America.

Pearl Jam happened because somebody died of a heroin overdose. Bassist Jeff Ament and guitarist Stone Gossard were partners in Green River and later in Mother Love Bone.

When the latter's vocalist, Andrew Wood, died in 1990, the most promising band on the West Coast scene died with him. The resulting tribute project – Temple Of The Dog – was put together by Gossard, Ament and Soundgarden's Chris Cornell as a way of saying farewell to their friend and collaborator. It is perhaps fitting that Andrew Wood will be remembered through his friends' songs, such as 'Say Hello 2 Heaven' and 'Reach Down'.

Whilst Temple Of The Dog were recording the album, Gossard and Ament were simultaneously working on material for Pearl Jam. Eddie Vedder was recommended to Gossard by the original Red Hot Chili Peppers' drummer, Jack Irons.

Vedder was a smouldering, hyperactive beach bum working the nightshift at a local San Diego gas station. He was sent three songs by the band ('Alive', 'Once' and 'Footsteps') and improvised the vocals onto a four-track machine. Vedder got the job and moved north to make a million.

After five days of intensive rehearsals Pearl Jam had written eleven songs.

"On the sixth day we played a show," Eddie Vedder said, "and on the seventh we recorded it all."

Pearl Jam called the album 'Ten' – the number of the shirt worn by their favourite basketball star. 16 months after its release the album was a hit. Ironically, it was the Temple Of The Dog album – with its highly emotional overtones – which stole much of 'Ten's initial thunder. But Pearl Jam's debut eventually broke through on a tidal wave of critical acclaim.

Pearl Jam are a hopeless Grunge band. 'Ten' is a hopeless Grunge record. Yet the band have been tagged with the same media-created label simply because they come from one particular rainy smalltown in North America. In the wake of Nirvana's runaway success with the 'Nevermind' set, this seemed like a good enough reason. Kurt Cobain, in one of his more precious outbursts which he might yet come to

EDDIE VEDDER (Pearl Jam): the sky (or the roof of the stage) is the limit

regret, accused Pearl Jam of selling Grunge out by making it commercial. It was also an accusation he laid at the feet of the Nymphs. Both refused to rise to the provocation.

Pearl Jam are a remarkable band because they made it okay to like the sound of Big Melodic Rock again. 'Ten' is a New Metal masterpiece with none of the old school's overblown gestures and banal platitudes. It is as accessible as Journey (a comparisson the band detest!), yet deeper and more thoughtful than Alice In Chains or Soundgarden. Unafraid of melody and real emotion, 'Ten' is a beautiful album for very stark reasons.

"God, I wish we weren't on MTV, man," Eddie Vedder once said, as the band's first single ('Alive') finally crashed into the Top 30 on both sides of the Atalntic.

Their commercial success has not been an easy pill for the band to swallow. The entire, communal Seattle scene was originally created as an alternative. Now it had become the mainstream. Pearl Jam's music is accessible, but Vedder felt uncomfortable about his growing stature as a bona fide pop star. Instead he chose to use his platform to rally for change and tolerance.

"You get a chance to say something on national TV," he once said, "and I'm not gonna keep my mouth shut."

In 1992, Vedder's growing notoriety as the consumate live performer and communicator began to take its toll. In the first half of the year a lengthy European tour was cut short due to the singer's complete physical exhaustion. It had been a ground-breaking tour for the band, but not without its problems. The media was still undecided about Pearl Jam's cause. In Manchester a local gang had stolen amps and equipment from the back of the band's bus, threatening one of the entourage with a six inch blade! The band flew home from the Roskilde Festival to rest and dig in for the summer months of extensive festival touring.

Their outspoken views on such issues as American unemployment, homelessness and the Pro-Choice organization, made them an ideal addition to the cross-cultural Lolapolooza tour. It was a successful trek for Pearl Jam and finally established them within the New Age hierarchy.

After the summer months of live activity, work began on the second album behind closed doors. Stone Gossard took time out from the machine to record an album with friends and associates under the moniker Brad. The whole band were also featured alongside Matt Dillon in the movie 'Singles' (also cruelly dubbed 'Grease Goes Grunge'), an ironic appearance in the light of the city's re-birth as the new Jerusalem for the world's media.

Pearl Jam's second album will not be an easy one to make. Expectations are high and the pressure is on. But Eddie Vedder is tougher than most.

"Getting a Gold record was cool for about two-and-a-half minutes. It doesn't seem real. The media and critics are gonna come down on the second album and dissect it. I can't care about any of that stuff though, so I hope people have a field day – I really don't give a fuck."

The only album, but essential nonetheless:
TEN (Epic, 1991 – KKKKK) *"A moody, evocative album, introspective and charged with a quiet emotional force that's more subtle and perhaps richer than Mother Love Bone's starstruck flashiness. They rock in a unique, spontaneous fashion that promises many great things."*
– Kerrang! 361, October 5. 1991

IN THEIR OWN WORDS...

"It'd be really depressing to be promoted as the next big thing. We're not treating this band like some blockbuster film. It's just more like a small firm that's just really nice to come and get into." – Eddie Vedder, Kerrang! 360, September 28, 1991

"Great-grandpa was an Indian and totally into peyote and hallucinogenics. Great-grandma Pearl used to make this hallucinogenic preserve that's just legendary. Shame we don't have the recipe..." – Eddie Vedder, Kerrang! 380, February 22, 1992

"I definitely think that there's someone up there looking out for us..."
– Jeff Ament, Kerrang! 380, February 22, 1992

"Some people might say that I have a death-wish. That's wrong. I have a total life-wish." – Eddie Vedder, Kerrang! 380, February 22, 1992

"Pearl Jam is a pure thing - kind of. What I do is pure, I think. I guess I'm okay as long as I keep thinking that!" – Stone Gossard, Kerrang! 341, February 20, 1993

"I hope there's one song on (the second album) that's just way out there. Either really, really not clever, or full-blown disco, or something just to make sure we're not taking ourselves too seriously." – Stone Gossard, Kerrang! 341, February 20, 1993

PEARL JAM

Pandora PEROXIDE

UK, comic strip character (1984-present)
THE HIGH Priestess of Rock. The Metal Queen

Bitch. The scourge of the species of vermin often referred to as 'Rock Stars'. After origins in the *Islington Gazette*, she appeared in the former *K!* supplement *Extra Kerrang!* (issue one) in 1984, going into main magazine, issue 76, September 6-19, 1984. Her exploits have featured regularly ever since, making Pandora Peroxide the longest running and most successful Heavy Metal-related comic-strip of all time.
Pandora recommends her favourite album:
NO SLEEP 'TIL HAMMERSMITH, *Motörhead*

Joe PERRY PROJECT

USA, solo (1980-1983)
TUT, TUT! Smacked-out, drunk, tired and emotional, guitarist Perry sensationally left Aerosmith during the recording of their '79 'Night In The Ruts' album, to pursue a solo career. Using a variety of virtual unknowns, he made three albums – 'Let The Music Do The Talking' ('80), 'I've Got The Rock 'N' Rolls Again' ('81) and 'Once A Rocker, Always A Rocker' ('83). It was all good stuff, and sold reasonably well, but it was obvious Perry's career wasn't going to take off in a big way as a solo artist. His marriage was over, he was sleeping on his manager's couch, and was about to work with Alice Cooper. Next thing, Aero-frontman Steven Tyler got in touch, and the idiots realised they needed each other... The original Aerosmith line-up reformed for 1984's 'Back In The Saddle' tour, and we all rocked happily ever after.
Recommended album:
LET THE MUSIC DO THE TALKING *(CBS, 1980 – KKKK)*

PESTILENCE

Holland, four-piece (1986-present)
INFLUENCED BY Death in the early days, Pestilence have matured into an altogether more Progressive outfit, while retaining the traditional Death Metal vocal style. The first two albums feature Martin van Drunen on vocals, who now fronts his own band, Asphyx. 1991's 'Testimony Of The Ancients' saw main Pestilence man/guitarist Patrick Mameli have a go at the vocals himself.
Recommended album:
TESTIMONY OF THE ANCIENTS *(Roadrunner, 1991 – KKKK)*

PHANTOM BLUE

USA, five-piece (1989-present)
PERHAPS THE most under-rated all-female band in this entire volume, Phantom Blue have sadly failed to build upon the favourable reaction to their sole album released so far, despite constant rumours of a deal with Geffen and an album supposedly produced by Don Dokken being in the can since they returned to the States from a successful European tour.
  Believed to have undergone slight line-up change in their time away but planning to return by the end of 1993 with that long-awaited second album.
Recommended album:
PHANTOM BLUE *(Roadrunner, 1989 – KKKK)*

PIGFACE

USA, any-piece (1990-present)
PIGFACE ARE an occasional Industrial supergroup, with such scene figures as Martin Atkins (Pil/Murder Inc/Killing Joke/ Hyperhead...) and Chris Connelly (Murder Inc/ Revolting Cocks/Ministry...) as mainstays.
  Characters come and go from album to album, and from gig to gig. Unsurprisingly, considering Pigface's haphazard nature, it wasn't until 1992 that they released anything worth even the slightest toss.
Recommended album:
FOOK *(Devotion, 1992 – KKKK)*

Germany, four-piece (1987-present)
BIG STARS in Germany but despite supporting
Europe once, Pink Cream 69 in the UK is a
cocktail of 90 per cent pineapple juice, 10 per
cent cream with a dash of grenadine.
Recommended album:
GAMES PEOPLE PLAY *(Epic/Sony, 1993 –
KKK)*

Robert PLANT

UK, solo artist (1981-present)
FOR A guy who in 1964 was still training
to be a chartered acountant, Robert
Plant has really rather well with his
chosen alternative career as a
singer. He'll forever be thought of
primarily as the bare-chested,
navel-flaunting frontman of Led
Zeppelin, but in reality, the seven
albums he's made to date since Zep's demise in
1980 have proved that there's much more to
him than those 12 years of glory.

Born in the Black Country town of West
Bromich on August 20, 1948, his first solo work
was actually pre-Zep, in the form of two
woefully unsuccesful solo singles 'Our Song'
and 'Long Time Coming' on CBS in 1967. CBS
gave him the break after he'd made a name for
himself singing in various West Midlands
R'n'B/Blues bands including one called Listen
with whom he made his recording debut on the
single 'You Better Run', also on CBS, in '66.

1968 to 1980 saw him attain legendary status
alongside Messrs Page, Jones and Bonham so
when he played a few low-key pub/club dates
fronting an R'n'B/Blues/swing outfit called The
Honeydrippers in April 1981, interest was
intense – and overshadowed what was
something he really only planned to do for fun.
After the hugely successful Zeppelin, something
as low-key as The Honeydrippers was all Plant
could face, afraid as he was, that his next
venture would be compared to the legend he
had been part of. Ironically, the sound on his
first solo album, 'Pictures At Eleven', was not a

million miles from latter day Led Zeppelin.
Released in July '82, the album featured Robbie
Blunt (guitar, also of The Honeydrippers), Paul
Martinez (bass) plus guest drummers Cozy
Powell and Phil Collins. It was and met with
worldwide approval, charting Top Five on both
sides of the Atlantic.

But Plant wanted to push himself further
musically and on its follow-up, 'Principle Of
Moments' ('83), he distanced himself from his
past. The album had an altogether mellower feel
than the debut – with Jezz Woodruffe's
keyboards coming to the fore – and produced
the hit single, 'Big Log'.

Late '84 found Plant touring again with
The Honeydrippers then recording a mini
album, 'Volume One' featuring
contributions from Robbie Blunt – and
Jimmy Page. The record even spawned
a hit in the States, 'Sea Of Love', but Plant
was again at pains to play down Page's
involvement and stress that the project was just
a side-project.

The release of 'Shaken 'N' Stirred' in June '85
showed just how much further Plant wanted to
take his music. On it, he and Blunt were
experimenting with guitar synthesisers, studio
techniques and musical structures. highly
complex, even today, much of it is inaccessible
compared to any of his other works. The
struggle in the studio also put his relationship
with the band in general, and Blunt in particular,
under intolerable strain. They toured to promote
it – playing encores as The Honeydrippers,
augmented by the Big Town Playboys' horn
section! – but disbanded at the end of '85.

At a February '88 one-off show in Folkestone
billed as The Band Of Joy (an alias pinched
from a group he and Bonham played in prior to
Zeppelin) he debuted a new band of Phil
Johnstone (keyboards), Doug Boyle (guitar),
Charlie Jones (bass) and Chris Blackwell
(drums) – musicians he recruited after being
impressed by their demo. Writing mainly with
Johnstone, the band recorded the album, 'Now
And Zen' ('88). On it, Plant was inspired enough
by his backing musicians' enthusiasm to

IN HIS OWN WORDS...

"...Because of what I'd been involved with in Zep... Because I loved what I did before so much, it was a case of things happening slowly but surely... I mean, I didn't want to play with anyone initially and then The Honeydrippers sort of got me at it again." – Kerrang! 18, June 17-30, 1982

"I probably was going up my own ass a bit in trying to be different, in trying to keep away from the mainstream." – Kerrang! 171, January 23, 1988

"What we've got now is something that is bursting with energy, brimming with animal cunning and produced really well. Fatigue may come in about three years time, but I can jump off the horse and run with another one. Until then it sounds bloody great!" – Kerrang! 171, January 23, 1988

"I spent so much time pretending I wasn't the singer with Led Zeppelin and looking at David Coverdale and wondering where I was. I thought, what a wanker, I could do that. In fact, I DO do that. That's me! I want my money back! And when I find him I SHALL get my money back..." – Kerrang! 171, January 23, 1988

"Unfortunately, there's an air of cynicism now, with hard rock sticking its big tongue out and wiggling its all-too lurex-clad ass. We've moved away from that..." – Kerrang! 282, March 24, 1990

"When I'd got a big audience I brought two or three Zep numbers back in. I didn't want to get five or six thousand people waddling in just to hear 'Battle Of Evermore', I wanted them to hear 'Little By Little' or some other anti-Pop" – Kerrang! 293, June 9, 1990

"I don't subscribe to the idea of winning accolades merely because you've been around long enough to get 'em! I mean, I'm glad I've been around a long time: it gives me great scope in music, but I don't wanna end up doing TV shows with Adam Faith..." – Kerrang! 441, May 1, 1993

"A bob or two has never entered into it!" – Kerrang! 441, May 1, 1993

ROBERT PLANT

acknowledge his past with Zeppelin. The record featured numerous samples of Zep riffs and even a guest appearance by Jimmy Page on the stand-out track, 'Tall Cool One'. Coincidentally, its release came not long after Whitesnake's '1987' LP, tour and MTV successes and prompted Plant to question publicly (and bitterly) it and David Coverdale's thinly-veiled Zep/Plant styling...

'Now And Zen' was quite a turnaround after 'Shaken 'N' Stirred' and led to some stunning gigs where Plant stopped people shouting for old Zep songs by actually playing them! He later explained that until that point he'd felt the need to prove himself as a solo artist in his own right. But in '88, having played gigs of 10,000 people and more in Europe and the States, he could now play Led Zeppelin songs without being accused of using them as a crutch.

On the next album, 'Manic Nirvana' ('90) samples were still to the fore, but old Zep riffs less so, with the band honing their songwriting talents instead. The live show, also, had improved and in interviews Plant spoke of his contentment with, and respect for, the band. Midway through sessions for what was to become 'Fate Of Nations', however, things weren't going so well. Plant went from being a big fan of studio trickery and a man happy to let everyone in the band have their input to someone faced with an album starting to sound only a little like he wanted it to. Out went Blackwell and Boyle and in came a variety of drummers and guitarists Frank Dunnery (ex-It Bites) and Kevin MacMichael (ex-Cutting Crew), plus various guests.

Despite the fraught and lengthy recording process, 'Fate Of Nations' proved to be probably his finest ever work, certainly dispelling any thoughts of a return to the world of accountancy for good...

ALBUMS

PICTURES AT ELEVEN (Swan Song, 1982 – KKKK) "It's certainly taken him a while to get his solo career officially under way (but this) shows that it's been well worth the wait." – Kerrang! 19, July 1-15, 1982

PRINCIPLE OF MOMENTS (Atlantic, 1983 – KKKKK) "Strange, brooding, electrifying... Robert emerges as a man with so much more to say than perhaps he was given the chance in the last five years." – Kerrang! 47, July 28-August 10, 1983

VOLUME ONE (Es Paranza, 1984 – KKK) Strictly speaking, a Honeydrippers not a Robert Plant record. A complete side-step from his solo career. Doo-wop R'n'B which swings and boogies with a huge grin on its face...

SHAKEN 'N' STIRRED (Es Paranza, 1985 – KK) "Strange days for Robert Plant. He floats into his future with dreamy musings and sudden outbursts..." – Kerrang! 96, June 13-26, 1985

NOW AND ZEN (Es Paranza, 1988 – KKKKK) "A highly palatable reconciliation of old and new... Kicks a-plenty... Plant's best release in some wee while, and accepting the lack of lemon juice at last, (sees) the man back at the forefront." – Kerrang! 174, February 13, 1988

MANIC NIRVANA (Es Paranza, 1990 – KKKKK) "Planty's cooking... He's back and he's bastard-well good. Ooh, let the sun beat down on his face." – Kerrang! 281, March 17, 1990

FATE OF NATIONS (Es Paranza, 1993 – KKKKK)

P.M.R.C.

USA, watchdog committee (1982-present)
EVER-GROWING council of strident conservative censors with a worryingly strong political platform, especially since Bill Clinton's election victory. The wife of his vice-President is also the head of the Washington-based group.
Recommended for members: **GETTING A LIFE**

POISON

USA, four-piece (1983-present)
ALONG WITH Guns N' Roses, the ozone unsociable Poison – Bret Michaels (vocals), CC Deville (guitar), Bobby Dall (bass), and Rikki Rocket (drums) – were spawned outta the post Ratt/Crüe LA scene brat-pack... GN'R guitarist Slash having actually auditioned for the lipstick killers at one point! Sounding like classic bubblegum-era Kiss, their debut album 'Look What The Cat Dragged In' ('86) fully captured their wham-bam-don't-give-a-damn persona.

Although subsequent releases saw a more 'we wanna be taken serious now' attitude, and in terms of success – many say through pure dumb luck and Michael's face-ache pout – they got away with it!

In 1991, however, bad boy guitarist Deville left their ranks amidst mucho ballyhoo, to be replaced by the more muso-minded Richie Kotzen, who made his debut on the well recieved 'Native Tongue' ('93) album.
Recommended album:
LOOK WHAT THE CAT DRAGGED IN (Enigma, 1986 – KKKKK)

POISON in '87: what self-respecting cat would drag this lot in?!?

POISON IDEA

USA, five-piece (1980-present)

WITH A combined weight roughly equal to that of a fleet of pregnant Sherman tanks (guitarist Pig Champion weighs 500lbs), Poison Idea are perhaps unlikely candidates for the self-awarded title of Kings Of Punk... but hey, are you gonna tell them?

Actually the title is more than justified by a back catalogue of ferocious albums and live shows that sometimes include their lunatic frontman Jerry A firebreathing and slicing his forehead with broken glass!

Not many people are man enough to stick with Poison Idea for too long (somehow they seem put off by drug abuse, alcoholism, fist fights, hospitalisations and the like), but the present line-up – completed by Myrtle Tickner (bass), Mondo (guitar) and Thee Slayer Hippy (drums) – proved more constant than most, if terminally unhealthy!

Recommended albums:

IAN MACKAYE *(In Your Face, 1988 – KKKKK)*

FEEL THE DARKNESS *(Vinyl Soloution, 1990 – KKKKK)*

Iggy POP

USA, vocalist/legend (1968-present)

BORN JAMES Jewel Osterberg on April 21, 1947 (which makes him really bloody old), Iggy Pop has always been the embodyment of the rock 'n' roll animal! Since the late '60s when he lead the legendary and highly influential Iggy Pop And The Stooges, the Ig has been carving himself up on stage, picking fights with whole chapters of Hell's Angels in the audience – the latter immortalised on the infamous 'Metallic KO' live album (Skydog, '76), where you can actually here the bottles breaking – and generally behaving badly!

Like most rock stars who stop abusing the ol' nasal powder, Iggy's music went rapidly downhill when, with the help of David Bowie, he cleaned up his act. Thankfully, although he remained straight, he regained much of his former attitude and to this day is still completely hatstand. Unlike many of the pretenders to the throne in this book, Iggy Pop can reasonably claim to be some kind of god!

Recommended albums:

NO FUN *(Elektra, 1980 – KKKKK) compilation of the two 'Stooges albums 'The Stooges' and 'Funhouse'.*

RAW POWER *(CBS, 1973 – KKKKK)*

INSTINCT *(Virgin, 1988 – KKKKK)*

PORNO FOR PYROS

USA, four-piece (1992-present)

FORMED BY ex-Jane's Addiction frontman Perry Farrell after the split of the controversial LA rockers, Porno For Pyros also include Jane's Addiction drummer Stephen Perkins, Peter DiStefano (guitar) and Martyn Lenoble (bass). The band released their eponymous debut LP in April '93, following a delay after Farrell ran into trouble with record company Warner Bros over album artwork which featured swastikas, albeit reversed swastikas.

Farrel stressed these were commonly used in Eastern mysticism, but Warners still said no. On its release, the eponymous debut received a lukewarm response, and was generally seen as a poor man's version of its singer's previous much-respected outfit.

Recommended album:

PORNO FOR PYROS *(Warner Bros, 1992 – KKK)*

POSSESSED

USA, four-piece (1984-present)

SEMINAL DEATHSTERS with a debut album generally considered to be an evil classic, flawed only by a fairly weak production job. Possessed's career concluded with an EP, 'Eyes Of Horror', produced by none other than Joe Satriani, for some strange reason. The bestial boys split up in 1987 but went back on the rampage in 1992.

Recommended album:

SEVEN CHURCHES *(Roadrunner, 1985 – KKKK)*

Cozy POWELL

UK, drummer (1971-present)

OFTEN CRITICISED for doing anything for money, his critics tend to forget that bands pay highly for good drummers – of which Mr Powell is undoubtedly one. His role of honour started in '71 with The Jeff Beck Group, then Cozy's own bands Bedlam and Hammer – with whom he had three hit singles 1973-1974 – then Rainbow, MSG, Whitesnake... He played on Robert Plant's first solo album, became the new 'P' in ELP in '84, and joined Black Sabbath. Has also made four patchy solo albums, some featuring Gary Moore...

Recommended solo album:
TILT *(Polydor, 1981 – KKK)*

POWER STATION

UK/USA, five-piece (1984-1986)

POP/ROCK crossover outfit featuring guitarist Andy Taylor (ex-Duran Duran) who went on to greater fame as a producer, and singer Robert Palmer – later replaced by ex-Glam Rocker, Michael Des Barres. They had three hit singles in '85 – including cover of T Rex's 'Get It On', re-christened 'Bang A Gong' so as not to offend US audiences!

Recommended album:
THE POWER STATION *(Parlophone, 1985 – KKKK)*

PRAYING MANTIS

UK, five-piece (1978-1982)

NWOBHM OUTFIT with quasi-Pomp Rock leanings, featuring the Troy brothers Tino (guitar/vocals) and Chris (bass/vocals). Bernie Shaw (later of Uriah Heep) sang for them. Used to support the likes of Iron Maiden and Samson but could never make the step up into the big league and after a couple of compilation appearances and just one full release, they split.

Still big in Japan though, where the name was briefly revived for a 1990 revival tour...

Recommended album:
TIME TELLS NO LIES *(Arista, 1981 – KKK)*

PRETTY BOY FLOYD

USA, four-piece (1988-present)

NOT TO be confused with the Canadian act of the same name, this LA strip act arrived in a hail of publicity, as was the case with many of the Glam bands of the late '80s, however, despite unleashing a fairly commendable album, very typical of the genre, seemingly disapeared from the face of the earth after being dropped by MCA due to poor sales (not helped by dismal promotion and no tour support).

Having since contributed the song 'Slam Dunk' for a basketball sequence in the Ellen Barkin movie 'Switch', the band are still believed to be an ongoing concern with a revised line-up but low-visibility.

Recommended album:
LEATHER BOYZ WITH ELECTRIC TOYZ *(MCA, 1989 – KKK)*

PRETTY MAIDS

Denmark, five-piece (1981-present)

WANNABE DEEP Purple clones who, unlike their heroes, have two guitarists and no Hammond organ player. But one of the guitarist has the Very Metal name of Ken Hammer and they did persuade Roger Glover to produce their fourth LP, 'Jump The Gun' in '90.

Recommended album:
RED HOT AND HEAVY *(CBS, 1984 – KKK)*

PRIMUS

USA, three-piece (1984-present)

ABSOLUTELY INSANE avant garde power trio with mainman Les Claypool's bass and Popeye-style vocals very high in mix. Current line-up completed by Larry Lalonde (guitar) and Tim Alexander (drums). They write bizarre lyrics, lots of songs about fishing, and are much admired

by Rush – who booked them as a support band on the 'Roll The Bones' tour.

Recommended fourth album:
PORK SODA *(Interscope, 1993 – KKKK)*

PRONG

USA, three-piece (1987-present)
CRUNCHY THRASH with uncompromising lyrics
coming out of New York's Lower East Side...
fighting! Two albums for NY indie label Spigot –
'Primitive Origins' ('86) and 'Force Fed' ('88) –
brought them to the attention of major labels of
whom Epic was keenest.
Recommended third album:
BEG TO DIFFER (Epic, 1990 – KKKK)

PRONG: uncompromisingly crunchy!

QUARTZ

UK, four-piece (1977-1983)
PUB ROCKERS who failed to cash in on the
NWOBHM despite landing a support slot with
Brummie neighbours Black Sabbath (when
Quartz were still called Bandylegs). Quartz
made four albums but went nowhere. Their
second did include a mean re-working of
Mountain's 'Nantucket Sleighride', though...
Barely recommended album:
LIVE SONGS *(Logo, 1979 – KK)*

QUEEN

UK, four-piece (1970-present)
THE CHAMPIONS! The roots of Queen
begin to flourish in the dawn of the
'70s, although guitarist Brian May
and drummer Roger Meadows
Taylor were previously bandmates
in an outfit called Smile (who
released one relatively obscure 45 in
the shape of 'Earth', which had a US-
only release on Mercury). Interestingly, it was
another member
of Smile, one
Tim Staffell, who
on leaving the
act persuaded
his flatmate
Freddie Mercury
(real name:
Frederick
Bulsara) to join
their ranks.
Then, come Feb
'71, science
graduate John
Deacon
completed the
quartet as
bassist. As if to
prove that
fairytales do
come true, the
recording of a
demo, led to the
studio engineers
(one being Roy
Thomas Baker –
the producer

QUEEN in 1975: classic shot from the 'Bohemian Rhapsody' video

TRIBUTES FROM THE STARS
(Kerrang! 372, December 21–28, 1991)

"Queen had an individual sound that no one else could ever duplicate."
– Ozzy Osbourne

"A lot more bands could do with being influenced by them."
– Sean Harris (Diamond Head)

" 'Bohemian Rhapsody' was a landmark in rock music. There was nothing like it before nor since."
– Danny Bowes (Thunder)

"Queen were unique because they never compromised in their attempts to push forward the boundaries of rock – and usually did!"
– Toby Jepson (Little Angels)

QUEEN

who would play a major part in Queen's recording career) recommending to their employers, Trident Audio Productions, that they get Queen on their books. After witnessing the band live, Trident astutely signed Queen for production, publishing, and management. A 24-track demo was recorded at Trident's studios, using vacant time, and the finished tape captured the imagination of EMI who swiftly collared the band. The slippers fit, and for the ball, Queen were definitely on the guest-list!

Strangely, before EMI release Queen's eponymous '73 debut album, Mercury manages to release a solo single, 'I Can Hear Music', under the frightfully camp pseudonym of Larry Lurex! Queen's first single, 'Keep Yourself Alive', failed to chart, but the band built up an amazing live reputation supporting the likes of Mott The Hoople, and were even described as 'Britain's answer to the New York Dolls'! 1974 saw the release of the imaginatively-titled 'Queen II'. As fate would have it, a David Bowie promo clip was unavailable for use on 'Top Of The Pops', so Queen were slotted in to perform their 'Seve Seas Of Rhye' single. They made a considerable impact and things really start to take off for our black 'n' white clad heroes – Mercury, with his flamboyant demeanour, had naturally become the central figure. Their third album, 'Sheer Heart Attack' ('74), touched Number Two in the UK charts, and with the release boasting two classic hit singles in 'Killer Queen' and 'Now I'm Here', Queen's status as a force to be reckoned with, was cemented. Despite excursions into pomp and whimsicality, Queen were still considered primarily a heavy rock band, but the release of the transitional (to say nothing of phenomenal!) 'A Night At The Opera' ('75), put them in a whole new league. Actually, their own league. As for the single 'Bohemian Rhapsody'... Despite its epic length, the song, with its lavish blending of classical pastiche and blistering Heavy Rock, topped the UK charts for a staggering nine weeks. With the accompanying promo-film inciting new trends in promotional ploys. Video launched the radio star?

With a die-hard following Queen transcended mere trends, becoming a law unto themselves, releasing numerous albums as well as the individual members dabbling in all manner of relating projects over the next 10 years. Then, Queen's spectacular performance at the Live-Aid concert at Wembley Stadium on July 13, 1985 appeared to further escalate the popularity of a band who were already sitting on a cosy throne.

Their success never waning for a second, come the late '80s and the press begin to cast aspersions on the increasing ill-health of Freddie Mercury. Mere days before the star's death on November 24, 1991, it was officially announced that Mercury had the AIDS virus. A major talent had been taken from us. A Freddie Mercury Memorial Tribute took place on April 20, 1992 to raise funds for AIDS Awareness. A multitude of stars, including Extreme, Def Leppard, Guns N' Roses and Metallica, took part. The Mercury legacy will live on. In addition tp the above, rumours persist of more material he worked on with Queen up until his death...

ALBUMS

QUEEN *(EMI, 1973 – KKK) A hit and miss affair, but with oodles of promise...*

QUEEN II *(EMI, 1974 – KKKK) Realises what their debut only hinted at, running the whole gamut of rock...*

SHEER HEART ATTACK *(EMI, 1974 – KKKKK) meaner, Queen's heaviest approach to date...*

A NIGHT AT THE OPERA *(EMI,1975 – KKKK) It kicks in places, but here Queen's pomp leanings really come to the fore...*

A DAY AT THE RACES *(EMI,1976 – KKK) The storming 'Tie Your Mother Down' aside – '...Races' is a weak relative to '...Opera'*

NEWS OF THE WORLD *(EMI, 1977 – KKKK) Queen beef up the drums as the champs come up trumps...*

JAZZ *(EMI, 1978 – KKK) Wacky, but not without its entertainment value...*

LIVE KILLERS *(EMI, 1979 – KKKKK) Confirmation, if any were needed, that Queen are a shit hot live rock act...*

THE GAME *(EMI, 1980 – KKKK) Overtly commercial with blatant stabs at pop and disco, but none-the-less a strong record...*

HOT SPACE *(EMI, 1981 – KK) Dance-based pap...*

FLASH *(EMI, 1982 – K) Title-track aside, a rather weak movie soundtarack...*

THE WORKS *(EMI, 1984 – KK) 'Radio Ga Ga' and some top quality rock...*

A KIND OF MAGIC *(EMI, 1986) Heaviest Queen LP for some time. Includes tracks from the 'Highlander' movie...*

LIVE MAGIC *(EMI, 1987 – KKKK) Updated live set to complement the 1979 double...*

THE MIRACLE *(Parlophone, 1989 – KKK) Patchy and eccentric...*

QUEEN AT THE BEEB 1973 *(Band Of Joy, 1990 – KKKKK) "The release of this material serves to illustrate just how bland and mundane recent Queen have become." – Kerrang! 226, November 25, 1989*

INNUENDO *(EMI,1991 – KKKK) Totally eccentric. Kaleidoscope of styles. Pure Queen brilliance. "You don't have to be mad to like it, but it'll probably help... – Kerrang! 326, February 2, 1991*

QUEENSRŸCHE

USA, five-piece (1981-present)

ARGUABLY THE biggest thing to come out of Seattle since the first Boeing 747 rolled from the production line, Queensrÿche still boasts the original line-up – Geoff Tate (vocals), Chris DeGarmo and Michael Wilton (guitars), Eddie Jackson (bass) and Scott Rockenfield (drums) – 'discovered' way back in early '83 by *Kerrang!*. The band took some time in converting the masses to their cause afte that, but their persistence paid off... They had briefly dallied with using the handle of The Mob, while spending months

QUEENSRŸCHE: from basements to empires...

QUEENSRŸCHE

rehearsing in a basement. But as Queensrÿche, they released a self-financed four-track EP on their then manager's 206 label, later re-issued with the might of EMI America behind it.

Back then, Queensrÿche were playing a style of music on the pompous side of Judas Priest. By the time the band's first full album, 'The Warning', was issued in 1984, the band were seriously confused and more than intimidated by the record label. EMI America forced them to finish it well before it was really ready. They also dictated misguided choice of James Guthrie as producer. Nevertheless, the album did enlarge their cult following and with the follow-up, 'Rage For Order', the band were allowed to make the true progression from the EP. 'Rage...' was classily produced by Neil Kernon and advertised with the slogan, 'Every chord a power chord'! Queensrÿche's Glam image of the day didn't do them any favours, however!

It would be Queensrÿche's third and utterly conceptual 'Operation: Mindcrime' album (released in 1988, by which time the band had switched management to Peter Mensch and Cliff Burnstein at Q-Prime) that really established the band, hurling them to the forefront of technical Power Metal in an almost true-to- life tale of power, corruption, sex, drugs and murder, based around the central character of a young street punk called Nikki.

Described in *Kerrang!* as possessing a

"palapable story-line, strong secondary character themes, and dappled like poison between each track with an intertwining monologue of voices", '...Mindcrime' was lapped up in Europe. American audiences were slower on the up-take, until 'Empire' was issued two years later. 'Empire' was a tad more commercial, though nonetheless thoughtful lyrically and precise musically. Sales went through the roof, a multi-Platinum success.

Early 1993 found Queensrÿche recording basic tracks for their next album in each others home studios. How's that for art-rock?

ALBUMS

THE WARNING (EMI America, 1984 – KKK).
"The production and remix tend to fall over themselves." – Kerrang! 77, September 20-October 3, 1984

RAGE FOR ORDER (EMI, 1985 – KKKKK).
"Sheer chaotic intensity." – Kerrang! 124, July 10-23, 1986

OPERATION: MINDCRIME
(EMI, 1988 – KKKKK) "Every song is a monstrous achievement." – Kerrang! 188, May 21, 1988

EMPIRE (EMI, 1990 – KKKKK)
"You would be a full-on fool not to have it as part of your collection." – Kerrang! 306, September 8, 1990

QUIET RIOT

USA, four-piece (1975-1989)

ENJOYED SLIGHTLY more than 15 minutes of fame in 1983 when their 'Metal Health' album sold five million and spawned a handful of hits led by their cover of Slade's 'Cum On Feel The Noize'. But after that, the band receded quicker than singer Kevin DuBrow's hairline. Rudy Sarzo (bass, later Whitesnake) and Frankie Banali (drums, later W.A.S.P. *et al*) were lucky not to get dragged down with the sinking ship. In fact, disdain for DuBrow is about the only thing Axl Rose and Mötley Crüe agree on these days. Collectors chase this LA band's highly valuable pop/rock first two albums (on Columbia Japan) because the line-up then featured the late great Randy Rhoads, before he joined Ozzy Osbourne.

Recommended album:
METAL HEALTH *(Epic, 1983 – KKKK)*

KEVIN DuBROW (Quiet Riot): hair today, gone later today...

The QUIREBOYS

UK, six-piece (1984-present)

CLUB LEVEL heroes of the mid-'80s who got a shot at the big time, originally under the managerial guidance of Sharon (Ozzy) Osbourne. By the time of the release of their debut platter, 'A Bit Of What You Fancy' ('89), the London-based band's favoured pin-stripe jackets, cowboy boots 'n' bandanas had become the chic for the street-cool rock 'n' roller. Loved by the fans, the QBs did suffer a lot of (understandable) Faces comparisons from the press for their good-time, rollickin' brand of music, and more so for the gravel-laced larynx of vocalist Spike. But our lads persevered undaunted, and looked set to conquer the world at one point – their progress, according to general consensus, being halted by the arrival of the 'superior' Black Crowes.

The long (and questionably) awaited release of their second studio album, 'Bitter Sweet And Twisted' ('93), was dogged by studio technicalities and disagreements, yet the end product was a strong effort. But then the question of the band's relevancy arose, as Spike & Co found themselves slap bang in the middle of the 'Grunge' revolution.

The Quireboys are doing fine in many foreign territories, but whether they will regain their foothold on their own turf remains to be seen.

Recommended album:
A BIT OF WHAT YOU FANCY *(Parlophone, 1989 – KKKK)*

Trevor RABIN

South Africa, solo artist (1978-present)
ORIGINALLY A member of the ridiculously named Rabbit whilst in South Africa, he moved to Britain and won himself a deal with Chrysalis. Although primarily a guitarist, he can sing and played every instrument on his eponymous debut album, the first of four to date in a solo career interrupted by his invitation to join the reformed Yes in 1982.
Recommended second album:
FACE TO FACE (Chrysalis, 1979 – KKKK)

RACER X

USA, five-piece (1986-1990)
TECHNO METAL Los Angeles outfit which proved a breeding ground for talent. Guitarist Paul Gilbert (now Mr Big) is the real star of their alumni but the line-up also featured singer Jeff Martin (latterly Badlands' drummer), and drummer Scott Travis (who went on to Judas Priest and Fight).
Recommended debut album:
STREET LETHAL (Roadrunner, 1986 – KKK)

RAGE

Germany, three-piece (1986-present)
UNDERRATED SPEED Metal trio with the rare ability to actually pen a few memorable tunes.
Recommended album:
PERFECT MAN (Noise International, 1987 – KKKK)

RAGE AGAINST THE MACHINE

USA, four-piece (1991-present)
CONFRONTATIONAL REBELS of Rap Metal, Rage Against The Machine have been amazingly swift to carve their political manifestos in stone. Already, they've produced one of Rock's most striking slogans; "Fuck you, I won't do what you tell me!".

As great as that one is, it's likely that the strength and passion of Rage's music, including some highly creative guitar work from Tom Morello, will be enough to stop them from becoming a one-obscenity wonder.
Highly recommended album:
RAGE AGAINST THE MACHINE (Epic, 1993 – KKKK)

RAGING SLAB

USA, five-piece (1983-present)
SOUTHERN OUTFIT whose eponymous '89 RCA debut album took some unexpected Thrashy twists and led to some misleading comparisons with Metallica. Doubly confusing after their '87 indie label debut, 'Assmaster', had them pegged as more of a biker band... Second album proper, 'Dynamite Monster Boogie Concert' ('93), was more in keeping with their Lynyrd Skynyrd-style roots. The band features three guitars, including those played by singer Greg Strzempka and the impossibly skinny female slide guitarist Elyse Steinma. She wears nice hipster flares, too.
Recommended album:
RAGING SLAB (RCA, 1989 – KKKK)

RAGING SLAB: with the impossibly skinny Elyse Steinma second from right

RAINBOW

UK/USA, five-piece (1975-1984)

FORMED BY Ritchie Blackmore from the ashes of US band Elf, who supported Deep Purple in 1974. When he quit Purple in '75, Blackmore hired the whole of Elf (except their guitarist!) and renamed them Ritchie Blackmore's Rainbow. Main attraction for Ritchie was Elf's singer Ronnie James Dio, the only man to survive the wholesale personnel shuffle when the band took to the road after the debut album's release in late '75. At that point, the line-up peaked – with Blackmore and Dio complemented by Cozy Powell (drums), Jimmy Bain (bass) and Tony Carey (keyboards) – and made the seminal 'Rainbow Rising' album – featuring 'Stargazer' – released in '76. This band recorded the lacklustre – not to say premature – double live album, 'On Stage' ('77), but Bob Daisley (then ex-Widowmaker) and David Stone had replaced Bain and Carey respectively come 'Long Live Rock 'N' Roll' ('78).

After that tour, Blackmore's notorious perfectionism (his excuse) or moodiness (according to everyone he sacked) led to a radical re-think, with Dio being replaced by Graham Bonnet, former Purple cohort Roger Glover coming in on bass and Don Airey taking over on keyboards. The new album, 'Down To Earth' ('79) took a more commercial turn and produced the hits 'Since You Been Gone' and 'All Night Long' – but Blackmore remained unsatisfied and membership of the band became as precarious as a journey through a revolving door...

More to the point, he turned his back on the original epic/neo-Gothic Metal style of Rainbow and tried to create something closer to bands like Foreigner or Bad Company. In retrospect, it never really worked. 'Difficult To Cure' ('81), featuring new singer Joe Lynn Turner and drummer Bobby Rondinelli, was too radical a change and they just got slicker – but less effective – with 'Straight Between The Eyes' ('82) and 'Bent Out Of Shape' ('83), the latter featuring yet another new member, former

Balance man, Chuck Burgi on drums.

Live, Blackmore's brilliance rarely failed to impress, although he was often frustrated by the reaction of some UK audiences – most notably the one at Wembley Arena in 1980 which he deemed unworthy of an encore, sparking a riot and attracting coverage in the 'quality' daily press... The first couple of tours were the best, however, when above the stage curved a massive, computer-operated electronic rainbow, a brilliant mass of swirling colours. Er, perhaps you had to be there...

The band bowed out with the appropriately named double odds 'n' sods collection 'Final Vinyl' in '86, but an impressive double, 'Rainbow Live In Germany', emerged in '90.

Recommended albums:
RITCHIE BLACKMORE'S RAINBOW
(Oyster/Polydor, 1975 – KKKK)
RAINBOW RISING
(Polydor, 1976 – KKKKK)

RAM JAM

USA, five-piece (1977-1978)

FACELESS ONE-HIT wonders who made two albums but will always be remembered for just one Top 10 song...

Recommended single:
BLACK BETTY *(Epic, 1977 – KKKK)*

The RAMONES

USA, four-piece (1974-present)

THREE CHORDS, a handful of dumb lyrics, crap haircuts... it's hardly the stuff that legends are usually made of, but the Ramones didn't seem to notice and thus went on to become one of the world's greatest (Punk) rock bands. Maybe it's because they're from New York or something, but the Ramones just bash on blissfully unaware of changing trends in music, and, at times, blissfully unaware of anything else. Legend has it that vocalist Joey Ramone was once so out-of-it in Italy that he had to count his steps to cross the road; he lost count halfway across, turned back to start again, and was hit by a car!

Everything they ever record is about five times as fast when they play it live and it's almost compulsory to shout along to their imortal catchphrase "Hey ho let's go!" during 'Blitzkrieg Bop'. They influenced everyone from Skid Row to Nirvana, Motörhead wrote a song about them, and they were Sid Vicious' favourite band!

Recommended albums:
IT'S ALIVE (Sire, 1979 – KKKKK)
LOCO LIVE (Chrysalis, 1991 – KKKK)

RATT

USA, four-piece (1983-1992)
HOT ON the heels of pack leaders Mötley Crüe, Ratt – Stephen Pearcy (vocals), Robbin Crosby and Warren DeMartini (guitars), Juan Croucier (bass) and Bobby Blotzer (drums) – came out of the LA sleazola explosion of the early '80s. Their nice and, well yeah, 'ratty' eponymous debut mini-album (released in the UK on the Music For Nations label) was well received critically, and the band soon found themselves on the Atlantic label. With glossy production work from Beau Hill, the first two (full) albums, 'Out Of The Cellar' ('84) and 'Invasion Of Your Privacy' ('85), were *tres* successful. But come '86 and 'Dancing Undercover' (ironically the first albums to feature the band on the front sleeve), the art of Ratt-bashing seemed to have become a favourite pastime of certain factions of the music press, many seeming to consider the talents of vocalist Stephen Pearcy somewhat questionable. 'Dancing...' , actually a strong album, was panned. And the following two elpees, along with Pearcy's *faux pas* of admitting "... we know our limitations", did bugger-all to affect opinion. The rodent rockers' extermination was inevitable. Pearcy is the only Ratt who left Metal's answer to the Titanic to have surfaced so far, with his new oufit Arcade. James Hetfield is reportedly ecstatic...

Recommended album:
OUT OF THE CELLAR (Atlantic, 1984 – KKKK)

RAVEN

UK, three-piece (1976-1990)
GEORDIE NUTTERS who pretty much invented Speed Metal and enjoyed their best years, 1980-1984, with the line-up of John Gallagher (bass/vocals), his brother Mark (guitar) and Rob 'Wacko' Hunter (drums). John's high-pitched vocal were 'an acquired taste' to fans and 'bloody painful' to everyone else, but there was no denying the band's insane power and enthusiasm (live and on record). They described their style as 'Athletic Rock' – a bit like Wolfsbane in attitude – and you certainly needed to be fit to keep up. After four albums but only moderate success on Neat, they made the catastrophic error in '84 of signing to Atlantic and going more mainstream in an attempt to crack the States. It failed badly and although the band soldiered on in various guises, time has proved they should have stuck to what they were best at – and waited for the rest of the Metal world to catch up.

Recommended, anything on Neat, but particularly:
ROCK TIL YOU DROP (Neat, 1981 – KKKK)
Rough 'n' ready debut
ALL FOR ONE (Neat, 1983 – KKKK) *Better produced third LP*

RAZOR

USA, four-piece (1983-present)
IF YOU want violent Thrash, then Razor are up there among the best. The worst mistake they ever made was releasing albums too frequently in the mid-'80s, resulting in quality being sacrificed for the sake of quantity, not to mention them losing their deal with Roadrunner.

But since 'Violent Restitution', their awesomely heavy comeback platter of 1988, Razor have been consistently excellent, if far harder to find.

Most recommended albums:
VIOLENT RESTITUTION (Fist Fight, 1988 – KKKKK)
SHOTGUN JUSTICE (Fist Fight, 1990 – KKKKK)

RE–ANIMATOR

UK, four-piece (1988-present)
ABYSMAL EXAMPLE of directionless, trend-pandering UK Metal. Re-animator have gone through more stylistic changes than Axl Rose during a GN'R gig. In 1993, they're 'quite big in certain European territories'.
Utterly disposable:
THAT WAS THEN, THIS IS NOW *(Music For Nations, 1993 – K)*

RED HOT CHILI PEPPERS

USA, four-piece (1983-present)
IT'S BIZARRE to think that Los Angeles, the sprawling home to the most homogenised Metal hopefuls on the planet, should have spawned The Red Hot Chili Peppers, possibly the most eclectic rock act ever to trouble the scorers. In a town where Follow The Leader is the most popular participation sport, the Chilis have burnt as the brightest flame of non-conformism.

Vocalist Anthony Kiedis spent his formative years riding the wild horses of the LA hep-set. His father, little-known actor Blackie Dammett, introduced him to a life of weird and wonderful people doing even weirder and more wonderful things, which doubtless accounts for the man's more eccentric live performances.

The roots of the band, however, lay in the far more conventional roots of two laddies with stars in their eyes performing a Kiss tribute performance to wide-eyed school chums. Drummer Jack Irons and guitarist Hillel Slovaks obsession with all things Starchild and Demon was, however, soon allied to the prodigious talents of bassist Flea (born Michael Balzary) – the oddball offspring of jazz trumpeter Walter Urban Jr. Christened – in a band called Anthym. They performed standard hard rock unintentionally tinged with Flea's more obtuse musical style, with Anthony not involved in the musical proceedings, but acting as general sounding-board and live gig compere.

Anthym became What Is This? – with Kiedis becoming the singer – before The Red Hot Chili Peppers was eventually deemed the perfect hatstand name to define their perfectly hatstand music. A deal with EMI was struck, resulting in 1984's eponymous debut.

While the band's heady mix of Hendrix guitar and Funkadelic rhythm confused the hell out of most people, the band's commitment to the Chili cause never wavered. 1985's 'Freaky Styley' again failed to win friends and influence people, but 'The Uplift Mofo Party Plan' ('88) finally saw the band break the waters of that mother called success. The 'Fight Like A Brave', single/zany fancy-dress video, created a trickle of appreciation which would soon grow to a tidal wave...

The band's penchant for complementing their high octane fusion with hilarious visuals (who can forget the infamous 'cocks on socks' 'Abbey Road EP' cover?) hid a darker underbelly. Having never made a secret of their prediliction for narcotic experimentation, the whole shebang blew up in their faces with the death of Slovak from a heroin overdose and the departure of drummer Irons. Ironically, the arrival of John Frusciante on guitar and Chad Smith on drums heralded the major breakthrough of 'Mother's Milk' ('88). Chocked to the funky gills with fusionistic gems such as 'Subway

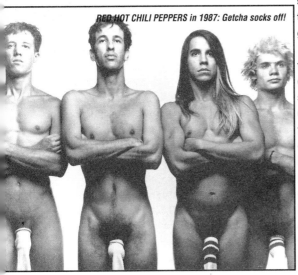
RED HOT CHILI PEPPERS in 1987: Getcha socks off!

To Venus' and 'Taste The Pain', it was a turbo-charged cover of Stevie Wonder's 'Higher Ground' which saw the band uplifted to high altitude stardom.

With the Metal community's perceptions of what constituted rock music ever-broadening, The Chili Peppers found themselves heading off into a 1920s mansion on LA's Laurel Canyon Boulevard with producer Rick Rubin (Slayer/The Cult) to lay down 'Blood Sugar Sex Magik' ('91). The was funky as fuck, with a heartful of soul and blessed with the kind of passion that Hendrix would have been proud of. It stormed the American charts, spouting hit singles and earning the Chilis headlining status on the 1992 Lollapalooza US tour.

But after the Japanese leg of the 'Blood Sugar...' tour, Frusciante quit amidst the predictable drug scaremongering, to be replaced by Arik Marshall, a long-standing friend of the band. How long he remains standing within the ranks of one of rock's party-hardyest bands remains to be seen, but despite rumours that the group are no longer the live tour-de-force they once were, the Chili Peppers' star remains firmly in the ascendant.

ALBUMS
RED HOT CHILI PEPPERS *(EMI, 1984 – KKK)* *"Songwriting shows impressive inventiveness (but) this debut lacks the muscular power that they would later develop." – Kerrang! 302, August 11, 1990 (re-release)*
FREAKY STYLEY *(EMI, 1985 – KK) "Teetering on being out-and-out (poor) mainstream funk, there's very little of what rock's all about here." – Kerrang! 302, August 11, 1990 (re-release)*
THE UPLIFT MOFO PARTY PLAN *(EMI, 1988 – KKK) First indication that the Chilis could successfully fuse rock energy with funky sass...*
MOTHER'S MILK *(EMI, 1989 - KKKKK) "(Proves) Funk doesn't have to be the lightweight, sickly smooth load of bollocks that is most often associated with the term." – Kerrang! 253, August 26, 1989*
BLOOD SUGAR SEX MAGIK *(Warner Bros., 1991 - KKKKK) "Blood, sugar, sex, magik,*

sadness, madness, elation, the spectrum ad infinitum. The Red Hot Chili Peppers have given us a wonderfully human record" – Kerrang! 359, September 21, 1991

Dan REED NETWORK
USA, five-piece (1986-present)
ALTHOUGH GENERALLY the band are considered to play funk-fuelled rock that defies categorisation, the Dan Reed Network have taken their cue from Mother's Finest – coming up with a sound that falls halfway between Prince and Bon Jovi. They sailed into view in the summer of 1988 with their eponymous major label debut for PolyGram, having already issued a now very rare indie EP in their native Portland, Oregon some time before.

Featuring a truly multi-racial line-up and fronted by the extremely enigmatic Dan Reed (former farm worker and Burger King employee!), the group have constantly received

critical acclaim for everything they've done. Yet despite a strong European following, major success seems to have passed them by. Having taken a break after the release of the third album, 'The Heat' ('91), one can only speculate as to whether DRN will return to fight another day. If they do it will surely be as much of a triumphant return as their original entry.
Recommended
DAN REED NETWORK *(Mercury, 1988 – KKKKK)*
SLAM *(Mercury, 1989 – KKKK)*

REVOLTING COCKS

USA, three/seven-piece (1984-present)
AL JOURGENSEN'S main hobby after Ministry, Revolting Cocks are weirder, wilder and more dance-oriented, but still pack a punch. Line-up varies, but revolves around a core of Jourgensen, Luc Van Acker, Paul Barker and Chris Connelly. Debut LP 'Big Sexy Land' ('86) named after brothel, setting the scene for follow-up live LP and video 'You Goddamned Son Of A Bitch' ('88) which displayed band's ironic embracing of pure gonzoid behaviour. When bizarrely named founding member Richard 23 (formerly of Electro/Industrial outfit Front 242) left, Jourgensen replaced him with Chris Connelly, whose first recording was the grinding biker anthem 'Stainless Steel Providers'.

Their hardcore/dance crossover sound wasn't fully realised until 'Beers, Steers & Queers' ('90); the accompanying tour, plans for which included strippers and live cattle on stage, saw the band discussed in The House Of Commons by shocked MPs.
Recommended album:
BEERS, STEERS & QUEERS *(Wax Trax/ Devotion, 1990 – KKKK)*

RHINO BUCKET

USA, four-piece, (1987-present)
ONCE SENT every *K!* scribe a tape of the band performing at the Coconut Teaszer club in LA. There was no info, no pic, no address – nothing. In fact, if it hadn't been for the downright daft name, the thing probably wouldn't have been played at all!

The tape revealed an AC/DC clone band featuring Georg Dolvio (vocals/guitar), a man with a filthier mind than Bon Scott, as evidenced by the immortal rap, "So who's gonna fuck me tonight then?". Their songs were actually pretty good but sadly, the 'magic' of Rhino Bucket never came over on studio product, and the band seem destined to stay in the clubs until they catch some horrendous social disease and become generally incapable.
Recommended offensive demo:
LIVE AT THE COCONUT TEASZER – UNCENSORED *(Rhino Bucket/Amazing Girth Music, 1990 – KKKKK)*

Randy RHOADS

USA, guitarist
(December 6, 1956-March 19, 1982)
BRILLIANT LEAD guitarist who shot to fame in 1980 as a member of Ozzy Osbourne's band but was tragically killed when their tour-plane crashed in Florida in '82. He started playing when he was seven, but made his recording debut on the self-financed Quiet Riot single 'Slick Black Cadilac'/'Killer Girls' ('78) and also featured on 'Quiet Riot' ('78) and 'Quiet Riot II' ('79) – both LPs recorded for Sony Japan and originally released in that territory only. Since Randy's death, Ozzy has often spoken, with great fondness, of a young man who hadn't yet fulfilled his potential and who would spend all his spare time practising, often falling asleep cradling one of his beloved guitars. Undoubtedly, a major loss...
Recommended album:
TRIBUTE *(Epic, 1987 – KKKKK) Collection of live recordings with Ozzy*

RICH RAGS

UK, four-piece (1989-present)
HULL HERBERTS whose persistence seemed finally to have paid off when they signed a deal with the Games Workshop's label Warhammer to release their debut album. The 'Rags – Ian Hunter (vocals, no relation to anyone who was

ever in Mott The Hoople), Jon Stewart (guitar), Paul Harrison (formerly 'Angel' – cough! – bass) and Dave Carter (drums) – released an indie EP, 'Bedlam', in '89 and a succession of three rapidly improving demos that peaked with 1992's streetwise 'White Punks On Dole'.
Recommended album:
PSYCHO DEADHEADS FROM OUTER SPACE *(Warhammer, 1993 – KKKK)*

RIOT

USA, five-piece (1976-present)
A HUGELY underrated US Metal band, Riot were amongst the bands who were on 1980's very first Donington Monsters Of Rock bill. At the time, they had already released two albums and gone through rapid personnel changes before settling, for two years, on what many people consider to be the definitive line-up – Guy Speranza (vocals), Mark Reale and Rick Ventura (guitars), Kip Leming (bass) and Sandy Slavin (drums). They toured the UK with Sammy Hagar and Saxon and released the 'Fire Down Under' album before falling out with Speranza. His place was taken by the gruff voiced Rhett Forrester.

Problems with record labels forever plagued their career and it was after falling from grace with the majors, leading to the 'Born In America' album only coming out on the Canadian independent Quality Records in 1984, that the band called it a day. That is, until 1988 when guitarist Reale, now Texas-based, decided to change the handle of his band Narita (in honour of Riot's second album, not the Tokyo airport) to Riot, although Reale is the only original member. Secured a deal with CBS and there have been three albums released by the band in the present incarnation, although success seems to be limited to the German market.
Riotously recommended:
ROCK CITY *(Ariola, 1977 – KKKK)*
RIOT LIVE 1980 *(Metal Blade, 1993 – KKKK)*

ROCK-AID ARMENIA

Global, 14-piece (1989)
CHARITY ENSEMBLE put together by Jon Dee to raise funds for the victims of December '88, Armenian earthquake. Over five sessions, July-September '89 in West London, the all-star cast re-recorded Deep Purple's 'Smoke On The Water'. Ritchie Blackmore and Ian Gillan, who featured on the original, dropped by to help, as did Brian May and Roger Taylor (Queen), Dave Gilmour (Pink Floyd), Chris Squire (Yes), Geoff Downes (Asia, co-producer with Gary Langan), Keith Emerson (ELP), Paul Rodgers, Bruce Dickinson, Bryan Adams, Tony Iommi (Black Sabbath), Alex Lifeson (Rush), Jeff Beauchamp of, er... Patsy Kensit's Eighth Wonder. The track featured on several remixed singles, a compilation video and album.
Recommended video (especially for rare Led Zeppelin footage):
SMOKE ON THE WATER – THE VIDEO COLLECTION *(Virgin, 1989 – KKKK)*

ROCK GODDESS

UK, three-piece (1977-1987)
SCARILY UNDERAGE all-girl Trad Metallers who never quite matched Girlschool for either credibility or tunes.
Recommended debut album:
ROCK GODDESS *(A&M, 1983 – KKKK)*

The RODS

USA, three-piece (1980-1987)
BULLISH POWER trio whose lengthy career never produced a true killer album to remember them as anything except a wannabe-Raven.
Loud but underwhelming album:
LET THEM EAT METAL *(Combat, 1984 – KKK)*

Henry ROLLINS

USA, solo artist (1981-present)
HENRY ROLLINS' first stage appearance was at a gig by hardcore LA Punk band Black Flag in 1981, when, as a fan, he got onstage and grabbed the mike off the singer. Weeks later they asked him to become their new vocalist.

HENRY ROLLINS: Manic Persona

Rollins stayed with Black Flag for five years, developing both his muscled physique and his intense stage performance. In '86, he formed his own band and put out the first Rollins Band LP, 'Hot Animal Machine'. Several albums followed, and the Rollins Band toured endlessly; their fierce work ethic, extremely tight, heavy Blues-based sound and Henry's manic persona won them fans the world over. 'The End Of Silence' ('91), and the accompanying world tour, consolidated the appeal. Henry has also become a crowd-puller in his own right as a spoken-word performer.

Recommended album:
THE END OF SILENCE (Imago, 1991 – KKKKK)

Mick RONSON

UK, guitarist (1974–1993)
NEVER QUITE cutting it as a solo performer (his tour of '74 being written off as something of a joke), guitarist Mick Ronson will always be remembered as the sometimes partner and friend of ex-Mott The Hoople frontman Ian Hunter, and even more so as the axe-wrenching peroxide-blond demi-god who stole a sizeable portion of David Bowie's limelight in the Ziggy Stardust-dominated early '70s ('Ziggy...' being Bowie's '72 album-turned-Frankenstein). Yet 'Ronno' did release two elpees under his own name – 'Slaughter On Tenth Avenue' ('74) and 'Play Don't Worry' ('75) – and at the time of his tragic death was working on his third, tentatively-titled 'Heaven Or Hull'.

Mick Ronson died from liver cancer at the age of 46 on Thursday, April 29, 1993. The rock world mourns his passing.

Recommended album:
PLAY DON'T WORRY (RCA, 1974 – KKKK)

ROMEO'S DAUGHTER

UK, five-piece (1988-present)
MELODIC ROCK outfit fronted by the sultry and smouldering Leigh Matty. Early involvement of 'Mutt' Lange and early-'80s AOR star John Parr promised much, but the band have failed to become household names. They did, however, get 'Heaven In The Back Seat' onto the soundtrack of the 'Nightmare On Elm Street V' movie and have had songs covered by Heart and Eddie Money. Thus inspired, they've plugged away on and off and despite being totally unfashionable, haven't given up yet.

Only album:
ROMEO'S DAUGHTER (Jive, 1988 – KKK)

ROSE TATTOO

Australia, five-piece (1977-present)
ALTHOUGH ACTIVITY since 1987 has been sporadic to say the least, this band are too much of an institution to have ever died away completely – reforming periodically, most recently at the request of Guns N' Roses for their January 1993 shows in Australia. Four of the classic line-up took the stage – Angry Anderson (vocals), Pete Wells (slide guitar), Mick Cocks (guitar), Geordie Leech ((bass) – and showed that age had reduced little of their legendary anger and power. Got their initial break when picked up by AC/DC producers Vanda and Young, who would have had to have been deaf, dumb and blind not to have been blown away. On stage, Rose Tattoo looked like a gang of brawlers looking for a damn good ruck (which wasn't far from the truth for anyone who crossed them), but they could also play some truly hard-as-nails rock 'n' roll. You wouldn't have guessed it from listening to the 'Southern Stars' ('84) or 'Beats From A Single Drum' ('87) albums. Avoid those and go instead for the three early LPs, or at *least* these two...

Highly recommended albums:
ROCK 'N' ROLL OUTLAW (Streetlink, 1990 – KKKKK) Re-issue of Albert Records' 1978 debut
ASSAULT AND BATTERY (Streetlink, 1990 – KKKK) Re-issue of second LP (1981)

David Lee ROTH

USA, solo (1985 – present)

CALL HIM Mr Total And Utter Spontaneity In A Perfect Pair Of Jeans, yet if you but merely mention the magic word 'Dave' in a rock crowd – five will get you 10 that those in earshot will know you ain't talkin' about no Megadeth frontman or Iron Maiden guitarist! Nope, they'll think of DAVID LEE ROTH (...always works better in big block capitals), ex-frontman with Van Halen, the rule-bending band he made six spectacularly wonderful albums with before he waved bye-bye in early '85, to be 'replaced' by one Sammy Hagar. It was not an amicable split. Hyper-active Roth needed his action fix, but the rest of the Halen troupe were happy to dawdle over the recording of their final vinyl together '1984'. So packing his get-up-and-go, Roth got up and went. The Halen corner bitched, the Roth corner said: 'Sticks 'n' stones...'

Interestingly, Van Halen producer from day one Ted Templeman took Roth's side. And there was his credit stamped on Roth's debut solo excursion; the almost un-rock yet totally 'Dave', 'Crazy From The Heat' EP ('85) – a record probably noted more for the gloriously OTT videos it spawned in 'Californian Girls' and 'Just A Gigolo'. Roth and partner/buddy/manager Pete Angelus (aka 'The Fabulous Picasso Brothers') also worked on, and casted for, a movie boasting the same name as the EP, a project it is said the duo were entrusted with 10 million dollars to produce. But, alas, the demise of the CBS film company involved appears to have halted the project till this very day..:.

Then came the 'supergroup'. Ex-Zappa/Alcatraz guitarist Steve Vai ("We split a sandwich and started a band" – Dave), ex-Talas bassist Billy Sheehan ("His original band opened for the old act, and they were so good we had to let them go... but I kept Billy's phone number" – Dave), and drummer ("The Prince Of Pound" – Dave) Gregg Bisonette. Their combined talents came to create the Templeman-produced 'Eat 'Em And Smile' ('86), which was as imposing and dazzling as the cover close-up shot of Roth in tribal warpaint. The blink-and-you'll-miss-it video to the bombastic opening cut 'Yankee Rose' sold the band to his adoring public, *no problem*... yet astoundingly, the song was not a hit (further salt in the wound for our Dave being Halen's debut 45 devoid of his delicate tonsilisin', 'Why Can't This Be Love', flying to Number One Stateside!).

'Skyscraper' ('88), found Sheehan on the album, but out of the band. Roth insinuated he

---

IN THEIR OWN WORDS...

"Some of us in Van Halen forgot that people still work for a living, still take the bus."
– David Lee Roth, Kerrang! 111, January 9-22, 1986

"A lot of what I do is not technical singing. But I don't think anybody else is going to sound like me. I'm not sure anybody else would want to!" – David Lee Roth, Kerrang! 125, July 24-August 6, 1986

"DRAMA! CHAOS! and ORGANISATION! It's a hell of a soundtrack to live by..."
– David Lee Roth, Kerrang! 173, February 6, 1988

"Jesus, I feel high! I'm fuckin' flying here!... It musta been that orange I ate before coming down to the gig..." – David Lee Roth, Kerrang! 200, August 13, 1988

"The guy who said that money can't buy you happiness didn't know where to go shoppin'!" – David Lee Roth, Kerrang! 324, January 19, 1991.

DAVID LEE ROTH

DAVE LEE ROTH (1986 vintage): Curve ball supremo (any vintage)

greatest entertainers of our time – now has to re-evaluate his strategies while pale imitators such as Vince Neil, and the imitators' imitators like Bret Michaels, are faring well. In a genre which at times forgets to laugh at itself we truly need Roth's curve-balls, but it would also be nice if we could come close to catching the occasional one...

ALBUMS

EAT 'EM AND SMILE *(Warner Brothers 1986 – KKKKK) "Now the party can REALLY begin!!" – Kerrang! 124, July 10-23, 1986*
SKYSCRAPER *(Warner Brothers 1988 – KKK) "A huge erection slicin' through the clouds... it's just that the elevator can't seem to find the right floor." – Kerrang! 172, January 30, 1988*
A LITTLE AIN'T ENOUGH *(Warner Brothers 1991 – KKKK) "Has almost everything and a pinch of something more." – Kerrang! 323, January 12, 1991*

had to let him go, Sheehan made it clear he wanted to. And after all, it was an odd album. Interesting, brave, not a little clever, and produced by Roth and Vai, it was possibly Dave's sharpest left-turn to date, but still... odd. Greg's bass-slappin' younger brother Matt Bisonette took on tour duties, a worldwide live trek which incorporated such spectacles as giant surfboard (!) and a boxing ring (!!)... also reports of dwindling audiences...

Roth's third album, 'A Little Ain't Enough' ('91), was Vai-less. The recording and touring musicians (which still included the Bisonettes) were now background fixtures, and this time out Dave was demanding full attention – and who can blame him with ex-hired guns Vai and Sheehan (with Mr Big) cleaning up elsewhere! The new record, produced by Bob Rock, was back to good ol' Blues-based rock, but the material was hardly division one Roth standard. In that year of '91, Dave's world tour (along with Alice Cooper's – obviously 'props' were out!), was a financial disaster.

Ironically, Diamond Dave – one of the

ROX

UK, five-piece (1980-1984)
WHAM-BAM shock glammers who idolised Kiss but could never sustain their initial stakk-heeled orgy.
Stupidly recommended album:
VIOLENT BREED *(Music For Nations, 1984 – KK)*

ROXX GANG

USA, five-piece (1985-present)
TERRIBLY INEPT Sleaze Metal band from Florida fronted by the ridiculous Kevin Steele. Their sole album to date is laughably full of every hoary old Glam cliché known to mankind.

Roxx Gang are, incredibly, still active despite 'walking out' of their deal with Virgin.
Not at all recommended:
THING'S YOU'VE NEVER DONE BEFORE *(Virgin, 1989 – K)*

RPLA

UK, five-piece (1989-present)

MASSIVELY OVER-HYPED and decidedly weak-kneed, this paper-thin pose of Cult-esque clichés are signed to EMI, but still not ready for a *Kerrang!* cover. Not a good day at the beach.
Amusingly derivative single:
SHE TALKS TO ANGELS *(EMI, 1991 – KKK)*

The RUNAWAYS

USA, five/four-piece (1976-1979)

PIECED TOGETHER by music guru/Hollywood oddball Kim Fowley with teenage girls who answered a music rag ad, The Runaways perpetuated the myth that all female rock bands are brainless, sex-crazed bimbos.

The band did, however, provide a start for guitarists Joan Jett and Lita Ford who were to become two of the leading female hard rock artists in the '80s. Ironic, then, that it is alleged that most of the actual playing on The Runaways' first two albums was undertaken by session musos.

Of the other members in the band, only original singer Cherie Currie – who quit in an egotistical rage in 1977 – ever made anything of herself with two solo albums (the second in cahoots with sister Marie, now Mrs Steve 'Toto' Lukather) and a brief movie career.

It's also worth noting that Kim Fowley did try to orchestrate a Runaways sequel in 1987 with a new set of girls. Nobody took the blindest bit of notice...
Recommended albums
QUEENS OF NOISE *(Mercury, 1977 – KKK)*
LIVE IN JAPAN *(Mercury Japan, 1977 – KKKK)*

RUNNING WILD

Germany, four-piece (1980-present)

ENDURING BUT incredible Power Metal cartoon of pirate-fixated bombast, fronted by the ridiculous Rockin' Rolf and still adored in their homeland.
Recommended album:
UNDER JOLLY ROGER *(Noise International, 1987 – KKK)*

RUSH

Canada, three-piece (1968-present)

FEW BANDS can claim to have played in such a variety of styles as Toronto-based Rush, and probably none could be said to have played them so well.
Recent works have drifted from their hard rock roots but their following remains no less fanatical, almost a subculture among rock fans. Having proven themselves as accomplished musicians and songwriters, Rush are now in the enviable position of having fans happy to watch them experiment and take turns up whatever musical avenues they choose...

The early days of Rush were a little different. They began as a basement band heavily influenced by English groups like Cream and Led Zeppelin, varying their line-up between three and four members. Founders were Alex Lifeson (guitar, born August 27, 1953) and John Rutsey (drums). Geddy Lee (bass/vocals, born Gary Lee, July 29, 1953) joined soon after on a less than permanent basis. Other bassists, keyboard players, singers and second guitarists came and went until mid-'71 when they pretty much settled on being a power-trio.

In 1973, with five years' bar and club experience under their belts, Rush decided to record a single, covering Buddy Holly's 'Not Fade Away' and backing it with 'You Can't Fight It', and release it on their own Moon label. It sold poorly and completely failed to impress the A&R men it had primarily been recorded for. Undeterred, the band soon took the next step and cut an album, 'Rush'. Manager Ray Danniels enlisted ex-pat Englishman Terry 'Broon' Brown to oversee remixing and a little re-recording. Still no record companies were interested – due, probably, to Lee's very high-pitched vocals – so it came out on Moon, distributed by London. Soon after, the band boosted their profile by opening for the New York Dolls in Toronto. They started playing bigger gigs in Canada and venturing across the border to play a shows in Cleveland, Ohio with ZZ Top. Word of mouth and a copy of the Moon Records album eventually reached Mercury Records where the interest of one Cliff Burnstein (who would later sign Def Leppard) led to a deal with the label.

Mercury re-issued 'Rush' – changing the logo colour from the original red to pink – while John Rutsey decided to opt out, citing musical differences. His replacement was Neil Peart (born September 12, 1952), then playing in a band called Hush, where he used to impersonate The Who's Keith Moon during their covers of songs from 'Quadrophenia'... To Rush, however, he brought more than brilliant drumming skills, he could also write lyrics.

Initially, his style was based very much on sword and sorcery fantasy, but over the next 20 years his interest in 20th-century novelists such as Ayn Rand, John Barth, Gabriel Garcia Marquez and John Dos Passos would become more of an influence. Peart made his live debut for Rush when they opened for Uriah Heep on August 14, 1974 in Pittsburgh. His first album with the band was 'Fly By Night', released in March '75 as the band toured the States, opening at dates for Aerosmith and for Kiss. Following the dates, they rushed back into the

studio to record a third album, 'Caress Of Steel', out in November '75.

On it, Rush took the concept of the epic 'By-Tor And The Snow Dog' from the previous album one step further and recorded a side-long conceptual cut called 'Fountain Of Lamneth'. This style of lengthy songwriting was a Rush trademark until 1980 and reached its peak on LP number four, '2112', with its side-long title-tack. The album was the first to enter the US *Billboard* Hot 100 (peaking at 61) and generated no small amount of interest as an import in the UK. In June '76, a month after its release, the band recorded three 4,000-seat sell-out shows at their home town's Massey Hall for a double live album, 'All The World's A Stage'.

Lavishly packaged, this too sold well in the UK on import (while it reached Number 40 in the States) and persuaded the band to make their debut European visit. The first of seven sold-out dates was at Manchester's Free Trade Hall on June 2, '77. With the tour completed, the band remained in the UK, travelling to Rockfield Studios in South Wales to record their next album. When released in October of that year, 'A Farewell To Kings' received rave reviews, giving the band their UK chart debut (peaking at Number 22) and establishing strong ties with a UK fan-base that remains to this day. After it was issued, Phonogram, who handle Mercury releases in the UK, gave all their previously import-only albums a UK release, initially gathering the first three together as a triple compilation, 'Archives'.

Late in '78 came the 'Hemispheres' album, the last to feature the by-then traditional 'epics'. The album consolidated the band's standing as a major act both sides of the Atlantic. Every date they had ever played in the UK had sold out and 'Hemispheres' rose as high as Number 14 in the UK, an impressive feat for a band who were almost totally unknown outside the cult world of heavy rock.

For studio album number seven, 'Permanent Waves' ('80), Rush streamlined their approach to songwriting and even happened upon a freak

RUSH: Discussing plans for a return to side–long epics about inter–dimensional travel?

hit single in 'Spirit Of Radio'. It was such a success that they were able to sell-out five nights at the Hammersmith Odeon. Lee's vocals had by now mellowed and were delivered in a more comfortable register; he and Lifeson were playing keyboards in addition to their guitars (double-necked for some numbers); and Peart had a spectacular array of percussion instruments mounted behind his already impressive kit. Rush prided themselves on being able to reproduce all the complexities of their albums on stage without the use of tapes, and needed all that hardware to be able to do so. As their music changed over the years to come, they did succumb to technology and let sequencers do some of the work, but always insisted that whatever came over the PA was originated and triggered by the three of them on stage...

On their next album, 'Moving Pictures' ('81), the band hit a peak: eight songs, each superbly crafted and performed which held together as a compact unit or stood alone individually. Even today, songs from 'Moving Pictures' still feature strongly in the live set... but the band saw the tour to promote it as the end of an era. They celebrated this with a second double live album, 'Exit... Stage Left' (November '81), cut their hair a little more and prepared to return with 'Signals', 11 months later. It, and subsequent albums, 'Grace Under Pressure' ('84) and 'Power Windows' ('85), portrayed the band working hard to second-guess musical trends, working within economical short time-spans but using studio technology to create ultra-modern rock. On both, Rush finally abandoned long-time producer Terry Brown in an effort to move forward. Each record took them further from their hard rock roots but they still scored highly with 12th studio album, 'Hold Your Fire' ('87), boosted in the UK by dates in '88 – their first tour in Europe since the 'Signals' album. Whilst away, it emerged later, the band had considered splitting up as time spent enjoying family lives and personal freedom became more precious than that spent making records and undertaking tours of the States and Canada.

They were welcomed back with open arms, however, by fans and reviewers delighted to note that here were a band not trying to recreate past glories but who had genuinely matured and were looking ever forward.

Following earlier precedents, their third batch of four studio albums was summarised on a third double-live album (and video), 'A Show Of Hands' ('89), after which the band ended their longstanding relationship with Mercury – originally just for two albums in the States! – and signed to Atlantic

The first LP for this label was 'Presto' (December '89), followed in October '90 by a double-CD compilation, 'Chronicles' – released and put together by their former label – and then in '91 by 'Roll The Bones'.

Whether the band will make it to studio LP number 16, let alone a fourth double-live is far from certain but if they do, and as long as they play live, there'll be no shortage of people waiting to hear and watch.

ALBUMS

RUSH (Mercury, 1975 – KKKK) Raw and aggressive Led Zeppelin-styled hard rock laced with helium-fuelled vocals...

FLY BY NIGHT (Mercury, 1975 – KKK) The first to feature Peart's drums and lyrics. Much more varied than above with an excruciating six-minute acoustic called 'Rivendell'...

CARESS OF STEEL (Mercury, 1976 – KK) Some good moments but the band were over-stretched, especially on Side Two's sole track 'Fountain Of Lamneth'...

2112 (Mercury, 1976 – KKKKK) All-time classic thanks mainly to Side One's unequalled 20-minute title opus. No rubbish on the flip, either...

ALL THE WORLD'S A STAGE (Mercury, 1976 – KKKKK) Double-live featuring the very best of Rush's early work. Dripping with atmosphere...

A FAREWELL TO KINGS (Mercury, 1977 – KKKKK) Brilliant change in pace and direction. Acoustic guitars alongside their first real use of keyboards...

HEMISPHERES (Mercury, 1978 – KKKK) On which Rush bade farewell to epics with two more(!); the title-track and the complex instrumental 'YYZ' inspired by one of Lifeson's nightmares...

PERMANENT WAVES *(Mercury, 1980 – KKKK)* First to feature simpler, short-form songs – although three of these were gathered together as the semi-epic 'Natural Science'!

MOVING PICTURES *(Mercury, 1981 – KKKKK)* Filled to the very brim with power, inventiveness and sound. The supreme example of techno-rock...

EXIT... STAGE LEFT *(Mercury, 1981 – KKK)* Patchy collection of live recordings from many different gigs. Flow interrupted by gaps between tracks...

SIGNALS *(Mercury, 1982 – KKKK)* "Appreciate the beauty of Rush's acceptance of the mantle of middle-age..." – Kerrang! 25, September 23-October 6, 1982

GRACE UNDER PRESSURE *(Mercury, 1984 – KKK)* "Always a pleasure to hear master craftsmen at work..." – Kerrang! 65, April 5-18, 1984

POWER WINDOWS *(Mercury, 1985 – KKK)* "I have agonised long and hard... and I still can't honestly say I'm much wiser as to what is going on here overall."– Kerrang! 105, October 17-30, 1985

HOLD YOUR FIRE *(Mercury, 1987 – KKKKK)* "Once again, an album of class, quality and consistency... 10 grade 'A' songs." – Kerrang! 156, October 3, 1987

A SHOW OF HANDS *(Mercury, 1988 – KKKKK)* "Elegant, vibrant and alive... All grace, no sweat!" – Kerrang! 221, January 14, 1989

PRESTO *(Atlantic, 1989 – KKKK)* "Rush won't make a bad album. The worst they'll do is merely make another one. 'Presto' is somewhere between the two." – Kerrang! 265, November 18, 1989

CHRONICLES *(Mercury, 1990 – KKKK)* Sensible collection of the best (shorties) from each LP...

ROLL THE BONES *(Atlantic, 1991 – KKKK)* "Rush have rediscovered rock 'n' roll... Songwriting is sharp, the playing fiery... the best Rush album for a long time." – Kerrang! 356, August 31, 1991

IN THEIR OWN WORDS...

"A lot of our early work was pure escapism and at the time it was right. We were teenagers growing up in the suburbs and we needed to escape. I really dwelled on Science Fiction and fantasy which I've outgrown. I can smile at my naivety but I can't sneer."
– Neil Peart, Kerrang! 188, May 21, 1988

"To me things are moving along a lot better now that some of the older, longer pieces aren't there any more. The show itself has a totally different feel to it. The band has a different appearance, the sound has taken a step forward... I feel really good, almost reborn!"
– Alex Lifeson, Kerrang! 26, October 7-20, 1982

"As much as our fans think they know all about us, know who we are and everything, they don't and never have."
– Neil Peart, Kerrang! 44, June 17-30, 1983

" 'Intellectual' is an ugly word, let's face it, unless you're a particularly dried up stick of a person... it's not an epitaph I would choose for myself." – Neil Peart, Kerrang! 44, June 17-30, 1983

"We are all in Rush because we like what we do and not because we want to influence people to believe or do things through our lyrics or whatever... I think our lyrics should be classed as a 'discussion' rather than anything else."
– Alex Lifeson, Kerrang! 107, November 14-27, 1986

"All musical parts are produced by us three onstage. But sound effects, in the manner of Pink Floyd, we feel quite happy with in pre-recorded fashion... Some music is produced by sequencers and that is treading a fine line ethically."
– Neil Peart, Kerrang! 224, February 4, 1989

"The main reasons (we have remained such close friends after 20 years of working together) are that we have remarkably similar tastes in music, we have the same level of ambition, and a healthy sense of humour..." – Geddy Lee, Kerrang! 388, April 18, 1992

RUSH

SABBAT

UK, five-piece (1985-1991)

SABBAT WERE criticised for attaining a two-page *Kerrang!* feature before having even issued vinyl, but in truth they pretty much deserved it. They were a fresh example of British Power/Metal Thrash, and certainly one of its best bets.

Pagan imagery was very much their thing, and this was mainly down to singer Martin Walkyier, now in the altogether stranger Skyclad. However, disagreements between Walkyier and guitarist Andy Sneap led to the former being replaced by the far less exciting Richard Desmond in 1990.

That final version of Sabbat released one album, 'Mourning Has Broken' ('91), and promptly disbanded. Look out for Sneap's latest endeavour, Godsend.

Recommended album:
DREAMWEAVER – REFLECTIONS OF OUR YESTERDAYS *(Noise, 1989 – KKKK)*

Paul SABU

USA, AOR god (1980-present)

CLAIMING TO be a direct decendant of the original Elephant Boy is not normally a guarantee of rock superstardom, and neither is releasing two albums called 'Sabu' in the same year (1980) – one hard rock, the other pure disco. Just ask Paul Sabu...

In '84 he stopped using just his surname and assembled a band called Kidd Glove. This failed too. In 1985 he released another solo album, 'Heartbreak'. Nope, no luck there either.

Then in '88, with the formation of Only Child and the whole-hearted support of *Kerrang!*, he tried again. Er... currently residing in the 'unquestionably brilliant but where are they now?' file.

Totally recommended album:
KIDD GLOVE *(Morocco, 1984 – KKKKK)*

SACRED REICH

USA, 1986-present (four-piece)

THRASH METALLERS from Arizona who debuted with the well-respected 'Ignorance' ('87) after a slot on the eighth of Metal Blade's legion 'Metal Massacre' compilation albums, then earned many more friends with the 'Surfing Nicaragua' EP ('88). Led by Jason Rainey (guitar) and Phil Rind (bass/vocals), the band have recently signed to Hollywood Records.

Recommended album:
IGNORANCE *(Roadrunner, 1987 – KKKK)*

S.A.H.B.

Scotland, five-piece (1972-1982)

FULL TITLE of The Sensational Alex Harvey Band was the invention of legendary Glaswegian rocker Alex Harvey. He died following a heart attack, very probably brought on by excessive drinking, on February 4, 1982 – one day short of his 47th birthday. The band was completed by Zal Cleminson (guitar and clown face-paint, later of Nazareth), Chris Glen (bass and leather underpants over his jeans, later of MSG/Ian Gillan), Ted McKenna (drums, later of MSG, Rory Gallagher and Ian Gillan) and Ted's brother Hugh on keyboards. S.A.H.B. were at their best live where Alex would lurch around the stage, acting out the lyrics and even crucifying himself for that extra dramatic effect. Had a hit with Tom Jones' 'Delilah' in '75.

Recommended album:
LIVE *(Vertigo, 1975 – KKKK)*

SALTY DOG

USA, four-piece (1989-1991)
MIDWEST MINIMALIST blues-laden rock 'n' rollers with a bassist, Mike Hannon, who used to eat spiders at school. Issued just one album, on Geffen, that shoulda made them household names. Recorded that album at Rockfield Studios in Wales but never played live in the UK despite a cover feature in *Kerrang!* 274 in 1990. After sacking original singer Jimmi Bleacher in '91, Hannon – then claiming to be down to his last 10 bucks and in desperate need of a hamburger – started to spread rumours of a return.

These proved exaggerated, as in '93 Hannon joined LA-based hooligans Bogus Tom. Lock up yer daughters (and your spiders)...
Highly recommended album:
EVERY DOG HAS ITS DAY *(Geffen, 1990 – KKKKK)*

SAMSON

UK, guitarist (1979-present)
ONE OF the more enduring also-rans from the NWOBHM boom, Samson never achieved the success many thought they deserved. Led by Paul Samson, the band cranked out several albums of Metal-tinged rock with a Blues edge ripped off from Mountain. Although they toured extensively with Iron Maiden, financial and label insecurity prevented Samson from achieving the same status. When Bruce Dickinson left to join Maiden in 1981, many considered it to be the end of the band.

Undeterred, Paul re-assembled his troops with heavyweight Blues vocalist, Nicky Moore, and replaced his ludicrously fright-masked drummer Thunderstick with the infinitely more talented Pete Jupp (now of FM). Despite three major label releases, throughout the '80s Samson's credibility and fanbase dwindled. Eventually Paul split the band and took to the pubs with a power-trio. He is currently out there somewhere and, allegedly, big in Yugoslavia.
Recommended album:
BEFORE THE STORM *(Polydor, 1982 – KKKK)*

SANTERS

Canada, three-piece (1980-1986)
A TRADITIONAL and ultra-tuneful hard rock band whose lack of image eventually sank their career.
Worth hearing if bored:
RACING TIME *(Heavy Metal Worldwide, 1982 – KKK)*

SARAYA

USA, five-piece (1988-1992)
CHICK-FRONTED and very sensible rockers, Saraya piddled about in the American clubs for what seemed like decades before running out of steam. They left one so-so album and one crap album, and most will remember the band for Sandi Saraya and her budget-Pat Benatar appeal. Ultimately Saraya was another case of all mouth and no trousers.
Recommended so-so album:
SARAYA *(Polydor, 1989 – KKK)*

SATAN

UK, five-piece (1984-1987)
FORMED FROM the ashes of NWOBHM act Blitzkrieg, Satan are now remembered really only for two things: releasing a now highly collectable single on Guardian called 'Kiss Of Death' and having a really wicked name. Unfortunately, they changed it in 1987 to Blind Fury and promptly sank without trace.
Recommended album:
COURT IN THE ACT *(Neat, 1984 – KKK)*

Joe SATRIANI

USA, guitarist (1984-present)
A NATIVE Long Islander, Satriani's prodigious digits found their way around a fretboard early in life. From teaching another guitar maestro in the making, one Steve Vai, while still at high school, Satriani graduated to solo recording artist via self-financed debut album, appropriately titled 'Not Of This Earth'. Despite a purportedly uncommercial style (full-on widdling, no vocals), second album 'Surfing With The Alien' achieved major mainstream

success and paved the way for non-train-spotterish reaction to totally Techno Metal! Joe Satriani – a pioneer who made it pay! Majorly Metal fact: also taught monster Metallica's Kirk Hammett!

Recommended album:
FLYING IN A BLUE DREAM *(Food For Thought, 1989 – KKKK)*

SAVATAGE

USA, five-piece (1983-present)
CULT LEVEL Metal band who have tried long and hard to crack the big time with no great success. Signed to Atlantic in 1985 after their '83 debut, 'Sirens' (Par, '83) and 'The Dungeons Are Calling' (Music For Nations, '85). With that label, the band attempted to refine their mix of high-pitched vocals (by Jon Oliva), Priest-style rifferama and quasi-Dio-esque lyrical imagery. Not always as horrible as it sounds, Savatage actually got rather good at it on 'Hall Of The Mountain King' ('87) then peaked with 'Gutter Ballet' ('90). They went barking mad a year later, issuing the concept album 'Streets: A Rock Opera' after which Oliva checked out. He has since remained involved in a mainly writing capacity with his replacement, Zachary Stevens, debuting on 'Edge Of Thorns' ('93).

Recommended album:
GUTTER BALLET *(Atlantic, 1990 – KKKK)*

SAXON

UK, five-piece (1979-present)
DESPITE STARTING life not only in Barnsley but also as Son Of A Bitch, Saxon soon came to embody all the strengths of the NWOBHM. They were late for the party, but they soon scorched into the charts with 'Wheels Of Steel' ('80).

Saxon's major weapons were a truckload of simple, highly melodic Metal anthems and a *Boys Own* approach to Heavy Metal. Motörhead had a bomber. Maiden had Eddie. Saxon, typically, had a fucking great eagle as a lighting gantry, known to the roadcrew as 'Biff's Budgie'. Saxon were a credible ticket draw on the Odeon circuit and an entertaining night out. Envious of Iron Maiden's growing status in America, however, Saxon's attempts to cross the pond with 'Crusader' ('84) saw them struggle. America was largely underwhelemed by Saxon. Thrash Metal was looming on the horizon and Saxon were seen as a cliché. Instead the band concentrated on the lucrative European market (particularly Germany) where antics such as spinning guitars and songs about Real Men will always be remarkably popular.

A back-to-basics UK club tour in 1990 proved an unexpected success. Buried alive by the press and radio, Saxon have nonetheless continued to fight for their right to party long after many expected them to give up. The records have become steadily weedier, but the live show can still boast a clutch of memorable hit singles and epic set pieces. Listen out, too, for Biff singing: *'Another town, another place/ Another woman to sit on my face'* during 'Rock 'N' Roll Gypsies'...

Recommended albums:
WHEELS OF STEEL *(Carrere, 1980 – KKKKK)*
DENIM AND LEATHER *(Carrere, 1981 – KKKK)*

SCORPIONS

Germany, five-piece (1971-present)
DESPITE ITS obsessive interest in heavy rock, Germany still boasts but one internationally-acclaimed Metal act. Formed by Flying V-handed brothers Rudy and Michael Schenker, in the early '70s, the band's first recorded  output attempted to put a Teutonic twist on the psychedelic meanderings of Pink Floyd and fellow-countrymen Eloy. The results sound painful when heard with today's sonically aggressive ears, but the seeds were sown by debut album, 'Action' (later re-released in the UK as 'Lonesome Crow') for the forthcoming Hendrix-tinged hard rock assault.

Michael, the younger of the two brothers, was filched from the band when Brit rockers UFO found themselves without the services of short-stay guitarist Bernie Marsden. He stepped in

SCORPIONS contemplate (but decline) another death-defying human pyramid

worship, aided and abetted by a completely hatstand personality disorder, involving drugs, psychedelic hallucinations and frequent disappearing acts! Scorpions battled manfully on, being touted rather dismissively as 'big in Japan', a status confirmed by their last album for RCA, 1978's double live opus, 'Tokyo Tapes'. The album featured the seminal battle cry: "Doo jew feel like a leetel rock ant roll?"

The band felt that they needed a more turbo-charged approach to their music and rang the changes by signing to EMI, allowing Roth to disappear into a pall of pot-induced navel contemplation and recalling a disenchanted Michael Schenker to the fold. The liaison proved short-lived with Schenker upping sticks, cutting his barnet and riding off into the sunset on a low-powered motorcycle. However, his legacy to the band was a writing and playing hand on 'Lovedrive', Scorpions' 1979 breakthrough album.

and UFO wouldn't let him leave. Scorpions replaced him with the slightly bonkers Ulrich Roth, a man whose obsession with Jimi Hendrix led to him eventually living with erstwhile Jimi-chick Monika Dannemann.

With a sound defined by the caterwaul vocals of the diminutive Klaus Meine and Roth's free-form axe-pertese, the band signed to RCA and released a plethora of progressively harder-edged albums as the tone of the times shifted towards Metal with a capital M.

The band courted controversy on more than one occasion with their somewhat saucy albums sleeves. 'Virgin Killer' featured a particularly 'right off' shot of a naked pre-pubescent girl, overlain with a sheet of strategically-positioned broken glass. *Ouch!*

While Scorpions toured Europe consistently and achieved mediocre success, their status was always perceived as secondary to that of guitar maestro Michael and his UFO cohorts - and not necessarily for his music. His flowing blond locks, crouched playing style and stylish leather cat-suit immediately attracted hero-

With a fistful of granite-edged hard rock stompers such as 'Another Piece Of Meat' and the instrumental 'Coast to Coast', plus the addition of the less mentally-challenged guitarist Matthias Jabs, the band arrived in a big way. It was the classic line-up of Meine, Jabs, Rudy Schenker, bassist Francis Buchholz and drummer Herman 'The German' Rarebell which saw Scorpions mutate from mid-table also-rans to championship-winning rock stars.

State-of-the-art hard rock albums flowed thick and fast, based around a riff-mongous selection of melody-orientated ditties which covered such subject matter as tranvestites and excessive drinking habits. However, the band also proved that they had a keen ear for the commercially adroit ballad and scored their biggest world-wide hit with 'Still Loving You', an emotionally-draining effort from 1984's 'Love At First Sting' album. The States reeled under the weight of such European blubbing and the band moved into the superheavyweight Metal league.

The double 'World Wide Live' the following year confirmed their status as a major attraction and the band went from strength to strength, amassing Platinum albums and immensely elongated tours with ease. Highlight of the live show had to be the feat of daring which was the human pyramid, featured on the cover of the live album.

'Savage Amusement' marked the end of the band's long-standing relationship with EMI but continued their impressive run of hit singles, with 'Rhythm Of Love' scoring high marks.

PolyGram ran out triumphant winners of an aggravated bidding war and were more than happy to have their Vertigo label embossed on 1990's 'Crazy World'. The record also marked the long-anticipated removal of Dieter Dierks from the band's production chair. Word had it that contractual difficulties had meant that the band were forced to remain with the German knob-twiddler for far longer than they had wished. Keith Olsen gave the group a more contemporary sound and assisted Scorpions in releasing their biggest hit to date, the astonishing 'Wind Of Change'. Not only did the

song emerge as an anthem for the re-unification of Germany, but more importantly marked the first recorded example of whistling in a Heavy Metal tune! The band's heightened profile also resulted in a spate of myriad compilations, begun by 'Best Of Rockers And Ballads'.

1992 saw another bizarre twist in the history of this exceptional band. Rumours flew thick and fast of major tax irregularities in the group's affairs, which have been rigorously denied, and the surprising departure of bassist Buchholz, to be replaced by Ralph Rickermann in time for the 12th studio album.

Despite the onset of advancing years, Scorpions remain at the forefront of the hard rock genre. The hair may have receded, but their passion for the fight remains intact.

ALBUMS
ACTION/LONESOME CROW (Brain, 1972 – KK) *Winsome, eclectic fusion rock that meanders rather than mauls...*
FLY TO THE RAINBOW (RCA, 1974 – KK) *Hendrix with a German accent. Possibly useful for that once-a-decade spiritual chill-out...*
IN TRANCE (RCA, 1975 – KKKK) *The best example of the early Scorpions sound, mixing*

IN THEIR OWN WORDS...

" 'Taken By Force' was the first album I played on with the band, but it was still the old Scorpions basically. When I joined I had the feeling that the band was divided between Ulrich Roth and the others. To me the band really started to work as a unit after he left." – Herman Rarebell, Kerrang! 12, March 25-April 7, 1982

"I had a really serious drinking problem. I just had to stop everything and go to a clinic in Switzerland for six weeks where they treated me. It's okay now. I still drink, but I can stop when I want. One year ago, I couldn't. I used to wake up in the morning and have a half-bottle of champagne or some vodka or some whiskey." – Herman Rarebell, Kerrang! 59, January 12-25, 1984

"We are not in this for the fashion or the fame or any of that shit. We're here for the feeling." – Klaus Meine, Kerrang! 137, January 8-21, 1987

"We give the people all our energy every night. We'll go onstage and rock our ass off. That's what we do." – Klaus Meine, Kerrang! 226, February 18, 1989

"It's just like a marriage. We're very happy to have lasted this long, and we wouldn't have if there had been many arguments. Most bands break up because of ego problems, but we have it under control. We've 'grown up', as they say." – Herman Rarebell, Kerrang! 301, August 4, 1990

SCORPIONS

acid and testosterone to full hard rock effect...

VIRGIN KILLERS (RCA, 1976 – KKK) An album which saw the band honing an amalgam of styles into a potent and original whole. Killer cut: 'Pictured Life'...

TAKEN BY FORCE (RCA, 1977 – KKKK) Truly creative powerhouse of a record, uncompromising and melodious, epitomised by the lengthy and awesome classic, 'We'll Burn The Sky'...

TOKYO TAPES (RCA, 1978 – KKKKK) The zenith of the band's more experimental years. Everything you need to plot the band's early history. Lots of screaming Japanese...

LOVEDRIVE (EMI, 1979 – KKKKK) Probably the band's finest hour, featuring a collection of raucously rude, instantly addictive anthems...

ANIMAL MAGNETISM (EMI, 1980 – KKKK) A curious cover, featuring a dog fouling something other than a footpath, didn't mask the sustained impetus of the songs...

BLACKOUT (EMI, 1982 – KKK) "Words can't really describe the power evidenced on the record... a totally over the top rock 'n' roll album." – Kerrang! 12, March 25-April 7, 1982

LOVE AT FIRST STING (EMI, 1984 – KKK) " 'Love At First Sting' has emerged finally as a nut-ratting Scorpions recording. It'll rock you like a hurricane." – Kerrang! 64, March 22-April 4, 1984

WORLD WIDE LIVE (EMI, 1985 – KKKK) "In essence this is a tribute to the crustacea of the band... The Scorpions have chosen the right time to serve up a monster raving loony party." – Kerrang! 95, May 30-June 12, 1985

SAVAGE AMUSEMENT (EMI, 1988 – KKK) "The heavier songs have turned out to be some of the best the Scorpions have ever recorded... this is modern Metal with minimal experimentalism and superlative atmosphere." – Kerrang! 83, April 16, 1988

CRAZY WORLD (Vertigo, 1990 – KKK) "The production is certainly a whole lot better than the last few Scorpions releases. But despite that, there just isn't enough in there to make me want to play this album over and over." – Kerrang! 314, November 3, 1990

SCREAMING JETS

Australia, five-piece (1989-present)

STUNNINGLY OFFENSIVE yob rockers from Newcastle, New South Wales who echo fellow countrymen The Angels in delivery and attitude, if not style. Frontman is rent-a-quote motormouth Dave Gleeson, whose talents for upsetting people merely by speaking his mind are totally without equal – but even in a song called 'Fat Rich Cunts', he's only having a go at people who deserve it. Live, the Screaming Jets are a stunning outfit whose performances have been honed to a razor-sharp edge by incessant gigging in their native land – up to 20 shows a month in the two-and-a-half years before they were signed to RooArt. The rest of the band – Grant Walmsley (guitar), Richard Lara (guitar), Paul Woseen (bass) and Brad Heaney (drums) – are great songwriters but have (not surprisingly) yet to make an album that captures their on-stage energy. When they do, the band will become an unstoppable force. Until then, you could do a lot worse than wrap your ears around their debut...

Recommended album:

ALL FOR ONE (RooArt, 1991 – KKKK)

SCREAMING TREES

USA, four-piece (1987-present)

HAILED AS Grunge's secret weapon, Screaming Trees are in fact nothing of the sort. Highly tuneful, Country-edged rock 'n' roll with an acute sense of melancholy and a typical anti-pop stance. They're also very fat.

Essential album:

SWEET OBLIVION (Epic, 1992 – KKKKK)

SEA HAGS

USA, four-piece (1985-1991)

"THERE'S ONLY so far you can get with three junkies and one alcoholic," said the manager of these San Francisco-based sleaze-bags. He was morbidly close to the truth as in '91, bassist and founder member Chris Schlosshardt was found dead from a suspected drug overdose in LA. He and former rock-photographer Ron

Yocom (vocals) had put together what was doomed from the start, but came close to their heroes Aerosmith – especially the Toxic Twins bit. A demo produced by Kirk Hammett led to interest from Ian Astbury who wanted to produce their album, but the job went to Mike 'Appetite For Destruction' Clink. Drummer Adam Maples later nearly replaced Steven Adler in GN'R , and Perry-clone Frank Wilsey (now with Stephen Pearcy in Arcade) completed the line-up for album and tour and helped leave stunned faces and the smell of real destructiveness behind.

Highly recommended album:
SEA HAGS *(Chrysalis, 1989 – KKKK)*

SEPULTURA

Brazil, four-piece (1984-present)
SEPULTURA DRUMMER Igor Cavalera was only 14 years old when he first positioned himself behind a makeshift drum-kit. The poor lad could barely reach those tubs. His brother Max handled rhythm guitar from the start, and together with lead axeman Jairo T and bassist Paulo Jnr, Sepultura began adding substantially to noise levels in the city of Belo Horizonte.

They'd been fiercely inspired by the new poundings of bands like Slayer and Metallica; anything fresh and violent that trickled through the labyrinthine underground scene to their stereos. However, to listen to their first demos, you'd be hard pressed to recognise them as the innovative Thrash act that they are in the '90s.

Neither does their first ever vinyl appearance stand as anything like an achievement by today's standards. It was on a split-LP with their fellow countrymen Overdose, released through the minuscule Brazilian label Cogumelo, which cursed Sepultura's rabid Discharge-flavoured Death with a remarkably poor production job.

Nevertheless, it made a decided impact among the subterranean tape trading fanatics, and led to the creation of Sepultura's debut LP, 'Morbid Visions' in 1986, again via Cogumelo. The band's musical progression was hardly marked, and displayed plenty of dodgy Satanic imagery, which was soon to be ditched in later years. In late '87, Jairo T was replaced with the excellently-named Andreas Kisser, who brought some much needed musical class into the proceedings. This showed itself quite blatantly on the band's 'Schizophrenia' LP – an impressive display of brutality locking horns with melodic quality.

Yet Sepultura's records were still only available as hard-to-find imports outside of their own country. That all-important international market seemed a long way away. Until...the 'major indie' label Roadrunner stepped in with contracts outstretched. They had been monitoring Sepultura's movements in the underground scene, and 'Schizophrenia' was the album that

SEPULTURA: boys from Brazil turned men of (fearsome Thrash) Metal

made them bite. The necessary agreements were finalised against odds posed by the incredibly dodgy mail service from New York to South America.

The subsequent Roadrunner Records debut was 'Beneath The Remains' – still Sepultura's finest, even though the circumstances during recording were limiting to say the least. Today, Scott Burns is seen as one of the best Thrash/Death producers, but back in 1989, he was virtually a novice, forced to work with the outmoded resources of a Rio De Janeiro recording studio. This considered, 'Beneath The Remains' seems even better, although it was re-released with a slightly different, bassier mix after its initial pressing. The riffs had been honed to hard-edged perfection, and were present in numbers beyond comprehension. Once again, Andreas Kisser's lead-work added

further dimensions and colour, taking Sepultura's work beyond the massed ranks of pretenders and copyists. The Brazilian Death Metal scene, in particular, churned out badly-produced junk for quite some time.

'Beneath The Remains' became one of Roadrunner's best-selling debut albums ever, prompting the label to release 'Schizophrenia' worldwide; re-mastered, and complete with a bonus track – the 1990 version of 'Troops Of Doom' from the 'Morbid Visions' album.

'Arise' came next, almost two years later. Scott Burns remained in control of the mixing desk, but the difference was that he and the band were recording in America this time around. Although the song-writing wasn't quite as strong as that of its predecessor, 'Arise' went on to do marvellously well, and the Seps toured non-stop after its release.

Max Cavalera also had the birth of his first son to slot into the band's schedule, and the babe's heartbeat was recorded for use on the band's fifth studio album before he was even born! The album, scheduled for September 1993, would no doubt see the 'Jungle Boys' rise to even greater levels of acclaim.

IN THEIR OWN WORDS...

"You wonder why we sound the way we do? We are born in scum, we live in filth and we die in dirt. This is the only way we know how to express ourselves."
– Max Cavalera, Kerrang! 334, March 30, 1991

"If we get really big in Brazil, we're going to fight the bullshit hard-time, the things that have been f**ked up for so many years now. I guess I'm talking about a musical revolution..." – Max Cavalera, Kerrang! 334, March 30, 1991

"MTV totally freaked out (over the promo for 'Arise')! They said there's too much blood, too much fire and too much Jesus!" – Max Cavalera, Kerrang! 376, January 25, 1992

"Maybe we take it to heart too much, but we get pissed off when people always talk about Rio, soccer, Pele and Copacabana Beach when they talk about Brazil." – Andreas Kisser, Kerrang! 382, March 7, 1992

"If it's heavier, we're happier!"
– Max Cavalera, Kerrang! 292, June 2, 1990

SEPULTURA

ALBUMS
MORBID VISIONS (Cogumelo, 1986 – KKK) "A fetid, evil-smelling chunk of history, even if it doesn't make for easy listening, and isn't... uh... great." – Kerrang! 360, September 28, 1991
SCHIZOPHRENIA (Cogumelo, 1988 – KKKK) "A slightly darker, dirtier and slightly Deathlier affair than the subsequent 'Beneath The Remains' opus that so many know and love." – Kerrang! 316, November 17, 1990 – KKKK)
BENEATH THE REMAINS (Roadrunner, 1989 – KKKKK) "Time to take Sepultura seriously – dead seriously. Total f**kin' hate, man!" – Kerrang! 237, May 6, 1989
ARISE (Roadrunner, 1989 – KKKK) "A bold step forward, not as arrogantly experimental as, say, Slayer's 'South Of Heaven', but clearly a progression in both ideas and execution. And the friggin' thing works." – Kerrang! 333, March 23, 1991

SEX PISTOLS

UK, four-piece (1975-1978)

CONSIDERING THEY were supposedly intent on destroying the rock business it's rather ironic that these foul-mouthed yobs should be the most influential band since The Beatles and The Rolling Stones.

Much of the attraction of course, was the fact that they were so badly behaved. They hijacked the stage at St Martins College of Art for their first gig and had the plugs pulled after a few songs... which caused various punch ups. They said words much ruder than 'bottom' on Bill Grundy's live early evening TV show and made national headlines. They got to Number One in the Queen's jubilee week with an unpleasant ditty called 'God Save The Queen'. They got chucked off EMI and A&M record labels for being naughty. And they kicked bassist Glen Matlock out for not being very 'ard and for liking The Beatles, then replaced him with Sid Vicious!

In retrospect it's probably a good thing that the band fell apart when they did (their last gig was at the Winter Ballroom in San Francisco, January 14, 1978), otherwise they would have become a bad joke. As it is, though, they made history. In case you didn't know, they were Johnny Rotten (vocals), Steve Jones (guitar), Paul Cook (drums) and Sid Vicious (bass). Sid died on February 2, 1979 of a heroin overdose whilst on bail charged with the murder of his girlfriend Nancy Spungen...

Recommended album:
NEVER MIND THE BOLLOCKS *(Virgin, 1977-KKKKK)*

SHARK ISLAND

USA, four/five-piece (1986-present)

SHARK ISLAND evolved from the LA club band Sharks, who had released a pop-tinged album on their own label in 1982, vocalist Richard Black (considered to be the man from whom Axl Rose stole all his stage moves) and guitarist Spencer Sercombe piecing together a new line-up of bassist Tom Rucci, second guitarist Michael Guy and ex-Americade drummer Walt Woodward under the new handle.

Releasing an album of demos, 'S'Cool Buss' (sic) in 1987, Shark Island signed a development deal with A&M which led to two of their songs being included on the 'Bill And Ted's Excellent Adventure' soundtrack. Black and Sercombe recruited a new band of drummer Greg Ellis and ex-Tormé bassist Chris Heilmann. Epic then released second album, 'Law Of The Order' in 1989.

Despite an initial spate of livework the band has been strangely inactive giving rise to rumours of their demise, especially since Black turned up fronting the Contraband project alongside Michael Schenker and Ratt's Bobby Blotzer. More recently Sercombe appeared with Schenker and Robin McAuley doing some acoustic MSG shows.

Sparklingly recommended:
S'COOL BUSS *(Shark, 1987 – KKKK)*
LAW OF THE ORDER *(Epic, 1989 – KKKK)*

SHOTGUN MESSIAH

Sweden, four-piece (1989-1993)

WAY BACK in the mind-mangling mists of 1989, the band were called Kingpin, and made an album of pure sleaze called 'Welcome To Bop City'.

Kingpin relocated to Los Angeles, changed their name to Shotgun Messiah, and in 1989 'Welcome To Bop City' was finally released in the UK, re-titled 'Shotgun Messiah'.

This shag-tastic four-piece – self-credited as 'Harry K Cody (guitarmageddon), Zinny J San (provocals), Tim Tim (basstard) and Stixx Galore (drum 'n' coke') were plagued by bad luck but in 1991 came up with the consummate 'Second Coming' album.

By this time Zinny had gone, Tim had changed his surname to Skold and taken over vocals, and they'd recruited a new bassist, Bobby Lycon. Confused? You soon will be...

Despite 'Second Coming' being a god among records, big bucks and megafortune still avoided Shotgun Messiah, and come early '93 the band had fallen apart – ironically, on the eve of the release of their new mini-album 'I Want More'.

Recommended album:
SHOTGUN MESSIAH (Relativity, 1989 – KKKKK)

SHY

UK, five-piece (1983-present)
CLICHÉD PUB rockers, almost universally known as Shyte, who still can't get over the fact that they will never be American. Plenty of Trad Metal glitz and posing, but very little substance.
Almost worth hearing but not quite:
BRAVE THE STORM (RCA, 1985 – KK)

SILVERHEAD

UK, five-piece (1971-1973)
GLAM METALLERS years ahead of their time, fronted by Michael Des Barres (later of Power Station *et al*). Also included Nigel Harrison (bass, later of Blondie). Second LP, '16 And Savaged', featured a less than tasteful sleeve and Robbie Blunt – later of Robert Plant – on guitar. First one pictured Des Barres in unfeasibly large flares.
Recommended album:
SILVERHEAD (Atlantic, 1972 – KKKK)

SILVERWING

UK, four-piece (1980-1983)
RIDICULOUS BUT highly entertaining, Kiss-inspired Shock Rockers from Macclesfield.
Recommended party bomb single:
ROCK AND ROLL ARE FOUR LETTER WORDS (Bullet, 1980 – KKKKK)

SISTER DOUBLE HAPPINESS

USA, four-piece (1985-present)
PROMISING BUT rather anonymous New Metal quartet, led by a former Buddhist monk and so far not getting the breaks they deserve.
Recommended album:
HEART AND MIND (Caroline, 1992 – KKKK)

SKID ROW

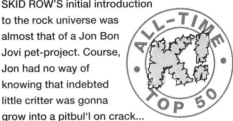

USA, five-piece (1988-present)
SKID ROW'S initial introduction to the rock universe was almost that of a Jon Bon Jovi pet-project. Course, Jon had no way of knowing that indebted little critter was gonna grow into a pitbul'l on crack...

Almost like something outta 'Butch Cassidy And The Sundance Kid' (or at least Tom Sawyer and Huckleberry Fin), the story goes that Dave 'The Snake' Sabo and Jon Bon Jovi grew up, lost their virginity together (not to each other, natch), etc, in New Jersey, and the pair made a vow that if one should make it to the big time – he'd come back and help out the other. Thus, with the eventual success of Jon's band Bon Jovi (trust us, they sold a disc or two), and true to his word, Jon rode back into town with enough gold to launch Dave's band Skid Row's career.

Skid Row had come into being after guitarist Sabo and bassist Rachel Bolan (he of the infamous nose-chain) got serious about this rock *thang*, sacked the remainder of their existing band, and roped in second guitarist Scotti Hill and drummer Rob Affuso. Then along came one, nay... *young* Sebastian Bach. A demented stick insect, high on youthful enthusiasm, and with a mouth that could swallow a planet. The Skids had sent the Toronto-based Seb (then in an incarnation of Glam nightmares Madam X) a tape. "When I heard 'Youth Gone Wild'," said Bach of the demo, "I knew it had been written for me to sing!" So, fully-manned, and under the 'tutelage' of Jon Bon Jovi, faster than you could say: "I'm your Fairy Godmother!", Skid Row were signed to both McGhee Entertainment and Atlantic Records! Natch, the media smelled hype, but come the release of their eponymous '89 debut, Skid Row proved that not only could they deliver the goods, but they could cook and force-feed you them as well! The recipe of

SKID ROW

Bach's cover-star looks and vein-exploding vocals combined with the high-octane toons of Sabo with his Metal leanings and Bolan with his Punk edge proved irresistible. The album charted Top 10 Stateside, spewing hit singles aplenty. Then, after their appearance with Bon Jovi at Milton Keynes (still '89) the British rock fans were likewise converted.

Ah, but things got sticky in 1990. There was the incident in Boston where a bottle was thrown at the stage and Seb, in the heat of the moment, stupidly threw it back – resulting in a fan's injury. Our boy found himself in court over that *faux pas*, and banned from his homeland Canada! And then, of course, there was the verbal going down in the press between Jon Bon Jovi and

Seb over an incident at the tail-end of the '89 Bon Jovi tour where our heroes (who each have their own story...) came to blows. And out of it too came to light the fact that Jon, along with his guitarist Richie Sambora, held a contract which entitled the pair to 100 per cent of Skid Row's publishing royalties – an agreement made early in the band's career in return for Bon Jovi's help; financial, support slot on the tour, etc. It was ugly. Sambora eventually returned his cut...

Mid '91, and the long-awaited second Skid

SKID ROW: fronted by a demented stick insect, backed by Jon Bon Jovi (once upon a time)

Row album, 'Slave To The Grind', hit the shelves. The release, to the surprise of many, found the Skids refusing to exploit the lucrative commercial direction past US hits like 'I Remember You' could have taken them, for material of monstrously heavy proportions. And their no-compromise policy even copped them a ban from Wembley's Brent Council who declared Wembley Stadium a 'no foul language' zone when the Skids appeared there with Guns N' Roses. Of course, asking Seb to hold back on the colourful patter was like asking a goldfish to breathe air!

Will Skid Row be the only rock band to survive a nuclear holocaust? Possibly. As Seb once claimed: "We're the cockroaches of Heavy Metal!"

ALBUMS

SKID ROW (Atlantic, 1989 – KKKKK)
"Giant vocals, straight but skin-snagging arrangements and a host of hooks that rise high and drag the standard of every song up with them." – Kerrang! 223, January 28, 1989

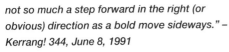

SLAVE TO THE GRIND (Atlantic, 1991 – KKKK)
"For Skid Row this is not so much a step forward in the right (or obvious) direction as a bold move sideways." – Kerrang! 344, June 8, 1991

SKREW

USA, seven-piece (1991-present)
FORMERLY ANGKOR Wat, Skrew are one of the finest exponents of Industrial Thrash around, and are often compared to Ministry, from whom they've clearly gained spirit. Featuring leader Adam Grossman's macabre voice in a churning hell of huge drum beats and guitar, their debut album was one of 1992's major highlights.
Recommended album:
BURNING IN WATER, DROWNING IN FLAME
(Devotion, 1992 – KKKKK)

SKYCLAD

UK, six-piece (1989-present)
IT CAME to pass that Mad Martin Walkyier left the Sabbat fold with the intention of forming his own venture. Skyclad was that venture – an insane hybrid of Folk and Thrash, which has since mellowed somewhat, and drifted more towards the former.

With Fritha Jenkins a mainstay on the fiddle, Skyclad are more than well equipped to become even madder before the century's end. Bow down to 'The Earth Mother, The Sun And The Furious Host'.
Most recommended album:
THE WAYWARD SONS OF MOTHER EARTH
(Noise, 1990 – KKKK)

SLADE

UK, four-piece (1966-present)
THESE WOLVERHAMPTON noise merchants spent the first four years of their career with no record deal, which is hardly surprising since they went by the abysmal name of The N' Betweens. In 1969, however, they became Ambrose Slade and then in 1970 they shaved their heads and became Slade. The rest, as they say, is history – once their barnets grew back.

Well, if there was any justice in the world it would be, but alas Slade are often overlooked as the magnificent and awesomely successful band that they were. Instead they're sometimes remembered as a trivial Glam band who recorded the much overplayed 'Merry Xmas Everybody', and for things like vocalist Noddy Holder's hair-do and guitarist Dave Hill's retarded platform boots. In fact, Slade had 16 boot-stomping Top 20 hits between 1971 and 1976, including six Number Ones and three Number Twos, and they were *very* good...so there!
Recommended album:
WALL OF HITS
(Polydor, 1991 – KKKK) compilation...

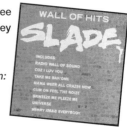

SLAMMER

UK, five-piece (1987-1991)
SIGNED BY major label, WEA, when known only by their mothers, Slammer was a classic case of much ado about nothing. Dropped after one album, the band released 'Nightmare Scenario' on FM/Revolver, the Metal graveyard, and dutifully split within weeks.
Slightly recommended album:
THE WORK OF IDLE HANDS *(WEA, 1989 – KKK)*

SLAUGHTER

USA, four-piece (1989-present)
FORMED BY the duo of bassist Dana Strum and vocalist Mark Slaughter after their ill-fated liaison in ex-Kiss guitarist Vinnie Vincent's band, Invasion, Slaughter's American-ised Stadium Metal reaped huge rewards with the Platinum-selling debut 'Stick It To Ya'. Noted for competence rather than inspiration, the band have suffered setbacks with the second studio album, 'The Wild Life' failing to match the success of the first release, and a worrisome cocaine-related drugs charge which hangs over the head of guitarist Tim Kelly. Heavy irony, given the band's oft-stated anti-drugs stance. May result in less dude-isms from Strum.
Recommended album:
STICK IT TO YA *(Chrysalis, 1990 – KKK)*

SLAVE RAIDER

USA, five-piece (1985-1990)
EXUBERANT US club band featuring the eye-patched Chainsaw Caine, an image unable to sustain the band's catchy Yob Rock for long.
Surprisingly recommended album:
TAKE THE WORLD BY STORM *(Jive, 1988 – KKK)*

SLAYER

USA, four-piece (1982-present)
"DO YOU wanna die?!" rages Tom Araya at one point during the mammoth 'Reign In Blood' album of '86. It's a brutal tornado of Thrashing pain which has yet to be equalled, let alone surpassed. Slayer conceived the world's greatest Death Metal album, even before the genre became truly prominent.

The quartet began terrorizing the LA club scene around '82, playing covers and wearing some of the most ludicrous 'evil' make-up imaginable while onstage. This led to some extremely memorable (not to mention regrettable) promo shots at the time, and gave the anti-Thrash critics even more to laugh behind their hands at.

Nevertheless, Slayer went on to make their first vinyl appearance with 'Aggressive Perfector' on the 'Metal Massacre III' compilation – a series of albums which Metallica had already debuted on. Later in 1983, the world shook as a full-blown album rose up from the Depths of Hell.

'Show No Mercy' had arrived, and songs like 'Crionics', 'Black Magic' and 'Die By The Sword' instantly grabbed the attention of most hardcore Metal disciples. This was different – faster, meaner and more downright Satanic than even Venom had been with their first two albums, 'Welcome To Hell' and 'Black Metal'.

It was followed up with the 'Haunting The Chapel' EP in 1984, with an A-side which many consider to be one of Thrash Metal's great moments: the fast and furious 'Chemical Warfare', which amply demonstrated how Slayer had taken Venom's evil fury to new limits.

'...Chapel' paved the way for a live EP, 'Live Undead', and the band's second piece of full-length Devil's work, 'Hell Awaits' ('85), which begins with one of the most ludicrous Satanic build-up intros ever heard. Marvellous stuff, and this one made the critics finally start to take Slayer at least half-seriously.

The lyrics were getting sicker, and reached their objectionable apex with the song 'Necrophiliac': *'I feel the urge, a growing need, to fuck this sinful corpse'.*

'Hell Awaits' shifted 100,000 units, paving the way for a contract from Rick Rubin's Def Jam

"To a Journey fan we suck, but to a fan who appreciates fast Metal, it's great, it's phenomenal. Humbly said..." – Kerry King, Kerrang! 91, April 4-17, 1985

"We didn't draw (people) for a long time. But now we draw really well. Now the Metal scene's gotten so big they want something heavier than Twisted Sister. We're, er, strange, I think." – Kerry King, Kerrang! 91, April 4-17, 1985

"Slayer? Our whole lifestyle is one big joke!" – Dave Lombardo (then ex-drummer), Kerrang! 138, January 22-February 4, 1987

"If you wanna call us anything, let it be purveyors of a New Age Of Music." – Tom Araya, Kerrang! 138, January 22-February 4, 1987

"The four of us know that, without each other, it really couldn't work as well. There's a deep understanding between the four members of this band, and we don't feel we have to prove anything to anybody." – Tom Araya, Kerrang! 308, September 22, 1990

"War is man's favourite and most elaborate sport..." – Jeff Hanneman, Kerrang! 308, September 22, 1990

"There's always been some vibe against me. I really don't know what it was, but those guys - there was always something about me that bothered them..." – Dave Lombardo, ex-Slayer, Kerrang! 437, April 3, 1993

SLAYER

Recordings label. It was an unusual occurrence, considering Def Jam's roster at the time: Run DMC, Beastie Boys and LL Cool J!

Nevertheless, the first product of this new arrangement was the Godly 'Reign In Blood', in 1986 – an album which sold half-a-million, and strangely didn't receive a domestic release in the UK, but was backed up with some blinding live shows, despite drummer Lombardo's temporary departure.

It's never seemed like Slayer are blood brothers, exactly, and they've always freely admitted that they probably wouldn't socialize together if they weren't playing violent Thrash together.

'Reign...' also managed to cause a bit of fuss among the moral majorities, particularly because of the song 'Angel Of Death', which laid out the atrocities of Auschwitz in grisly detail. Many had the band written off as Nazis, but the reality seems to be their mere interest in the whole phenomenon, and guitarist Jeff Hanneman's modest memorabilia collection.

The album's obsession with frightening speed and aggression led to Slayer slowing things down on their next outing two years later. 'South Of Heaven' saw Slayer as a more accessible unit, with Tom Araya toning his vocal style down, and actually attempting to sing occasionally. The Black Sabbath influence was all the more apparent on this one.

1990 was the year that unleashed 'Seasons In The Abyss' – an album which Slayer themselves described as a cross between 'Reign In Blood' and 'South Of Heaven'. Songs like 'War Ensemble' and 'Spirit In Black' certainly had more of that earlier flame, while the subtler 'Dead Skin Mask' simultaneously chilled and impressed.

After a weighty double-live package ('Decade Of Aggression'), Slayer promptly sacked Dave Lombardo once again, presumably for the last time. They played Donington in '92 with ex-Forbidden man Paul Bostaph behind the kit, and Bostaph remains with them as they reportedly attempt to concoct a 'Reign In Blood' Part Two.

Hell awaits once again. Be very afraid.

ALBUMS

SHOW NO MERCY (Metal Blade, 1984 – KKK) *"This is crap, pure unadulterated junk – NOT what Magick is all about!" – Kerrang! 62, February 23-March 7, 1984*
HELL AWAITS (Metal Blade, 1985 – KKKK) *"The most threatening, subversive band on the face of the planet at this particular moment in time. 'Hell Awaits' is*

the product of sick minds. It reeks of evil intent and rattles your walls with its fuck 'em all frenzy" – Kerrang! 92, April 18-May 1, 1985
REIGN IN BLOOD (London, 1986 – KKKKK) "The best Frash/Death/Hate/Speed Metal you're likely to hear this year. Satan's most loyal servants have kome good on their third and easily most accessible outing to date. AAAAAHHHHH!" – Kerrang! 130, October 2-15, 1986
SOUTH OF HEAVEN (Def American, 1988 – KKKKK) "They're like a video nasty on record. EVIL, DARK and TWISTED!" – Kerrang! 195, July 9, 1988
SEASONS IN THE ABYSS (Def American, 1990 – KKKKK) "This is basement zero, a cartoon cliché hell for your wildest, stupidest escape. It's all there, just

like you hoped... and it's thicker and stronger than ever." – Kerrang! 308, September 22, 1990
DECADE OF AGGRESSION (Def American, 1991 – KKKKK) "This is raw power, right in yo' face, from the greatest Heavy Metal band on the planet" – Kerrang! 363, October 19, 1991

SLAYER (Tom Araya): the greatest HM band on the planet?

UK, three-piece (1978-1981)
ONE HIT wonders from the NWOBHM whose eponymous single dominated the upper reaches of HM charts for much of 1978.
Recommended single (for the line 'She hit me... like a sledgehammer'):
SLEDGEHAMMER (Sledgehammer, 1978 – KKKk)

S.O.D.

USA, four-piece, (1985-86)
PART-TIME Hardcore/Metal crossover outfit, formed by Anthrax men, Scott Ian (guitar) and Charlie Benante (bass). They released a record (shortly after recording 'Spreading The Disease'), with a line-up completed by Nuclear Assault's Dan Lilker (bass) and ex-Psychos singer Billy Milano – but the two 'Thrax-based members found less and less time for the project as a European tour with Metallica loomed. Reformations have sporadically popped up since the riotous agitators split, however, and will no doubt continue to do so.
Recommended (and indeed only) albums:
SPEAK ENGLISH OR DIE (Megaforce, 1985 – KKKKK)
LIVE FROM BUDOKAN (Megaforce, 1992 – KKKKK)

SODOM

Germany, three-piece (1981-present)
PART OF the German Thrash explosion in the mid-'80s, Sodom never reached the same heights as Kreator or Destruction, and were often regarded as a joke. With early song titles like 'Volcanic Slut' and the meaningless 'Burst Command 'Til War', this was perhaps understandable. Sodom continue to release albums, the most recent being the Death Metal-tinged 'Tapping The Vein'. But it seems unlikely that the war-obsessed die-hards will ever make that important break from the German market.
Recommended album:
BETTER OFF DEAD (Steamhammer, 1991 – KKK)

SOHO ROSES

UK, five-piece (1986-1989)
SNEERING, SNOTTY, punky glamsters fronted
by excruciating Mike Monroe impersonator Paul
Blittz, who also featured Joolz on bass and Pat
on drums, later to become the original rhythm
section of The Wildhearts.
Recommended album:
THE THIRD AND FINAL INSULT *(Trash Can,
1989 – KKK)*

SONIC YOUTH

USA, four-piece (1983-present)
SEMINAL POST-PUNK American artcore
underground band led by the arrogant bravado
of Thurston Moore (guitar/vocals). Spent a
decade creating obscure music which was
hailed by the cognoscenti as ground-breaking.
Finally moved into a more public spotlight when
Nirvana's 'Nevermind' album went supernova,
with band leader Kurt Cobain citing the Youth
as primary influence. Bands toured Europe
together in '91, finally releasing home movie of
the gigs, '1991: The Year That Punk Broke', in
'93(!). Second Geffen album, 'Dirty', was hailed
as a masterpiece, yet failed to capture the
general public's imagination, sticking too rigidly
to their unwieldy style.
Recommended album:
DIRTY *(Geffen, 1992 – KKK)*

SOUNDGARDEN

USA, four-piece (1984-present)
THE MOST Metal-oriented of all the Seattle
bands, Soundgarden's initial line-up was Chris
Cornell (vocals), Kim Thayil
(guitar), Matt Cameron
(drums) and Hiro
Yamamoto (bass). The
band released a handful
of singles on the then-
fledgling Seattle label
SubPop, before moving to
another hardcore indie, SST, where they
released their debut LP 'Ultra Mega OK'.
Following an SST single, 'Flower', the band

SOUNDGARDEN: Seattle's most Metal...

signed to a major, A&M, the first SubPop band
to do so. The second LP, 'Louder Than Love',
was released in 1989, and showcased the
band's fiercely idiosyncratic sound – heavily
influenced by '70s hard rock and psychedelia,
but set apart by Thayil's excellent guitar work
and Cornell's distinctly modern world-view. The
album and accompanying singles, particularly
'Loud Love', saw Soundgarden move to the
forefront of the 'alternative' Metal scene.
Following the recording of this second LP,
bassist Yamamoto departed, to be replaced by
Jason Everman, formerly of Nirvana (and now in
Mind Funk). Soon after the LP's release, Cornell
and Cameron teamed up with future Pearl Jam
members Stone Gossard and Jeff Ament to
record the 'Temple Of The Dog' LP, a tribute to
friend and former Mother Love Bone frontman
Andrew Wood, who died of a heroin overdose.

Soundgarden continued to win over new fans
with some thunderous live performances, but it
wasn't until the release of the third LP
'Badmotorfinger' in 1991 (featuring Everman's
replacement on bass, Ben Shepherd, a friend of
the band) that Soundgarden soared to arena

size. They opened for Metallica at the Oakland Coliseum in San Francisco in front of 65,000 in the Summer of '91, then played to approximately one-and-a-half million people over the next two months while supporting Guns N' Roses. 'Badmotorfinger' was the band's best yet, a twisted sonic assault that, stylistically, was unique. By now used to critics pointing out the obvious Black Sabbath influences, Soundgarden flicked the Vs to one and all when they recorded the Sabs' 'Into The Void' for the flipside of the single 'Jesus Christ Pose' (the video for which featured a Terminator-style robot nailed to a cross). A slot on the bill of Lollapalooza II in '92 cemented Soundgarden's widespread appeal, and they remain one of the most innovative and striking modern rock bands around.

IN THEIR OWN WORDS...

"It was neat that the majors were waving this money in our face, but it was important to us to establish ourselves with the people that like us. We've got a foundation, and we didn't jump to a big label just for the bucks." – Matt Cameron, Kerrang! 233, April 8 1989

"Obviously we're not gonna come out with all the Metal clichés that have been put on the radio for the past eight years. If the suburban Metal guy likes it, and the college guy who buys Red Hot Chili Peppers or The Sugarcubes, so be it... but I can tell you, we don't get a lot of feminists and we don't get a lot of yuppies." – Chris Cornell, Kerrang! 259, October 7 1989

"There are always going to be certain degrees of showmanship but as for saying, 'C'mon Matt, do a drum solo', or 'Kim, how about a 12-string arpeggio in D-minor' or 'Chris, nice falsetto!'... that's the sort of thing that pushed us into playing in punk rock bands because we hated what was on the radio. Still do." – Kim Thayil, Kerrang! 356, August 31 1991

"It's impossible for me to step back and really understand or know what impact I've had. For the band, as well, I can't really tell where Soundgarden fit into music or how Soundgarden are really perceived. A lot of people get it and a lot want to get it and don't." – Chris Cornell, Kerrang! 414, October 17, 1992

SOUNDGARDEN

ALBUMS

ULTRA MEGA OK *(SST, 1989 – KKKK) "Brutally heavy, louder than hell, and explosively dynamic are the best ways to describe Soundgarden. They're as honest and raw as rock 'n' roll gets." – Kerrang! 221, January 14, 1989*

LOUDER THAN LOVE *(A&M, 1989 – KKKK) "Dark, Brooding. Hip-swingingly perverse. Soundgarden are light years removed from the Zeppelin-esque revisionism they are so often tagged for." – Kerrang! 253, August 26, 1989*

BADMOTORFINGER *(A&M, 1991 – KKKK) "Hints at the absolute emergency of an album Soundgarden have inside them... a massive brooding slab of grunge surfing on Cornell's bleeding heart... 'Jesus Christ Pose' and 'Holy Water' could crack skulls at a thousand yards." – Kerrang! 359, September 21, 1991*

SPIDER

UK, four-piece (1977-1986)
EIGHT-LEGGED boogie merchants Sniffa (guitar), Col Harkness (vocals/guitar), Rob E Burrows (drums) and Brian Burrows (bass/vocals) – were Status Quo clones who received plenty of attention at the time of their 1982 debut album 'Rock 'N' Roll Gypsies'.

Two years later they put out 'Rough Justice' (A&M), sticking pretty much to that four-bar, Quo-static formula, but by this time the Mötley Crües and Ratts of the world were making their made-up mark, leaving trad Brit bands like Spider well and truly down the plughole. Split after LP number three, 'Raise The Banner' (Mausoleum, '86).
(Slightly) recommended album:
ROCK 'N' ROLL GYPSIES *(RCA, 1982 – KKK)*

SPINAL TAP

UK, four-piece (1984-present)
PAINFULLY ACCURATE spoof of a hideously clichéd Metal band performed in-character by a group of sharp satirists. The American-made  film, rockumentary if you like, traced the band's comeback US tour in fly-on-the-wall style, and was an instant cult success within the music industry. 'This Is Spinal Tap' was so acutely observed that some audiences believed it to be a real documentary, and several accomplished Metal bands walked out of screenings with their egos truly flattened. Although the video is practically essential on-tour entertainment for any band, Spinal Tap themselves pushed the joke too far. A 1992 LP, 'Break Like The Wind' garnered little interest and subsequent live shows were weak and tired compared to the film. Turning a one-off masterpiece into a commercial bandwagon ruined the joke, but Spinal Tap are still a giggle when they turn up at all-star *charidee* benefits.
Essential video:
THIS IS SPINAL TAP *(Channel Five, 1984 – KKKKK)*

SPREAD EAGLE

USA, four-piece (1989-present)
NEW YORK noise boys who deliver basic, honest gutter-level rock 'n' roll with Paul DiBartolo's guitar honed like a razor and Ray West's vocals dripping sleaze and sex at every turn... at least until they grew up a bit with 1993's second album 'Open To The Public', and decided to claim that people had misunderstood first album classics like 'Back On The Bitch', and failed to notice that 'Hot Sex' was actually about brain surgery. Shame.
Recommended, not sexist at all, debut album:
SPREAD EAGLE *(MCA, 1990 – KKKK)*

Billy SQUIER

USA, solo artist (1979-present)
BOSTON-BORN singer/songwriter/guitarist formerly of New York bands Magic Terry and The Universe, The Sidewinders and Piper, the latter managed by Bill 'Kiss' Aucoin. After Piper split, Squier signed to Capitol Records and made a strong solo debut with 'Tale Of The Tape' ('80).

His big breakthrough came a year later when the triple Platinum 'Don't Say No' album (produced by Mack of Queen fame) spawned the hits 'The Stroke' and 'My Kinda Lover'. Big Stateside success was followed by an invitation to tour the UK with Whitesnake. But after a good show at the 1981 Reading Festival, his profile over here began to lapse.

In the States, however, his increasingly AOR-flavoured career went from strength to strength so that, come 1993 and the release of his eighth LP, 'Tell The Truth', he could look back on 11 million sales worldwide. The latter record was his first since 1986's 'Enough Is Enough' to get a full UK release and thankfully found him returning to his earlier 'big beat' commercial hard rock style.
Recommended albums:
TALE OF THE TAPE *(Capitol, 1981 – KKKKK)*
DON'T SAY NO *(Capitol, 1980 – KKKK)*

STAR STAR

USA, four-piece (1988-present)
GLAM-ISH METAL band who live for the 'Rocky Horror Show', a brash combo with just one album under their mucky belts, the wonderfully-titled 'The Love Drag Years', featuring one of the greatest empty-head tracks of all time: 'Groovy Guru Gangster Girl'.

Vocalist/guitarist Johnny Holliday is a promising frontman, and when backed up by guitarist Jay Hening, bassist Weeds and drummer Deon, Star Star become a package well worth opening for closer inspection.
Recommended album:
THE LOVE DRAG YEARS *(Roadrunner, 1992 – KKK)*

STARCASTLE

USA, six piece (1972-1980)
PRIME PURVEYORS of the overblown pomp rock style popularised throughout the '70s, Starcastle were keen to tout their musical pedigree with four... er, pompous albums. Almost famous for vocalist Terry Luttrell having performed with REO Speedwagon, Starcastle never leapt over the ocean to wow their UK fanbase, preferring to hone their musical talents in the American Midwest, where they achieved moderate success. Whereabouts of the band members are currently unknown.
Recommended album, if only for the painting on the sleeve:
CITADEL *(Epic, 1978 – KKK)*

STARZ

USA, five-piece (1975-1980)
INTIALLY UNDER contract to Arista, under their original name of Fallen Angels, Starz got out of the deal after discovering the label had no intention of releasing any product, to hook up with Capitol Records, with whom the band recorded four albums (five, if you include the sought-after promotional live album) but failed to really breakthrough in a market largely dominated by Kiss, despite generally being considered musically superior. It was more than ironic that they shared Bill Aucoin as manager!

Record label problems prevented singer Michael Lee Smith and guitarist Richie Ranno's post-Starz band, The Hellcats, from gaining any further ground, but it is to Ranno's eternal credit that he's seen fit to release an interesting array of Starz live and demo material on various labels in recent years.
Utterly recommended:
STARZ *(Capitol, 1976 – KKKKK)*
VIOLATION *(Capitol, 1977 – KKKKK)*

STATUS QUO

UK, four/five-piece (1966-present)
SINCE 1987, when they reformed for the money after vowing in 1983 they were too old to continue, Status Quo have been crap.

No question. As anyone who saw them in their heyday (1971-1977) will testify. Live they could cut it right up to their 'farewell' 'End Of The Road' tour in '84 but they were a spent force on record after 'Rockin' All Over The World' ('77). The classic line-up of Francis Rossi (guitar and vocals), Rick Parfitt (guitar and vocals), Alan Lancaster (bass and vocals) and John Coghlan (drums) found longterm success after a couple of mid-'60s flash-in-the-pan pop hits, by growing their hair and going on stage wearing denims and T-shirts – basically looking exactly like the club and college crowds they were playing to. They then expanded their simplistic heads-down, no-nonsense 12-bar boogie to bigger and bigger crowds and through a series of albums that were nowhere near as one-dimensional as many reviewers suggested. After 1977, the band enjoyed ever more success as a singles act but ironically, they played very few of these on stage and their albums got steadily weaker and poppier. Really, Rossi and Parfitt – the only two surviving founder members – should have knocked it on the head when they said they would.
Recommended albums:
PILEDRIVER *(Vertigo, 1972 – KKKK)*
LIVE *(Vertigo, 1977 – KKKKK) But skip the drum solo*

Jim STEINMAN

USA, composer/instrumentalist (1974-present)
ROSE TO fame in 1978 as Meat Loaf's right-hand man/the writer of the fat one's 'Bat Out Of Hell' masterpiece. The pair first met in 1974 when Meat Loaf worked in a Steinman musical called 'More Than You Deserve'. He wrote 'Bad For Good' as 'Bat...'s follow-up but this was released as a Steinman solo project due to Meat Loaf's vocal problems. Their subsequent 1981 collaboration 'Dead Ringer' was a relative flop also but Steinman enjoyed much critical acclaim with the 'Original Sin' epic – a magical mystery tour through the madness and hysteria of the man's musical mind. The record is credited to Pandora's Box, a supposed 'band'

fronted by *four* female vocalists to exorcise his visions; and the sounds of Elaine Caswell, Ellen Foley, Gina Taylor and the gloriously-named Deliria Wilde make for uneasy listening. Todd Rundgren also makes an appearance. At once terrifiying, desperate and heartbreaking, this anguished catharsis could only belong to Steinman.

Recommended album:
ORIGINAL SIN *(Virgin, 1989 – KKKKK)*

STEPPENWOLF

USA, five-piece (1967-present)
HAD MONSTER hit with 'Born To Be Wild' from the soundtrack of biker movie 'Easy Rider' in 1969 but have done absolutely bog-all of interest ever since. Gotta hand it to John Kay (vocals/guitar) for flogging it for all he's worth ever since, though...

Recommended:
*Putting **BORN TO BE WILD** on any jukebox and watching others play air guitar to it...*

STONE TEMPLE PILOTS

USA, four-piece (1989-present)
SUPERLATIVE, POST-PUNK craftsmen from LA who have so far scored a hit with the Grungetastic 'Sex Type Thing' single, and who are currently being bad-mouthed as a new Jane's Addiction/Nirvana/Pearl Jam *bla-bla-bla*.

Essential album:
CORE *(Warner Bros, 1992 – KKKKK)*

Izzy STRADLIN

USA, guitar/vocals (1991-present)
FOUNDER MEMBER of Guns N' Roses hailing from the same town – Lafayette, Indiana, as Axl Rose. Quit that band after completing work on their 'Use Your Illusion' albums and a final UK date at Wembley Stadium on August 31, '91. Izzy laid low for about a year, travelling the world, then re-emerged in 1992 fronting the Ju-Ju Hounds, a band including Rick Richards (guitar, ex-Georgia Satellites), Jimmy Ashurst (bass, ex-Broken Homes) and Charlie Quintana (drums, ex-Bob Dylan). Away from GN'R, Stradlin (real name Jeffrey Isabell) has finally

dropped the rather silly apostrophe at the end of his adopted surname and has turned to music strongly influenced by reggae and the Rolling Stones, as evidenced on his first release, the EP 'Pressure Drop' (September, '92) and much of the album 'Ju Ju Hounds'.

Recommended album:
JU JU HOUNDS *(Geffen, 1992 – KKKK)*

STRANGEWAYS

UK, five-piece (1986-1989)
SHORTLIVED BUT highly rated – by the AOR anorak brigade – part-Scottish outfit fronted by Atlanta-born singer Terry Brock. Made three albums, including an eponymous debut produced by Kevin 'Journey' Elson, then disappeared despite connoisseurs' assurances that they should have been as huge as Journey or Foreigner...

Recommended second album:
NATIVE SONS *(RCA, 1987 – KKKK)*

STRYPER

USA, four-pious (1983-present)
CHRISTIANS WITH attitude! Formerly Roxx Regime, they have become the world's leading White Metal band – with a penchant for yellow and black. Frontman Michael Sweet's vocals get a bit histrionic at times but the music is melodic Metal which has helped them cross over into the secular market, where mainstream fans have listened to them religiously. HA! This peaked with 1986's 'To Hell With The Devil' which went Platinum and prompted a world tour where the band became legendary for tossing bibles into their audience and selling T-shirts bearing 777 logos. Mysteriously, with Him Upstairs so obviously on their side, they went for a complete change of image on 'Against The Law' ('90) dropping the yellow and black and growing beards. This failed horribly and in 1992 things got horribly worse when Sweet quit.

Recommended album:
SOLDIERS UNDER COMMAND *(Enigma, 1985 – KKKK)*

STYX

USA, five-piece (1971-1984)
POPULARISED POMP Rock, employing lashings of keyboards and spartan power chords to produce a commercially acceptable hard rock sound. Unafraid of eating quiche in public, Styx grew from obscure Chicago roots to dominate the American charts in the late '70s and early '80s. Having broken with the syrupy ballad, 'Lady', from 1973's corny 'Styx II' album, it wasn't until 'The Grand Illusion' ('77) album that the band achieved lasting popularity.

Styx often seemed torn between vocalist/keyboardist Dennis de Young's pop leanings and the twin guitar attack of James Young and Tommy Shaw, yet 1978's 'Pieces Of Eight' captured the perfect blend of styles to produce a classic hard rock showcase. Perhaps more importantly, the band's 'Paradise Theater' album is one of the first recorded sightings of etching on vinyl! Since the band's split, only Shaw has remained in the public eye with Ted Nugent in Damn Yankees.
Recommended album:
PIECES OF EIGHT *(A&M, 1978 – KKKKK)*

SUGAR

USA, three-piece (1992-present)
THE RETURN of the Godfather of Grunge. Ex-Hüsker Dü frontman Bob Mould formed Sugar in '92 after several years – and two albums – as a solo performer.

The trio launched Sugar with a summer tour that had journalists running out of superlatives and audiences going apeshit. The debut album 'Copper Blue', released in autumn '92, lived up to expectations – as well as Mould's past – proving that he hadn't lost his touch for catchy melodies, soaring vocal harmonies and intense guitar mangling.

As usual, Mould's prolific songwriting was in evidence; the follow-up mini-album 'Beaster' released in March '93 contained songs left out from 'Copper Blue'.
Recommended album:
COPPER BLUE *(Creation, 1992 – KKKKK)*

SUICIDAL TENDENCIES

USA, five-piece (1982-present)
ORIGINALLY STARTED as a four-piece Hardcore band, but over the years ST have progressed through Skate Thrash to being simply a very good rock band. Rumours about the band's involvement with notorious LA street gangs have always been rife, even to the extent that vocalist Mike Muir had supposedly killed several people. But to this day many of these stories remain unsubstantiated; it's all a load of bollocks in other words! Apart from the fact that Muir often wears a blue bandanna normally associated with street gang The Crips.

Although their records have been consistently good, the best way to experience the band is live, when they really come into their own and could undoubtedly wipe the stage with most bands. Funny they never seem to have got much bigger.
Recommended album:
LIGHTS, CAMERA... REVOLUTION *(Epic, 1991 – KKKKK)*

SURVIVOR

USA, five-piece (1978-present)
SURVIVOR WERE dragged along in the AOR slipstream created by the likes of Foreigner and Journey, but despite having released their debut album in 1979, didn't make any commercial headway until recording the theme song for Sylvester Stallone's hit movie, 'Rocky III', in 1982. 'Eye Of The Tiger' went on to be a massive worldwide hit and still accompanies boxing footage on TV everywhere. The mainstay of the band is keyboardist Jim Peterik, whose ear for melody ensured a string of minor UShits. Original vocalist Dave Bickler was replaced by Jimi Jamison, formerly of Cobra, for 1984's 'Vital Signs' album. Jamison was once tipped to join Rainbow. The band reformed in 1993 when they toured Europe with Bickler back in charge of vocal duties.
Recommended album:
EYE OF THE TIGER *(Scotti Brothers, 1982 – KKK)*

SVEN GALI

Canada, five-piece (1987-present)

BIG IN Southern Ontario but almost unknown everywhere else until signed by BMG Canada in 1991. Their home country remains their main market but first moves to break worldwide began in 1993 with the release of their Skid Row- and Love/Hate-sounding debut...

Only album to date:
SVEN GALI *(BMG, 1993 – KKK)*

SWEET

UK, four-piece (1970-1979)

THE NAME still exists today but the band bears little resemblance to the classic line-up of Brian Connolly (vocals), Andy Scott (guitar), Steve Priest (bass) and Mick Tucker (drums). Although initially a lightweight bubblegum pop band they slowly evolved into outrageous Glamsters (contemporaries of Slade, Gary Glitter and T Rex), then to a nearly full-on hard rock act. Between 1971 and 1977 they chalked up 16 hits, winning favour with rock fans mainly for their more Metalised B-sides, written by themselves and not by their producers Chinn and Chapman. In December '74, the band split with their producers in the hope of establishing their own rock cred. But the hits all but dried up, and Sweet ran out of steam. Got big in Germany but fell apart when Connolly quit to go solo in '79. Scott is now an occasional member of UK pub rockers Paddy Goes To Holyhead. Connolly is a regular at many UK pubs.

Recommended album:
DESOLATION BOULEVARD *(RCA, 1974 – KKKK)*

SWORD

Canada, four-piece (1981-1991)

ONE OF the original Power Metal bands, Sword's 1986 debut 'Metalized' was way ahead of the trend that was to come.

In 1987 they supported Motörhead in the UK and sadly, that was the only time the Montreal-based quartet made it over here. Their Hammersmith Odeon show was certainly impressive, with blond vocalist Rick Hughes almost taking the roof off with his volcanic warblings.

During '88 the follow-up, 'Sweet Dreams', was born, once more sticking to a heavier-than-thou philosophy. However, Sword remained no more than moderately successful, and eventually the band – Dan Hughes (drums), Mike Larock (bass) and Mike Plant (guitar), decided to call it a day.

Recommended album:

TAD

USA, four-piece (1988-present)
SEATTLE SCUMBAGS named after their extremely large frontman Tad Doyle. A better idea might have been to name themselves after their debut album 'God's Balls' (SubPop, '89). But they didn't, and instead built themselves a sizeable following with their over-the-top blend of sicko lyrics and fuzzy hardcore riffing. After the 'Salt Lick' EP ('90), they issued the bizarrely-titled 'Eight Way Santa' LP, by which time the rest of the world had gone Seattle mad and they found themselves, uncomfortably, in vogue.
Recommended album:
EIGHT WAY SANTA (SubPop, 1991 – KKKKK)

TALAS

USA, four-piece (1979-1985)
NOTED FOR numbering bass virtuoso Billy Sheehan (later to find fame with David Lee Roth and Mr Big) in their ranks, Talas never achieved success despite their technical capabilities. Two studio albums, a live opus and a compilation remain as a legacy to unfulfilled talent. Sheehan performed Talas song 'Shy Boy' in both his following bands.
Recommended 'Shy Boy'-featuring album:
SINK YOUR TEETH INTO THAT (Food For Thought, 1982 – KKK)

TANK

UK, three-piece (1980-1988)
MOTÖRHEAD SOUNDALIKES who even got to support their heroes on the 'Iron Fist' tour in 1982. Actually, Tank were a natural progression for bassist/vocalist Algy Ward who formed the band. Having first gained notoriety in Punk band The Saints, he went on to join even better Punk band The Damned and played on arguably their best album 'Machine Gun Etiquette'. All the time though he talked about Metal and his love for Motörhead.

Alas, having developed a decent style of their own, Tank split up allegedly because nine times out of 10 they were too drunk to play anything when they got on stage.
Recommended album:
FILTH HOUNDS OF HADES (Kamaflage, 1982 – KKKK)

TANKARD

Germany, five-piece (1982-present)
BEER-SWILLING Thrashers who like beer even more than Thrash. Second demo was called 'Alcoholic Metal', then made a number of heavily beer-soaked albums for Noise including 'Chemical Invasion' ('87) (about pollutants in beer).
Recommended hangover cure:
THE MORNING AFTER (Noise, 1988 – KKK and two aspirins)

TATTOOED LOVE BOYS

UK, four/five-piece (1987-1992)
CHIRPY AND confident good-time chancers who scored points for longevity but none whatsoever for their fashion sense. They split up before they could take LA by storm.
Kind of recommended album:
BLEEDING HEARTS AND NEEDLE MARKS (Episode, 1988 – KKKK)

TEMPLE OF THE DOG

USA, five-piece (1991)
FORMED AS a one-off project by a host of Seattle luminaries-to-be in deference to their

departed friend, Mother Love Bone singer Andrew Wood, this tribute album became more influential than anticipated when band members, guitarists Stone Gossard and Mike McCready and bassist Jeff Ament ,went on to massive success with day job band, Pearl Jam. Vocalist/guitarist Chris Cornell and drummer Matt Cameron had already found fame with Soundgarden.

Wood's highly Glam-orientated style which he employed to great effect in Mother Love Bone is hardly to be heard on this melancholy musical stroll, but considering his untimely death from a heroin overdose, the sombre yet sensitive mood fits the picture well.

Recommended (and only) album:
TEMPLE OF THE DOG (A&M, 1991 – KKKK)

TEN YEARS AFTER

UK, four-piece (1966-1975)
PROGRESSIVE BLUES rockers who were essentially a vehicle for the blinding guitar work of Alvin Lee. Lee continued to tour after the band – completed by Chick Churchill (keyboards), Leo Lyons (bass, later to produce UFO *et al*) and Ric Lee (drums, no relation) – broke up, trying again as Ten Years Later (!), before reforming the original line-up in 1989 for the 'About Time' album and tour. Alvin Lee has spent most of the latter part of his career trying to be famous for something other than the stunning version of 'Goin' Home' in 1969's 'Woodstock' movie.

Recommended:
*The stunning version of **GOIN' HOME** in 1969's 'Woodstock' movie*

TERRAPLANE

UK, four/five-piece (1981-1988)
THE BAND that became Thunder. After much glowing press in *Sounds* and early *Kerrang!*, they released indie single 'I Survive' in '83. A deal with Epic followed – as did a radical change in image and style as the label steered them towards the pop market until the press pilloried them to oblivion.

Current Thunder boys Danny Bowes (vocals),

Luke Morley (guitar) and Gary 'Harry' James (drums) were then accompanied by Nick Linden (bass) and, for the latter days, Rudy Riviere (guitar). Terraplane fought bravely against the odds, and many of their songs were pure brilliance – 'Dirty Love' was originally by them, not Thunder – but in the end they decided to do things their way, not Epic's, and started again as Thunder.

Recommended album:
BLACK AND WHITE (Epic, 1985 – KKKK)

TERRORVISION

UK, four-piece (1986-present)
IT WAS said that Terrorvision's 'Formaldehyde' opus "...holds hours of strangely dark fun". Hailing from somewhere near Bradford, Tony Wright and his troupe are throwing rock some truly interesting twists and turns, while evolving into a force to be reckoned with.

Recommended album:
FORMALDEHYDE (Total Vegas, 1993 – KKKK)

TESLA

USA, five-piece (1983-present)
TAKING THEIR name from a barmy scientist who insisted on cleaning his cutlery with at least 18 napkins and who discovered electricity in his spare time, Tesla spent their early days poncing around playing weak-kneed wimp rock before getting wise and going back to their Blues-encrusted roots. The result was a management contract with the powerful Q-Prime organisation, a deal with Geffen Records and a wedge-generating debut, 'Mechanical Resonance'.

Perhaps more than any other band, Tesla represented the shift back towards more roots-orientated rock. No gimmicks, no outrageous quotes. Simply power rock played with feel and focus.

The band proved that they weren't afraid to experiment by releasing the self-explanatory 'Five Man Acoustical Jam' in 1990, but last album, 'Psychotic Supper', failed to capitalise on Tesla's previous achievements. Little-known facts fans note: drummer Troy Luccketta played with seminal, if terminally obscure, AOR acts The Eric Martin Band and Breathless in the late '70s.

Recommended album:
MECHANICAL RESONANCE (Geffen, 1987 – KKKK)

TESTAMENT

USA, five-piece (1985-present)
LEADERS OF San Francisco's Second Wave Of Thrash bands, Testament's opening gambit was a stunning collection of ravaging riffs and rhythms, titled 'The Legacy'.

After maintaining the quality level with 1988's 'The New Order', they seemingly began to compromise over the course of the next three albums. 1992's 'The Ritual' saw them virtually bereft of their original Thrash fire.

1993 sees them preparing for a comeback, with new members, and a new attitude. The world awaits the New Testament...

Recommended albums:
THE LEGACY (Megaforce/Atlantic, 1987 – KKKKK)
THE NEW ORDER (Megaforce/Atlantic, 1988 – KKKKK)

THEE HYPNOTICS

UK, four-piece (1989-present)
IGGY POP And The Stooges wannabes who never will be, but do a good enough job of trying to have impressed The Black Crowes.

Recommended album:
COME DOWN HEAVY (Situation Two, 1990- KKKK)

THERAPY?

Ireland, three-piece (1989-present)
THE JOVIAL trio's simultaneous love of Techno and classic Punk singles has resulted in a formidable arsenal of tuneful white noise as well as a massive live audience. Tuned into the post-Manic Street Preachers-sloganeering, as well as keeping a firm lid on pretention and glamour, Therapy? were the '90s most welcome chart success. Inroads into North America have only just begun, but their material has continued to

grow at an astonishing rate. The last great hope for national Heavy Metal.

Essential Therapy?:
NURSE (A&M, 1992 – KKKKK)
SHORT-SHARP-SHOCK EP (A&M, 1993 – KKKKK)

THIN LIZZY

Ireland, three/four/five-piece (1969-1983)
"IS THERE anybody here with any Irish in them? Is there any of the girls who'd like a little *more* Irish in them?" – Philip Lynott. The son of Brazilian and Irish parents, Lynott didn't always have his 'right on'

house in order, but there can be no denying that the leather-trousered, mirrored bass-wielding frontman was to many the epitome of a rock star. Thin Lizzy's unique combination of heavy rock power, linked with an irresistible passion for 'the song', set them apart from many of the more technically enraptured musos of the '70s.

Lynott formed the group in his native Dublin in 1969 with schoolfriend and drummer Brian Downey. After toying with keyboards in a four-piece line-up, Lizzy settled on being a trio with Eric Bell on guitar – a man still to be seen playing gigs in numerous low-class London hostelries.

Lizzy caused something of a stir in their homeland which led to them being signed by the London-based Decca records label in 1970. The band immediately moved to London and released a self-titled debut in 1971, which was greeted with an overwhelming tide of apathy. Lizzy were looking conspicuously as if they were to be a heavy rock also-ran in a league of thoroughbreds when 'Tales From A Blue Orphanage' failed to attract attention. However, their skinny asses were saved by the unexpected success of the 'Whisky In The Jar' single in February of 1973. The tricky third album, 'Vagabonds Of The Western World', proved to be mightily tricky indeed and the band returned to Ireland with its proverbial tail between its legs. The bell tolled for guitarist Eric, who cut his losses while Lizzy recruited Gary Moore as his replacement. The virtuoso guitarist with the rather unfortunately defaced visage, hung around for a mere four months before buggering off to join tosh jazz rockers Coloseum II. Lynott recruited Andy Gee and John Cann (currently residing in the 'Where are they now?' file) to fulfil touring commitments, before finally employing the talents of guitarists Brian Robertson and Scott Gorham in June '74.

With a line-up finally stabilised, Lizzy signed a new deal with the Vertigo label in August of the same year, releasing 'Nightlife' to no reaction once again. Despite the public's crippling apathy, the band were beginning to show signs of real songwriting abilities, including a tear-jerking 'Still In Love With You' (featuring guest vocals from Frankie Miller) on the album.

With the band still running on empty, Lynott's fortunes took a turn for the worse when he contracted hepatitis. Just as well that the band's 'Fighting' album ('75) provided a glimmer of hope, charting at Number 60 in the UK.

PHIL LYNOTT of Thin Lizzy: a much-missed rock legend

July 1976 marked the time when the misfit Irishman and his group of hard-drinkin' hard rockers finally came of age. 'Jailbreak' proved to be the band's breakthrough release, staying in the UK album charts for a mammoth 50 weeks and going Gold in America. The band then provided a convincing double whammy with the release of the follow-up, 'Johnny The Fox'. No doubt the hard-won success encouraged the band to indulge in their passion for hard drinking, hard drugs and even harder women. Having a bit of a knock when the need arose wasn't off the agenda of extra-curricular activities either, which resulted in Robertson departing after cutting his hand in a night-club brawl. Moore filled Robbo's shoes and acquitted himself admirably in the drinking stakes before the itinerant Scot returned to record 'Bad Reputation', released in the summer of '77. Again, the album proved a convincing success with the UK and US charts crumbling under the weight of Lizzy's assault. Lynott was steadily etching himself as a performer of some versatility, the wild boy bravado masking a craftsman of no little sensitivity.

On the crest of a creative wave, the band released their *piece de resistance*, the double 'Live And Dangerous' in 1978, but found themselves having personnel problems yet again when Robertson quit, later to form Wild Horses, leaving the way clear for Moore to re-join the ranks yet again.

1979 saw the release of 'Black Rose (A Rock Legend)', the only Lizzy album to feature Moore as a full-time band member, a year after the success of his solo single, the perennial 'Parisienne Walkways', which had featured Lynott on guest vocals.

Trouble, however, followed the band with an unerring relentlessness, with Moore being sacked during a US tour. Allegedly, the man was so hacked off with the band's persistent drug abuse that he deliberately shunned a show, resulting in dismissal. In a particularly bizarre twist, Lizzy recruited erstwhile Slik and Rich Kids popster guitarist, Midge Ure, but he soon quit to join Ultravox. His replacement was the highly unexciting Snowy White.

Quite out of character with his brazenly birding ways, Lynott married Caroline Crowther, daughter of the master of the TV quiz show, Leslie Crowther, and immediately set to work on his first solo album, 'Solo In Soho', released in May '80.

Back with his day job, Lynott and Lizzy released 'Chinatown' (October '80) and caused something of a minor furore with the single, 'Killer On The Loose', deemed tactless at the height of the Yorkshire Ripper killings.

1981's 'Renegade' marked the last appearance of Snowy White, who left for a solo career (which peaked with the unremarkable 'Bird Of Paradise') and the feeling was that Lizzy needed something remarkable to revive a flagging career. It arrived in the form of flaxen-haired John Sykes, guitarist in the NWOBHM act The Tygers Of Pan Tang. Lynott seemed distracted from his main priority. 1982's solo effort, 'The Philip Lynott Album' stunned the world with its eccentric title and failure to chart.

Sykes, however, provided Lizzy with exactly the right impetus, and when 'Thunder And Lightning' was released in March of 1983, the rejuvenation of Lizzy (since 1981, also featuring keyboardist Darren Wharton) seemed complete.

Considering that the aforementioned album had injected some venom back into Lizzy, there were more than a few raised eyebrows when Lynott split the group for good in August of 1983, cheifly because Gorham and he needed to dry-out and clean-up...

Thin Lizzy released a second live double, 'Life' (the *Oirish* for 'Live'!), as a posthumous gesture in 1984. It featured a fourth side of encores which highlighted all the guitarists who had recorded with the band.

Following the demise of Lynott's great love, it felt as if he was drifting aimlessly without any real musical focus. His new act, Grand Slam, which initially also featured Downey, failed to secure a deal and a solo single, 'Nineteen' didn't ignite any long-term sparks.

Rumours of Lynott's prevailing ill-health, which had been circulating for some time, finally became apparent when he lapsed into a coma after overdosing. Philip Lynott died eight days later, on January 4, 1986 of liver, kidney and heart failure and pneumonia., leaving a legacy of life lived hard and music played in the same uncompromising fashion.

Philip Lynott: The Black Rose – A Rock Legend.

IN THEIR OWN WORDS...

"They'd had one sort of fluke hit with 'Whisky In The Jar' but by the time I joined that was already a couple of years old. Everybody was considering them one-hit wonders and people were actually advising me not to join the band." – Scott Gorham, Kerrang! 9, February 11-24, 1982

"I am egotistical, that I won't deny. I do think I'm good – in fact I know I'm good – but I know that I don't appeal to everybody." – Phil Lynott, Kerrang! 20, July 15-28, 1982

"They were a little mellow and even they themselves agreed. I think they got into a rut and I've come along and given them a boot up the arse. It sounds good now." – John Sykes, Kerrang! 27, October 21-November 3, 1982

"I'm still a bit sick Lizzy's ending really... but you can't hold people together by force." – Phil Lynott, Kerrang! 49, August 25-September 7, 1983

"I always wondered what some of those Lizzy songs would sound like if you took them into the studio today and re-mixed them... but there's no point. They are what they are and they were what they were. It was a real different time." – Scott Gorham, Kerrang! 326, February 2, 1991

"Lizzy was absolutely Phil Lynott's whole life, no doubt about it. That's what makes me feel that maybe his death was a little bit my fault." – Scott Gorham, Kerrang! 326, February 2, 1991

THIN LIZZY

ALBUMS

THIN LIZZY *(Decca, 1971 – KK) Anonymous, eponymous debut which hasn't weathered the storms of time too healthily...*

SHADES OF A BLUE ORPHANAGE *(Decca, 1972 – KK) A record possibly more intriguing for its title than its musical output...*

VAGABONDS OF THE WESTERN WORLD *(Decca, 1973 – KKK) The seeds of the band's future success were being gradually sown, and the songwriting talents of Lynott are more apparent here...*

NIGHTLIFE *(Vertigo, 1974 – KKK) Not the classic that the new record label had been hoping for, but worthy of casual investigation...*

FIGHTING *(Vertigo, 1975 – KKKK) The band's style is finally thoroughly defined here, best highlighted in standouts 'Rosalie' (by Bob Seger), 'Suicide' and 'Wild One'...*

JAILBREAK *(Vertigo, 1976 – KKKKK) Possibly the finest example of Lizzy's lads-together bonhomie, exemplified no better than the 'one fist in the air, one hand on the glass' anthem, 'The Boys Are Back In Town'...*

JOHNNY THE FOX *(Vertigo, 1976 – KKKKK) Yet another full-on Lizzy opus, revelling in the band's delicate match of Metal and melody. Standout cut: 'Don't Believe A Word'...*

BAD REPUTATION *(Vertigo, 1977 – KKKK) Crazy album title, crazy guys. 'Dancin' In The Moonlight' has proved to be one of Lizzy's most enduring anthems...*

LIVE AND DANGEROUS *(Vertigo, 1978 – KKKKK) Indisputably right up there amongst the all-time classic live albums of all time, mate!*

BLACK ROSE – A ROCK LEGEND *(Vertigo, 1979 – KKKK) Notable for the excellent guitar performance from Gary Moore and certainly possessed of an even more Celtic feel than previous releases.*

CHINATOWN *(Vertigo, 1980 – KKK) Not the most consistent of Lizzy albums, but still possessed of some dynamite monster boogie...*

RENEGADE *(Vertigo, 1981 – KKK) A slightly more introspective album, reflecting Snowy White's more mellow style of play...*

THUNDER AND LIGHTNING *(Vertigo, 1983 – KKKKK) "This album reeks with an enthusiasm and sweet arrogance that can only come from a collective who have found a new source of strength to unleash on unsuspecting lobes." – Kerrang! 34, January 27-February 9, 1983*

LIFE *(Vertigo, 1983 – KKKKK) "This is undeniably a superb collection of some of Lizzy's finest songs performed by, arguably, their greatest ever line-up with John Sykes stamping his furious authority over many of the numbers." – Kerrang! 57, December 15-28, 1984*

DEDICATION – THE VERY BEST OF THIN LIZZY *(Vertigo, 1991 – KKKK) "As the title suggests, 'Dedication...' is a compact jukebox. A safe, sensible collection that is open to only the meanest of nit-picking." – Kerrang! 326, February 2, 1991*

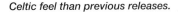

.38 SPECIAL

USA, six-piece (1977-present)

FRONTED BY Donnie Van Zandt, brother of Lynyrd Skynyrd singers Ronnie and Johnny, .38 Special added mainstream AOR numbers – such as the big 1980 US hit 'Hold On Loosely' – to the Southern-style boogie and twin drum attack they were more famous for. Up to 1982 and their fifth album 'Special Forces' this worked well enough but gradually the AOR took over and the band lost direction. In '88, the band lost guitarist Don Barnes, one drummer, and their career-long deal with A&M. The time had clearly come for a rethink and come 'Bone Against Steel' (Charisma, '91), doubtless inspired by the return of Lynyrd Skynyrd, .38 Special had returned to their roots if not former glories.

Recommended album:

WILD-EYED SOUTHERN BOYS *(A&M, 1980 – KKKK)*

THOR

USA, solo artist (1978-1985)
UNBELIEVABLY COMIC freak-show featuring
Thor as a former Adonis turned Metal
muscleman, remembered not for his lame
anthems but for blowing up hot water bottles
and bending iron bars with his teeth on stage.
Aided and abetted by his buxom wife,
Rusty/Pantera.
Definitely worth a laugh:
ONLY THE STRONG *(Roadrunner, 1985 – KKK)*

THUNDER

UK, five-piece (1989-present)
THUNDER WERE formed in 1989 by the unholy
triumvirate of vocalist Danny Bowes, guitarist
Luke Morley and drummer Gary 'Harry' James.
All three had served time in cheesy pop/Metal
combo Terraplane, finally throwing in the towel
after falling decisively between two stools.

Thunder displayed a far rootsier appeal,
resulting in the band finally finding their niche
somewhere between Bad Company and British
music hall (James occasionally feels the need to
fly across the stage in tutu and green fright wig,
or sing Frank Sinatra songs). Debut album,
'Back Street Symphony', went Gold in the UK as
a direct result of constant touring, but follow-
up, 'Laughing On Judgement Day', also failed to
unlock the States. Original bassist Mark 'Snake'
Luckhurst left the band under somewhat
acrimonious circumstances in 1993, to be
replaced by former Great King Rat bassist
Mikael Hoglund. Luckhurst is went on to the
Coverdale Page touring unit.
Thunderously recommended album:
BACK STREET SYMPHONY *(EMI, 1990 –
KKKK)*
LAUGHING ON JUDGEMENT DAY *(EMI, 1992
– KKKKK)*

Johnny THUNDERS

USA, living wreck (1976-1991)
AFTER SELF-STYLED svengali Malcolm
McLaren spray-painted a jaded and label-less
New York Dolls red on red, guitarist and
drummer Johnny Thunders and Jerry Nolan
slipped outta their garish patent leather strides
and formed The Heartbreakers. More wham-
bam and less careering than the 'Dolls, by late
'76 Thunders and his troupe were in Britain and
sucked into the tail of the Punk comet. Johnny
became merely another player in the game he
had practicaly created, the Pistols cleaning up
because McLaren utilised what he had learned
from his stint with the 'Dolls. Thunders
eventually went solo, releasing the guest-star
pregnant and wondrous 'So Alone' album – the
one true constructive testament to the talent of
the guitarist/songwriter/vocalist he recorded
post-Dolls. Thunders was an addict. He died in
New Orleans on April 22, 1991.
Recommended album:
SO ALONE *(Sire/Warner Bros, 1978 – KKKKK)*

THUNDERSTICK

UK, idiot (1982-1986)
HILARIOUSLY CAMP NWOBHM-bred drum
clown whose days in Samson were followed by
a dreadful solo career featuring a succession of
ropey leading ladies and Hack Metal sidemen.
Worth looking at the cover and weeping:
BEAUTY AND THE BEAST *(Thunderbolt, 1984
– K)*

TIGERTAILZ

UK, four-piece (1984-1993)
FORMED IN Cardiff, Wales in 1984, although the
concept really didn't slip fully into gear until the
duo of bassist Pepsi Tate and guitarist Jay
Pepper teamed up with the vocalist Steevi
Jaimz and American drummer Ace Finchum
who had previously worked together in post
NWOBHM act Treason and Mötley Crüe clones
Crash KO.

Big on image and not short of ideas Tigertailz
released a self-financed EP in early 1987. By the
time they were signed to Music For Nations and
cut the 'Young And Crazy' album later in the
year, they had become a popular draw on the
UK club circuit. They parted company with the
human dynamo Jaimz in 1988 . "He IS Mr Rock
'N' Roll", Tate was quoted at the time, "but

unfortunately it can conflict with what you're trying to do as a band."

Jaimz, who went on to form his own band St Jaimz, was replaced by former Rankelson bassist Kim Hooker with whom Tigertailz went on to record the 'Bezerk' album, although eventually parting company with Music For Nations and striving to break free of the constraints of being a Glam band with progressively heavier demo material.

With Ace Finchum leaving the band in early 1992, Tate (left), Pepper and Hooker finally decided to knock the whole concept of Tigertailz on the head, taking a year off to work on new material, eventually reappearing in 1993 under the handle of Wazbones and an interesting Thrash/Industrial/ pop combination.

Recommended albums:
YOUNG AND CRAZY *(Music For Nations, 1987 – KKK)*
BEZERK *(Music For Nations, 1990 – KKK)*

TOOL

USA, four-piece (1990-present)
FORMED BY guitarist Adam Jones and singer Maynard James Keenan after the pair met in LA, Tool work up an intense storm of twisted Metal that was displayed starkly and viciously on their excellent debut EP 'Opiate', released through RCA/Zoo Entertainment in '92. Dubbed by some as 'hatecore', Tool have been compared to the likes of Helmet and the Rollins Band – Henry Rollins appears on the follow-up to 'Opiate', the full-length LP 'Undertow', released April '93.

Recommended album:
UNDERTOW *(Zoo Entertainment, 1993 – KKKK)*

TORANAGA

UK, four-piece (1982-1991)
WAKEFIELD WARRIORS with a Manowar-esque approach to Power Metal, Toranaga fell victim to the usual chain of events between major labels and British Thrash bands. The lads were dropped after just one album – perhaps they should have stayed in their original Peaceville Records fold...

Semi-recommended album:
GOD'S GIFT *(Chrysalis, 1990 – KKK)*

Bernie TORMÉ

Ireland, guitarist (1976-present)
IRISH-BORN Tormé came to London in 1976 to form first Scrapyard, then his own Bernie Tormé Band. His rough-edged, heavily-distorted sound found favour with the burgeoning punk movement, but it wasn't long before Metalheads took interest in his OTT playing style, including a certain Ian Gillan; Tormé appeared on the Gillan albums; 'Mr Universe', 'Glory Road' and 'Future Shock'. In early '82 Tormé went on tour with Ozzy Osbourne as a temporary replacement for Randy Rhoads, a partnership that lasted two weeks. Tormé then returned to his own band, Electric Gypsies. They disbanded, and the guitarist linked up with ex-Girl vocalist Phil Lewis under the name Tormé, but success never followed.

Recommended album:
LIVE *(Zebra, 1982 – KKK)*

TORONTO

Canada, six-piece (1980-1985)
AN ACCOMPLISHED and relatively boring mini-Heart, Toronto were never able to capitalise on the vocal strength of Holly Woods and drifted aimlessly around the Canadian clubs in search of a hit single. Eventually Lee Aaron took over the mantle of Most Promising Canadian Bird and Toronto were history.

Recommended album:
HEAD ON *(Solid Gold, 1981 – KKKK)*

TRAPEZE

UK, three/four/five-piece (1971-1982)
BEST WORK recorded with the line-up of Glenn Hughes (vocals/bass), Mel Galley (guitar/vocals) and Dave Holland (drums) – but began as a quintet signed to the Moody Blues' Threshold label and ended as a quartet featuring Pete

Goalby (vocals). At their best, Trapeze pioneered some amazingly powerful funky hard rock but – despite various attempts to reform over the last 10 years – will always be remembered for its ex-members going on to bigger things: Hughes joining Deep Purple and enjoying some solo success, Galley going to Whitesnake and Holland warming the Judas Priest drumstool.

Recommended album:
YOU ARE THE MUSIC... WE'RE JUST THE BAND (Threshold, 1972 – KKKKK)

Pat TRAVERS

Canada, guitarist (1976-present)
LONG-PAST-his-prime axeman who came to fame after he came to London in 1976. Polydor signed him up and he made nine albums which gradually deteriorated from bluesy, hard rock 'n' roll to something altogether less impressive. His label noticed this too and dropped him after sales bottomed out on 'Hot Shots' ('84). With him on all albums was the very excellent (but very non-rock 'n' roll) bassist Mars Cowling plus people like Nicko McBrain – drums on 'Putting It Straight' ('77) – Pat Thrall and Tommy Aldridge – guitars and drums respectively on 'Heat In The Street' ('78) and 'Go For What You Know – Live' ('79). But sadly when he wrote the song 'Snortin' Whiskey, Drinkin Cocaine' in 1978, Travers dropped a sizeable hint about his future career prospects.

Recommended (second) album:
MAKIN' MAGIC (Polydor, 1976 – KKKK)

TREPONEM PAL

France, five-piece (1988-present)
MAD AGITATORS and proud of it, Treponem Pal are the only European band worth going to see. Led by a shortsighted, slaphead conscientious objector with manky ratlocks, the band's three albums to date have been refreshing and challenging. The live show is a gruelling exorcism at extreme volume, a psycho-sexual baptism of mud.

In 1992, Marco and Michael were temporarily drafted into the high-profile Ministry line-up for that year's Lollapalooza tour, and Treponem Pal are a name to drop within the precious Industrial Metal circle.

Recommended albums if you're not after a shag:
TREPONEM PAL (Roadracer, 1989 – KKKKK)
AGGRAVATION (Roadracer, 1991 – KKKK)

TRESPASS

UK, five-piece (1976-1983)
NWOBHM HEROES from the unlikely Metal hotbed of Suffolk who made a big impression with the absolutley spiffing 'One Of These Days' which inspired one Lars Ulrich to join their official fan club. Er, that's about it really. Later metamorphosed into the spectacularly unremarkable Blue Blud.

Recommended single:
ONE OF THESE DAYS (Trial, 1979 – KKKKK)

TRIUMPH

Canada, three-piece (1975-1988)
SECOND ONLY to Rush in terms of international stardom, Triumph once dominated the North American arena circuit with their super-commercial rock anthems and lavish stage shows. Guitarist Rik Emmett left in 1988 to work with Lee Aaron and he has since become something of a spokesman for the Canadian music industry.

Recommended album:
NEVER SURRENDER (RCA, 1984 – KKK)

TROUBLE

USA, five-piece (1979-present)
CHICAGO SABBATH fanatics who debuted with a track on 'Metal Massacre IV' (Metal Blade, '83). The same label put out three so-so records plagued by over-indulgences with drugs but which attracted the attention of fellow Sabs-nut Rick Rubin. In 1990, he produced and released their eponymous fourth album on his Def American label which was an improvement on their earlier works but paled into insignificance (almost) alongside the awesome follow-up 'Manic Frustration'.

Line-up of Eric Wagner (vocals), Rick Wartell

and Bruce Franklin (guitars), Ron Holzner (bass) and Barry Stern (drums, ex-Zoetrope) is definitely one to be watched.

Highly recommended album:

MANIC FRUSTRATION (Def American, 1992 – KKKKK)

TRUST

France, four/five-piece (1979-1992)

A BAND out of time, Trust were the first Metal act to acknowledge the influence of punk in their music. Fronted by the balding yet barbed Bernard Bonvoisin, the group pumped out furiously spiky riffs which added real musical fire to the vocalist's highly political lyrics. Writing songs about jailed killers did little to endear Trust to the French authorities, but the country's disaffected youth lapped up such albums as 'Repression' and 'Marche Ou Creve' (released in the UK as 'Savage').

Iron Maiden's Steve Harris brought the band to the UK to support Maiden on their 'Killers' tour in 1981, but Bonvoisin's attempts to sing in English – even with translations by Sham 69's Jimmy Pursey – didn't cut *la moutarde*. Trust's drummer, Nicko McBrain, joined Iron Maiden in 1983, with erstwhile Irons sticksman Clive Burr heading the other way for the 'Trust' album.

In 1989, following a lengthy hiatus, the band returned with a double-live set recorded in Paris, but the famed Trust anger and passion had all but expired.

Recommended album:

MARCHE OU CREVE (Epic, 1981 – KKKKK)

Joe Lynn TURNER

USA, singer (1977-present)

MADE FOUR albums with Fandango (1977-1980) before hooking up with Ritchie Blackmore in Rainbow. Upon leaving Rainbow, he secured a solo deal with Elektra for his 1985 AOR-mungous 'Rescue You' album, then went on to work with Yngwie Malmsteen, before rejoining Blackmore (unbelievably) as Deep Purple singer in '90. Since that sojourn ended, he has been threatening another solo album but what everyone really wants to know is: does he wear a wig? The answer is yes, because he suffers from alopecia.

Recommended album:

RESCUE YOU (Elektra, 1985 – KKKK)

TWISTED SISTER

USA, five-piece (1981-1988)

ORIGINALLY A New York freak/joke act, playing strip clubs and places equally salubrious, Twisted Sister 'refined' their anything-goes presentation into a macho Ugly Sister Metal assault. With this outrageous image combined with the mile-wide mouth and in-your-face arrogance of frontman Dee Snider, their impact in Britain was instant. Their first full album 'Under The Blade' ('82), produced by UFO man Pete Way, was a heady mix of 'real man' Metal and pop-tinged anthems. It wasn't perfect, but they were onto something. And after their manic appearance on TV's 'The Tube', Atlantic Records were down on the Twisted ones with their cheque book like a ton of bricks. Snider & Co were happening, and their home country thought Twisted Sister were a British act! The 'You Can't Stop Rock 'N' Roll' elpee in '83, an appearance at Castle Donington that same year, and then their second Atlantic release 'Stay Hungry' ('84), and the Sisters unstoppable. Yet the poorly received 'Come Out And Play' ('85) found our boys taking an abrupt U-turn in the opposite direction to the signpost marked 'popularity'. No one could quite explain it, but thus are the mysteries of rock 'n' roll...

Recommended album:

YOU CAN'T STOP ROCK 'N' ROLL (Atlantic, 1983 – KKKK)

TYGERS OF PAN TANG

UK, five-piece (1978-1987)

ABOVE AVERAGE NWOBHM warriors who somehow evaded the big time, but did once boast in their ranks flash sod guitar-slinger John Sykes (later to join Thin Lizzy), original (non) singer Jess Cox, second singer Jon Deverill, and one-time Penetration guitarist, Fred Purser.

Recommended album

THE CAGE (MCA, I982 – KKKK)

UFO

UK, four/five-piece (1969-present)
UNDOUBTEDLY ONE of the best hard rock bands the UK has ever produced but spent far too much time enjoying themselves to secure the kind of respect, not to mention bank balance, that should – by rights – have set them up for life (peerages).

Their origins were dodgy, to say the least, beginning in August '69 as the quartet of Phil Mogg (vocals), Pete Way (bass), Andy 'No Neck' Parker (drums) and Mick Bolton (guitar), playing extended jams which later could most kindly be described as space-rock. This phase, wholly unremarkable if not for what was to follow, lasted until January '72 and produced three very amusing albums (but for all the wrong reasons): 'UFO', 'UFO 2 – Flying' and 'Live In Japan'.

Bolton quit to be replaced (for eight months)

by Larry Wallis (ex-Pink Fairies and later in the original Motörhead line-up) then Bernie Marsden (of Babe Ruth, later Whitesnake) for another eight months until June '73 when the band went to tour Germany. They were supported there by the Scorpions featuring a teenage Michael Schenker. He deputised for Marsden when the latter failed to show up at one gig... and promptly kept the job.

With Schenker in tow, the band signed to Chrysalis and began a stream of brilliantly crafted hard rock albums with 'Phenomenon' ('74) featuring 'Rock Bottom' and one of the greatest guitar solos of all time. The same line-up recorded 'Force It' ('75) but had been augmented by a keyboard player – Danny Peyronnel (ex-Heavy Metal Kids) on 1976's 'No Heavy Pettin''. But Peyronnel didn't like touring and so was replaced by Paul 'Kipper' Raymond, ex-Savoy Brown, on keyboards and rhythm guitar. Raymond really filled UFO's sound out, giving freer rein to both the songwriting arrangements and Schenker's stunning lead work. Their first album together, 'Lights Out' ('77), was arguably their finest – but 'Obsession' ('78) could lay almost as strong a claim.

Together, the records helped UFO reach a peak in terms of ticket sales both at home and in the States. This success, coupled with the band's naturally excessive personalities, led to an escalation in alcohol and drug consumption – not to mention some

UFO (Phil Mogg and Pete Way): high flying wind-up merchants

IN THEIR OWN WORDS (HIC)...

"We have to keep an eye on Neil Carter, because we never know what he's going to wear next. You should see one thing he's got – talk about Star Trek! It's covered in ruffles and things..."
– Paul Chapman, Kerrang! 10, February 25-March 10, 1982

"There's been enough personnel changes (but) the crunch never actually came until after Pete Way left. It's one of those points where you're faced with going on a downhill path – and no one wants to do that." – Phil Mogg explaining the decision to quit (!), Kerrang! 40, April 21-May 4, 1983

"I think it's time people knew: we weren't the blokes that made Michael Schenker mad. He made us mad! We were the sensible ones. When I saw two Kentucky policeman escort him off a balcony, goosestepping, I thought, I've arrived!" – Pete Way, Kerrang! 356, August 31, 1991

"We'll support Thunder, I don't care! I dare anyone to follow us and 'Doctor, Doctor', 'Lights Out', 'Love To Love' and 'Rock Bottom'..." – Pete Way, Kerrang! 356, August 31, 1991

"I've got no time to be serious. Life's too short." – Phil Mogg, Kerrang! 386, April 4, 1992

UFO

of the wildest after-show activities known to man, beast or Mötley Crüe. Hotels would welcome the band cordially, then write their names on a blacklist after they checked out. Backstage riders would disappear faster than Linford Christie out of a starting block... and numerous dodgy characters would follow the band around to supply them with nefarious chemical stimulants. It all seemed like a whirlwind of fun but eventually the craziness led to paranoia, rows and eventually to sporadic performances. Schenker, the brunt of most of Mogg and Way's wind-ups, cracked first,

bowing out in November '78 after a stunning live album, 'Strangers In The Night' (released 1979), had been recorded in the UFO hotbed Chicago.

Schenker's replacement was mad Welshman Paul 'Tonka' Chapman (ex-Lone Star) who had also drifted through the UFO ranks a couple of times earlier, even playing alongside the Schenk' during much of '74. On a good night, Tonka (nicknamed after the supposedly indestructible kids' toys) could play as well as his German predecessor, but – as he could also party just as hard – he seldom did. Nevertheless, he was good in the studio, as can be heard on his debut with the band, 'No Place To Run' ('80). After that, 'Kipper' Raymond grew tired of Mogg, Way and the whole circus and was replaced by Neil Carter, ex-Wild Horses. Carter had a perm and an even larger nose than his predecessor so was subjected to far more abuse – but he survived three albums: the barnstormer 'The Wild, The Willing And The Innocent' ('81), the very under-rated 'Mechanix' ('82) and the patchy-to-sad 'Making Contact' ('83). The band fell apart during the recording of the latter with Way the first to jump ship, leaving Chapman to play most of the bass. Paul Gray (ex-Damned and Eddie And The Hot Rods) joined for the tour but it was far from good. Mogg, was often too out-of-it to play soundchecks and not much better come showtime. Finally, after some gigs in Greece, the band knocked it on the head in April '83 and a legend died, not with a bang but a whimper. A bizarre compilation, 'Headstone' – featuring tracks by some member's other bands and four live cuts recorded at Hammersmith on the final tour – was the last nail in the coffin.

In all sensible universes, that would have been it. But the universe occupied by Phil Mogg dictated that in 1985 he should keep the name UFO going with a succession of sidemen – including bassist Billy Sheehan at one point. Gray was still there for 'Misdemeanour' ('85) alongside Japanese guitarist Atomik Tommy M and Jim Simpson (drums, ex-Magnum). But a mini-album of demos called 'Ain't Misbehavin'' ('88) brought the name of UFO to an all-time low and finally persuaded Mogg that the band couldn"t continue as it was.

In 1990, a knock at his door from Pete Way persuaded him of a better idea. Legend has it that Pete came for the evening and stayed six weeks. It's probably untrue but fact and fiction get pretty blurred in UFO circles. Plans to work together were just for fun initially, but eventually a band was formed with the addition of Clive Edwards (drums, ex-Wild Horses) and Laurence Archer (guitar, ex-Stampede) and it seemed quite natural to call it UFO. The line-up re-emerged with 'High Stakes And Dangerous Men' ('92) and a tour that was well received but marred (slightly) by Mogg and Way's continued predilection for the ol' devil juice...

After the dust settled, two momentous decisions were taken. First, that if UFO were to continue, they should contact and attempt to work again with Messrs Parker, Raymond and Schenker. Second, that if UFO were to continue, Messrs Mogg and Way should stop drinking. As of 1993, the impossible had happened – and whilst executives from Carlsberg watched share prices with more anxiety than usual – contractual negotiations with ex-members of the band proved the only stumbling block to a serious reformation. In the meantime, check the record racks for most of the above plus various other live sets and compilations...

ALBUMS

UFO (Decca, 1971 – K)
UFO 2 – FLYING (Decca, 1971 – KK)
LIVE IN JAPAN (Decca, 1972 – KKK)
All three of the above are prone to extended bouts of rambling, bluesy 'space rock' jamming-type numbers. Now described by Way as "best forgotten", they did at least produce the spectacularly titled, 'The Coming Of Prince Kajuku' and a blistering cover of Eddie Cochran's 'C'Mon Everybody' on the latter.
PHENOMENON (Chrysalis, 1974 – KKK)
Stunning in places – 'Doctor Doctor' and 'Rock Bottom' – but overall only a pointer to the glories to come...
FORCE IT (Chrysalis, 1975 – KKKK) Blistering

hard rock, raw and punchy songs, short and very much to-the-point...
NO HEAVY PETTIN' (Chrysalis, 1976 – KKK) Apart from 'Natural Thing', the songs are a little too dominated by Peyronnel's keyboards. Still a good effort, though...
LIGHTS OUT (Chrysalis, 1977 – KKKKK) An indispensable tour-de-force. Contains title-track, 'Too Hot To Handle, 'Love To Love'. Nuff said...
OBSESSION (Chrysalis, 1978 – KKKKK) Another masterpiece. Includes 'Only You Can Rock Me', 'Cherry'. Schenker's last studio LP before forming MSG...
STRANGERS IN THE NIGHT (Chrysalis, 1979 – KKKKK) Seminal double live. Storming performances in front of a rabid Chicagoans...
NO PLACE TO RUN (Chrysalis, 1980 – KKKK) Lightweight production by George 'Beatles' Martin but songwriting as strong as ever. First to feature Paul Chapman...
THE WILD, THE WILLING AND THE INNOCENT (Chrysalis, 1981 – KKKKK) Probably Mogg's finest hour: stunning, almost Springsteen-esque songs and brilliant arrangements...
MECHANIX (Chrysalis, 1982 – KKKK) Hard-as-nails rock with some beautiful lighter moments. Often overlooked, but unjustly so...
MAKING CONTACT (Chrysalis, 1982 – KKK) "Whatever happens, UFO have emerged with a powerful salab of vinyl..." – Kerrang! 35, February 10-23, 1983
HEADSTONE (Chrysalis, 1983 – KK) Baffling compilation to be avoided except by completists...
MISDEMEANOUR (Chrysalis, 1985 – KK) "The new UFO is a show that should run and run..." (!) – Kerrang! 107, November 14-27, 1985
AIN'T MISBEHAVIN' (FM/Revolver, 1988 – K) "This has done the enigmatic singer no favours..." – Kerrang! 181, April 2, 1988
HIGH STAKES AND DANGEROUS MEN (Essential, 1992 – KKK) "A long way from being the kind of limp, half-hearted affair that regroupings after a length 'sabbatical' often throw up." – Kerrang! 386, April 4, 1992

UGLY KID JOE

USA, five-piece (1990-present)
THE BAND who at first seemed to be something
of a goofy gimmick, what with their name itself
being a parodoxical send-up of bad Crüe-
clones, Pretty Boy Floyd. And even the
irritatingly catchy smash hit 'Everything About
You' from their 'Ugly As They Wanna Be' EP
('92) reeked of a freak one-hit-wonder novelty
toon. But come their first fully-fledged album
'America's Least Wanted' (also '92) and it was a
hot poker up where the sun never shines for
their doubters, as UKJ proved themselves a
rock band of unconsidered versatility. Not to
mention they've accumulated a sizeable
following of baseball-cap-wearing, sidewalk-
surfing little upstarts.
Recommended non-Satanic album:
AMERICA'S LEAST WANTED (Mercury, 1992 –
KKKK)

UNCLE SAM

USA, four-piece (1985-present)
PRE-GRUNGE and outrageously underrated
early Alice Cooper/Stooges-fuelled garage
gargoyles... perhaps more infamous for their
day jobs as Rochester, New York milkmen...
Recommended album:
FOURTEEN WOMEN, FIFTEEN DAYS
(Comminique, 1993 – KKKK)

URIAH HEEP

UK, five-piece (1970-present)
FORMED BY moustachioed guitarist Mick

''Appy Days' Box, a man blessed with the kind
of dogged never-say-die determination that, if it
could have been transformed into songwriting
talent, would have made Uriah Heep one of the
biggest bands in the world today.

Instead, they are a once very good band now
woefully unaware that their sell-by date is so far
behind them it would take a reasonably skilled
palaentologist several months to uncover. To
save time, let's just say it was in 1973, one tour
after the release of the magnificently raucous
double album, 'Uriah Heep Live!', recorded one
steamy Friday night in their hometown of
Birmingham and featuring the classic line-up of
Box plus David Byron (vocals), Ken Hensley
(keyboards/guitar), Lee Kerslake (drums) and
Gary Thain (bass).

Tragically, booze and drugs killed Byron (in
'85, nine years after leaving the band) and Thain
(in '75). Sadly, after '73 Heep soldiered on, with
a plethora of different line-ups, usually writing
only two or three good songs per album and
only rarely coming close to their classic early
albums like 'Look At Yourself' ('71), 'Demons
And Wizards' ('72) or 'Magician's Birthday' ('72)
– records which earned them the unfair tag of 'a
poor man's Deep Purple'. Today, over 20 Heep
albums languish in the racks whilst the band
play to vast crowds in places no other bands
visit. A definite case of when they were good,
they were very very good, but when they were
bad, they didn't know when to stop...
Recommended album:
URIAH HEEP LIVE! (Bronze, 1973 – KKKKK)

Steve VAI

USA, guitarist (1981-present)

BY HIS late teens, Long Island resident Steve Vai had already turned his precocious talent to writing full orchestral pieces for guitar, trading licks with his mentor and best buddy Joe Satriani. At 18, Vai became the youngest-ever member of the Frank Zappa ensemble, staying for 15 albums and four years, before leaving and recording his debut solo effort 'Flex-Able'. He followed this with a stint in Alcatraz, replacing the departed Yngwie J Malmsteen, before hooking up with Johnny Lydon for the PiL LP 'Album'. Then came an appearance as Satan's own guitar-slinger (!) in the film 'Crossroads', before signing on as David Lee Roth's right-hand man for two LPs, 'Eat 'Em And Smile' and 'Skyscraper'. In '89, Vai deputised for injured guitarist Adrian Vandenberg on the Whitesnake LP 'Slip Of The Tongue' – then played alongside Vandenburg as replacement for Vivian Campbell. In 1990, Vai released his masterpiece 'Passion And Warfare', then began 1993 working with Jeff Beck drummer Terry Bozio.

Recommended album:

PASSION AND WARFARE *(Food For Thought, 1990 – KKKKK)*

VAIN

USA, five-piece (1985-1991)

WHEN FRONTMAN Davy Vain first showed his messily made-up face (and black-painted toenails!) on the scene, everyone sat up expectantly, waiting for something a little bit different. They got it.

With their 1989 album 'No Respect', Vain blasted away rock's cobwebs and boasted the kind of energy that makes you think they had at least five Shredded Wheat for breakfast.

The Vain live show that always springs to mind is the one they did with Skid Row at the Hammersmith Odeon. The combination of Davy Vain followed by Sebastian Bach was almost too much to take – and almost too bloody good to be true! The rest of the band – guitarists Danny West and James Scott, bassist Ashley Mitchell and drummer Tom Rickard – provided the perfect foil for dishy Davy's onstage antics, making Vain a pretty sure bet to put your money on. Sadly, the Vain dream was short-lived. They made a second album which their record company, Island, tragically rejected. Unsurprisingly, the band split up with Messrs Vain, Scott and Mitchell linking briefly with ex-Guns N' Roses drummer Steven Adler in the short-lived Roadcrew. Less surprisingly, Vain began plotting their reformation in 1993.

Recommended album:

NO RESPECT *(Island, 1989 – KKKKK)*

VAN HALEN

USA, four-piece (1975-present)

THE MIGHTY Van Halen were originally a covers band going under the lumbering handle of Mammoth and playing the Pasadena club circuit. In '74 the Halen brothers, guitarist Eddie and drummer Alex (who'd moved to Pasedena from their native Holland in '65) and their diagnosed hyperactive vocalist David Lee Roth, latched onto bassist Michael Anthony and by '75 humbly established themselves as the loudest and heaviest band in Los Angeles. They flirted with the idea of Rat Salade as a new monicker, but

"I feel like a shining example... but I'm not sure of what!"
– David Lee Roth, Kerrang! 61, February 9-22, 1984

"I told the truth in that Rolling Stone interview. David Lee Roth is an asshole! Look, we don't want to talk about the past..." – Eddie Van Halen, Kerrang! 110, December 26-January 8, 1986

"For me there never really was a pressure, we just jammed and made records, so for me it's that cut-and-dried simple. It's our life, we're musicians and we love making music."
– Eddie Van Halen, Kerrang! 345, June 15, 1991

"There are some old songs I don't wanna do, not because I don't like them – I think Van Halen have been a great group forever – but I just don't relate to some of the lyrics, and some of the registers they're sung in are too low for me."
– Sammy Hagar, Kerrang! 428, January 30, 1993

VAN HALEN

eventually settled on Van Halen (quite amazing really, taking into account Lee Roth's ego!). Kiss bassist Gene Simmon was impressed enough by a live set he caught at the Starwood in '76 to finance and produce a demo. Including 'Running With The Devil' and 'House Of Pain', this was touted around the majors, yet despite the Simmons connection no one took the bait. It wasn't till 1977 when Warner Bros producer Ted Templeman was likewise blown away by the Halen's (again at the Starwood), that our boys would get their big break. The Van Halen eponymous debut ('78) with its dazzling sense of dynamics was a breath of much-needed fresh air into a genre which was looking conspicuously dinosaur-ish alongside the excitement being generated around the rise of Punk Rock. Here was a science age Jim Dandy (he of Black Oak Arkansas) fronting a bunch of crazies who included one who would prove to be the most innovative guitarist since Hendrix! And more important than all that shit – they were fun! With consecutive releases, while their lethargic contemporaries plodded on with their banshee vocalising, pained grimaces, and dot-to-dot riffs, Van Halen were having a field day nukin' the HM cliché. Even Ozzy Osbourne admitted the Halen troupe wiped the floor with the Sabs when VH supported them in Britain in 1978!

In 1984, Van Halen released their sixth chart-busting album, '1984— (natch!). A single culled from the release, 'Jump', became their first UK hit (despite Warner Bros having a £6,000 fine imposed on them for hyping the disc!), which was not a bad thing considering it was the same year the band were to debut at the Donington Monsters Of Rock festival. Yet, as it turned out, things were not well in the Halen camp. Although it hadn't been officially announced, at the time of the release of Roth's solo EP in early '85 – Dave and Van Halen had definitely had a split of the acrimonious kind. The rock world was stunned to say the least! After all, wasn't Roth without Halen like a joke without the punchline?!

Van Halen's new punchline was soon revealed to be one-time Montrose man turned successful solo artist Sammy Hagar – ironically a verbal sparring partner of Roth's (although a long-time friend of the VH muso contingent, aside from 'playfully' belittling each other in the press, it seems Dave and Sammy had never actually met!). This seemed to be a more comfortable arrangement for Messrs Halen, Halen, and Anthony, as thereafter, unlike with Mr Charisma Roth hogging the spotlight, the individual members could share equal billing within the unit and concentrate on becoming a musical force as opposed to a vehicle for you-know-who's shenannigans. This comparatively sober arrangement paid off big time as the debut from this line-up '5150' ('86) nailed the US Number One position, with accompanying hit single action from the likes of 'Why Can't This Be Love' and 'Dreams'.

After a two year break from the live arena, Van Halen hit the US road in 1988 as part of the ambitious 'Monsters Of Rock' package which included Metallica, Scorpions, Dokken and Kingdom Come. Early into the tour (most gigs were, suprisingly, under-attended) 'Van Hagar' – as the press would 'affectionately' refer to 'em – released 'OU812' ('88). This opus also walked over any opposition in the US charts. And even in recession ravaged '91 the VH success chain-reaction continued as third album with Sam The Man, 'For Unlawful Carnal Knowledge' (better known as 'F.U.C.K'!), glided to the top of the pile, the accompanying tour raked in big bucks whilst every other bugger (including Roth!) was running at a financial loss. A live double album and 'souvenir' of their lengthy touring was released in '93, as Van Halen hit Britain for the

first time with Hagar and since their Donington appearance in '84. Obviously the VH machine can do no wrong. An undisputed supergroup.

ALBUMS
VAN HALEN (Warner Bros, 1978 – KKKKK) *Quite simply one of the greatest Heavy Rock albums of all time...*
VAN HALEN II (Warner Bros, 1979 – KKKK) *More swagger and less 'Metal' than the debut, but the new horizons it reveals are irresistible...*
WOMEN AND CHILDREN FIRST (Warner Bros, 1980 – KKKKK) *Big Rock! Big Fun!...*
FAIR WARNING (Warner Bros, 1981 – KKKK) *Lots of bounce, but with a gritty backbone...*
DIVER DOWN (Warner Bros, 1982 – KKKK) *"It's all good fun!" – Kerrang! 15, May 6-19, 1982*
1984 (Warner Bros, 1984 – KKKKK) *"Some truly classy melodic hard rock." – Kerrang! 61, February 9-22, 1984*
5150 (Warner Bros,1986 – KKK) *"This is a highly conservative, sanitised rock album..." – Kerrang! 118, April 17-30, 1986*
OU812 (Warner Bros, 1988 – KKKK) *"Loud, rude, dirty and very much a Van Halen album." – Kerrang! 190, June 4, 1988*
FOR UNLAWFUL CARNAL KNOWLEDGE (Warner Bros, 1991 – KKKK) *"Van Halen '91 have their steel wheels firmly on the rails, as their annoyingly incessant rhythms chug-along at mid-tempo..." – Kerrang! 346, June 22, 1991*
LIVE: RIGHT HERE, RIGHT NOW (Warner Bros, 1993 – KKKK) *'"Big, brash and colourful." – Kerrang! 431, February 20, 1993*

VANDENBURG

Holland, four-piece (1982-1985)
NAMED AFTER precocious guitar upstart, Adrian Vandenberg, the Euro commercial rockers soon found a home within the American legion of aspiring Melodic Metal ex-pats. The band had already fallen apart when Adrian jumped ship to join the far more lucrative position as David Coverdale's fall-guy in the revitalised Whitesnake corporation. *Recommended album:*
HEADING FOR A STORM (Atco, 1983 – KKK)

EDDIE VAN HALEN: *the most innovative guitarist since Hendrix – and good fun too!*

VARDIS

UK, three-piece (1979-1985)
YORKSHIRE-BASED boogie maestros
recognised for guitarist Steve Zodiac's snow-
white, flowing hair, a frenetic cover of
Hawkwind's 'Silver Machine' and an
unspectacular, four-album career.
Recommended live-in-Lowestoft album:
100MPH (Logo, 1980 – KKK)

VENOM

UK, three-piece (1980-present)
MANY BANDS have claimed responsibility (or
blame, depending on your view point) for the
Black Metal scene, but only one band truely
brought this festering wound of a genre to the
public's attention. Formed in Newcastle upon
Tyne by vocalist/bassist Cronos (rabid captor of
bestial malevolence), drummer Abaddon
(barbaric guardian to the seven gates of hell)
and guitarist Mantas (grand master of Hades
and Mayhem), Venom unleashed the debut
opus 'Welcome To Hell' on the world in 1981.

That in itself was rather remarkable, because
apart from the fact that it was a great album
recorded in just three days, the band had never
played any gigs! Indeed, since legend has it
they refused to support any others bands,
Venom played their debut UK gig at
Hammersmith Odeon on June 1, 1984 –
supported by Dumpy's Rusty Nuts! – a night
billed as the 'Seventh Date Of Hell'. The gig was
completely sold out, but perhaps more
surprising was the fact that the audience was a
mixture of Punks, Headbangers, Skinheads,
Bikers... all had come to witness this crazed
spectacle, making Venom one of the few Metal
bands of their time to attract such a crowd. Only
the likes of Hawkwind, Motörhead and Rose
Tattoo had previously attracted such diversity.

As you'd expect from such a brutally over-
the-top outfit, the show was a massively
overblown and seriously loud affair with flame
throwers going off on stage that could be felt
right at the back of the venue, and climaxing
with just about everything on stage being
smashed to pieces!

Venom were not in the least bit
subtle, and just to prove the point,
their second vinyl splatter was a
ridiculously menacing effort called
'Black Metal', featuring such dangerous
classics as 'Leave Me In Hell' and 'Raise The
Dead'. Perhaps the heaviest Heavy Metal record
of its time, its sleeve bore the legend "home
taping is killing music... so are Venom".

Stories circulated of the band attacking radio
DJs on air, dealing out demonic curses to any
unfortunates who had the misfortune to stand in
their path and of how Cronos allegedly used to
climb onto the roof of his house every full moon
and howl like a wolf. Barking mad, but
unfortunately their third vinyl excursion, 'At War
With Satan', which began with the dying chords
of the song of the same name that featured on
the previous album, showed far more musical
tendencies than would have been believed of
this raging three-piece. Venom were learning
how to write proper songs, and though '...Satan'
was a fine record, it lacked some of the band's
trademark unnecessary aggression, and thus
was far less memorable. 'Possessed' ('85) was a
slight return to form but still never touched the
previous lunacy that was
expected of them.

Pretty much the final nail in
the coffin, as far as many fans
are concerned, was
hammered home when
Cronos admitted that he
actually knew very little about
the black arts, and had *not*
sold his soul to the Horned
One from Downstairs. People
simply lost interest. And as
the style changed from hard
to harmless, eventually so did
Cronos himself when he left
to form an AOR band called,
er... Cronos.

Venom plodded on
aimlessly with a new vocalist
called Demolition Man but

alas, they were reduced to playing half-empty gigs in the clubs and never regained the former attitude that had made them so attractive in the first place. Later albums are not worth bothering with, but the fitness classes that Cronos now runs in Newcastle are highly recommended.

EARLY ALBUMS

WELCOME TO HELL (Neat, 1981 – KKKKK) "In the world invoked by Venom, virgins get the sacrificial chop, bodies are invariably headless (or at least limbless), teeth are ground with Black and Decker fury, and Satan always wins!" – Kerrang! 11, March 11-24, 1982
BLACK METAL (Neat, 1982 – KKKKK) Thoroughly obnoxious from start to finish. The classic Black Metal album of all time, which is just as well really considering the title...
AT WAR WITH SATAN (Neat, 1984 – KKKK) "Something of a disappointment, it's bottom line proving generally less secure tha the asphalted aft of it's predecessor." – Kerrang! 66, April 19-May 2, 1984
POSSESSED (Neat, 1985 – KKK) A slight return to the old Satanic form, but unlikely to scare your kid sister too much...

VENOM (Mantas): inventors of Black Metal, since turned crap

IN THEIR OWN WORDS...

"No one stands at the front and stays on their feet at the beginning of the set, no one. I don't care how big they are, they'll duck, and that's a challenge!" – Cronos, Kerrang! 29, November 18-December 2, 1982

"There's a local radio DJ called Alan Robson... Well, all I can say is, when we get rich enough to afford his hospital bills, we'll fucking have him!" – Cronos, Kerrang! 50, September 8-21, 1983

"Anything to do with Venom is there because we wanna be the biggest and the best, simple as that!" – Cronos, Kerrang! 94, May 16-29, 1985

"To put the record straight, the Devil was me dad and I have got long pointed horns!" – Cronos, Kerrang! 103, September 19-October 2, 1985

"Well fuck you, WE like it!" – Cronos, Kerrang! 161, November 7, 1987

"This band is fucking brain-melting. At Hammersmith we were recorded at 147 decibels onstage before they switched the PA on!" – Abaddon, Kerrang! 265, November 18, 1989

VENOM

VICIOUS RUMORS

USA, five-piece (1983-present)
LEGENDARY SAN-FRAN Power Metal band most noted for having featured axe-pert Vinnie Moore in their line-up for first album, 'Soldiers Of The Night'. Signed to major label, Atlantic, in 1989 and released two good hard rock albums. Dropped in 1992 due to lack of interest. Demos have been shopped but the signs are not good. *Recommended album:*
DIGITAL DICTATOR (Roadrunner, 1988 – KKKK)

Vinnie VINCENT INVASION

USA, four-piece (1985-1988)
DUMPED BY Kiss in 1984, Vinnie Vincent suddenly found himself with a Chrysalis deal and thus engaged one-time Journey and

Channel vocalist Robert Fleischman to join a rhythm section of bassist Dana Strum and drummer Bobby Rock. But after their debut album was released, Fleischman – the only one of the quartet not to adopt an outrageous Glam image – was replaced by former X-Cursion vocalist Mark Slaughter for live work.

After recording 'All Systems Go' ('88), Vincent, by then declared a bankrupt, was on his own. Slaughter and Strum went on to enjoy success with Slaughter and Rock, certainly no slouch either, joined Nelson. Vinnie has actually recorded a third album, with Fleischman once more, but it remains unreleased.

Recommended albums:
VINNIE VINCENT INVASION *(Chrysalis, 1986 – KKKK)*

VIO-LENCE

USA, five-piece (1985-present)
ARCHETYPAL BAY Area Thrashers. Mechanic Records had a good go at marketing Vio-lence, what with sending out free samplers and equipping a 10-inch single with an attractive see-thru bag of 'puke' – but they never really caught on (!). Their second album, 'Oppressing The Masses', never got a European release, due to a split between Megaforce and Atlantic Records, but Vio-lence nevertheless soldiered on. Both 'Oppressing...' and a new album, 'Nothing To Gain', were slated for 1993 release.

Recommended album:
OPPRESSING THE MASSES
(Megaforce/Atlantic, 1990 – KKKK)

VIXEN

USA, four-piece (1986-1991)
ASSEMBLED IN LA, the all-girl rockers will be principally remembered for looking like rock babes and playing like men. Big deal! Vixen were culled in an ever-strengthening mood of anti-glamour, the sight of drummer Roxy Petrucci perched on a motorbike drum-stool proving too ridiculous for the band to weather the storm. Despite the fact that the majority of their material was penned by outside writers, Vixen failed to score much in the way of commercial success.

Big girly rock album:
REV IT UP *(EMI, 1990 – KKK)*

VOIVOD

Canada, four-piece (1982-present)
CYBER-HEADED LOVERS of the bizarre, VoiVod have consistently baffled people with their convoluted sci-fi epics and dischordant musicality.

When they released their 'War And Pain' debut in 1984, they were more Punk than anything else, and the subsequent 'RRROOOAAARRR' opus contained the charming 'Fuck Off And Die'. After having created such peculiar albums as 'Nothingface' ('89) and 'Angel Rat' ('92), however, VoiVod are less obnoxious, if altogether stranger. What will they think of next?

Most recommended album:
KILLING TECHNOLOGY *(Noise, 1987 – KKKK)*

VOW WOW

Japan, four-piece (1976-1990)
FORMERLY BOW WOW, the band were forerunners of the futile Jap Metal invasion but noted primarily for recruiting journeyman bassist, Neil Murray, who was taller than the entire band put together.

Recommended funny accent comedy album:
SUPER LIVE *(Invitation, 1978 – K)*

WARFARE

UK, three-piece (1983-present)
LESS THAN totally-serious raucous act led by stickily-monikered vocalist/drummer Evo. Have released a gargantuan six albums to date, most interesting of which, 'Hammer Horror', was funded by the gore-geous Hammer film house. Lemmy contributed to second album, 'Metal Anarchy', but the band remains a curio.
Recommended album:
CRESCENDO OF REFLECTIONS *(Kraze, 1992 – KKK)*

WARRANT

USA, five-piece (1987-present)
IN THE slipstream of Poison, Warrant hooked up with Ohio-born drummer-turned-singer/ songwriter Jani Lane, and found themselves the biggest draw on Sunset Strip. CBS didn't fail to take notice, releasing the quintet's 'Dirty Rotten Filthy Stinking Rich' debut and its slick pop-rock follow-up 'Cherry Pie'. But finding themselves having to compete with the Grunge boom by the time the band's third album, 'Dog Eat Dog', was issued in 1992 proved difficult. The album, although by far the best of the three, failed to ignite America. And in early '93 worse was to follow when the underrated Lane quit to pursue a solo career. Warrant have vowed to continue with a new singer, but for how long?
Recommended album:
CHERRY PIE *(CBS, 1990 – KKKK)*

WARRIOR

USA, five-piece (1985-1986)
MARGINALLY BETTER than a combined plate of rice pudding and custard, Warrior were a grossly over-hyped LA arena rock band whose demos were far better than the one and only album released.

Vocalist Parramore McCarty went on to work with Steve Stevens' Atomic Playboys along with the band's somewhat veteran bassist, Bruce Turgon, who was last seen with his old Black Sheep colleague Lou Gramm in Shadow King.
Barely recommended:
FIGHTING FOR THE EARTH *(10 Records, 1985 – KK)*

WARRIOR SOUL

USA, four-piece (1988-present)
ONE OF the original ambassadors of the East Coast New Age Metal boom, Warrior Soul are outspoken underdogs on a mission. Led from the front by Kory Clarke, the band play gleaming, streamlined agit-rock with soul and intelligence. Live shows have been unreliable, but when Warrior Soul hit their stride there are few around today who can touch them for sheer emotion.

Kory's lyrics lie at the heart of the band's three albums. Some have called him obsessive and even insane, but such songs as 'The Losers' and 'Drugs, God And The New Republic' have won him a passionately loyal following.

Management by Q-Prime and enormous European support has yet to be fully tapped, but Kory will probably visit each and every one personally with his sensible Manifesto for Change.
Highly recommended albums:
LAST DECADE DEAD CENTURY *(Geffen, 1989 – KKKKK)*
SALUTATIONS FROM THE GHETTO NATION *(Geffen, 1992 – KKKKK)*

W.A.S.P.

USA, four-piece (1982-present)
FORMED FROM the bizarre workings of ex-New York Doll Blackie Lawless' mind, W.A.S.P. attempted to instigate a 1982 revival of the glam rock theatre popularised by Kiss almost a decade earlier. Self-titled debut album released in '84 with final hometown show dubbed 'LA finally gets rid of W.A.S.P.'. Possibly not the best news for the rest of the world. From the OTT beginnings of exploding codpieces and lobbing raw meat into the audience to the strains of their most famous ditty, 'Animal (Fuck Like A Beast)', the band attained reasonable record sales by parting with original members Tony Richards (drums) and Randy Piper (guitar) and allowing guitarist Chris Holmes to drink and fornicate his way around the world.

Albums such as 'Inside The Electric Circus' and 'The Headless Children' found the band caught between shock tactics and a desire to break the commercial strata. Lawless dismissed the incorrigible alcoholic Holmes in 1991 and attempted a concept album, 'The Crimson Idol', in 1992. The 'Who on steroids' approach was severely flawed. Currently deal-less in the States, the future looks bleak.
Red-raw recommended album:
W.A.S.P. (Capitol 1984 – KKKK)

WAYNE'S WORLD

USA, rock basement, (1980s-present)
BEGAN LIFE as a sketch on USA cult TV show 'Saturday Night Live' then took on a life of its own leading to the 'Wayne's World' movie ('92). Wayne (Mike Myers) and Garth (Dana Carvey) are not worthy – but managed to persuade Aerosmith to appear on their rock show presented from the basement of their Midwest home. Mom upstairs was not impressed...
Recommended viewing:
THE ORIGINAL TV SKETCHES. No way? Way!

WAYSTED

UK, four-piece (1983-1988)
APPROPRIATELY-MONIKERED UK act formed by notorious substance abuser and occasional bassist Pete Way after his acrimonious departure from seminal hard rockers, UFO. Originally featuring Scottish vocalist Fin (ex-Flying Squad – the band not the police department), Ronnie Kayfield (guitar) and Frank Noon (drums), they released a cool debut, 'Vices', in 1983.

The band then underwent miriad line-up changes during their five-year career, including erstwhile UFO-ers, keyboardist Paul Raymond, drummer Andy 'No Neck' Parker and guitarist Paul Chapman. Three labels, four albums and a lot of empty bottles is the legacy of a band that created some excellent gritty rock and some even better tales of excess. Way later re-united with his former sparring partner, vocalist Phil Mogg, in a re-formed UFO.
Recommended album:
THE GOOD, THE BAD, THE WAYSTED (Music For Nations, 1985 – KKKK)

WHITE LION

USA, four-piece (1985-1991)
FORMED IN Brooklyn, New York by the former lead singer of Danish pop band Mabel, Mike Tramp and American guitarist Vito Bratta. Initial media interest actually centred on the short-lived employment of ex-Angel bassist Felix Robinson who played on the band's debut album, 'Fight To Survive', but he was out by the time it was released. White Lion were subsequently dropped by Elektra and picked up by JVC Victor in Japan (Grand Slamm released the record in the USA, by which time they'd signed a new deal with Atlantic). Phew!

A number of bassists and drummers flitted in and out of the group before it settled on the definitive rhythm team of James Lomenzo (bass) and Greg D'Angelo (drums). Shortly afterwards 'Pride', White Lion's second album, broke in the States and the band toured extensively. Its follow-up, 'Big Game', was considered lame in comparison and when White Lion did hit back on a heavier note with 'Mane Attraction', few people wanted to know.

A brief US club tour with replacements for

Lomenzo and D'Angelo failed to improve matters and the band split, Bratta retaining the Atlantic deal whilst Tramp set about forming the excellent Freak Of Nature.

Recommended album:
FIGHT TO SURVIVE (JVC/Victor, 1985 – KKKKK)

WHITE SPIRIT

UK, five-piece (1975-1983)
TRADITIONAL HARD rockers who dealt out lashings of Purple-esque fodder. Signed to MCA in 1980 as part of the NWOBHM fall-out and released one album before crumbling into dust. Most famous for spawning Gillan and Iron Maiden guitarist Janick Gers.

Recommended album:
WHITE SPIRIT (MCA, 1980 – KKK)

WHITE ZOMBIE

USA, four-piece (1987-present)
FROM OUT of New York and now signed to Geffen, White Zombie have been very muddy, very Metal and very hairy throughout their three-album, sub-Grunge career. Whether their major label status will kick-start their world domination game-plan remains to be seen. Most interestingly, the band possess a female bassist named Sean!

Recommended album:
LA SEXORCISTO: DEVIL MUSIC VOL 1 (Geffen, 1992 – KKK)

WHITESNAKE

UK, six/five-piece (1978-1989)
FORMED BY David Coverdale, erstwhile vocalist in Deep Purple. Whitesnake officially arrived with the 'Snakebite' four-track EP in 1978, on the tail-end of two solo albums from the Saltburn By The Sea-born gentleman of British hard rock ('David Coverdale's Whitesnake' and 'Northwinds'). The band's initial line-up fetaured Micky Moody and Bernie Marsden (guitars), Neil Murray (bass), David Dowle (drums) and Pete Solley (keyboards). The latter was replaced in late '78 by the addition of Coverdale's former Purple colleague Jon Lord.

Travelling a distinctive blues road (with brief, early forays into R'n'B for good measure), they built a loyal following on the strength of the first two albums 'Trouble' and 'Lovehunter' (memorable for its so-called 'sexist' cover, the first of many!), by which time another ex-Purple man had signed up: Ian Paice replacing Dowle. As the new decade arrived, so did a remarkable surge in popularity for Coverdale beginning with a Top 20 hit single in the excellent 'Fool For Your Loving' which increased sales of the 'Ready An' Willing' album, prompting the release, later in 1980, of a live album 'Live... In The Heart Of The City', initial UK copies also included the 'Live In Hammersmith' album, recorded in 1978, and previously only available as a Japanese import – much to the disgust of those hardcore fans who'd already splashed out for it.

Although having been affected by a number of line-up reshuffles that brought the likes of Cozy Powell and John Sykes into the group, Whitesnake's popularity throughout Europe and the UK (where the band headlined Castle Donington in 1983) had increased rather than waned, although little had been achieved in the lucrative American market.

WHITESNAKE: 1989's elegantly-permed and eminently-presentable final line-up, as adored by the Americans

"I do not like being an opening act, I'm sorry." – David Coverdale, Kerrang! 3, September, 1981

"Actually, I'm something of a private 'guitar hero' myself, though I don't think I've got the bottle to throw shapes on stage." – David Coverdale, Kerrang! 30, December 2-15, 1982

"Unless you hear it from me, it's bullshit." – David Coverdale on line-up changes within the group, Kerrang! 60, January 26- February 8, 1983

"Whitesnake couldn't go any further in Europe. We were doing sell-out tours and smashing records for attendances and merchandising sales and still only breaking even or losing money..." – David Coverdale, Kerrang! 143, April 2-15, 1987

"I think I'm actually starting to get a little tired of standing out there screaming my lungs out.." – David Coverdale, Kerrang!, August 18, 1990

WHITESNAKE

This was a situation that was to change with Coverdale cunningly signing a solo deal with the then still fledgling Geffen label in 1983, and the then current album, 'Slide It In', being issued in America in remixed and, on some tracks, re-recorded form. Curiously this was to be the last Whitesnake album for four years as a number of niggling problems, not least of which included Coverdale experiencing trouble with his throat, severely disrupting Whitesnake's schedule.

Their return to the fray in 1987 was nothing short of triumphant – even if the band behind Coverdale were little more than hired guns. Throwing aside the often plodding, hoary old Bluesy numbers aside for a more majestic, huge Cock Rock sound of the '1987' album (featuring Sykes on guitar and Aynsley Dunbar on drums) transformed Coverdale's career, netted him a rather nice Jaguar and a B-movie actress for a wife, both of which would soon appear cast together in one of Whitesnake's no-expense-spared promo videos.

Touring with a line-up of Adrian Vandenberg and Vivian Campbell (guitars), Rudy Sarzo (bass) and veteran drummer Tommy Aldridge encouraged sales to go through the roof, although the band wouldn't play in the UK until making their seemingly final live appearance headlining Donington in 1989. By then, Steve Vai had replaced Campbell, who had quit before the recording of Whitesnake's final album, 'Slip Of The Tongue', Coverdale announcing that he would be putting the band 'on ice' whilst he went off to pursue a real solo career. He never did, and instead teamed up with ex-Zeppelin guitarist Jimmy Page in Coverdale Page.

ALBUMS

TROUBLE *(EMI, 1978 – KKK) "An honest, entertaining British rock album." – Kerrang! 3, September, 1981 (Whitesnake retrospective)*
LOVEHUNTER *(United Artists, 1979 – KKKK) "Mucho macho music, indeed!" – Kerrang! 3, September, 1981*
READY AN' WILLING *(United Artists, 1980 – KKKK) " 'Ready An' Willing' proved they meant business." – Kerrang! 3, September, 1981*
LIVE... IN THE HEART OF THE CITY *(United Artists, 1980 – KKKK) "A thank-you to Whitesnake's fans." – Kerrang! 3, September, 1981*
COME AND GET IT *(Liberty, 1981 – KKKK) "A cleanly, powerfully produced record."– Kerrang! 3, September, 1981*
SAINTS 'N' SINNERS *(Liberty, 1982 – KK) "The emotional weight which normally stacks itself up to sound in a Whitesnake record seems strained and drawn thin." – Kerrang! 30, December 2-15, 1982*
SLIDE IT IN *(Liberty, 1983 – KKK) "They might still conquer America this year." – Kerrang! 61, February 9-22, 1983*
1987 *(Liberty, 1987 – KKKK) "An album compiled before a backdrop of problems." – Kerrang! 141, March 5-18, 1987*
SLIP OF THE TONGUE *(EMI, 1989 – KKK) "A decent album – for the wrong reasons." – Kerrang! 264, November 11, 1989*

The WHO

UK, four-piece (1964-1989)
PHENOMENAL INFLUENCE on a generation of
Metal acts. The Who's music veered
spectacularly across the entire spectrum of
rock, and when they had the urge, they could
powerchord with the most potent. Check out
'Live At Leeds' ('70) or 'Who's Next' ('71) for the
evidence. Led by trout-farming vocalist Roger
Daltrey and guitarist Pete Townshend, the
classic line-up was completed by bassist John
Entwhistle and drummer Keith Moon. Moonie
died in 1978 after battle against alcoholism, but
band soldiered on with ex-Faces drummer
Kenney Jones. Things were never the same and
The Who fizzled out, still leaving a spectacular
legacy of classic rock albums.
Recommended double concept album:
QUADROPHENIA *(Polydor, 1973 – KKKKK)*

WIDOWMAKER

USA, four-piece (1992-present)
NOT TO be confused with the late '70s UK band
of the same name which boasted ex-Mott The
Hoople guitarist Ariel Bender, this is the latest
mob to be fronted by ex-Twisted Sister bellower
Dee Snider. His previous project, Desperadoes,
featuring guitarist Bernie Tormé, having been
shelved despite the fact an album was recorded
and ready to go.
Recommended album:
BLOOD AND BULLETS *(Squirt, 1992 – KKKK)*

The WiLDHEARTS

UK, four-piece (1990-present)
IN ONE live review in the pages of *Kerrang!* of
an early incarnation of The Wildhearts, it stated:
"The Wildhearts transcend Metal and shatter
the foundations of pop...". Cataclysmic
sentiments, indeed, for a band formed by the
volatile Ginger, who was unceremoniously
jettisoned from The Quireboys and voted most
likely to self-destruct. After a spell in New York
vagabonds The Throbs, guitarist Ginger
returned to the UK to make his Wildhearts
dream a reality. After numerous line-up
changes, Ginger reluctantly accepted lead vocal
duties. With their high energy 'genre-hopping'
music, The Wildhearts have rapidly become
hotly-tipped contenders as well as being further
proof that Britain is hardly devoid of new world
class talent.
Recommended second EP (with free first EP!):
DON'T BE HAPPY... JUST WORRY *(EastWest,
1992 – KKKK)*

Wendy O WILLIAMS

USA, legend (1984-present)
DESPITE HER age, Wendy has long been
regarded as the Grandmother of Punk and has
resolutely refused to either settle or slow down.
Controversy dogged her career in The
Plasmatics thanks to her on-stage penchant for
masturbation and destroying cars. Her solo
career has been no less confrontational. Famed
for her energy, enthusiasm and her body,
Wendy O is a porno vixen from outer space.
Don't argue.
Recommended splatter-Metal album:
W.O.W. *(Passport, 1984 – KKKK)*

WINGER

USA, four-piece (1987-present)
ALTHOUGH NICK-NAMED the blow-waved Bee
Gee by *Kerrang!*, vocalist/bass player Kip
Winger has a jolly nice sense of humour and
takes it all in his leather stride.
   His band's eponymous 1988 debut was
nothing too remarkable, but certainly no
disgrace; providing a firm footing for Kip – plus
Reb Beach (guitar), Paul Taylor (keyboards/
guitar) and Rod Morgenstein (drums). 1990's 'In
The Heart Of The Young', however, was a totally
different story. 'Miles Away' was adopted by the
American forces' wives as 'their' song during
the Gulf War. The LP became a huge seller, but
the majority of picky Brits have yet to warm to
them. Third LP, 'Pull' ('93), features Paul Taylor
in songwriting and recording capacity although
his touring commitment seems in doubt...
Recommended album:
IN THE HEART OF THE YOUNG *(Atlantic, 1990
– KKKKK)*

WISHBONE ASH

UK, four-piece (1969-present)
STANDING ON the periphery of the Metal
scene, Wishbone Ash were one of the first acts
to hone a two-guitar duelling style. Never heavy
enough to send headbangers into paroxysms of
ecstacy, 1972's 'Argus' (not to be confused with
the wholesale store!) proved to be the zenith of
their career, its gentler moments influencing the
likes of Steve Harris and Metallica. Line-up
changes have been frequent and unobtrusive
and the Ash have continued to survive in their
own, hermetically-sealed world.
Recommended album:
ARGUS *(MCA, 1972 – KKKK)*

WITCHFINDER GENERAL

UK, four-piece (1979-1984)
NWOBHM ALSO-RANS who played a Sabbath-
inspired doomy Metal which was overshadowed
by their highly tasteful album sleeve for 'Death
Penalty'. It featured the band in period dress
sacrificing an amply-bosomed wench in a
graveyard. Top tack!
Recommended album sleeve:
DEATH PENALTY *(Heavy Metal Records, 1982
– KK)*

WITCHFYNDE

UK, four-piece (1976-1985)
SATANIC METALLISTS fronted by guitarist
Montalo (not his real name) who once was once
pictured on a single sleeve dressed all in black
holding a broadsword poised above some poor
'virgin' lying prone in a graveyard. Best thing
about their early stage act was the six-foot
candelabra burning black candles...
Recommended debut album:
GIVE 'EM HELL *(Rondelet, 1981 – KKK)*

WOLFSBANE

UK, four-piece (1986-present)
PERENNIAL BRITISH hopefuls whose true
promise has only recently been realised with the
release of the unrelenting live album 'Massive
Live Injection' – bravely recorded in one night,
warts, scabs, dandruff *et al*, at London's The
Marquee. When the hard-touring band from
Tamworth were snapped up by Rick Rubin's
happening Def America label, Wolfsbane looked
set to explode. Yet in terms of what was
anticipated from the Wolfies with Rubin at the
helm, the debut 'Live Fast, Die Fast' ('89) was a
disappointment. The full power and personality
of Wolfsbane was not to be found betwixt
plastic grooves until 'All Hell's Breaking Loose
Down At Little Kathy Wilson's Place' EP ('90), a
release which coincided with a support slot on
Iron Maiden's UK trek. Yet, despite the breaks,
incessantly favourable press, and one of
Britain's most charismaticly manic frontmen in
the shape of the unshaven but suave Blaze
Bayley, Wolfsbane failed to achieve the level of
success originally predicted, resulting in the
eventual seperation from their label. Down, but
not out, the scuzzy wonders had the inspired
idea to go for a live album to hammer home
what all the fuss was about in the boggin' first
place! And it worked. God bless 'em.
Recommended album
MASSIVE LIVE INJECTION *(Bronze, 1993 –
KKKK)*

WORLD WAR III

USA, four-piece (1986-present)
CAME INTO their own when German-born
singer Mandy Lion hooked up in LA with former
Dio-ites Jimmy Bain (bass) and Vinny Appice
(drms) to conjure up some decidedly sexist and
OTT sonics.
Recommended album:
WORLD WAR III *(Hollywood, 1991 – KKK)*

WRATHCHILD

UK, four-piece (1980-89)
HAILING FROM sunny Evesham, Wrathchild –
with their 'Blue Peter'-level stage props and
costumes – were funny for a while back in the
mid-'80s as Britain's self-acclaimed Glam titans.
But the glitter faded and the gag went grey.
Recommended album:
STAKK ATTAKK *(Heavy Metal Records, 1984 –
KKKKK)*

XENTRIX

UK, four-piece (1988-present)
STALWART BRITS who've weathered the storm which laid waste to practically all of their fellow Thrashy countrymen. Started out as Sweet Vengeance, rehearsing doggedly away and playing the local pub once a month. A sprightly demo secured them as deal with Roadrunner Records, and the band's career was under way, if perhaps a touch prematurely. Since then, they've plodded on quite dependably, but hardly approached the real heights...
Recommended album:
KIN *(Roadrunner, 1992 – KKKK)*

Y&T

USA, four-piece (1974-1991)
SAN FRANCISCO hard rockers who were originally known as Yesterday And Today then shortened the name on third LP, 'Earthshaker' ('81). The album was well-named, a cult classic that suggested Y&T were a real force to be reckoned with – even if subsequent albums never matched it. For the next, 'Black Tiger' ('82), Y&T – Dave Meniketti (guitar/vocals), Joey Alves (guitar), Phil Kennemore (bass) and Leonard Haze (drums) – employed Chris Tsangarides as producer, then toured Europe to rave reviews due to the unbridled power of their delivery and Meniketti's impressive vocals. But follow-ups, 'Meanstreak' ('83) and 'In Rock We Trust' ('84), saw the band lose ground. In 1986 they lost Haze too (he would eventually hook up with Ian Gillan). Y&T never achieved the success they deserved – but their records remain very influential.
Recommended album:
EARTHSHAKER *(A&M, 1981 – KKKKK)*

Neil YOUNG

Canada, solo artist (1970-present)
MANIAC JOURNEYMAN and eccentric recluse, Neil Young has been blasting his Fender amps to bits for as long as anyone can remember. He is the Godfather Of Grunge, a genre he typically detests. Nonetheless his super-distorted guitar sound and an occasionally stadium-shredding riff has elevated the man to the status of a cult god.

His accoustic records have drifted at times towards the twee, but the electric albums with Crazy Horse have been about as rock 'n' roll as heroin. Such riffs as 'Hey Hey, My My (Into The Black)', 'Rocking In The Free World' and 'Fuckin' Up' could piss on Deep Purple for breakfast, whilst his extraordinary and anarchic solos have transformed the likes of 'Southern Man' and 'Cinnamon Girl'. The last rock god.
Essential electric albums:
RUST NEVER SLEEPS *(Reprise, 1981 – KKKKK)*
FREEDOM *(Reprise, 1989 – KKKKK)*

ZEBRA

USA, three-piece (1981-1990)
FRONTED BY guitarist/vocalist Randy Jackson, and coming on like a tasteful combination of Rush and Led Zeppelin. Zebra were originally from New Orleans, but relocated to New York. They made four albums, the first of which, 'Zebra' ('83), became one of the fastest selling albums in Atlantic Records' history.

The band reaching near perfection with their third album, '3.V' ('86), but sadly bowed out with the 'Live' album in 1990.
Highly recommended
3.V *(Atlantic, 1986 – KKKKK)*

ZED YAGO

Germany, five-piece (1985-1990)
CONCEPTUAL EURO rock act fronted by
gutterally-voiced female vocalist Jutta.
Released two albums in the late '80s and toured
the UK with W.A.S.P. in 1989 to massive apathy.
Recommended album:
FROM OVER YONDER *(SPV, 1988 – KKK)*

ZNOWHITE

USA, four-piece (1982-1990)
CHICAGO THRASHERS whose original line-up
comprised a white female singer and three male
black musicians. Over the years, the band's sole
mainstay was guitar cruncher Ian Tafoya, and
after the exceptional (if under-produced) 'Act Of
God' album, Znowhite became Cyclone Temple.
Recommended album:
I HATE...THEREFORE I AM *(Relativity, 1991 –
KKKK)*

ZODIAC MINDARP

UK, four-piece (1985-present)
WHEN ZODIAC and the boys first hit town they
were probably the most exciting band you could
wish to see. Cartoon character bikers who wore
Nazi helmets and played songs like 'Kick Start
Me For Love' and 'Holy Gasoline', and whose
audience was largely made up of real bikers and
scantily clad nubiles.

Unfortunately, the band got too much too
soon and things began to fall apart. Zodiac (real
name Mark Manning) started believing his own
press and became increasingly over the top,
spending most of the band's large advance
advance on beer and drugs. Once he forgot that
it was all supposed to be a piss-take and he
wasn't *really* the messiah, everything went
rapidly downhill.

Bassist Kid Chaos reverted to the name
Haggis and left to join the Cult, before leaving
them to form The Four Horsemen. His
replacements (a new bassist called Trash and
an extra guitarist called Flash Bastard) although
musically competent, simply didn't have the
same attitude and drinking ability.

Thankfully, failure brought them down a peg
or two and they dropped Flash, regained their
sense of humour, then shortened their name to
Mindwarp...
Recommended 12 inch:
HIGH PRIEST OF LOVE *(Food, 1987 – KKKKK)*

ZOETROPE

USA, four-piece (1981-1991)
MUCH-TOUTED Chicago band who were there
or thereabouts during the Thrash explosion, but
never graduated to the big league. Briefly
featured Mind Funk guitarist Louie Svitek, while
their long-term drummer Barry Stern has now
joined Doomsters Trouble.
Recommended album:
A LIFE OF CRIME *(Music For Nations, 1987 –
KKKK)*

ZZ TOP

USA, three-piece (1969-present)
TEXAN ODDBALLS Billy Gibbons (guitar/
vocals), 'Dusty' Hill (bass/vocals), and Frank
Beard (drums) are almost as well known for their
bizarre sense of humour as their music. If you're
looking for clues, bear in mind that of the three
– all born in the year of 1949 – Beard is the only
one without a beard...

Beard and Hill first played together in 1967 in
the Warlocks, later known as American Blues,
alongside Hill's brother Rocky. At that time, the
guitar playing of Gibbons was already
something of a legend in Texas. He was playing
in a Psychedelic Blues band known as The
Moving Sidewalks who in June '68 opened a
show for the Jimi Hendrix Experience. In '69,
both American Blues and Moving Sidewalks
split whereupon Gibbons enlisted Beard and
Dusty Hill for his new band, who allegedly took
their name from a brand of cigarette papers.

At this early stage, the band released their
first single, 'Salt Lick', on Scat, and hooked up
with manager/producer Bill Ham. He helped
them sign a deal with London Records who re-
issued 'Salt Lick' then their debut album, the
helpfully-titled 'ZZ Top's First Album', in 1970.
Initially, touring in Texas was enough to keep

the band solvent, but steadily they ventured into adjacent Southern states. This built them a reputation that was crowned in May '72 when they added the name of The Rolling Stones to the list of stars they had opened the show for. That same month saw the release of their second album, 'Rio Grande Mud', spawning their first national hit single, 'Francene' and helping them to pull over 100,000 to a July festival with the snappy handle of 'ZZ Top's First Annual Texas Size Rompin' Stompin' Barndance Bar-B-Q'...

Third album, 'Tres Hombres' ('73), was something of a triumph, containing the classic 'La Grange', about a brothel of the same name, later immortalised in celluloid in the Burt Reynolds/Dolly Parton movie 'The Best Little Whorehouse In Texas'. The album went Gold and reached Number Eight in the States.

Come May '75, and the release of 'Fandango', the band were big news and the word had spread to Europe where the album marked the band's UK chart debut, not least thanks to the inclusion of 'Tush', the three-minute or so belter that has since become a standard to covers (and major) bands all over the world.

To promote the next record, 'Tejas' – the traditional spelling of their home state's name – ZZ Top did something very odd: they took Texas on tour with them. Well, 75 tons of it... For the ensuing road trek, dubbed 'The Worldwide Texas Tour', the band performed onstage surrounded by large amounts of sand, cactus plants and even Texan buffalo and snakes – not to mention six buzzards, all called Oscar.

After the tour, the band took a two year break and the three members went off separately to travel the world. Whilst London

marked the end of the recording contract with the release of 'The Best Of ZZ Top', Gibbons was somewhere in the Himalayas hunting Yeti. Whether he actually saw one is uncertain, but he swears he saw something he wouldn't touch with a 'Ten Foot Pole'. Naturally enough, he would write a song of that title on a forthcoming ZZ Top album. First though, came their debut on Warner Bros, 'Deguello' ('79). (Warners later re-issued all their London back catalogue.) Backing 'Top on some tracks were The Lone Wolf Horns (aka Gibbons, Hill and Beard). At live gigs, The Lone Wolf Horns would accompany the band from a video screen behind the stage playing perfectly in synch...

Such technical wizardry would pale into insignificance alongside future albums, but some of it was in evidence on 1981's 'El Loco' – Spanish for mad – an album where the band appeared to, er... go mad, with some of their wackiest songs ever. It was a particularly unlikely precursor to the record which broke them worldwide on a scale they could never have predicted, the album called 'Eliminator'.

It was released in April '83 to almost universal acclaim – but its hi-tech sound did alienate the Blues purists who had followed 'Top from the

ZZ TOP: shufflin' outta Texas to go 'el loco' on a worldwide scale...

start. Rumours that Beard never played on the album and that all drum patterns were computer synthesised have, however, always been denied. More significantly, perhaps, the album was among the first to be sold via video technology and MTV: who blasted the promo clips for 'Gimme All Your Lovin'', 'Sharp Dressed Man' and 'Legs' for all they were worth. Instantly, the images of the beards, long-legged girls and the ZZ logo on the Eliminator Ford custom car turned ZZ Top into household names and the album into a seven million-selling blockbuster.

All of which made the follow-up, 'Afterburner' ('85), even more of a disappointment. Largely a caricature of its predecessor, it far from a creative peak. 1990's 'Recycler' found 'Top, if not exactly returned to their Blues roots, at least back on the right (on) road – recorded in memphis and featuring a whole host of Save The Planet references. After the tour which followed, the band laid low but rumours suggest they were anonymously backing acoustic Blues guitarist Rainer Ptacek on his very 'Top-esque album, 'The Texas Tapes' (Demon, '93)...

Around the time of that release, ZZ's new label BMG were looking forward to their first album by the band, after which anything could happen. ZZ Top are, after all, the only band in this book with reservations on the first passenger flight to the Moon. Over and out... of this world.

ALBUMS

ZZ TOP'S FIRST ALBUM (London, 1970 – KKKK) 'Abstract Blues' played with bucketfuls of emotion and spontaneity...
RIO GRANDE MUD (London, 1972 – KKKK) More honest down-home no-frills Blues and shuffles, plus the absolutely brilliant slowie 'Sure Got Cold After The Rain Fell'...
TRES HOMBRES (London, 1973 – KKKKK) Essential! The album that launched ZZ into stadium status. Every track a winner...
FANDANGO (London, 1975 – KKKKK) Half live, half studio. Short and to the point – just like its monster track, 'Tush'...

TEJAS (London, 1977 – KKKK) 'Top at their most mellow – plus stormers like 'El Diablo' and 'Arrested For Driving While Blind' (!)...
DEGUELLO (Warner Bros, 1979 – KKKKK) Stunning set of songs with magnificently zany titles. Includes 'Fool For Your Stockings' and 'Cheap Sunglasses'...
EL LOCO (Warner Bros, 1981 – KKKK) Relatively lightwieght and almost too wacky for words: contains 'Ten Foot Pole'...
ELIMINATOR (Warner Bros, 1983 – KKKKK) "Could well displace that scratchy old Stones album as the ultimate party record." – Kerrang! 40, April 21-May 4, 1983
AFTERBURNER (Warner Bros, 1985 – KKK) "Predictable, yes. But a good friend to have hanging around." – Kerrang! 107, November 14-27, 1985
RECYCLER (Warner Bros, 1990 – KKKK) "Halfway between 'Eliminator's commercial, boogie sensibilities and the jalapeno blues of 'Deguello'." – Kerrang! 312, October 20, 1990

IN THEIR OWN WORDS...

"I had an understanding with the buzzard behind me... but it didn't like me. Buzzards are really shitty birds. I walked back near him one day and he tried to throw up on me...." – Dusty Hill, Kerrang! 57, December 15-28, 1983

"One key to playing is to stay true to your art whatever it may be. ZZ Top will never be considered a Punk, New Wave or highly electronic band..." – Billy Gibbons, Kerrang! 39, April 7-20, 1983

"Someone said to me once: 'Where do you live?'. And I said: 'Some hotel'. But our hearts will always be in Texas." – Billy Gibbons, Kerrang! 130, October 2-15, 1986

"We take our music seriously. We're all good musicians but, y'know, I think some people take things just a little too serious. It's like, 'Lighten up and get a life'..." – Dusty Hill, Kerrang! 325, January 26, 1991

"I try to be a tourist, but it's hard with the beard!" – Dusty Hill, Kerrang! 325, January 26, 1991

ZZ TOP